D1083274

THE SURVIVAL OF EMPIRE

THE
SURVIVAL OF EMPIRE

PORTUGUESE TRADE AND SOCIETY
IN CHINA AND THE
SOUTH CHINA SEA, 1630–1754

GEORGE BRYAN SOUZA

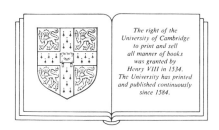

The right of the
University of Cambridge
to print and sell
all manner of books
was granted by
Henry VIII in 1534.
The University has printed
and published continuously
since 1584.

CAMBRIDGE UNIVERSITY PRESS

CAMBRIDGE

LONDON   NEW YORK   NEW ROCHELLE
MELBOURNE   SYDNEY

Published by the Press Syndicate of the University of Cambridge
The Pitt Building, Trumpington Street, Cambridge CB2 1RP
32 East 57th Street, New York, NY 10022, USA
10 Stamford Road, Oakleigh, Melbourne 3166, Australia

First published 1986

Printed in Great Britain by the
University Press, Cambridge

British Library cataloguing in publication data
Souza, George Bryan
The survival of empire: Portuguese trade
and society in China and the South China
Sea, 1630–1754.
1. Imperialism   2. Portugal –
Colonies – History.   3. China –
Politics and government – 1368–1644.
4. China – Politics and government –
1644–1912.
I. Title
325′.32′09469   JC359

Library of Congress cataloguing in publication data
Souza, George Bryan
The survival of empire.
Bibliography.
Includes index.
1. Portugal – Commerce – China – History.   2. China –
Commerce – Portugal – History.   3. Portugal – Commerce –
Asia – History.   4. Asia – Commerce – Portugal – History.
5. Portugal – Colonies – Asia – Commerce – History.
I. Title
HF3698.C6S68   1986   382′.09469′051   86-922

ISBN 0 521 24855 8

TO MY FATHER, IN LOVING MEMORY,
AND TO MY MOTHER

CONTENTS

FIGURES, MAPS AND TABLES

GLOSSARY

Aldeia: Village

Alfandega: Crown customs house, *almojarifazgo* in Spanish territories.

Bague: share-ticket in a joint enterprise.

Bakufu: Japanese, 'curtain government', term refers to military regime under the *Shogun* that ruled Japan during the period.

Bandos: groups – term applies to individual, familial or extra-familial groupings in Portuguese communities on social, political or economic grounds.

Caixas: base coin, prominent throughout Asia, made of iron, copper or alloys; used here primarily for copper coinage of Vietnam (Tonkin and Cochinchina).

Camara, Senado da: municipal council.

Capados: eunuchs.

Capitão: captain, governor.

Capitão-geral: captain-general, at Macao, title of the Crown governor and military commander of the city and its population from 1623 onwards.

Capitão-mor: captain-major as in the case of the Japan voyage.

Carrack: English term (*Kraak* in Dutch) used to describe the large Portuguese shipping of the *nao do trato* type.

Cartazes: sea passes, system of granting passes to Asian traders by the Portuguese in India to obtain revenue.

Casados: married settlers.

Chalupa: sloop.

Chapas: Chinese passes.

Chos: Macaonese word, derived from the Cantonese *t'so*, a sea-going junk.

Companhia das Indias: Portuguese Crown company in English/Dutch style active in Europe to Asia trade for a short period in the seventeenth century.

Conselho da Fazenda: Royal Treasury Council at Goa.

Conselho Ultramarino: Overseas Council, Lisbon-based.

Country: (ships, trade, traders) term used by English to distinguish private commercial activities from those of the English East India Company, used here in its broadest sense to describe the inter-Asian interport trade carried by non-Company shipping.

Cristão-novo: 'new Christian', crypto-Jew.

Dagh-registers: 'day registers'. Dutch Company reports on daily voyage or major port or fortress activity.

Daimyo: Japanese feudal and territorial nobility.

Desembargador: A high court magistrate.

Estado da India: 'State of India' name given by the Portuguese to their Asian empire from East Africa to Japan, with Goa as its centre.

Fidalgo: a nobleman or gentleman.

Feitor: 'factor', person in charge of a trading establishment or agency in an Asian port.

Foro do chão: 'land rent' fee paid by the Portuguese at Macao to Chinese authorities.

Galiotas: 'galliot', size usually between 3 and 400 tons.

Generale Missiven: 'general letters', annual letters from VOC representatives in Asia at Batavia detailing their activities to the home office.

Go-shuin-sen: Japanese shipping trading under the Shoguns pass, 'August Red Seal', in the South China Sea in the early seventeenth century.

Heeren XVII: 'Gentlemen Seventeen', the directors of the VOC in Holland.

Hoppo: Chinese Imperial Customs Commissioners at Canton and Macao.

Hong: guild or merchant association; *co-hong*.

Itowappu-nakama: cf. *pancada* in the Japanese case.

Juiz dos orfãos: Probate judge.

Karengs: Macassarese nobility.

Lançados: Literally 'thrown-out', used here to describe elements of Portuguese society that chose on their own, or were expelled from the centres of empire, to seek their fortunes independently from Crown efforts in different parts of Asia.

Lanteas: broad-beamed, river transport vessels used to bring merchandise purchased by Portuguese at Canton down to Macao.

Livro de rezão: merchant account books.

Lorchas do risco: Chinese shipping that risked confiscation by illegally trading with Macao.

Mas: gold coin in use in Macassar.

Mesa: Board of guardians in the *Santa Casa de Misericordia*.

Mestiço: Eurasian, half-caste or mixed-bloods.

Não do trato: 'great ship', the carrack whose size ranged from 1,200 tons to as large as 2,000, used on Portugal to India and India to Japan routes.

Naveta: swift ship of galliot type, around 300 tons.

Navio: ships, general and imprecise term, usually in the *galiota/naveta/pataxo* range.

Ouvidor: Judge with appellate jurisdiction; *ouvidor geral*, superior Crown magistrate in a High Court.

Padroado: Crown patronage of Catholic missionary activities; *Patronato* in Spanish territories.

Pancada: price fixing procedures; describes Japanese case, its use by authorities at Nagasaki for the bulk purchase of Chinese silk imports at regulated rates; also used at Manila.

Parian: Chinese section/area near to Manila.

Pataxo: pinnace, vessel of about 2–400 tons.

Pauta: At Macao, shipping list.

Procurador: legal represenative, person with powers of attorney.

Provedor-mor dos Defuntos e Ausentes: superintendent of interstate property.

Provincia do Norte: 'Province of the North', name given by the Portuguese to their fortresses and claimed territories in northern India (Diu, Daman, Bassein).

Quevees: apparently from the Cantonese. Chinese merchant.

Reinol: European-born Portuguese.

Relação: High Court, at Goa in the *Estado da India*.

Renda: quit-rent, method of selling offices for revenue, especially at Goa.

Respondencia: money borrowed on the goods and merchandise of a vessel.

Roteiros: 'rutters', written sailing and navigational directions.

Santa Casa de Misericordia: Holy House of Mercy, a charitable lay brotherhood.

Senado da Camara: municipal council.

Shabandar: port official in South China Sea.

Shogun: 'Generalissimo', head of Japan's military government.

Situado: 'aid', financial support sent annually to the Philippines from New Spain.

Vedor da Fazenda: Royal Treasurer at Goa.

Vereenigde Oost-Indische Compagnie (VOC): the Dutch East India Company.

Vrij-burgers: private Dutch traders.

Wakō: Japanese term for pirates who were active on the China coast in the sixteenth century.

Wankan: Chinese sailing vessel.

SPELLING AND CURRENCY, WEIGHTS AND MEASURES

Every attempt has been made to standardise the spelling of Portuguese, Dutch, Chinese, Malay, Indonesian and other Asian place and personal names. Seventeenth century Portuguese and Dutch pose few difficulties as most of the names are anglicised and follow commonly accepted spelling. There are a few exceptions in the Portuguese, Macao is retained instead of Macau.

The romanisation of Chinese terms is in the Wade-Giles system, which is still the most commonly used method of transliteration. It is also the method used in all of the quotations in the text. A Chinese emperor's reign title has been used as if it were his personal name.

An official system of spelling was adopted by the Indonesian and Malaysian governments in late 1972 and all quotations in the text follow the new system; some place names, Aceh instead of Atjeh, are written in the new style but others, such as those for Malacca, Macassar and the Celebes, that might confuse a non-specialist reader have been avoided.

CONVERSION OF CURRENCY, WEIGHTS AND MEASURES

Despite a number of admirable reference works, there are severe restrictions encountered by the modern economic historian in converting the currency, weights and measure, used in the pre-modern maritime trading world of Asia. All reliable information that could be established from the available records and references for the conversion of the currency, weights and measures used in this study is summarised below. If a value has been computed on a different rate of conversion, this is indicated in a note. Most of the conversions were made for the early seventeenth century. Later, the Dutch East India Company financial system dominates and no conversion to Portuguese or any other currency was attempted.

CURRENCY AND MONEY OF ACCOUNT
Portuguese

xerafim (pl. xerafines)	cruzado	tanga
= 1 pardão	= tael (rough equivalent)	= 60 reis
= 1 pataca	= 1.25 real	

= 0.75 cruzado   = 1.33 xerafines
= 300 reis   = 400 reis
= 2 guilders 7 stuivers

Chinese

tael = 10 mace = 100 conderin
  = 1.25 real
  = 1.33 xerafines
  = 1 cruzado (rough equivalent)
  = 3 guilders 2 stuivers (before 1636)
  = 2 guilders 17 stuivers (1637–40)

Spanish

peso = 8 reals   = 0.8 tael (ave.)
                     = 0.8 cruzado
                     = 1.07 xerafines
                     = 2 guilders 10 stuivers

Dutch

Rijksdaalder (rsd)   guilder = 20 stuivers
= 2 guilders 8 stuivers (until 1665)   = 0.33 rsd
= 3 guilders (after 1665 in Asia)   = 0.4 real
= 1.2 real   = 0.32 cruzado
= 0.96 cruzado   = 0.43 xerafim
= 1.29 xerafines   = 0.32 taels
                                               (before 1636)
                                             = 0.35 taels
                                               (1637–40)

WEIGHTS AND MEASURES

Bahar   Tonelada
= 3 picols   = 1 ton
= 1 candil   Last
= 400 pounds   = 2 tons

Picol
= 133⅓ pounds
= 124 Dutch ponds

Quintal [Port.]
 = 130 pounds
Quintale [Span.]
 = 100 pounds

Dutch Pond
= 1.09 pound
= 0.494 kilogram

Tael
= 0.0827 pound
= 0.0375 kilogram

PREFACE

This book has been written as a contribution to a specific field of European expansion. It is not a history of China, Southeast Asia or the Indian sub-continent during the seventeenth and eighteenth centuries. Asia is the centrepiece on which I chose to examine hypotheses about the nature of the Portuguese empire, its survival, its involvement in maritime trade, the role played by the private merchant, and early East–West relations.

Prevailing in this book are those ideas that were originally presented in my doctoral dissertation at the University of Cambridge. I have benefited from a period of reflection and rewriting in order to focus my argument and presentation. While a doctoral candidate, my work benefited from the guidance of my supervisor, Mr G. V. Scammell of Pembroke College. My thanks to Dr F. P. Bowser of Stanford University, who first guided my interest in Portuguese colonial society, Dr J. S. Bastin and Dr R. B. Smith of the School of Oriental and African Studies, who introduced me to the history of Southeast Asia. I have benefited from comments by Professors C. R. Boxer, D. C. Twitchett, T'ien Ju-Kang, and Dr G. Johnson, Dr A. das Gupta, Dr J. E. Wills, Jr, and Dr W. Atwell, who read early drafts of this work. In particular, Dr K. N. Chaudhuri elaborated a very useful and instructive critique.

My gratitude to Mrs Margaret King and Miss Elsa Streitman, lecturer in the University of Cambridge, for their introduction to the Dutch language. Their guidance opened a whole range of archival and secondary works that are fundamental to this study. Mr Nicolas Menzies, lecturer in the University of Cambridge, kindly translated several Chinese references.

The directors and the staff of archives on three continents graciously granted me all facilities and aid that the archival researcher requires. In particular, in the Netherlands, I wish to thank the staff of the *Algemeen Rijksarchief*. In India, my gratitude to the director and staff of the Historical Archive at Goa for their interest in my research. In Portugal, the director and staff of the *Biblioteca da Ajuda*, who over several long research stays, cheerfully provided access to the voluminous *Jesuitas na Asia* collection.

Financial support for my last visit to the Spanish and Portuguese archives was provided by a research grant from the Calouste Gulbenkian Foundation and a contribution from the Council of Trinity College, University of Cambridge.

My thanks to a myriad of friends and relatives in Europe, Asia, South America and the United States whose kindness re-enforced the spirit of research and writing. Finally, to my wife, Caroline, who participated in this process, occasionally as a scribe and always the best companion, I can only record her efforts and marvel at her patience.

While an enormous debt of gratitude is owed to many, the responsibility for any errors in fact is mine alone.

I

MARITIME TRADE IN ASIA

Maritime trade in Asia antedates early modern history. During the fifteenth century, intrepid Chinese mariners and ships sailed into the Indian Ocean. Chinese produce was sold in Indian ports and shipped into the Red Sea, Persian Gulf or along the east African coast. By the end of the fifteenth century, Ming China's official interest in these commercial and political links with India and the Indian Ocean had collapsed. Maritime trade between China and India was sustained by junk traders sailing, principally, to Malacca and other ports in the South China Sea. At Malacca, the Chinese encountered and traded with other Asian merchants who frequented that port.

The Asian, Chinese, Indian, Arabian, Malay and non-Malay indigenous merchants who traded at Malacca met on the periphery of one geographical region in which the Chinese perceived themselves dominant. Those Chinese merchants did not concern themselves over the commercial and religious penetration by Islamic traders and missionaries throughout the Indonesian archipelago. Neither were they particularly preoccupied with the competitive commercial activities of the Malay and non-Malay indigenous merchants. Sinocentric attitudes led the Chinese merchants to ignore the maritime and commercial acumen of the many merchants of the Indian Ocean who were present at Malacca.

The Indian Ocean and the South China Sea are terms recently created by geographers to delineate the physical boundaries between three regions, the Indian sub-continent, Southeast Asia and China. Asian and European merchants of the early modern period would not recognise the Indian Ocean and the South China Sea as those terms are currently used. Today's actual boundary of the Indian Ocean includes portions of the Indonesian archipelago.[1] But, it is argued that the Indonesian archipelago during the early modern period formed an integral part of the South China Sea. For those Asian merchants, the Indian Ocean and the South China Sea were a series of seas, bays, islands and coastal markets that stretched, respectively, from the east coast of Africa to the west coast of Malaya and Sumatra and from the south coast of China, including Taiwan, the Philippines, the Indonesian archipelago, to the west coast of Malaya and Sumatra.

The geographical range of the activities of those Asian and European merchants who participated in the maritime trade of China and the South China Sea focused upon China, encompassed the South China Sea, the Indian Ocean and, finally, Europe. It may be useful to mentally draw a series of more or less concentric arcs on a map of the world, with south China as the focal point, the first arc runs along the western border of the South China Sea and up to Japan. The second is drawn across the Indian Ocean, to the east coast of Africa; and the third in the north and south Atlantic to include western Europe. Within the first arc, Chinese junks dominated maritime trade. The Chinese were joined by Japanese, European and other Asian competitors, including Siamese 'tribute' traders. In the second arc, Asia and European country traders (those ship-owners and merchants involved in inter-Asian maritime trade) were active and the European Companies were also present. In the third arc, Europeans competed exclusively between themselves in supplying Asian commodities by sea via the Cape of Good Hope route to Europe.

THE MARITIME TRADING WORLD OF CHINA

Portuguese forces under the command of Alfonso Albuquerque conquered Malacca in 1511 and abruptly initiated early modern relations between Europe and China.[2] Although aware, according to Tomé Pires, of Malacca's political and economic relationship with China, the Portuguese did not expect Ming officials to respond militarily or act intransigently towards their overtures to trade with China from Malacca.[3] Despite such claims, the conquest of a tributary vassal of China potentially involved the Portuguese in confrontation. The reason why these two powers did not clash is based upon China's highly divergent view from those of the Portuguese on the ordering of state relations and the role of maritime trade.

The conquest of Malacca by the Portuguese disturbed China's 'world order' – a term used to describe a set of ideas and practices towards foreign relations developed and perpetuated by the rulers of China, based on the concepts of Sinocentrism, an assumption of Chinese superiority and the utilisation of an intricate series of tributary relationships to justify their claims to a predominant position in the world.[4] The Ming officials were not without aid in how to approach this new barbarian problem; in all probability, they had to determine the exact nature of China's relationship with the Malacca sultanate. Based upon historical and conceptual antecedents, they had to establish the extent of the threat posed by these new barbarians to China and her vassal states and had to decide upon the manner in which these new intruders were to be controlled. They would have read the Emperor Yung-Lo's inscription where he commented that 'Malacca wished to be better than barbarian and wanted to be permanently part of the imperial domain.'[5] Malacca paid tribute to Ming China, whose frontiers were stabilised by this relationship. Ming policy, no 'outer-separation' for Malacca, had also been supported if not fostered in China by eunuch diplomats and naval commanders. Malacca was the gateway to the Indian Ocean and as a tributary state became involved as a useful support base for Ming naval expeditions.[6]

TRADITION, GEOGRAPHY AND OFFICIAL ATTITUDES

South China's maritime tradition existed prior to the naval expeditions of the early Ming dynasty. The conflict of Chinese public and private participation in the exercise of maritime trading privileges touched many facets of local Chinese

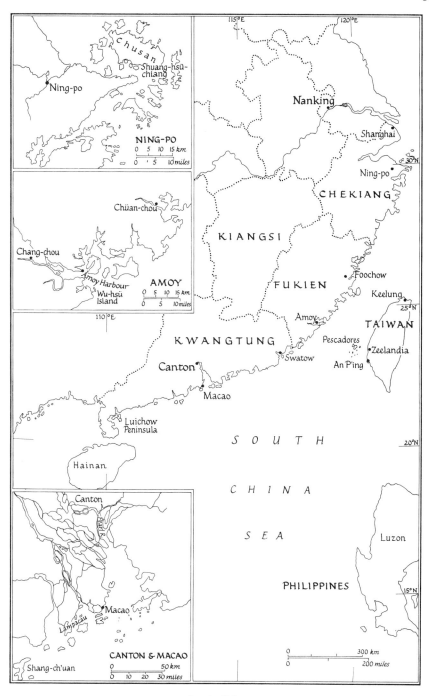

1 South China

society.[7] The maritime trade of China was not confined to Chinese participants alone; the tributary missions of the vassal states of the South China Sea to China had an economic as well as diplomatic and political purpose.

Geographical location, familial and occupational connections influenced the development of Chinese commercial and maritime trading practices and are a factor in the development of the south China ports as foci or enclaves of commerce and manufacturing.[8] Most of China's maritime merchant activity originated in the ports along the coast of Chekiang, Fukien and Kwangtung provinces. Merchants were mobile; Chang-chou merchants, for example, resided at Canton. Individual merchants from Chang-chou competed against each other, yet they did form a trade association based upon geographical location and type of product traded. Consequently, Chang-chou merchants at Canton defended their home port's commercial interests *vis-à-vis* those of Canton's merchants and Ming officials.

The ports of Ning-po in Chekiang, Amoy (a term used for the major ports Chang-chou and Ch'uan-chou) in Fukien, and Canton in Kwangtung, were the principal Chinese maritime commercial centres involved in trade to the South China Sea.[9] Shanghai, in Kiangnan, during the seventeenth and early eighteenth centuries, had not yet emerged as a major competitor to these ports' trade in the South China Sea. The geographical, historical, administrative and economic characteristics of these ports are factors which explain why they developed in the late Ming.

Ning-po, Amoy and Canton, in an age when fluvial transport was fundamental to the marketing of goods over almost any distance, were river-based, slightly in-land from the open sea and in the vicinity of island or estuary anchorages which offered protection from the elements, especially typhoons, and provided opportunities for smuggling. Only Canton was at the confluence of many river systems and had a large, productive delta region.

Geographic proximity to the South China Sea also aided Canton's development in that maritime tributary trade missions were received at that port. In the eyes of officials, management of overseas barbarians should occur as far away as possible from the centre of the empire. This fact and Canton's expansion in maritime trade had important repercussions on Portuguese involvement in China's trade.

Surrounding most of these south China ports were large, flat, farming areas with fertile alluvial soils which had highly developed, or soon to be developed, flood-control irrigation and canal systems that insured the production and marketing of agricultural produce. The adjacent river systems provided navigable points of penetration into the interior which permitted the movement of handicraft products in various stages of completion, and agricultural and mineral resources to the port areas. With sufficient arable land, under food crop cultivation, hydraulic control and fluvial transport, the population of these ports grew. This population was also involved in the development of maritime technology and the application of improved agricultural, manufacturing and handicraft techniques.[10]

Official attitudes, the Ming bureaucratic view of the world, and the Confucian-trained scholar-gentry antipathy towards merchants, meant that the Chinese merchant interested in maritime trade usually encountered vigorous bureaucratic constraints. These constraints were diminished either by bribery or the formation of a partnership between the merchants and officials. When such constraints and the cost of overcoming them were too high, the local merchant had to decide whether to divest his involvement in maritime trade and invest in more secure forms of financial activity, such as real estate.[11] The merchant also had the option of opposing the official and participating in non-social activities. Maritime trading opportunities, however, in the late Ming were on a scale that generally encouraged merchants and investors at Canton, Amoy and Ning-po to overcome bureaucratic constraints.

PARTICIPANTS, SUPPLIES AND DEMAND

The participants in the maritime trade of south China in the sixteenth century were Chinese merchants, investors, and junk owners who traded openly in the South China Sea and clandestinely with Japan. Others involved were the tribute traders from Southeast Asia, the Portuguese, and the Spanish. The economic development of the south China ports and their hinterland regions significantly benefited from the addition of these European participants.

The direct benefactors of the maritime trade that entered these ports were the Chinese merchants, the middlemen and the regional producers and the purchasers of the articles that were sold for export and bought for import. Beyond the creation of wealth and profit for a few merchants and officials, maritime trade had a fundamental role in the transformation of agricultural, mineral and handicraft production.

China's major exports in the late Ming were divided into three categories: precious metals, textiles and ballast goods. Gold bullion, one of three principal metals used in coinage and by weight in the large-scale transfers of wealth, was exported in significant quantities to Japan, India and the Philippines. Textiles, especially raw silk, and different varieties of silk and cotton piece-goods, were in increasing demand for export within Asia and to Europe. Ballast cargoes were supplied primarily from expanding export-oriented agricultural production, sugar in particular, and other commodities, such as alum, porcelain and zinc.[12]

There were regional differences in the supply of these goods dictated by geographical proximity, differences in pricing, and at times governmental controls. Zinc was mined near Canton and as a result was cheaper there. Large-scale sugar production for export first developed in Fukien province and stimulated Fukienese trade to Japan. The cultivation of cotton fibre for sale within China and the specialisation of cotton textile manufactures for the internal and overseas markets had emerged by the late Ming with Ning-po and Amoy deriving a slight pricing and ease of supply advantage over Canton.[13]

China's major imports in the late Ming may also be divided into three categories: metals, spices, and ballast commodities. Since China's silver production was very small and its requirements so large, the merchants of south China imported and purchased tremendous quantities of silver from Japan and the New World via the

Philippines, India and Europe. Previously, China was self-sufficient in copper production and copper coinage was exported; this trend reversed and sizeable quantities of copper were imported from Japan in the late Ming.

China's consumption of spices, pepper, cloves and nutmeg, probably increased in the last quarter of the sixteenth century. Portuguese traders were encouraged to bring spices to China; spices enjoyed a good market and were accepted for payment of customs duties, until 1582 when silver was demanded by Chinese authorities.[14] The Portuguese encountered difficulties in securing supplies of cloves and nutmeg directly from Ambon and Banda in the Indonesian archipelago as a result of the successful indigenous rebellion against the Portuguese on those islands in the late sixteenth century. With the arrival of the Dutch and English in the Indonesian archipelago, the competition for spice supplies in the South China Sea intensified and Portuguese spice sales fluctuated in China.

The historical characteristics of the south China ports refer to those maritime traditions, skills and technical capacities developed on the Fukien coast in the fifteenth century that built the ships and supplied the manpower that sailed into the Indian Ocean. Although some of these skills may have been lost, the sailors and shipbuilders from these ports certainly retained the memory of their heritage. The Ming naval expeditions were state-financed and from the available descriptions were carried out in rather large junks. The Chinese junks encountered by the Portuguese at Malacca in the early sixteenth century and the Dutch in the early seventeenth century underwent changes in their size and ownership. The large junks of the Ming naval expeditions reportedly equalled the size of a Portuguese *carrack*; the size of the majority of the vessels described in European reports in the seventeenth century ranged from one hundred tons to a maximum of two hundred tons.

Ship-owning and building in south China by the mid sixteenth century was no longer dominated by the state and returned to a form of economic activity for the very wealthy and powerful individual group, or association of individuals or groups. Since ship-owning and investing was in competition with other forms of risk-taking, the Chinese junk-owners diminished the size of their ships in order to gain advantages in their operating and investment costs. These Chinese ship-owners and investors found in their illegal and banned trade to Japan that their small and more numerous ships could attain a significant market share equal to, or greater than, their European and internal Japanese competition in the supply of raw silk.[15]

THE MARITIME TRADING WORLD OF THE SOUTH CHINA SEA

The conquest of Malacca also brought the Portuguese into confrontation with the state systems in the immediate vicinity and those which had political and economic relationships with the Malacca sultanate. The Portuguese encountered three major categories of state systems: Sinitic, Buddhist and Malay as they expanded through the South China Sea in the sixteenth century.

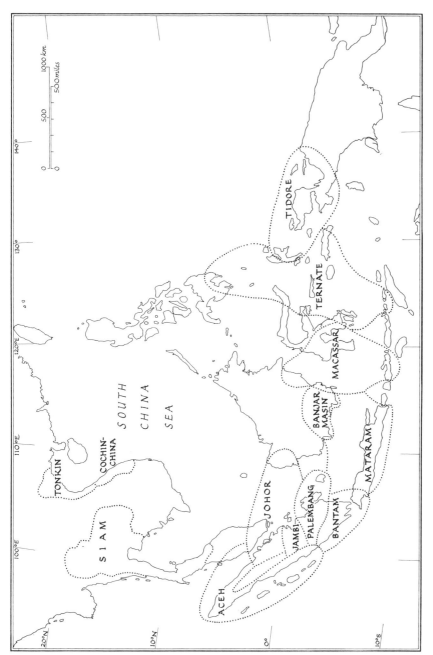

2 The South China Sea

Kings, sultans and views of the world

The Sinitic states, Tonkin and Cochinchina, possessed a set of ideas and practices towards foreign relations which were adapted from the Chinese model and developed by the rulers of Vietnam. Although based upon the Chinese pattern, the Vietnamese view was tempered by strongly held mythopoeic and religious views on the authoritarian role of the monarch.[16] The ruling families of Vietnam, the Trinh in Tonkin (northern Vietnam), and the Nguyen in Cochinchina (central Vietnam), employed Sino-Vietnamese bureaucracies that were Confucian in orientation and replicated dynastic courts which were heavily influenced by China's view of the world.

A protracted civil war, 1620–70, and its stalemate, reinforced the existence of two separate state systems in Vietnam. They simultaneously developed tributary systems based on a modified Chinese pattern of international relations. Tonkin by necessity and interest was an active participant in China's world order; the Trinh's claim to rule Vietnam was legitimised by Ming and, later, Ch'ing imperial investiture which aided the Trinh in its efforts to enlist foreign support for the conquest of the south.[17]

Cochinchina, in contrast, was not an active participant in China's world order; the Nguyen concentrated upon creating foreign relationships which would permit the continued existence of their regime and the expansion of their power into the lowland rice-producing regions of Champa and Cambodia. The slow territorial absorption of the present day southern regions of Vietnam, the *nam-thien* (southward) movement, was described by one Nguyen general as, 'the policy of slowly eating silkworms.' This expansionist Vietnamese policy began in the mid seventeenth century and lasted for well over a century.[18]

The Buddhist state systems, Siam and Cambodia, despite close contacts with China in the early fifteenth century and Siam being a tributary of Ming and Ch'ing China, practised a set of ideas towards foreign relations based upon Buddhist concepts of order. In their view the role of the ruler was dominant and relations with other states were governed by a system of overlord–vassal obligations.[19] The King of Siam was considered, 'a reincarnated deity, a chakravartin or universal emperor. Moreover, he was a bodhisattva, a being destined to be a Buddha. His authority was absolute, his person was both sacred and unapproachable.'[20] Siam's monarch received tribute from Laos and various Malay state systems; he claimed and received tribute whenever possible from Cambodia and Burma, states with similar perception of the world.[21]

The Malay encompassed the vast expanse of land and sea, known today as Malaysia, Singapore, Indonesia and the Philippines. It was divided into state systems, some of which were influenced to a variable degree by Islam and others which retained almost intact their non-Islamic traditions. Its rulers practised sets of ideas towards foreign relations that drew upon Islamic and non-Islamic traditions towards order and its maintenance through overlord–vassal relationships. In the Islamic state systems, the pre-eminent authoritarian figure was the sultan, 'whose right to the throne was primarily based on his unbroken descent from a glorious ancestor. While in theory no further justification for total authority was needed, in practice a ruler's power was directly related to his material resources.'[22] In the non-Islamic state systems, the authority of the ruler depended upon the sophistication of the society and the extent of Hindu influence. This contrast is best exemplified by a comparison of Bali's highly Hindu-influenced society with parts of Timor in which Indian influence were entirely absent.

Although continental in scope, possessing abundant mineral and other natural resources, the South China Sea state systems failed, in comparison to China, to establish a 'universal empire.' The region remained highly bifurcated and China through its 'tributary system' projected in stark contrast, 'a very real cultural and economic dominance and magnetism in East and Southeast Asia'.[23] The Malay ruler in Aceh expanded his control over the pepper ports of north Sumatra, which were located at the confluence of one or more river systems. The ruler of Johor, in the early seventeenth century, made his kingdom the new centre of the old Malacca sultanate; Johor continued to be a maritime state highly dependent upon the rivers and the sea which were its principal means of communications and livelihood. In terms of distance Johor could very well be termed a 'far-flung' kingdom; but with the sea and the rivers providing easy access to even the most remote dependency, 'Johor was a much closer-knit kingdom than the distance would indicate.'[24] The Buddhist ruler, the King of Siam, recurrently claimed overlordship of various neighbouring Malay and Buddhist state systems. The Sinitic rulers, contrary to their claims, did not maintain the unity of Vietnam nor could the Trinh in Tonkin overtly limit the expansion of the Nguyen in Cochinchina.

Limits to expansion, diplomacy and maritime trade

The physical and political geography, as well as the demography, of the South China Sea in the seventeenth and eighteenth centuries, especially after the arrival of the VOC (the *Vereenigde Oost-Indische Compagnie*, the Dutch East India Company), hampered tendencies within certain indigenous state systems towards their imperial expansion and did not permit the creation of a single-state universal empire. Consequently, divergent theoretical attitudes towards diplomacy and maritime trade within the region in practice succumbed to the more pragmatic exigencies of the exercise of state power.

The attitudes of the Sinitic, Buddhist and Malay rulers towards diplomacy and maritime trade may be characterised only in a general manner when discussing highly disparate societies over a century or more of intense political and economic development, confrontation with European interests and different perception of time and space. The theoretical purpose of diplomacy in the state systems of the South China Sea, as in China, was to reinforce the state's perception of its position in the universe. Elaborate overlord–vassal relationships, the exchange of gifts, and formal patterns of behaviour in the reception of ruler-to-ruler correspondence and ambassadors was in evidence in all of the Sinitic, Buddhist and Malay states.[25]

In the political theory of the individual state, the outward form of acceptance of a diplomatic message was maintained as well as the reception of an ambassador from a ruler who entertained a different political ideology, or was of a different status in a tributary relationship. What was necessary, and perhaps this in part explains the frequency of diplomatic activity in the South China Sea region, was the internal political and ideological requirement to receive and send diplomatic missions. The internal representation of embassies from non-tributary states was evidence of the power and prestige of the host state. In addition to the substantive political deliberations and the trade that might be carried out, these exchanges were interpreted or modified to coincide with that state's perception of the world. Vassalage was less onerous than is imagined and in certain unstable areas of the region was secretly negotiable; in some cases, it was a method of offsetting the encroachment of a powerful neighbouring state with another more distant powerful state.

The state systems of the South China Sea had varying attitudes to, and economic interests in, maritime trade. Consistent with the supremacy of the ruler, royal authority in theory was often equated with royal monopoly in the production, collection or sale of stipulated commodities. The regulation of maritime trade was controlled by the various courts and the indigenous ruler was usually the major participant in maritime trading ventures. Despite the apparent supremacy of the indigenous ruler and his domination of maritime trade, in practice there was a greater divergence on account of differing geographical, ideological and economic characteristics.

In the Malay and Buddhist states, with the major exception of Mataram, the political and commercial centres were combined and located either on or near a river system which provided fluvial access into the interior. In the Malay world, the *kampong* (village) formed the basic expression of socio-political organisation on account of the mountainous terrain and tropical vegetation and fluvial transport proved to be a relatively easy means of communication between the Malay peninsula and the multitudinous islands of the Indonesian archipelago as a result of relatively mild and protected sailing conditions. In the Buddhist states, the political centres of Siam and Cambodia were also the major maritime commercial centres and located on the Chaopraya and Mekong rivers. In the Sinitic world, by contrast, the political centres of Tonkin at Hanoi (Ke-cho) and Cochinchina at Hue, although located on river systems that had access to both the interior and the exterior, they were not the major maritime commercial centres. In Tonkin, Pho-hien (near modern H'ung Yen) and in Cochinchina, Fai-fo (Hoi-an) were the principal maritime centres of those states.

The harsher geographical characteristics of China were only one reason for its reliance upon foreign merchants in the development of its maritime trade; another, and perhaps the predominant, characteristic was ideological. The ideology of the Sinitic state was Confucian which conflicted with the development of mercantile endeavour; the Malay and Hindu state systems embraced an ideology which did not impede the direct participation of the ruler or bring the state officials in ideological conflict in the development of maritime trade. The degree to which there was an absence of ideological hostility to the merchant in the Malay and Buddhist world is startling. The Confucian orientation of the Hanoi and the Hue courts brought about a bureaucratisation of government and led to a theoretical contempt for merchants. In practice, however, there was some difference between the Chinese and Vietnamese views. In China, 'court ideology scorned merchants (overtly but not covertly) because it considered them parasitic and unproductive, compared to scholars and farmers.' In Vietnam 'rulers and bureaucrats tended to discriminate against merchants more because successful merchants commanded immoderately large resources in a poor society. In Nguyen Vietnam, it was as much the visible results as the functions of entrepreneurship that were invidious.'[26]

The theoretical attitudes of the Malay, Buddhist and Sinitic worlds towards maritime trade in the seventeenth and eighteenth centuries, when examined in an empirical fashion, demonstrated that the ruler's power was only occasionally so absolute as depicted; participation in maritime trade was not an exclusive domain of the ruler. Various powerful political and social elements in local society, either as bureaucrats, administrators, nobles or merchants, in joint or separate ventures, with or without the ruler, participated in trade. The granting of permission to trade by the indigenous rulers to these elements in local society and foreign merchants served as a means of patronage, a form of increasing wealth for the state and the individual involved, which occasionally caused internal political strife.

By the early seventeenth century, the states in the South China Sea had diminished their participation in international maritime trade. These states reveal an absence of significant structural economic change and development when compared with China and India. This has intrigued historians interested in examining the nature of premodern Asian society and the extent to which the Europeans influenced its development.[27] The curtailment of these states' participation in international and inter-regional maritime trade has been linked to their ideological, economic, and geographical characteristics. Additional reasons include the disruptive influence of and competition from the Portuguese and the Dutch upon the existing trade, the region's restricted and limited export and import commodity composition and requirements, and more controversial, the persistent perception that the region lacked sufficient technological advancement to sustain international maritime trade.

With the forcible intrusion of the Portuguese, Asia confronted an alien European society that was experienced in extending its political influence and power by sea. The Portuguese encountered in the East societies that equalled and surpassed their own in cultural richness and material splendour. The strengths and weaknesses of this Iberian society in Asia depended upon the organisation, utilisation, and maintenance of their resources in the complex trading worlds of China and the South China Sea.

2

IMPERIAL FOUNDATIONS: THE ESTADO DA INDIA *AND MACAO*

After their arrival in the Indian Ocean in 1498 and a short period of operation in southern India, the Portuguese established the administrative and political centre of their Asian empire at Goa. The *Estado da India*, the State of India, the name given by the Portuguese Crown to this imperial enterprise, was not a unitary state but a collection of forts, fleets, and communities that stretched from east Africa to Japan.

The Crown's representatives were preoccupied with the construction of an economic system of empire and their personal enrichment. Their basic objective was to dominate Asian maritime trade in spices, pepper in particular, and to force existing maritime trading activities to pay for permission to trade in the Indian Ocean; their energy, exchequer and manpower were committed ostensibly to this enterprise. The economic benefits to the Crown in establishing the Estado da India were obvious and the benefit to its supporters was to be ensured by patronage.

There was, also, a strong religious objective in the establishment of the Estado da India. Portugal, as a major Catholic power and with the major role of the Catholic Church in that society, possessed a real interest in the propagation of the Christian faith and a crusading zeal against Islam. With the Counter-Reformation, the Crown re-doubled its involvement and support for Catholic missionary activity in Asia.

Despite startlingly successful initial naval and military activities, the Crown's principal economic objective of establishing a Portuguese monopoly over the supply of spices to Europe was impossible to fulfil. Asia was too vast, her merchants too resilient and capable and Portuguese resources, especially in shipping and manpower, were limited. The voyage to India wreaked havoc upon the manpower sent out to garrison the Estado da India.[1] The men who did arrive sound and healthy were not always interested in staying in Crown service or in the formal centres of empire where their economic activities were restrained by a highly hierarchical society.

By the end of the sixteenth century, the Estado da India was involved, and had been almost from its inception, in 'redistributive enterprises' such as the collection of revenue from the sale of *cartazes* (sea passes).[2] Furthermore, the Crown sold the right to sail various inter-Asian maritime trading routes to members of local Portuguese societies. The Crown's monopoly system did not seek to stimulate economic activity, it was patently a method of raising revenue and

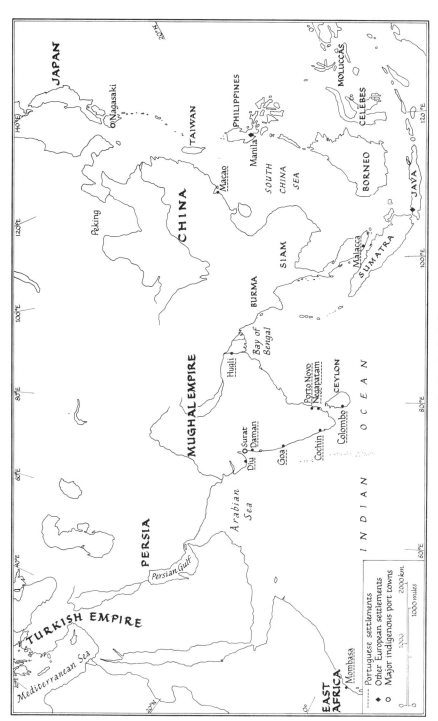

3 The Estado da India

Map labels:

JAPAN
Nagasaki
TAIWAN
PHILIPPINES
Manila
Macao
CHINA
Peking
MOLUCCAS
CELEBES
SOUTH CHINA SEA
BORNEO
JAVA
SUMATRA
Malacca
SIAM
BURMA
Bay of Bengal
MUGHAL EMPIRE
Hugli
Porto Novo
Negapatam
CEYLON
Colombo
Surat
Daman
Diu
Goa
Cochin
Arabian Sea
INDIAN OCEAN
PERSIA
Persian Gulf
TURKISH EMPIRE
Mediterranean Sea
EAST AFRICA
Mombasa

--- Portuguese settlements
♦ Other European settlements
○ Major indigenous port towns

1000   2000 km
1000 miles

providing patronage. Crown administrative involvement in such practices and its failure to establish a spice monopoly has led to the characterisation of Portuguese involvement in Asia's maritime trade and its impact on local society as minimal.[3]

The Estado da India, as well as other parts of Portugal's empire, was not 'just a string of fortresses and *feitorias* united by the departure and the arrival of the *caravelas* and *naus*.' The Portuguese empire was 'also and perhaps even principally, the married householders (*casados*) who so frequently adapted themselves to indigenous life' and 'already distant from political control,' it was 'those *lançados* on three continents.'[4] In the formal centres of empire, such as Goa and Malacca, the Crown's representatives dominated and attempted to husband their manpower resources.

Throughout the trading world of Asia in the sixteenth and seventeenth centuries, there were a sprinkling of Portuguese communities with an overwhelmingly male, European population. The inhabitants of these Portuguese communities consisted of small numbers of *reinois* (persons born in Portugal) augmented by *mestiço* (Eurasian) and slave populations. For the Portuguese Crown authorities, the reinois and mestiços, who in theory were under their total control, were grouped by marital status. Both the *casados* (married householders) and the *solteiros* (bachelors) or those Portuguese whose wives were elsewhere, kept large slave-holding households. When these groups lived outside of the formal centre of the Empire and those communities in which the Portuguese Crown representatives were in control, they were collectively known as *lançados*. Whether as lançados or under the aegis of Crown authority, in almost every maritime trading state in the South China Sea region in the sixteenth and seventeenth centuries, the Portuguese resided in a quarter in or near the major urban political or financial centre.

In their quarter, the Portuguese built residences, warehouses and Catholic churches, either for the trading season or on a permanent basis. This system of granting a quarter of a town for the residence of foreign merchants was not exclusive to the Portuguese but was already customary prior to their arrival in Asia.[5] The dispersal of the limited reinois and mestiço population, along with a small number of Catholic missionaries, out of the formal centres of the Empire, Malacca and the fortresses in the eastern Indonesian archipelago, to the more informal, Macao, Nagasaki, Manila, Siam, Cambodia, Tonkin, Cochinchina, Macassar and northern Java, was opposed by the Crown but impossible to control.

The Portuguese Crown and country traders were initially concerned with the procurement of spices for Europe and the re-orientation of maritime trade from the eastern Mediterranean, Red Sea, Persian Gulf supply routes to that of the Cape of Good Hope. Within Asia, the Crown sought to control existing trade by monopolising certain routes and re-directing existing trade into the ports dominated by Portuguese forces. By the end of the sixteenth century, the Portuguese Crown and country trader involvement in inter-Asian maritime trade dwarfed in volume and value the trade between Cochin–Goa and Lisbon via the Cape of Good Hope.

At the same time, the structure of Portuguese trade in Asia demonstrated the incorporation of totally new routes and the intensification and unification of others.

With their involvement in the supply of Japanese and New World silver to China from Manila and via India, the movement of silver bullion on a world scale was established as was the sale of Chinese raw silk and piecegoods in Europe, Asia and the New World. The Portuguese participated intensely in the inter-Asian trade; in which Indian goods, especially cotton textiles, were freely exchanged in the South China Sea for spices, especially cloves from the Spice islands. Silver and spices were exchanged for silk and gold from China for the Indian market.

THE PORTUGUESE AND THE TRADING WORLD OF THE SOUTH CHINA SEA

Throughout the sixteenth and into the early seventeenth centuries, the Portuguese expanded and, alternately, defended their political and economic interests in the South China Sea. Contemporaneously, the Sinitic, Buddhist and Malay worlds continued to develop and consolidate; other European powers, the Dutch East India Company primarily, emerged as fierce adversaries and competitors, first against the Portuguese and, subsequently, the indigenous state systems.

At Malacca, the Portuguese claimed the sultanate's overlordship of several small tin-producing states on the Malay peninsula, Perak and Kedah. In the Moluccas, in the eastern Indonesian archipelago, the Portuguese embarked upon a policy of conquest and occupation of various spice-producing islands in the hope of obtaining a European monopoly of the supply of cloves, nutmeg and mace. Pepper, on account of its widespread production in Sumatra, Java and Borneo, despite the Portuguese position at Malacca and their trade in that commodity on the Kanara and Malabar coasts of India, was a non-monopolisable commodity. Other spices, such as cloves and nutmeg, also resisted monopoly; by the last quarter of the sixteenth century, the Portuguese faced indigenous revolts in the Moluccas aided by Johor and other sultanates. In contrast and in part on account of the success of Catholic missionaries in the non-Islamic states in the Lesser Sunda islands on Solor and Timor, the Portuguese established themselves and derived benefit from their trade in sandalwood, wax and slaves.

Aceh, Johor and Mataram were the major indigenous power centres of the Malay world in the sixteenth century; Macassar joined them towards the end of that century or in the early seventeenth century. In the extreme western corner of the Indonesian archipelago on the island of Sumatra, the sultanate of Aceh, by a policy of diplomacy and force absorbed a number of smaller port states, and seriously contested the Portuguese attempt to establish a pepper monopoly, by reviving its trading relations with the Red Sea. Aceh's power was such that they periodically imperilled the Portuguese at Malacca.

Johor, and the successor of the Malacca sultanate, suffered perhaps more from continued Portuguese antagonism and attack than other state systems. From its shifting location on the southern Malay peninsula, it maintained for most of this period its influence over portions of Sumatra and protected its contacts with Borneo from encroachment by the Portuguese and Aceh. Johor, also, participated in attacks upon Malacca and provided aid for anti-Portuguese revolts in the Moluccas.

Mataram, as the most powerful sultanate on the island of Java, in contrast with the maritime-oriented sultanates of Aceh and Johor, retained its preoccupation with the extension of its sovereignty on that island. Consequently, their relations with the Portuguese from Malacca were minimal. After Mataram absorbed several north Java port-states, Japara and Griesik, and the Dutch occupied Batavia in 1619, Mataram explored the potential of an alliance with the Portuguese.

THE PORTUGUESE AND THE TRADING WORLD OF CHINA

After the conquest of Malacca, the Portuguese Crown's representatives in Asia, headed by the Viceroy of the Estado da India at Goa and the Governor at Malacca, were confident that they could initiate political and economic relations with China. Portuguese Crown efforts occurred after Ming official involvement in maritime enterprise had diminished dramatically. The Ming officials also perceived the Portuguese military threat to the security of China as limited.

Consequently, from 1513 to 1520, Ming officials at Canton implemented a policy towards official Portuguese overtures which may be construed as a form of appeasement supported by feelings of Chinese superiority.[6] After the death of the Emperor Cheng-te and the ill-conceived martial actions of the Portuguese forces under the command of Simão de Andrade at Canton in 1520, Ming officials reassessed and reformulated their policy towards the emergence of this new group of foreigners on the southern periphery of the Chinese Empire, ordered the exclusion of the Portuguese and implemented a ban on all dealings by the inhabitants of China with the barbarian devils.

Trade with China in the eyes of the Portuguese Crown's representatives had to be obtained by attracting Chinese junk traffic to Malacca. This policy was followed with some success by Portuguese governors of Malacca. It was replaced by direct trade links after Sino-Portuguese commercial competition developed in the South China Sea markets.

Those members of Portuguese society who were primarily responsible for the expansion of direct commercial contacts with China in the 1530s and the 1540s were the lançados from other Portuguese communities in Asia and who had congregated on the Fukien coast in hopes of pecuniary gain.[7]

The Crown and the Church, who were later to figure so prominently, at this point in time were not the driving force behind Portuguese efforts in China. Malacca and the Crown's authority and ability to control fractious commercial and communal elements was too distant; the Church, present to attend communal requirements, did not yet demonstrate the missionary zeal that emanated from the Counter-Reformation and is readily associated in Portuguese society with the activities of the Society of Jesus.[8]

Conditions on the south China coast by the 1530s and into the 1560s permitted and prompted a rise in lawlessness, corruption and those forms of marginal social behaviour so common to maritime regions, smuggling and piracy. The Portuguese, who arrived on the Fukien and Chekiang coasts from Malacca, were, according to the Imperial edict, to be excluded from the normal forms of commerce and correspondence with China. Since there were few constraints either from Chinese or Portuguese society, these Portuguese participated and sustained themselves by piracy and smuggling.

The process of legitimisation of the Portuguese in the eyes and minds of Chinese officials began at the time of the *wakō* (Japanese, *wo-k'ou* in Chinese) crisis and after the Portuguese initiated trade with Japan with Chinese products. The wakō crisis, the so-called invasion of south China by 'Japanese' pirates, the majority actually being Chinese, emerged perhaps even earlier than 1540.[9]

From 1549 to 1561 the incidence of violent pirate activities in the hinterland and against the cities on the lower Yangtze and on the south China coast was at its height.[10] Although the Portuguese may have utilised Wang Chin, a prominent pirate leader at Shuang-hsu, in some type of merchant–mediator role in one of their first visits to Japan in 1543, by late 1548, after Ming forces under Lu T'ang attacked the pirate base at Shuang-hsu and Portuguese ships skirmished with Lu T'ang's pursuing naval forces off Wu-hsu island in the bay of Amoy, the Portuguese were beginning to fear that the new Chinese Viceroy of Fukien and Chekiang, Chu Wan, really was dedicated to suppressing smuggling and piracy on those coasts. Additional proof of Chu Wan's dedication, as described by Gaspar da Cruz, came in 1549 when Galeote Pereira and other Portuguese leaders and sailors ventured on the south Fukien and Kwangtung coasts and were captured.

Under Ming military pressure, if the Portuguese were to continue their illicit activities, it was obvious to them that they had to establish themselves at an unobtrusive site and one where the local Ming officials would envision the financial benefit of having them present. By the mid-1550s, Ming officials permitted the Portuguese to use sites on the Kwangtung coast, first at Shang-ch'uan, then Lampacau and finally Macao. In 1554, the Portuguese commander, Leonel de Sousa, claimed to have negotiated a verbal agreement with Wang Po, the acting commander of the coastguard fleet, permitting the Portuguese to trade in Kwangtung on terms similar to those of the Siamese.[11]

When Chinese governmental forces established their control on the Fukien (1564) and the Kwangtung (1566) coasts, the Portuguese at Macao had sufficiently legitimised themselves with local Ming officials so that their community could begin to establish a more definite municipal formation. The incipient Portuguese community also benefited from the Ming decision to permit the partial legalisation of maritime trade in 1567.

Chinese maritime activity on the south China coast responded positively to the suppression of the wakō. The reasons for south China's prosperity from 1570 to 1620 in particular and the Ming economy in general are only in part explained by the establishment of peaceful and orderly conditions along the coast from the mouth of the Yangtze to the Pearl River and down to the Luchow peninsula and including Hainan island.[12]

The importation of silver bullion from Japan, the New World via the Philippines, and India stimulated the Ming economy and promoted the expansion of exports from certain sectors of Chinese regional economies. The late Ming economy 'witnessed a quickening in agricultural specialisation and commercialisation, rapid growth in the handicraft industries, a significant expansion in the volume and extent of interregional trade, and the widespread implementation of changes in the system of taxation.'[13] Silver, for example, became the basic form of paying land taxes. It was via maritime trade that silver was imported; the importance of maritime trade, as a consequence, upon the whole Ming economy is being recognised as one, if not the single, most significant factor in late Ming economic expansion.

Portuguese involvement in the maritime trade of China and the South China Sea was dispersed through the Estado da India. Although Portuguese society in China participated in trade in the South China Sea, Macao's early efforts were focused primarily on their trade with Japan, Manila and India. After the establishment of a Portuguese community in China, the Crown and the Church sought to introduce royal government and integrate Catholic religious observances and missionary efforts in the regions. The success or failure of the Estado da India and Macao revolved around these issues of royal government and communal organisation and administration.

THE ESTADO DA INDIA AND MACAO

The Estado da India was not different from other areas of the world in which the Portuguese established themselves, in that, the institutions which were established and which governed this and other overseas Portuguese societies reflected the administrative structure of continental Portugal. The ideology and political culture of these communities was the heritage of the manner in which different social and economic groups organised themselves, defended their economic interests and maintained their social mores and prejudices in sixteenth-century Portugal.

The representatives of the Portuguese Crown gradually implanted a system of royal government in China with the intension of protecting the monarch's interests and concentrated their efforts in three major overlapping bureaucratic areas: administration, finance and justice. A fourth area of interest was centred on the Crown's *Padroado* (patronage) of the missionary activities of the Catholic Church in China and the South China Sea. The Crown's administration in Macao was served first by the *capitão-mor* of the Japan voyage and subsequently by a *capitão-geral*. Crown finances, especially in the 1630s with the increased preoccupation for revenue and regional sources of finance for the prosecution of its war against Holland, became the subject of scrutiny by the administrators of the Japan and Manila voyages who reported to the *vedor da fazenda* (the royal treasurer) and the *Conselho da Fazenda* (the Council of the Royal Treasury) in Goa. The Crown's judicial representative in Macao was the *ouvidor* (judge) who was responsible to the *Relação* (High Court), which was composed of the *ouvidor geral* (superior judge), and the *desembargadors* (high court judges) in Goa.

THE CAPITÃO-MOR

Upon their arrival in Japan, which first occurred in 1542–3, the Portuguese, some of whom had already settled on the south coast of China and were to move to Macao, initiated an unfettered trade at various Japanese ports. Little record of these early efforts exists but Portuguese Crown representatives in Malacca and Goa were pleased when Lisbon announced its monopoly over the trading activities of Portuguese merchants to Japan. The Crown, in an effort to control its monopoly, established the position of *Capitão-mor da Viagem da China e Japão* (the Commander of the Voyages of China and Japan) which was to be conferred on an annual basis, usually by the Viceroy in India, upon a worthy applicant. In theory, the capitão-mor was the Crown's supreme representative and was to be acknowledged as such by all Portuguese shipping and settlements east of Malacca.

The creation of the position of capitão-mor suited the Portuguese Crown's purpose as a source of revenue and a method of patronage. The observable trends in the appointment of the capitão-mor were that the Crown, prior to its unification with Spain in 1580, rewarded applicants almost exclusively from the nobility.[14] From 1580 until the mid-1620s, there was a marked proliferation in the number of successful applicants, again mostly from the nobility, which led to requests that the right to the voyage could be bequeathed; the Japan voyage was involved in explosion of demands for and the rewarding of patronage by the Habsburg monarchy.[15]

By the early 1600s and especially in the 1620s, as increased difficulties in imperial finances in Europe and in the Estado da India became manifest, a new trend in the Crown's utilisation of the Japan voyage emerged. Revenues derived from the sale of the voyage and the customs duties collected by the vedor da fazenda in the East were earmarked for defence projects. It was especially during this period, although not exclusively, that the Crown granted voyages to various municipal councils with the intention that the revenue would be allocated for the construction of city defences and the supply of armaments.

After 1601 the revenue from the sale of the China and Japan voyages on account of the VOC threat was requested by various *camaras* of Portuguese ports in the Estado da India to be given to them by Crown grant and these funds were to be used for the fortification of these ports. The municipal councils of Goa, Cochin, Chaul, Daman, São Tomé de Meliapor, Malacca and Macao are some of these mentioned as either requesting or having been given Crown grants but the revenue from the sale of the voyage was withheld by the Viceroy or local *capitão*. In the case of Macao, prior to 1622, the Crown's suggestion and offer of a grant of a voyage to fortify the city was neglected by the local inhabitants for fear of adverse Chinese reaction; after 1622, the city involved itself in petitioning for various grants and in 1628 they transferred their grant for a Japan voyage to the camara of São Tomé.[16]

Two additional trends developed in the late 1620s and 1630s. The first trend which really re-emerged, was the naming of the Crown's favourites, such as the

Queen and the Monastery of Encarnación in Madrid, as recipients of grants for voyages; these grants were auctioned in Goa. The second trend was that prominent merchants in the East, for example Lopo Sarmento de Carvalho, were permitted to purchase the voyage.[17]

The successful applicant possessed the option to sell or take up his position as capitão-mor. Later, when the voyage was sold and allocated for the fiscal requirements of various municipal councils in the East and other institutions, the purchaser could also make the voyage in person, by proxy or sell it yet again. East of Malacca, the capitão-mor could enter into diplomatic and economic negotiations with the Crown's authority. He also acted as the *Provedor-Mor dos Defuntos e Ausentes* (Custodian of the Property of Dead and Absent Persons) until 1589 when it became a municipal appointment.[18] This meant that if any Portuguese in his region of authority died intestate, the capitão-mor was responsible for settling the probate and the transfer of the estate to India where arrangements for its dispersal to inheritors in Portugal or elsewhere were made. This is one example of the privileged access by the capitão-mor to the capital resources of the Portuguese settlements east of Malacca which could and on occasion did lead to his malfeasance of funds.

The reality of the capitão-mor's authority differed substantially from his theoretical powers. According to Goa, he commenced the outfitting of his own ship or the ship provided by the Crown on loan against adequate security. Although the capitão-mor's life-and-death powers over the crews on his shop or squadron was unquestioned, the potential restrictions upon his authority caused by his dependence on a good working relationship with the Viceroy, other Crown representatives, municipal council, the religious orders (especially the Jesuits), and the merchants at Macao and Nagasaki, as the voyage progressed, generally dissuaded him from any overbearing authoritarian role.[19]

After the establishment of a Portuguese settlement at Macao in 1557 and until the creation of the *Senado da Camara* (municipal council) in 1583, the capitão-mor faced little, if any, open questioning of his authority over Portuguese diplomatic and commercial interests in China and Japan. After 1583 and until his replacement by a permanent capitão-geral (governor) in Macao in 1623, the capitão-mor had to take much greater account of the political interests of the Portuguese country traders and the Jesuits. The Jesuits had to be considered not only because of their political position in Japan but also on account of their economic interests in the silk and other trades.

CAPITÃO-GERAL

The Crown's desire to establish a permanent representative in Macao antendated by several decades the actual appointment of the first capitão-geral, D. Francisco Mascarenhas, in 1623. In the sixteenth century, when the Spanish Governor of the Philippines encountered difficulties in obtaining a satisfactory response from the Portuguese concerning the structuring and the limitation of trade between Macao and Manila, he advocated the establishment of a capitão in China.[20] This recommendation, first made in 1592, was to recur in correspondence between the Crown to the Viceroy of Portugal, the Viceroy of the Estado da India and representatives of the Crown and the Senado da Camara of Macao for the next three decades.[21] It was only after Macao's successful defence against a VOC attack in 1622 that the Senado da Camara members allowed their fear of an adverse reaction from Chinese officials, the cost of supporting the office and garrison and the diminution of their privileges in government to be overcome and petitioned the Viceroy of the Estado da India for a military commander.

The capitão-geral's authority and responsibilities were defined in his instructions: he replaced the capitão-mor, who retained his titular rank but whose authority was now confined to his ship, as the Crown's most powerful representative east of Malacca.[22] The advantage for the Crown of appointing a capitão-geral, whose normal term of office was three years, was that he resided permanently in Macao and could be responsible for its defence and finances. The capitão-geral held ambassadorial rank and was empowered to negotiate for the Crown, a power which could directly interfere with similar privileges of the Senado da Camara.

Friction between the capitão-geral and the local country traders in the Senado da Camara developed because of his ample powers, his personality on account of his social background and temperament, and his activities in country trade. The observable trends in the appointment of the capitão-geral were that the successful appointee was usually a *fidalgo* (noble) and almost always from a military background. Some were members of one or more of the three prominent military orders of Portugal.[23] They were from a class that out of ideological conviction distained mercantile endeavour, but in practice were involved in trade which prompted complaints from Portuguese country traders at Macao. One of these complaints arose because of the inability of the country traders to recover the loans that they made to this official. Others were more general and included the country traders' belief that this official intentionally interfered in their trading operations.

During several critical periods of Macao's history, the capitão-geral was selected from available reinois candidates in the local citizenry by the Viceroy of the Estado da India; one of the better examples of this phenomenon was the appointment of Manual Tavares Bocarro from 1657–64. The reasons for these internal appointments stemmed from a scarcity of qualified administrative manpower, Crown preoccupation with the defence of Ceylon and India and the obvious capabilities of men such as Bocarro.

The Crown attempted via its royal orders and other correspondence to resolve the differences between the capitão-geral and the Senado da Camara, but these could only be effectively diminished on a personal level and on an individual issue basis. Defence was, for example, one of the capitão-geral's principal concerns but the financing of the fortification and the garrison at Macao was in the hands of the Senado da Camara based on the collection of custom receipts. The Crown, in the person of the capitão-geral, and the Senado da Camara were to haggle over the additional financial burden that had to be imposed upon Macao's revenues for defence schemes. By the mid-1630s, the capitão-geral's position on defence and military expenditure gained ground with the Senado da Camara's temporary acquiescence to the Viceroy of India's scheme to place Crown fiscal authorities in Macao to control the collection of revenues from the voyages to Japan and Manila and to pay for the military garrison from receipts. The Senado da Camara, however, never lost its financial position entirely as the customs receipts from the other voyages to the South China Sea were still collected under that institution's authority.

ADMINISTRADORES DA VIAGEM DE JAPÀO E MANILA

In 1634, dissatisfaction over the absence of sufficient Crown fiscal control of Macao's merchants, led the Viceroy, Dom Miguel de Noronha, the Conde de Linhares, to order the modification of the city's financial arrangements with the Crown by appointing administrators of the Japan, Manila and Macassar voyages.[24] Similar plans were debated in Macao in 1629, as was the idea of including the voyage from India to China in the *Companhia das Indias* (a company formed on the lines of the VOC and the English East India Company [the EIC] with the intention of reversing and renovating the Crown's declining economic position *vis-à-vis* the Protestant powers).[25]

These new offices were viceregal nominations and were not for sale. The Conde de Linhares encountered stiff opposition to the creation of an administrator of the voyage from Macao to Macassar, which had not previously been a Crown monopoly, and terminated this appointment in 1635. The positions as administrators of the Japan and the Manila voyages were filled, and met with notable success for the Crown in the provision of desperately needed revenue. Manoel Ramos was the first administrator of the Japan voyage and operated the voyage's finances and transactions to the Crown's benefit.[26] The administrator of the Manila voyage served a similar purpose and reported at Macao to the administrator of the Japan voyage.

This system of financial control was designed as a result of a row between Macao and the Crown over differing viewpoints of fiscal responsibilities towards the method of payment of the garrison. By installing these administrators, the Crown accepted responsibility for paying the garrison through a portion of its interest in the operating profits of the Japan and Manila voyages. By the mid-1640s, after the cessation of these voyages and the murder of one of the administrators in Macao, the intensity of the Crown's interest and its capability in maintaining this position diminished to the point that the Viceroy ceased to appoint these officials and the Senado da Camara reclaimed total control over Macao's finances.

OUVIDOR

The structure of the Estado da India's judicial system was based upon an elaborate organisational model found in continental Portugal.[27] At Goa, the Relação, which was created in 1544, served as the highest court of appeal and the ouvidor-geral and the desembargadores (the superior court judge and his colleagues) were the Crown's most powerful juridicial representatives in Asia.[28] To administer justice in Macao, the Viceroy and the ouvidor-geral appointed an ouvidor (judge) to visit and reside in the city for a period which was usually three years.[29] These judges were *letrados* (learned persons) on account of their relatively high standard of education.

The ouvidor was empowered to investigate claims of official impropriety and adjudicate capital crimes, such as murder. Since his was a Crown appointment, he also fulfilled a political and administrative function; in the absence of the capitão-mor, the ouvidor was the most important Crown representative in Macao. In communities with a Senado da Camara in addition to the ouvidor, two elected magistrates judged misdemeanour offences. After the capitão-geral was appointed, the ouvidor's role as an administrative figure diminished, but his influence in judicial matters and as an investigator of fraudulent and criminal activities was maintained.

Although Macao experienced periods of extreme internal unrest occasionally culminating in riots and murder, the ouvidor's presence as a peace-keeper, in general, functioned throughout the seventeenth and eighteenth centuries. By the 1740s, the ouvidor's activities had diminished to that of a referee in cases to the Relação which prompted the Crown to order the Viceroy to replace the ouvidor's office with the magistrates of the municipal council.[30]

PADROADO

An intimate and formal relationship between the secular and religious powers characterised Portuguese society; this formal relationship, the Padroado, founded in the fifteenth century, was the 'combination of the rights, privileges and duties granted by the Papacy to the Crown of Portugal as patron of the Roman Catholic missions and ecclesiastical establishments in vast regions of Africa, of Asia, and in Brazil'.[31] The Crown supported a number of religious orders and their missionary activities in China and the South China Sea. It is not within the compass of this study to discuss the activities of all the religious orders in the Padroado, their organisation or the various jurisdictional and doctrinal controversies that surrounded them. I shall concentrate upon the most important order in the Padroado in the Estado da India, the Society of Jesus, and its financial and political role in Portuguese society in China and the South China Sea.

The Society of Jesus was founded in 1540 and served in Europe as a primary force in the Counter-Reformation; its establishment in Portugal and throughout the Portuguese Empire quickly followed and by the late 1540s the Jesuits were at Malacca, the south China coast and preparing to enter Japan.[32] Their military-like organisation found a wide number of admirers as well as detractors when compared to the mendicant orders. Led by an elected 'General' who resided in Rome and who retained his position for life, the Society was strictly ordered, regimented and trained for Catholic missionary activity. The organisation of the geographical areas, into province and vice-province, in which the Society was to evangelise was simple and direct; the provinces which were involved in the Padroado in the East were established in Portugal in 1540, Goa in 1542, Japan in 1549, and the vice-province of China in 1583.

Within the Portuguese Padroado, unlike the Spanish *Patronato*, the Jesuits relied heavily upon non-Portuguese manpower for their missions in Asia. Those who were not Portuguese 'acknowledged the validity of the Portuguese claims, and since the mission largely depended for its existence on the resources and facilities by Goa, Macao, and Malacca, Portuguese influence was naturally predominant.'[33]

Macao served as the centre for the missionary activities of the Jesuits in China, the South China Sea and Japan; 'both provincials and vice-provincials were directly subordinated to the general at Rome, who, in addition, exercised control over the provinces and vice-provinces by the periodic dispatch of specially appointed visitors.'[34] In the first half of the seventeenth century, Catholic missionaries in general and the Jesuits of the Province of Japan were severely persecuted in that country; consequently, they expanded their missionary activities in the South China Sea.[35] After their subsequent total expulsion from Japan, these Jesuits relocated all of their members at Macao and expanded the Vice-Province of China and the missions in the South China Sea.

This hierarchical organisational framework has to be understood, in general terms, in order to comprehend how each province, vice-province and mission financed itself. In general, vice-province and mission kept their accounts separate. A Jesuit representative of the Province of Japan was present at Lisbon, Goa, and northern India to oversee their property and investments. This system sounds complicated but with the Society's communication talents, bureaucratic stamina and economic modernity, it functioned and adapted itself in time when funds for missionary work were difficult to locate.[36]

The Jesuits, as with other missionary orders within the Padroado, were meant to be supported in their efforts by the Crown allocating sufficient funds by grant or other forms of payment from the Royal Treasury. The Crown rarely met its financial obligation to the missionaries on time or with the promised sum; its failure led the Jesuits to lobby intensely in Europe and Asia in order to resolve or ameliorate their fiscal dependence.

A varied pattern of decisions emerged over the later half of the sixteenth and seventeenth centuries, some of which were unilateral actions and after the fact accepted by the Crown, which helped the Jesuits to lessen their dependence and finance the missions. In the case of the Province of Japan, the Vice-Province of China and the South China Sea missions, the Crown agreed to pay their daily expenses and the King, Dom Sebastião, in 1574 donated an additional sum to found a college. These contributions were to be paid on an annual basis at the Crown's customs house at Malacca. A major financial breakthrough for the Jesuits occurred when the Crown gave them permission to purchase real estate in the form of villages in western India.[37]

There were other financial practices in which the Jesuits participated that did not require Crown permission but led to complaints by local and royal government; one such practice was their administration of funds received as gifts, legacies and as the administrators of the estates of deceased persons. These funds formed the capital which was loaned at interest to local inhabitants who could provide adequate security, usually to reinois or mestiços, but in Macao there were regular instances of loans to Chinese inhabitants. Finally, the financial practice most central to this work, which the Crown and local society reluctantly approved, was the Jesuit investment and participation in maritime trade.

Representatives of the Crown – viceroys, governors, and ouvidors – were posted to India and Macao, served their term of office and were then recalled to India and Portugal. Their influence on the social and economic activities of the Portuguese communities in China and the South China Sea, while important and formative in restricted areas, was generally slight. The lançados, along with the religious community, constructed in Macao what has been called the epitome of casado society, a communal structure which revolved around the activities of the Senado da Camara and the *Santa Casa da Misericordia* (Holy House of Mercy).[38]

SENADO DA CAMARA

Although the Senado da Camara formed the basic framework for local government throughout Portugal and her Empire, the lançado community in Macao was determined not to form any type of government over which Crown officials in Malacca and Goa could exercise authority. When confronted with the news of the accession of Philip II in June 1582, they agreed to swear their allegiance to the new monarch; in almost the same breath, they petitioned the Crown for permission to form a Senado da Camara in order to protect their community and its trading position from Spanish encroachment from Manila. The Viceroy on 10 April 1586 confirmed the rights of the inhabitants of Macao to form this institution and granted that municipal council the same powers as those possessed by the municipal council of Evora in Portugal.

The structure of office-holding in the Senado da Camara of Macao was modified from the Evora model. In Portugal, with demands for representation by larger and more diverse population and socio-economic groupings, there was a tendency to allocate a greater number of offices. In Macao, the voting members of the Senado da Camara comprised three councillors, two magistrates and a municipal attorney. There were a number of non-voting office holders, but such positions were relatively unimportant. The level at which office holders could benefit either in terms of finance or of prestige was confined to the voting members.

The selection of lists of electors and the actual election of Senado officers was an extremely complicated affair; every three years the electors were selected from the eligible office-holding populace by a secret polling among the electorate. Once thus empowered, these electors, who were six in number, then compiled a list of the persons they thought were capable of governing. In theory, they were to exclude the outgoing officials and anyone related by consanguineous or occupational links but in reality in Macao this was difficult if not impossible. Lists of candidates were obtained by this indirect method, and each year as the tenure of various offices terminated, usually on New Year's Day, a ballot from these lists was held, which in some ways resembled a lottery. Officers were selected and they were presented at a general assembly of Macao's populace.[39]

The Senado's officers usually met twice a week but in Macao, because many officers were involved in maritime trade and were away for several months, there were periods of the year when the Senado would meet with greater frequency and with larger attendance. After an issue was brought to the Senado's attention and freely debated, decision-making within this group was by majority vote.

Active participation by Portuguese merchants in this institution and the Santa Casa da Misericordia in Macao was largely for financial reasons. The Senado da Camara's control over the diplomatic and commercial relations with China and the South China Sea, although contested by some of the Crown representatives, ensured that local, long-term, individual and group commercial interests were maintained. The authority of the Senado in municipal matters was superior to that of the representatives of the Crown, the capitão-geral and the ouvidor, and it 'could not be set aside or revoked by superior authority, save only if they involved unauthorised innovations which might adversely affect the Crown's finances.'[40] There were areas, such as Macao's contribution to the financing of defence, and the capitão-geral's involvement in commerce and in diplomatic efforts, that resulted in friction between the members of the Senado and the Crown's representative.

The Senado da Camara had to finance the local garrison and defence projects, with the exception of the years of the Crown's administration of the Japan and Manila voyage; they had to contribute to the support of the Padroado and pay for the diplomatic missions sent by the Senado da Camara and the Crown to Peking, Canton, Japan and the South China Sea region. To meet these expenditures, the Senado da Camara relied entirely upon the collection of import and export duties. Import duties were 'levied on all goods imported into Macao in Portuguese ships'. The Portuguese paid export duties levied by the Chinese custom-house from 1688 onwards, and the municipality collected a 'tax known as the *caldeirão* (cauldron). This was originally a duty of about 3 per cent levied on all goods exported to Japan, which was increased to 8 per cent in 1634, and transferred to other goods after the loss of the Japan trade in 1640.'[41]

The percentage of duties was decided by the Senado da Camara based upon the calculation of the city's annual expenditure, outstanding financial obligations, and the estimated revenue receipts available from the season's voyages. Prior to 1640, the Senado da Camara was able, on the whole, to meet these expenditures with relative ease but with the loss of the direct trade to Japan and Manila, the duty percentage rates increased and forced the city to arrange loans from the Santa Casa da Misericordia and borrow from Asian rulers, such as the King of Siam, and merchants in Nagasaki, Canton and elsewhere to find sufficient funds for its administrative costs.[42] This power to set the rate for import duties at the lowest possible figure and still ensure the survival of Macao was of fundamental importance to the local shipowner, merchant and investor, whose ships were regularly departing and returning from various ports in the South China Sea and the Indian Ocean.

SANTA CASA DA MISERICORDIA

Charitable lay brotherhoods were firmly established in Portugal before 1498, the year of the foundation of the Santa Casa da Misericordia of Lisbon.[43] Through royal patronage, this institution came to fulfil a major role in the provision of social assistance in continental Portugal. Consequently, when the Portuguese arrived in the East, the Santa Casa da Misericordia was embraced by the Portuguese Crown and casados as the institution to provide for their minimal social service requirements. Although they emulated the model of the Lisbon chapter of the brotherhood as embodied in its statutes, this institution in Asia developed an economic role in local society remote from its exclusively charitable purposes.

The first Santa Casa da Misericordia in Asia was established at Cochin in 1505 and the second at Goa during the governorship of Lopo Soares, 1515–18.[44] The social composition of the membership of these chapters mirrored Portuguese hierarchical and class attitudes; nevertheless, the relief provided by these meagre social services should not be underestimated in the maintenance of Portuguese society in Asia. Throughout the sixteenth century as Indo-Portuguese communities were formed, the pre-eminent expression of that society's institutional interest was in the formation of a Santa Casa da Misericordia and a Senado da Camara, in that order, to claim, represent, and defend communal interests *vis-à-vis* the Crown or the Church. This communal reliance upon the Santa Casa da Misericordia is witnessed by its widespread establishment over the sixteenth century from the Persian Gulf throughout the Indian Ocean and the South China Sea to Japan.[45]

The Santa Casa da Misericordia at Macao was founded in 1569 and quickly became the most important branch east of Malacca.[46] It still exists and operates many social services in that city. The brotherhood operated a hospital, a leprosarium, which in 1726 accommodated over one hundred patients, and an orphanage. Its organisation was modelled upon the statutes of the Lisbon and Goa chapters with modifications to take into account local social conditions. In theory, according to the Macao statutes of 1627, the membership of the brotherhood was to total three hundred males, one half to be selected from the nobility and the other from the artisans. In practice, however, since the Portuguese claimed that no persons in that city were artisans and all of the members were of equal social status, it was over the social composition of the brotherhood that Macao differentiated itself from Goa.

The activities of the brotherhood were administered by a board of guardians composed usually of thirteen members with one secretary who kept the minutes of meetings and financial records and ledgers. This board was led by a president whose election was on an annual basis. The members of the board were elected indirectly through an electoral committee of ten members chosen from the total brotherhood. On account of this selection and election process, simultaneous or alternate office-holding on the board of this institution and as a voting official in the Senado da Camara of Macao was common.

The Santa Casa da Misericordia of Macao derived its main source of capital from legacies, in the form of cash or properties, which were given outright or with stipulations, such as an obligation to have a number of masses said over a period of time in the brotherhood's church. Three courses of action were open to anyone who wished to make a bequest: the testator could nominate the brotherhood as heir or executor, grant a sum of money to cover the costs of administration, or nominate a relative as heir or executor who would make a donation to the brotherhood. The testator could elect to endow the brotherhood with a sum of money which that institution was to administer on a once-and-for-all basis or to loan at interest which would be applied towards a stipulated end. Legacies in kind were rare in Macao and if made were converted at public auction into cash. Dowries and provisions for the care of orphans and widows, in a city were a large percentage of the male population was engaged in maritime enterprise and shipwrecks regularly claimed victims, were prominent stipulations in the last wills and testaments registered at the Santa Casa da Misericordia of Macao. There were two categories of legacies which were deposited with the brotherhood for the provision of dowries and funds destined for orphans and widows: funds that were to be distributed immediately, and those to be administered and distributed according to the stipulations of the testator's last will and testament.

The Santa Casa da Misericordia derived its main source of income from its financial activities with its own funds and those it administered from legacies. With these fiscal resources this institution became one of the major local European-dominated sources of capital and after the provision of adequate security and a financial guarantor, its funds were sought by Portuguese country traders for loans for shipping ventures, the purchase of limited amounts of available property and for capital improvements in Macao.

An additional fiscal responsibility of the Santa Casa da Misericordia was to transfer the estate of deceased persons from China to Portugal. This service animated and reassured the small but influential segment of the community that was mobile between the Estado da India and Portugal that their gains of a lifetime in the East would be repatriated to their family and relations. The procedure for administering these funds was developed in the sixteenth century. In India, depending upon where the individual resided, when a Portuguese died and had his last will and testament registered with the brotherhood, or with one of the religious orders (usually the Jesuits), after all of his debts were liquidated and distributed as bequeathed, his estate was forwarded by the local brotherhood to one of the two most important branches of that institution in that region, Goa or Cochin. Upon the arrival of the particulars of the estate, the Goa or Cochin branch entered into correspondence and repatriated to the Santa Casa da Misericordia of Lisbon by letter of exchange, the estate of the benefactor which was to be distributed either by the Lisbon branch directly or via another nearer to the inheritor's home. When a member of Portuguese society died intestate his estate was assumed by the Santa Casa da Misericordia.[47]

In Macao, the procedure for the transfer of an estate was slightly revised, in that the brotherhood would correspond directly to the Santa Casa da Misericordia in Portugal which would handle the distribution of the estate. They also repatriated estates to inheritors in Cochin and other parts of the Estado da India. By the mid-1620s, all explicit archival references to this procedure in Macao cease to be mentioned, in part for demographic and economic reasons.[48] The *reinol*, the major participants in such a system, already thought of the Estado da India as home, their numbers were depleted and their personal fortunes were being diminished by financial losses on account of VOC naval actions. Consequently, fewer inhabitants were interested in, or able to avail themselves of, this service. Another reason, which was applicable to the entire Estado da India, if not all of the Portuguese Empire, was the expansion in the use of the legacies as a method of financing the Crown's defence projects and as a source of capital for trade.[49]

Armed with this legacy of bureaucratic and administrative structure from Iberia, the Portuguese society at Macao appears static and devoid of personality. The absence of Crown administrators, private merchants and others diaries, personal letters and business correspondence limits the possible depth of analysis and re-enforces this view. Other Portuguese societies in the Estado da India, with rare exception have been studied and as a result prejudice a comparative approach. Nevertheless, the quest for communal power, intriguing population patterns and strong personalities were present at Macao and within the Estado da India.

3

POPULATION, PERSONALITIES AND COMMUNAL POWER

Portuguese society in China was a highly diverse, multi-racial, communal aggregation. Through inter-racial marriage, concubinage, conversion to Catholicism and the attraction of commercial and political advantage, non-European elements joined this grouping of Portuguese Crown administrators, country traders and missionaries. Although Macao's European population were acculturated to many of the local conditions in China, the fundamental characteristics of the economic, political and social organisation in which these country traders participated remained Portuguese.

No attempt has been made to view as a whole the activities of a Luso-Chinese community or to stress the individual racial or religious inter-mixtures that were present at Macao.[1] The Portuguese community at Siam, for example, was largely *mestiço*, lived in the Portuguese quarter, and supported the largely Catholic missionaries that were part of the Portuguese Padroado; this community in the eyes of the Siamese and European observers was Portuguese. The conditions were similar in other Portuguese communities throughout the South China Sea and the Indian Ocean.

If we compare the casado's position within Portuguese colonial society at Goa and at Macao, we find a few major similarities and several sharp differences. The most important similarity was that of size; the total number of individuals was very small. Although there were methods by which many segments of colonial society, including indigenous merchants, religious and Crown administrators, were involved, the casados provided the bulk of the resources and the impetus for Portuguese participation in inter-Asian maritime trade. In the 1630s, at Goa, there were 3,000 casado households reported; at Macao, the casados numbered 850.[2] A few individual casado country traders possessed astronomical fortunes and owned outright a relatively large number of ships; in Japan in 1633, four Portuguese traders declared bankruptcy in the amount of 1.25 million *taels* worth of silver![3]

The majority of Portuguese participants in inter-Asian trade, casados or otherwise, were less powerful, smaller investors. But, the activities of these more numerous smaller investors at Goa and Macao were similarly influenced by the concentration of political and economic power in the hands of a small number of casados, who commanded the respect and fear of others and prompted the formation of *bandos* or competing factions. The formation of different trading ventures was dependent upon the association of groups of investors and ship-owners who were either related by extended familial, *compradrazgo* (god-parent relationship) or racial affiliation. Reinois, those born in Portugal, usually worked together rather than with mestiços, those of mixed-racial heritage born in the East. These investors usually held similar political and commercial interests, were allied in the same bando, and were protégés of, or were themselves, Crown or Church administrators.

There were sharp differences in the composition of, and position occupied by, those who participated in inter-Asian maritime trade at Goa and Macao. The country trader at Goa was just as likely to be a Crown administrator, an indigenous merchant (Hindu and later, Armenian), or a *cristão novo* (new Christian, a converted Jew) than a casado. The casados at Goa occupied a political and economic position that may be best, and perhaps too favourably, described as a partnership, an amalgamation of three major participants: the Crown, indigenous merchants and casados, including cristão novos and non-married Portuguese inhabitants. Maritime trade was a major economic activity but other economic pursuits such as agriculture and the collection of rents and revenue from land favoured the Goa and the *Provincia do Norte* economies.[4]

In contrast, the country trader at Macao was more than likely a casado. The ethos of that society was so dominated by the casado that Crown administrators were continually frustrated in their numerous attempts to establish control over the political and economic activities of the municipality. The Senado da Camara of Macao jealously guarded the casados control over the negotiation of commercial and political relations with China and neighbouring Asian states. Dependent entirely upon maritime trade for their survival, the casados at Macao demonstrated a remarkable flexibility and adaptability in the face of adverse conditions.

THE DEMOGRAPHY OF MACAO

The number of Portuguese in China was never very large; various estimates of the total number of inhabitants at Macao from 1601 until 1669 are given in Table 3.1. There were practical reasons for the limitation of the size of the Portuguese, mestiço, slave and Chinese populations. There was limited living space at Macao which was exacerbated by the city's dependence upon foodstuffs from the Chinese hinterland. The involvement of large segments of its male population in maritime trade, an occupation which was highly susceptible to losses inflicted by enemy capture, sinkings, piracy and shipwreck, was hardly conducive to stable population growth. Furthermore, Macao's population was dependent upon Chinese supplies which were not controlled by the Portuguese and which made the city susceptible to Chinese controls and famine conditions in south China.

The racial composition of Macao's population is very difficult to comment upon in that census and parish records have not survived. It is clear from late eighteenth-century census reports sent to Lisbon from Portuguese Crown officials at Macao that reinois continued to arrive in small numbers and dominated the political and economic scene in the colony out of proportion to their numbers. Emmigration from Portugal to the Estado da India was heavily male oriented; from

Table 3.1. *The demography of Macao, 1601–69*

1601	600 Portuguese casados and visiting merchants
1622	700–800 Portuguese casados and mestiços
	10,000 Chinese
1624	840 Portuguese casados, mestiços, Chinese Christians
	10,000 Chinese
1634–37	600 casados
	About 600 young males (capable of bearing arms)
	600 *gente da terra* (mestiços or Chinese Christians?)
	5,000 slaves
1635	850 casados
	150 bachelors, married males with wives in Portugal
	5,100 slaves (6 slaves average/casado)
1640	600 Portuguese casados
	600 sons capable of bearing arms
	500 native born casados and soldiers
	5,000 slaves
	20,000 Chinese
1643	2,000 *moradores* (Portuguese inhabitants)
1644	40,000 total inhabitants
1648	Jesuits record 5,000 persons starve to death
1662	200–300 Portuguese and other Christian males
	±2,000 widows and orphans
1663	±2,000 widows and orphans
1669	300–320 casados

Sources: HAG, MR 8, fol. 88; AHU, Macao, I, 24/xii/1643; *DRB, 1663*, 75, 628 32; *DRB, 1668–9*, 297; Colenbander, *Jan Pietersz. Coen*, I, 690; Boxer, *Fidalgos*, 99–100, 143–4; Boxer, *Azia Sinica*, I, 224, Cardim, *Batalhas*, 21, 29–30; and Boxer, *Macau na Epoca de Restauração*, 28.

the Estado da India to Macao, it was almost unknown that a European female venture that far. There was, for example, only one Portuguese female at Macao in the 1630s.[5]

The resulting pattern for Macao emerged; the *reinol* arrived in the East in Crown service, sailed between Goa and Macao and, upon leaving Crown service, established himself at Macao. He married, as well as possible, and became a casado in China; reinois sought to marry eligible single women with dowries. A complaint in the mid eighteenth century was that the eligible single women entered the local convent denying impecunious bachelors their dowries.[6] Those reinois that did not find a wife, and even many that did, were likely to have sexual liaisons with female servants and slaves.

The women of Macao were predominantly Chinese. In the early years of the city, before a substantial Chinese population settled in the growing port, the women with whom the Portuguese 'lived were Japanese, Malays, Indonesians and Indians, many of them being slaves.' Although the Japanese Christian community remained a facet in Macao, which grew temporarily after the expulsion of the Portuguese from Japan in the late 1630s, after the establishment of a Chinese population in

Macao in the 1560s or so, 'the Portuguese men, therefore, soon started to intermarry with Chinese women and, still more often, to use them as concubines and indentured girl-servants, *mui-tsai*.'[7] Although enthusiastic about the Chinese women's many virtues, the Portuguese male community at Macao demanded that their women lead a highly restricted and confined life in the city.[8]

The offspring of the reinois and their wives or liaisons, the mestiços, receive much less attention by Portuguese Crown officials. Although active in ship-owning, it appears in the late eighteenth century, that they owned smaller and cheaper ships suggesting that reinols political domination of the Senado da Camara and the Santa Casa da Misericordia also limited the economic opportunities of the second or third generation mestiço, no matter how able or capable in maritime trade.[9]

At Macao, the casado households, formed either by reinois or mestiços, were large and included, according to one report, an average of six slaves per casado. Slaves, with the exception of Chinese female domestic servants whose employment conditions were slave-like, came from all over Asia and Africa; their numbers were influenced by the prosperity of their purchasers.

The size of the resident Chinese community was dependent upon the economic opportunities offered at Macao. There were instances, for example, when the VOC reported the exodus of Chinese weavers of silk piecegoods from that city on account of political turmoil and the absence of order. Their numbers were also dependent upon the treatment they received at the hands of the Portuguese casados and Crown authorities and the political instructions they received from Ming and Ch'ing officials.

Macao, in contrast to most Asian port towns dependent on seaborne trade, did not have a dense population. Restricted by their physical location and their sources of supply of foodstuffs controlled by the Ming and, later, Ch'ing officials, the Portuguese casado population at Macao could not sustain new unexpected large-scale arrivals. The 287 Japanese Christian and Portuguese casados that were forced to leave Japan in the late 1630s, for example, were received temporarily at Macao but by the late 1640 famine years in south China, the Senado da Camara had found homes for these refugees and other Macao families in Macassar, and Cochinchina. After their expulsion from Macassar, a portion of that Portuguese community initially arrived at Macao, another at Timor but on account of Ch'ing restrictions in China, it appears they were quickly relocated to Siam in the 1660s.[10]

The economic losses that the Portuguese at Macao suffered from shipwreck, piracies and capture were special, at times, only in their intensity and magnitude. It is difficult to quantify the decline and attach any great significance to the magnitudes. Nevertheless, several examples are illustrative; in 1603, in four separate actions, the VOC captured three major and one lesser Portuguese vessels, one at Macao and three *en route* from Macao to Malacca and India. The value of two of the four vessels' cargoes, when the goods sold at Amsterdam was 4.8 million guilders.[11] Obviously, a total loss of several million guilders was incurred by the owners of the shipping and freight shipped between Macao and India in that year. In 1633, the Portuguese from Macao and Goa destroyed four small ships that they had dispatched to the Estado da India from China and, slightly later in the year, one of the ships the Portuguese at Macao had outfitted to go to Japan capsized *en route*; the total loss in this year was 2.5 million guilders.[12] Unfortunately there are no records of such losses being directly responsible for the bankruptcy of Portuguese merchants, although Crown reports suggest that this occurred throughout the Estado da India, or having contributed to the social unrest present at Macao.

Although the material losses suffered by the Portuguese were, occasionally, astronomical, the social havoc wreaked through shipwreck or the loss of a casado life had a certain and immediate impact at Macao. The care for widows and orphans fell upon the Senado da Camara and the Santa Casa da Misericordia.[13] In a rare instance of female dominance over her environment, the Macao widow of Francisco Vieira de Figueiredo, Doña Caterina de Noronha, who had accompanied her husband to Macassar and Timor, took control over his business affairs after his death in 1667 and returned to Macao in 1670.[14] She arrived with her household and family and remained active in business for at least one more decade. In 1680, the Jesuits convinced her to make them a substantial donation of around 12,000 taels which they invested in India and maritime trade.[15] It is unfortunate that we know so little about her in that her direct participation in and active role as a ship-owner was, perhaps, unique for a woman at Macao.

Portuguese country traders were those groups from Portuguese society (the casados), the Church and Crown (administrators), that were involved in inter-Asian maritime trade in the Indian Ocean and the South China Sea. Participation by Crown administrators in this type of trade was on the individual's own account and did not have the support of the Crown's Treasury; the different missionary orders of the Catholic Church has separate views on their involvement as individuals and as a group in maritime trade.

The Jesuits allowed individual priests to invest and as an order also invested the financial resources of the Province of Japan and Vice-Province of China in country trade. Both Crown administrators and the Society of Jesus were ship-owners, although the Jesuits appear to have preferred part-ownership of the shipping in which they invested and contractual arrangements with different casado country traders.

The Crown administrators, such as the capitão-geral of Macao, upon his appointment, occasionally purchased his own ship for transport to China from where he operated his commercial ventures during the tenure of his appointment. It was more common for the Crown administrator not to own a ship whereupon he acted as an investor in freighting goods on Crown and country trader shipping. When the capitão-geral was appointed from one of the casados of Macao, who had held previous Crown appointments, such as Pero Vaz de Siqueira in the late seventeenth century, a Crown administrator could also be Macao's largest ship-owner.

Although the Church and Crown administrators participated, the casados were the group in Portuguese society whose investment in inter-Asian maritime trade was greatest. Their reliance at Macao upon the proceeds of their investment in maritime trade was almost absolute and they were all either directly or indirectly gainfully employed in the operation or the ancillary support activities in shipping.

European, especially Dutch, sources make it possible to examine Portuguese trade and society in China and the South China Sea from, perhaps, an impersonal systemic viewpoint. Our story of imperial foundation, growth, defence and survival appears devoid of the major personalities, not to mention the common man and woman, the Chinese and other Asian merchants views of this alien European culture. In part, this is intentional in that previous studies on the Portuguese in the East focused on the personality within Portuguese society.[16]

Without the corroborative evidence of other European sources, it has been difficult to focus upon Portuguese economic practices in China and the South China Sea and delineate the patterns of commercial growth, change and innovation in those markets in which the Portuguese were active and their contribution to Asia's maritime trade was evident. This evidence also permits the examination of several broad themes – the inter-imperial relations of Portuguese society; China during its transition from one dynasty to another; and the Portuguese confrontation with the other Europeans that came to trade with China – over the seventeenth to mid eighteenth centuries.

Although in part intentional, there is another reason for our treatment of Portuguese trade and society in this manner and that is the absence in Portuguese records of evidence from the period in the hand of the Portuguese inhabitants and merchants of Macao and other colonial cities. It was rare for a Crown administrator to keep a diary and only occasionally did their personal papers survive. For the casado, reinol or mestiço, or his wife, the habit of recording their real commercial transactions was rare and never in letter or diary did they record their personal feelings or reactions to their life in the East.

The Portuguese casado-country trader utilized a basic, if not rudimentary, form of accounting for his transactions. Devoid of any elaborate methodology, the necessity for double-entry accounting hardly existed, and wary of the Crown accurately computing their wealth, the account book or *livro de rezão* of the Portuguese country trader was more a compilation of personal data, records of transactions, outstanding investments, and notations of ownership or partnership in different ships. That such account books and papers were commonly used has been corroborated by Crown, Dutch and English reference to this practice and by examples that have survived for a slightly later time span.[17] A generalized appreciation of the importance of these account books in the early seventeenth century has, heretofore, been limited by virtue of the fact that none for that period or geographical location had survived. The secretiveness of the individual and family members who guarded such records along with the ravages of time, climate and other physical conditions certainly diminished the possibilities of encountering such data.

The livro de rezão of one Portuguese country trader, Francisco da Gama, who was active in maritime trade between India and Malacca in the first few decades of the seventeenth century, was found in the Netherlands.[18] Captured by the Dutch in late 1621 or shortly thereafter, a servant of the VOC retained this account book and dispatched it to his brother in the Netherlands in 1626 where it eventually was deposited in the Library of the University of Leiden. Da Gama's account book only covers his activities between 1619 and 1621. Consisting of a series of different personal papers and accounts organized in an indifferent manner and written in several different hands, this account book offers a unique opportunity to re-create the salient aspects of an individual Portuguese country trader's commercial activity in the early seventeenth century.

The livro de rezão of Francisco da Gama suggests a ship-owner/merchant/agent of some considerable capacity and individual wealth. As a ship-owner, it appears he owned at least one ship outright and was a part-owner in another; as a merchant, he invested in merchandise shipped on at least seven Portuguese country traders' ships, including his own, and as an agent, he received freight, bullion and letters of exchange destined for ports from Cochin to Malacca and return to Goa in a period of three years. The merchandise he exported from India on his own account and freighted for others consisted of cotton and silk piecegoods and silver bullion, which was transferred for members of Portuguese colonial society with the Society of Jesus a leader in this activity. Imports, purchased at Malacca from China and the South China Sea, consisted of cloves, gold, sugar, zinc and porcelain.

There is sufficient material on the fortunate within Portuguese colonial society, the Crown servants who became casados in the East and who requested and received Crown recognition and patronage, to comment upon the personalities and the broad trends that each career suggests for the change and stability within Portuguese society at Macao, over the sixteenth and into the eighteenth centuries. The careers of three major civic leaders, with some slight reference to others, form the basis for our comments: Bartholomeu Vaz Landeiro, António Fialho Ferreira and Pero Vaz Siqueira.

EARLY PIONEER AND COMMERCIAL GIANT: BARTHOLOMEU VAZ LANDEIRO

Bartholomeu Vaz Landeiro, native of Portugal, in Crown service, arrived from Europe to the Estado da India in 1557. He was active in India until 1569 when he arrived at Macao and became a casado. With whom he married is not recorded, it is speculated that she may have been a Japanese Christian based upon his contacts and his reception in that country; from this union, there were two daughters. Other familial members appear to have been present at Macao; Vincente Landeiro is mentioned in documentation that indicates some relationship.[19]

Landeiro, contrary to most of the Portuguese nobility, made no mention of his family's position or his possible membership in any of Portugal's military orders; the absence of any such claim suggests some impediment either cristão-novo (new Christian) Jewish blood which is improbable on account of his relations with the Jesuits or most likely a humble familial past. In his actions in the Estado da India from 1557 to 1585, if he lacked social and political antecedents these did not hamper this early pioneer and developer of Macao's commerce.

Landeiro demonstrated a pretentious, dynamic, quasi-visionary, outwordly religious but firmly pragmatic attitude towards the development of his and the Portuguese position in China, Japan, the Moluccas and the Philippines. Based at Macao, he was active in all of these areas; his personal fleet was at least three ships, two of which were large junks. His pretentions were fabled; he was known in Japan as the 'King of the Portuguese' and 'he went everywhere attended by a suite of richly-dressed Portuguese, and by a bodyguard of eight Muslim and Negro slaves, armed with halberds and shields.'[20]

Although his fortune was established from the Japan trade, his early success appears to have been derived from astute dealings with Ming officials at Canton. During an era when individual Portuguese country merchants at Macao had access to direct dealings with Chinese officials at Canton, Landeiro cultivated those contacts and claimed that it was he at Macao that received a request from, probably, the viceroy of Kwangtung in the 1570s to rid the Chinese coast of a pirate band. By dispatching two of his ships and crews at his personal expense, Landeiro not only eliminated this band but demonstrated he was a man, if not the man, in Macao with whom Ming officials could deal.

In Japan, his fortunes were strongly linked to the Jesuit presence; he was a major contributor to the Mission and 'placed his resources and shipping unreservedly at their [the Jesuits'] disposal.'[21] There were a number of instances in which this Portuguese merchant demonstrated his understanding of political and commercial power in his alliance with the Jesuits. On one occasion to support one of the Kyushu Christian *daimyo* (lords), he dispatched to Japan one of his ships, the size of which was 600 tons, all at cost borne by him. The Jesuits praised him and indicated that he was as knowledgeable about power as he was of profit; 'for he carried them [the Jesuits] in his great and powerful ships, and he would not enter with his merchandise into any port or region of Japan where the padres were not properly received and maintained.' And the Jesuits recorded that 'on one occasion he had sacrified 30,000 *ducats* in merchandise through not entering a port which he could have, and going to another solely for the sake of religion.'[22]

On account of his strong relationship with the Jesuits in Japan and his connections at Canton and Macao, Landeiro must have been fundamentally involved in negotiating and arranging the Jesuit participation in the silk trade. In 1578, the Jesuits concluded their agreement with Macao's merchants; 'the Japan Jesuits were allocated a share of 50 piculs (bought with the interest on d'Almeida's legacy), the proceeds of the sale of which at Nagasaki were automatically credited to them at the highest ruling prices.' In addition, 'another 50 piculs were allotted them on the same terms in the balance of the silk left behind for sale at the end of the season. Thus their whole share amounted to 100 piculs per annum, [the Portuguese total at this time was 1,600 picols] and their profits from 4,000 to 6,000 ducats a year.'[23]

In addition to Landeiro's involvement in the Japan trade, his political pragmatism as well as commercial acumen was revealed yet again, in the early 1580s via his role in initiating and amplifying Portuguese trade from China at Manila and his arrival from the Philippines with Father Alonso Sanchez who brought the news of the succession of Philip II to the throne of Portugal. By lobbying for Portuguese oaths of allegiance and obtaining Macao's acquiescence to this new imperial relationship, Landeiro coldly recognised that Macao could derive significant economic benefits from dealings with Manila with payment in New World silver.

It was in the pursuit of Iberian hegemony in the South China Sea that Landeiro responded, again in the early 1580s, to Spanish requests for aid from Macao in the Moluccas. Outfitting several ships, Bartholomeu Vaz Landeiro over-reached even his ample resources with the aid that he sent to the Moluccas to be used against Ternate. Losing, according to his petition to the Crown, one of his ships and facing overextended finances, he requested a Crown grant for services rendered of two Japan voyages.

It is not clear from the existing archival records if the Crown granted Bartholomeu Vaz Landeiro's requests and it is suspected that Landeiro died relatively soon after his request in 1585. By the mid 1590s it is clear that the early dominating role of the early pioneer magnates at Macao was being restricted by the establishment of broader merchant involvement in newly established communal institutions such as the Senado da Camara. When the Senado da Camara of Macao assumed responsibility in 1595 for the negotiation of silk and other merchandise supply contracts, from the Chinese at Canton, the individual country traders in their different bandos were involved in serious communal disturbances.[24] It appears that, by that date, the 'King of the Portuguese' was no longer living or on the scene.

The unregulated era of the early pioneers at Macao terminated with the establishment of the Senado da Camara. News of Macao's growth and the economic opportunities available in maritime trade attracted new arrivals, most of whom were reinois and, although not tremendously wealthy, with some personal funds or with access to capital and willing to invest in the Japan and Manila trades. These reinois became casados in Macao; collectively, their careers are exemplified by those of Lourenço Correia Ribeiro, Gonçalo Monteiro de Carvalho, Simão Vaz de Paiva, Pero Fernandez de Carvalho, Francisco Carvalho Aranha and Diego Vaz Bavaro and ranged, roughly, from 1580 to 1650.[25]

One Macao casado explained to the Spanish Franciscan friar, Juan Pobre de Zamora in 1597, the Portuguese anti-Spanish attitude, 'we have settled down in this place and married here; we have children and property.' He continued, 'if the Castilians come, since they are a restless race, they will try to enter the mainland. And if their Religious come to try to convert this kingdom, the Chinese will kill them and kick us out. And this is why we stand on our guard and don't allow any Spaniards to come here.'[26] Although dedicated to their new lives in the East, this was an era for those sharp merchants of immense possibilities to enrich themselves. Those with families in continental Portugal could and did remit portion of their fortunes by the execution of their probate and estate through the different offices of the Santa Casa da Misericordia's. Others through service to the

Crown received recognition and the patronage through the granting of official posts within the Estado da India and entrance into one or more of the military orders of Portugal, the most prestigious being the Order of Christ.[27] Some casados even received Crown permission to return to and live in Portugal in recognition of services rendered.

Although this system benefited the few, Portuguese casados at Macao participated in the pursuit of patronage. In addition, the casados, while attempting in the Senado da Camara to limit the aggrandisement and mis-appropriation of economic and political resources of Macao for the personal benefit of a few casado magnates, dreamt of becoming as wealthy and influential as, for example, Lopo Sarmento de Carvalho and Francisco Vieira de Figueiredo.[28]

SHARP MERCHANT AND RECIPIENT OF CROWN PATRONAGE: ANTÓNIO FIALHO FERREIRA

António Fialho Ferreira was a reinol from Sesimbra, the son of Pedro Fialho Ferreira and Clara Gomes; he was born towards the end of the sixteenth century and he arrived in the Estado da India around 1602. He arrived at Macao before 1620 and his career and those of his associates clearly demonstrates the dynamics of familial and geographical origin relationships upon casados economic activities. Arrogant, abrasive, capable, ambitious, opportunist and patriot, Ferreira was a sharp merchant in an era of sharp merchants and a recipient of Crown patronage for his pivotal role in announcing the news of the accession of King João and the restoration of the Crown of Portugal at Macao.

Married in Macao in 1620 or slightly later to Caterina Cerqueira; Catarina's family connections were important for Ferreira's maritime trading activities. Her father, Jorge Cerqueira was a reinol from Lamego and her mother was Maria Pires, a native of the city but Catarina's grandmother 'stated publicly in Macau, amongst high and low alike, to be a Moor, daughter of a Moorish lascar and a converted Jew.'[29] Catarina bore Ferreira a total of five sons and, at least, one daughter, Leonora, who entered the Poor Clares' Convent; Leonora's father was a generous benefactor to that Convent.

It was the marriage of Catarina's sister, Maria Cerqueira, to Lopo Sarmento de Carvalho that benefited Ferreira. By the late 1620s, Ferreira and Carvalho were associated and involved in at least one major project.

Lopo Sarmento de Carvalho was a reinol from Braganza, the province of Trás-os-Montes; his parents were Lopo Roiz de Carvalho and Maria Luis Sarmento. Arriving to the Estado da India in 1607, he served the Crown in numerous campaigns on the west coast of India and in 1614, he commanded a fleet of six ships from Goa to Macao via Malacca. He arrived at Macao in 1615, resigned from Crown service, and married Maria Cerqueira. They had three sons, all of whom served the Crown, two died fighting the VOC in Ceylon and the third, the eldest, Inacio, was the staunch governor and defender of Cochin against the VOC in 1659–63.

Carvalho's business concerns at Macao focused very quickly upon the Japan trade; the rapidity of his success suggests he arrived at Macao already possessing connections, political support and finance at Goa for his plans. That support at Goa, it is suggested, came from his and Ferreira's future formal associate in the late 1620s, Manuel de Morais Supico, a contemporary and a reinol from his native Trás-os-Montes. Carvalho was the capitão-mor of the Japan voyage of 1617 and lead the Portuguese embassy to the Court of the new *Shogun*, Tokugawa Hidetada; the Portuguese envoy sought, with no success, to intercede on the behalf of banished Catholic missionaries and to obtain the expulsion of the VOC from Japan. He was the last commander of the *não do trato* and, probably, as a result of a narrow escape from VOC capture, recommended the shift from the large and cumbersome *não* to the smaller swifter *galiotas*, in 1618.

In 1620, Carvalho prematurely demonstrated the extent of his ambition to the rest of Macao's casados and his existing or future associates; he negotiated and purchased from the Crown at Goa a three-year monopoly on the Japan voyage for 68,000 *xerafines*.[30] In 1621, Carvalho's voyage of six galiotas sold over three million guilders worth of raw silk and other merchandise in Japan. Piqued with envy and concern, the casado enemies of Carvalho in the Senado da Camara at Macao, via their representatives in Goa, petitioned the Crown's reversal of its sale.[31]

Carvalho's voyage of 1622 did not occur on account of the Dutch attack on Macao; as the capitão-mor of the Japan voyage Carvalho was the leading military commander which fortuitously but soundly defeated the VOC's forces. By the second year of his monopoly, the Senado da Camara's attacks had succeeded in reversing the Crown's sale. To defend himself and his project, Carvalho had arrived at Goa by 1623; after the Crown's decision, Carvalho departed Goa in one of his vessels in June of 1623 and was captured by the VOC in the Singapore straits. He was a prisoner of the VOC at Batavia.

With his brother-in-law absent and his enemies in the community busy, little is heard of António Fialho Ferreira until the return of Lopo Sarmento de Carvalho to Macao from his captivity at Batavia in the mid to late 1620s. The Crown also recognising Carvalho's services in the defence of Macao awarded him a knighthood in the Order of Christ in March 1629.[32] After Carvalho's return, these two Macao casado's together with a group of associates embarked upon their most ambitious joint venture. This Carvalho–Ferreira joint venture was an expanded version of an earlier project and involved additional associates: António Fialho Ferreira, Gaspar Homem, Andre Salema and Manoel de Moraes Supico. Carvalho and associates negotiated and purchased from the Viceroy, the Conde de Linhares, at Goa the monopoly of the Japan and Manila voyages for 306,000 xerafines for the years 1629–32.[33]

With Ferreira, Carvalho found a man of equal ambition and, it appears, experience at Canton and Manila. With Supico, Carvalho and Ferreira associated themselves with reputedly the richest Portuguese merchant at Goa. Supico arrived at the Estado da India at the turn of the sixteenth century. He exhibited an early interest in the Africa trade, operating as a factor in Mozambique around 1613 and despatching ships from Goa to Mozambique in 1626. Supico is primarily known for his involvement as leading local director in India of the Portuguese India Company of 1628–33. As a financier, he loaned funds to the Estado da India for use in Muscat and Malacca and also dealt in the diamond trade. Supico joined Carvalho in 1629 as a knight commander of the Order of Christ; he was active in the Senado da Camara of Goa and from 1629–30 was the president of the Santa Casa da Misericordia in that city.[34] By adding Supico and Ferreira, Carvalho consolidated his political connections at Goa and his capabilities in China and the Philippines.

Commercial opponents, other casados active in the Senado da Camara at Macao, reacted vehemently to the news of the Carvalho–Ferreira purchase of the Japan and Manila voyage monopolies. These opponents successfully opposed the execution of the Japan voyage portion of the contract for 1630 and 1631. It was during the execution of this project that Ferreira, who was responsible for the execution of the Manila voyage portion of the contract, emerged as a major figure in his own right in this transaction. His voyages to Manila were profitable and the Spanish reported that he annually exported raw silk and other merchandise from China valued at about a million and a half pesos.[35]

Carvalho and Ferreira via their support at Goa, despite the death of Supico, were subsequently able to enlist the Viceroy's, the Conde de Linares, aid in negating the Senado da Camara of Macao's opposition. The Viceroy's aid was nothing less than the appointment of one of his own relatives, Manuel da Camara de Noronha, to replace the capitão-geral of Macao. The new governor overrode Senado da Camara opposition in Macao in 1632, 1633 and 1634; Carvalho was able to execute the highly profitable Japan voyage of those years through his intervention. The 1634 voyage was not as successful as Carvalho and Macao had hoped although he returned with 490 chests of silver, on account of difficulties in negotiating supply contracts at Canton.

Subsequently, in 1635, Ferreira was responsible for negotiating an agreement with the Cantonese merchants. As Ferreira explained to the Crown, Ming officials at Canton had sold the office of collecting measurage and other duties on Macao's maritime trade, and the problem encountered by Macao was rate payment, increases and outstanding minor points of disagreement. The appointment of Ferreira and Vicente Roiz by the Senado da Camara demonstrates that despite commercial differences, the casados chose the 'two persons with the most practice and experience in dealing with this problem in the City.'[36]

Having made a fortune in business and demonstrated his talents in service to the City, Ferreira in 1636 focused on a method of evading losses caused by the VOC stranglehold over Portuguese shipping at the Straits of Malacca. It was in this last decade of his life, when his business and personal enemies in the city made his life so uncomfortable that Ferreira left Macao and emerged as a patriot and an early advocate for direct navigation from Europe to China.[37]

With the end of the Carvalho–Ferreira monopoly contract, these brothers-in-law became involved in financial and jurisdictional disputes with the city and Crown officials over the results of the voyages. Ferreira left Macao for Goa where the

Viceroy of the Estado da India received him in June 1638; with increasing VOC pressure on the Portuguese empire, Pero da Silva, the Viceroy sent Ferreira to Europe by the overland route to report the desperate position in which the Portuguese were and to request aid. Arriving in Lisbon slightly before the Restoration of the Crown of Portugal and advocating direct navigation from Europe to China, Ferreira was entrusted with a royal decree in January of 1641 as an envoy at his own cost to inform the Portuguese in the East of João's accession. Before departing Lisbon, he and one of his sons were admitted into the Order of Christ.

Although Ferreira's news and the acclamation of the Restoration of the Crown of Portugal was well received in Macao, Ferreira was not, although Lopo Sarmento de Carvalho was present and both of their political and economic positions were solid. Surveying Macao after the loss of the Japan trade and recognising that it would be difficult to deal with the Philippines directly, Ferreira boldly and wisely chose to return to Europe with his sons to garner Crown rewards for his services. At Lisbon, his other four sons were granted in October 1643 knighthoods in the Order of Christ; he joined with the Society of Jesus to lobby with the Crown for a Portuguese embassy to Japan. Nominated to command the ships to carry the Portuguese envoy to Japan, Ferreira returned to Macao after an extremely unfortunate attempted direct passage, with Capitão Gonçalo de Siqueira de Souza in 1645.[38] Requiring additional Estado da India support for the embassy, Ferreira departed Macao with his sons and family in late 1645 in command of a squadron hoping to obtain aid for the Japan embassy. His brother-in-law had died in Macao in 1645. Ferreira, amid controversy over his leadership of the Macao-to-Goa squadron died soon after his arrival at Goa in 1646; the Japan embassy failed and direct navigation to China from Europe was not achieved until the eighteenth century.[39]

The memory of the immense wealth that had been made by their participation in China's maritime trade during the era of the sharp merchants of Macao was still fresh in the minds of the local casados in the mid seventeenth century. Faced with a drastic reduction in their trade after the loss of the Japan and Manila trades, Portuguese society at Macao was under intense pressure to forestall further and, if possible, recoup their losses. With Ch'ing forces attacking the Ming, Macao became embroiled and, ultimately, its very survival was imperiled by the Manchu's rise to power in China.

With a colony of such strong, fractious personalities and the Crown and the Estado da India's resources focused in self-defence in Europe, Africa, Brazil and Asia, the Crown in a number of instances sought local administrators from casados; the Crown rejected the 1645 petition of the illustrious Salvador Correia de Sá e Benavides for the captaincy of Macao and their selection, Dom Braz de Castro, 'a fidalgo with a long record of service in the Orient,' as Professor Boxer points out, 'declined the post, on the grounds that conditions at Macao were too disturbed.'[40] From the mid seventeenth until the mid eighteenth century, a few prominent reinols, who had become casados at Macao, and on rare occasions their offspring, revealed the casado capable of being a stalwart communal defender and effective Crown servant. A famous example of the first was the invaluable communal service rendered by Manuel Tavares Bacarro, famous as the founder of the Macao cannon foundry, casado in Macao and its governor during the difficult years of 1657–64. The rare father-and-son combination was that of Pero Vaz de Siqueira (governor from 1698 to 1700 and 1702–3) and António de Siqueira de Noronha (1711–14).

STALWART COMMUNAL AND CROWN SERVANT: PERO VAZ DE SIQUEIRA

Pero Vaz de Siqueira was one of the sons of the Portuguese ambassador, Captain Gonçalo de Siqueira de Souza, to Japan in 1644–7. Arriving to the Estado da India in 1657, according to one of his service records, this reinol was active in Crown service, serving the fleet under Luis de Mendonça Furtado's command in 1657–9, participating in the re-capture of Coulão in 1659 and was a defender of Cochin.[41] In 1669, he was a capitão of Crown shipping active off Muscat.[42] Arriving at Macao in the early 1670s, he left Crown service and became a casado, marrying Ana Maria de Noronha.

Macao's very existence was threatened in the late 1660s by Ch'ing orders for coastal populations to evacuate the south China coast; with the actual destruction on the orders of Ch'ing officials, of eight Portuguese country trader vessels at Macao on the evening of 15 November 1666, prospects in the early 1670s for a new casado like Pero Vaz de Siqueira still appeared bleak. Slightly after this incident, the Senado da Camara and the Portuguese Crown prepared the embassy of Manuel de Saldanha to China in order to improve Sino-Portuguese relations but encountered that the city's revenues were insufficient to cover expenses. Two prominent casados, both of whom were ship-owners and active in the Senado da Camara, Miguel Grimaldi and Manoel Leal da Fonseca, were sent as the city's envoys to Siam to negotiate with King Narai a loan of 120,000 taels to defray Saldanha's expenses.[43]

The loan was authorised but an uncertain total amount was delivered by the two Portuguese emissaries to Macao, where the desperately required funds were employed with some, but not total, success. This loan to Macao served Siamese Crown interests; King Narai called upon and received support from the local Portuguese community at Ayuthia.[44] This local Portuguese community provided sailors and pilots for Siamese Crown shipping; when a Siamese Crown ship, for example, required repairs at Canton, the Portuguese captain of that local community, Francisco Barreto de Piña, a Macao casado then living in Siam, travelled to Canton and made arrangements for the appropriate repairs.[45]

Macao in the late 1660s and into the 1680s traded directly with Siam and with the Siamese Crown ships in the Macao islands; the Siamese Crown ships, upon occasion, called at Macao, where they took on provisions, cargo and sailors. Repayment of the loan to the Siamese crown was made during direct Portuguese trade from Macao to Ayuthia; in later years, the 1690s to 1720s, the Portuguese at Macao, while not trading directly with Siam on an annual basis, made occasional repayments to the Siamese Crown on this loan via the Portuguese payment of the customs duties of Siamese Crown ships at Canton, and dispatching on board the same shipping payment in kind, usually silk, when returning on the Canton–Macao–Ayuthia route.[46] Finally, the Senado da Camara completed the repayment of this loan in 1721, whereby the Portuguese were offered another on similar terms, but this was declined.[47]

This brief background to Portuguese–Siamese relations shows events which did not have an immediate effect, but were subsequently of direct relevance to the career of Pero Vaz de Siqueira, who by the late 1670s and throughout the 1680s operated two ships out of Macao dispatching them to the Banjarmasin, Timor, Batavia and Siam markets. With improved access to Chinese export production by 1683, the Crown and the Senado da Camara of Macao selected a number of casados to lead embassies to neighbouring South China Sea states in order to improve commercial relations; Pero Vaz de Siqueira was chosen to act as Macao's emissary to Siam and Fructuozo Gomes Leite to Cambodia, Cochinchina and Tonkin. Both emissaries had similar instructions, the main thrust of their mission was commercial and in the case of Siam, the Portuguese at Macao sought to participate via Siamese Crown shipping in trading ventures to Japan. Pero Vaz de Siqueira executed his instructions in 1684 but failed, apparently, to obtained Siamese Crown support for a scheme that would threaten Siamese trade to Japan.[48]

Despite his diplomatic failure in Siam, Pero Vaz de Siqueira's communal political and commercial activities at Macao flourished in the decade 1689–98; during this period, he was, it appears, a voting member of the Senado da Camara for seven out of the ten years and 1693–4 was also on the *Mesa* of the Santa Casa de Misericordia. By the 1690s and early 1700s, he was the largest single ship-owner in the city, owning and operating three vessels which made voyages to Goa and different Indian ports, Aceh, Banjarmassin, Timor and Manila. His position in the community was also recognised by the Crown through his appointment by the Viceroy of India as capitão-geral of Macao from 1698 to 1700 and a second term, 1702–3; it was during this last governorship that he died at Macao.

The public career of Pero Vaz de Siqueira may have been unusual in the length of his service and his probity in the early eighteenth century. But, as these glimpses into the three casado careers has shown, the Portuguese casados at Macao possessed strong personalities and persisted in the pursuit of their economic goals despite the adversaries or adversity they faced within Macao, in China or the South China Sea or in the Estado da India. These careers focus on the reinol dominance of Portuguese society in China in part because the reinois actively benefited from patronage from the imperial system. Social tensions between differing bandos and mestiços and reinois were present but communal power was never far from strong reinol influence if not control.

Office-holding in the Senado da Camara and the Santa Casa da Misericordia is a guide to the prominent Portuguese country traders, ship-owners and investors who lived in Macao. The municipal attorney, as Professor Boxer mentions, 'became the city's accredited representative in all dealings with the Chinese officials' and as a result 'he was the key man in the colony.'[49] If relative economic power and social position within local society are the criteria, all of the voting offices within these institutions were held by 'key' men; the municipal attorney's position in the Senado da Camara was closer to being *primus inter pares* or within competing commercial or political factions because of the short, one-year, duration of this office.

Almost all of Macao's population were involved in maritime trade, especially during the years of the Japan trade. But, the actual number of Portuguese casado country traders that were ship-owners, either entirely or in part, or major investors was quite small with the rest of the population providing the labour to man their ships. The loss of the Japan and Manila trades signified that the smaller investor's opportunity to participate in Macao's maritime trade diminished. In the 1680s and the 1740s, Macao's country traders' fleets fluctuated respectively between ten and eleven vessels and between nine and fifteen vessels.[50] The total number of ship-owners was very small and major Portuguese investors in Macao's maritime trade numbered probably fewer than thirty individuals.

A century or slightly longer after the Portuguese arrived in the Indian Ocean and the South China Sea, the maritime trade of Asia had adjusted and accommodated these European interlopers. In China and the South Sea, Asian attitudes and traditions towards maritime trade were unaltered but the markets and the economy in which Asian and Europeans traded had undergone modification. Whether this change was wrought by the European presence or by Asian merchants or in partnership may be determined by examining Portuguese trade in China and the South China Sea.

4

COUNTRY TRADERS
AND CROWN MONOPOLY

In China's foreign relations, there was no precise historical precedent to permit the Portuguese to establish themselves at Macao. Although there were similarities with the overland traders on the continental periphery, the Portuguese maritime traders' experience was unique in that their establishment was permanent. Aided, furthermore, by the Ming ban on all Chinese trade with Japan, the Portuguese fortuitously assumed the middleman role in the exchange of Chinese goods for Japanese silver.

By the late sixteenth century, these Iberian entrepeneurs had converted Macao into a major entrepôt and commercial centre in south China. Certain geographical features, its proximity to the Canton market, neighbouring islands which provided relatively secret rendezvous for smuggling operations and a safe harbour to protect their shipping, favoured Macao's development as a port and its involvement in maritime trade. Its major drawback, which none of the other Chinese ports faced, was the absence of space and a cultivable hinterland in the immediate vicinity of the city which left Macao entirely dependent upon Chinese producers in Kwangtung province for its food supplies.

A *modus operandi* between Ming officials and the Portuguese developed on account of Macao's dependence upon Chinese foodstuffs for its survival, and produce and commerce for its prosperity.

South China imported large quantities of spices (pepper, in particular, cloves and nutmeg) and aromatic woods (sandalwood, primarily) but silver, in specie and bullion, was the item in greatest demand. The Portuguese catered to China's voracious silver appetite with large-scale imports from Japan, the New World via Manila and a circuitous route from Mexico and Peru via Europe and the Estado da India. South China exported vast quantities of highly priced raw silk, silk and some cotton piecegoods and gold; it also provided enormous amounts of low-priced ballast goods (porcelain, zinc, alum, and radix China amongst others).

According to the Portuguese historian, António Bocarro, in the early seventeenth century, China produced an estimated 36–37,000 picols per year of silk; 24–25,000 picols were consumed within China and 12,000 picols were exported. By 1635, this export figure had been halved to an estimated 6,000 picols, most of which was destined for Japan and Manila; Bocarro attributed the decline, in part, to the diminution in Portuguese purchases of Chinese silk for export to India.[1] While it is impossible to reconstruct Bocarro's sources for such a report and his claim for the total silk-productive capacity in the late Ming, his figure of 6,000 picols

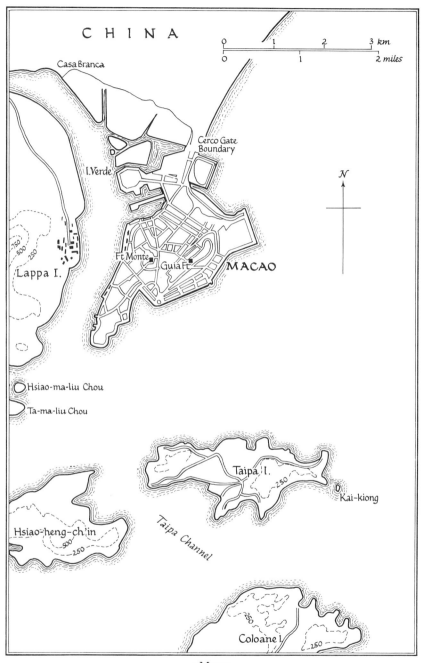

4 Macao

closely approximates the total amount of Chinese raw silk exported and sold in Japan and Manila by the Chinese, Portuguese, Japanese and the Dutch in the 1630s.

Earlier, the Portuguese had exported an average of 1,000–1,600 picols of raw silk to Japan.[2] Excluding any figures on Chinese silk sold at Manila by the Portuguese and depending upon which of Bocarro's figures (12,000 or 6,000 picols) are selected, the Portuguese exported around one-third to one-half of all of the silk that left China by sea. Even after the Portuguese ceased to export large quantities of silk to the Estado da India, in preference of gold, the Portuguese purchased a minimum of 2,000 picols of silk at Canton on an annual basis in the 1620s.[3]

The Portuguese involvement in the maritime trade of China and the South China Sea in the 1630s was linked to three markets, India, Japan and Manila. Owing to the loss of Portuguese archival records, Portuguese trade with India cannot be analysed. There is, in contrast, better documentation and detailed corroborative evidence for the Japan and Manila trades.

JAPAN

Portuguese trade to Japan from mid sixteenth century onwards, coincided with the discovery of large silver, copper and gold deposits in that country. There was a vigorous response towards the exploitation of these mineral resources and powerful groups within Japanese society embraced a favourable attitude towards foreign trade. Portuguese merchants first began to supply China's produce to Japan in the 1540s. When China promulgated edicts in 1557 prohibiting Chinese merchants to trade with Japan as a result of wakō activity on the Fukien coast, Portuguese merchants quickly seized and jealousy guarded the privilege to act as the exclusive official intermediaries in the trade between China and Japan. This privileged Portuguese position in the Japanese market was eroded before the arrival of the English and Dutch with the resurgence of trade by the Chinese, the emergence of Japanese and, to a much lesser degree, Spanish competition.

Japan's foreign trade in the late sixteenth century was firmly based upon the supply of Chinese raw silk and gold in exchange for silver bullion. By the 1630s gold was no longer as significant and silk piecegoods emerged as a major import. For the Portuguese, copper joined silver as an increasingly important export.

Innovations in the composition of Portuguese imports and exports to Japan occurred as the logical result of the astute commercial abilities and actions of their competitors, the necessity for Portuguese merchants to obtain higher profit margins and offset their losses, and the changing political attitudes of the Japanese towards foreign trade. Portuguese exports to Japan were not restricted to the commercial field; they exported Western military and mining technology that significantly changed Japanese society. The contribution of the introduction by the Portuguese of firearms to the martial arts and the *nanbanbuki* (an improved liquidation) process used in the refining of gold and silver had an important role in the incipient transformation of Japan's political and economic structures.[4]

5 Japan

Table 4.1: *Portuguese cargoes of Chinese goods to Japan, a comparison of*

Commodities	Sub-total quantities picols	*c.* 1600 Total quantities picols	Sale prices taels/picol	Sub-total sales taels	Total sales taels
Raw silk		900–1100			166,150
Chinese					
white	500–600		140–150	79,750	
retros, 1st			370–400		
retros, 2nd	400–500		100	86,400	
darca			90		
Silk piecegoods		1,700–2,000 pieces	2.5–3/piece		5,088
Cotton thread		200–300	16–18		4,250
Cotton piecegoods		3,000 pieces	0.23–1.7/piece		2,400
Gold		3–4,000 tael wt	7.8–8.3/ tael wt		28,000
Musk		2	1,120–1,280		2,400
Mercury		150–300	90–92		20,475
Radix China		500–600	4–5		2,475
Lead		2,000	6.4		12,800
Tin		500–600	12		6,600
Sugar		210–270			424
white	60–70		3–4.5		
black	150–200		4–6		
Others					5,300
			Total		256,362

Source: Boxer, *Great Ship.*

commodities, quantities, sale prices, and values, c. 1600 and 1637.

Commodities	Sub-total quantities picols	1637 Total quantities picols	Sale prices taels/picol	Sub-total sales taels	Total sales taels
Raw silk		1,736			368,135
Chinese					
white	373		287	107,186	
crimson	60		318	19,096	
pool (pouey)	56		305	17,096	
Tonkin	874		204	177,954	
twined	149		162	24,196	
raw twined	63		152	9,584	
floss (short)	11		131	1,445	
floss	30		112	3,446	
floss (coarse)	120		67.5	8,132	
Silk piecegoods		512,739 pieces			1,554,886
pangses					
white	294,875		2.3	679,622	
red, colrd	7,596		5.1, 1.9	38,559	
& plain			6.5		
gilams					
white	43,828		2.4	107,208	
red	10,936		4.4	48,979	
pelings					
white	49,665		4.3	215,628	
red	1,272		8	10,287	
satins	32,081			191,084	
damasks	41,513			143,656	
others	30,973			119,863	
Cotton piecegoods		16,259 pieces			16,827
cangas, Nanking & gauze					
Gold		60 tael wt	16.6/ tael wt		996
Musk		6	2,356		14,139
Mercury	181	86.8			15,716
Radix China		705	6		4,232
Zinc		2,953	8.3		24,589
Chintz, skins, wood & spices					62,865
Others					79,083
			Total		2,141,468

Observations upon the innovations in the export composition of Portuguese cargoes of Chinese goods to Japan were based upon contemporary Portuguese records and corroborated through VOC eyewitness reports. Table 4.1 compares the cargoes carried around the turn of the seventeenth century by the não do trato and the 1637 cargo carried by the galiotas. Appropriate comments are made in the examples of raw silk, silk piecegoods and gold.

In the case of sugar, the Fukienese had the advantage of a lower cost price because of their closer proximity to supplies; when the selling price declined in Japan as a result of the oversupply of this commodity, the Fukienese continued to trade in sugar despite the lower profit margins because of its importance as a ballast cargo. The Portuguese, the structure of whose trade required higher profit margins, ceased to compete against the Fukienese in the trading of sugar to Japan.

RAW SILK

The Kyoto silk textile industry had been in production since the fifteenth century. The demand for silk in Japan, which emanated from the feudal *daimyo* (lords) and the urban upper classes, continually exceeded domestic production capabilities both in quality and quantity. With the influx of revenues from silver, copper and gold mining and the resulting expansion of a monetary exchange economy, demand for the importation of raw silk was strong and continued to rise. Raw silk (bolted woven cloth, sold in bulk) as opposed to silk piecegoods (individual lengths of cloth) was the primary product imported into Japan throughout most of the sixteenth and seventeenth centuries.

Several varieties of raw silk were imported but the market preference was for Chinese white. The general trend in the importation of raw silk saw Chinese white remain the market leader with the addition of dyed raw silk from China, Tonkin and Cochinchina from the early seventeenth century. Raw silk, in addition to its utility in the manufacture of clothing, ceremonial and otherwise, was sold at high prices because of its rarity and amassed like money on account of its exchange value.[5]

The Portuguese recognised the importance of supplying Chinese raw silk and attempted to monopolise its supply to Japan. Their imports comprised almost the total market for imported raw silk which fluctuated between 1,000 and 1,600 picols per year. The Portuguese position in that market eroded in the early seventeenth century as a result of a combination of external political and economic factors. Portuguese shipping within the South China Sea region experienced difficulties in evading capture by the VOC.

Japanese officials, more importantly, perceived the liaison between the Japanese Christian daimyo and the Portuguese as dangerous. This perception led to a deterioration in relations and in 1610 the Japanese attacked the Portuguese não the *Madre de Deus*, which its capitão-mor scuttled along with himself and his crew in Nagasaki Bay. A reconciliation between the Portuguese and the Japanese was arranged and, although trade resumed, earlier economic decisions taken by the

Japanese remained. Those economic decisions which the Portuguese felt were inimical to their trade included the implementation of a price-fixing system on Portuguese imports of Chinese raw silk and the inauguration of despatching Japanese red-seal ships (*go-shuin-sen*) to ports in the South China Sea.

The impact of competition by the Chinese and Japanese upon the Portuguese position in the raw silk market was dramatic. Imports of raw silk increased, from the 1,000–1,600 picols the Portuguese supplied earlier to a total slightly less than 3,000 picols per year by 1610; the Portuguese maintained only thirty per cent of this expanded market.[6] Over the next decade, imports of raw silk from all competitors stabilised around 3,000 to 3,500 picols per year. The amounts of imported raw silk for the following two decades, 1620–4, fluctuated between 2,500 and over 4,000 picols per year. The VOC became a regular supplier and competitor during these decades and the market demonstrated oversupply conditions with the importation of over 4,000 picols of raw silk per year.[7]

GOLD

Although by the end of the sixteenth century there were some fifty gold mines in operation, the Japanese continued to purchase large amounts of gold imported by Portuguese, Chinese, other Europeans and their own shipping. The demand for gold in the Japanese market was widespread on account of the increased use of this precious metal as a medium of exchange, either in mint or bar, for payment of large financial transactions. Government and military expenditures, in particular, were high; after Hideyoshi's campaigns at home in 1590 and with the contemplated incursion into China, they became astronomical.

The high internal demand for gold in the early 1590s coincides with the high water mark of its import. This demand did not immediately decline after the establishment by Tokugawa Ieyasu of his *Bakufu* (the 'curtain government' or military dictatorship established by the Tokugawa) in 1603. Ieyasu maintained a policy of large-scale importations of gold, arrangements for which were done by the Jesuits, through Macao and the Portuguese. The moderation of demand, at least the demand for Portuguese participation in importing gold, may be explained in the continued opening of new mines after 1594 and increased competition in its trade from Japanese and other merchants.

In the middle of the sixteenth century, gold mines in Japan, principally in the provinces of Mutsu and Kai, benefited from new and improved methods of mining and refining. This trend of benefiting from technological innovation heightened towards the end of the sixteenth century and occurred contemporaneously with the initiation of mines on the island of Sado at the Nishi Mikawa and Aikawa. There was no further notable expansion in the numbers of mines in production in the seventeenth century with the exception of those in Satsuma province between 1620 and 1630.

Gold imports, as with raw silk, expanded as the go-shuin-sen traders to Faifo (major trading port of central Vietnam) and other ports of the South China Sea discovered that their silver bullion found ready markets for the purchase of this precious metal. Japanese transactions for gold in the Philippines began as early as 1572. At least forty-three go-shuin-sen made the voyage from Japan to Manila from 1596 to 1609; the Spanish, in particular, reported Portuguese merchants and goods on board the arriving go-shuin-sen of 1599–1602.[8] The Japanese and Portuguese maintained a vigorous trade at Manila exchanging silver, woven silks, weaponry, and bulk items such as wheat flour and salted meats with the Spanish and Chinese merchants for gold, raw silk, skins and woods to make dye.[9]

The importation of gold into Japan by go-shuin-sen and Chinese junks was probably one of the major contributing factors, along with the possibility of the stabilisation of internal demand, for the cessation of large-scale Portuguese participation in the trade in this commodity. Gold trading profit margins narrowed in Japan as a result of increased competition; Professor Kobata has observed that the profit margins on gold circa 1610 was 60 per cent. They declined circa 1620 to 30 per cent and after 1640, it ceased to be profitable.[10]

By the 1620s, the Portuguese, who in the later quarter of the sixteenth century had imported 3–4,000 taels (weight) of gold bullion as demonstrated in Table 4.1, no longer imported significant amounts of gold into Japan.

From 1629 until 1644, in China, gold was worth 1:10 silver but south of the Yangtze 1:13 silver; the probable cause, again, according to Professor Kobata 'was due to the export of gold to Japan and other countries by the Dutch and Chinese.'[11] To this observation, it must be added that Portuguese trade in gold, from China, directed towards India, where higher profit margins were apparently enjoyed, was very active in the 1620s and 1630. The Dutch in Surat in 1632 reported very competitive and aggressive Portuguese trading in gold supplied from China.[12] In the late 1630s, the VOC purchases of gold from China were adversely affected by widespread Portuguese purchases at Canton.[13] Japan continued to import gold in unknown total amounts from the Portuguese (until 1639), Japanese (until 1635), the Chinese and the VOC (until 1664), when it reverted to being a net exporter of gold.

SILVER AND COPPER

Silver bullion was the principal export from Japan in the sixteenth and most of the seventeenth centuries. Although the Portuguese had an early interest in trading for Japanese copper and sizeable exports were carried by them in the 1630s, that commodity, perhaps, did not truly become a major export item until the Bakufu embargo on copper exports, which was enacted in 1638, was lifted in 1645. Copper exports expanded dramatically as a result of the continued trading activity of the VOC and the Chinese.[14]

Silver and copper were, as was gold, in increased demand in the Japanese economy for identical reasons. Demand for precious metals and copper as a medium of exchange and the standardisation and centralisation of the minting of coin was on the upsurge in a society where military and commercial expenditures were

Table 4.2. *Departures of the não do trato from Macao to Japan, 1546–1617.*

Year of departure	Number of vessels	Year of departure	Number of vessels	Year of departure	Number of vessels
1546	3	1570	2	1594	0
1547	0	1571	2	1595	1
1548	1	1572	1	1596	1
1549	0	1573	2	1597	1
1550	2	1574	4	1598	3
1551	1	1575	1	1599	0
1552	1	1576	1	1600	1
1553	1	1577	2	1601	0
1554	1	1578	1	1602	1
1555	2	1579	1	1603	0
1556	2	1580	2	1604	1
1557	2	1581	2	1605	1
1558	2	1582	2	1606	1
1559	2	1583	1	1607	0
1560	3	1584	2	1608	0
1561	5	1585	1	1609	1
1562	3	1586	2	1610	0
1563	3	1587	2	1611	0
1564	3	1588	1	1612	1
1565	2	1589	2	1613	0
1566	2	1590	2	1614	1
1567	3	1591	1	1615	1
1568	2	1592	0	1616	0
1569	2	1593	1	1617	1

Sources: Boxer, *Great Ship* and Brown, *Money Economy.*

soaring. This growth in military and commercial expenditures was a consequence of increased liquidity after the expansion of silver mining in Japan.

Silver mining from the early sixteenth century on was centred in Iwami province. After the death of Hideyoshi, by 1602, the Iwami mines became the property of the central government. In the seventeenth century, the island of Sado, which recorded from 1613 to 1648 an annual production capacity of over half a million taels (weight), and the provinces of Iwami and Tajima were the major centres of silver mining.

Japanese economic historians have made invaluable contributions towards estimating the total value and the annual average of the foreign and go-shuin-sen export of silver bullion from Japan in the sixteenth and seventeenth centuries. Any estimate of the value of Portuguese exports of silver bullion must establish, first, the frequency of Portuguese arrival and departures in Japan during the period, second, determine the annual estimated and observed values of their commercial transactions and, third, ideally, add a variable rate of *respondencia* and consignment participation.

The frequency of Portuguese shipping arrival and departures in Japan is available and presented in Tables 4.2 and 4.3. Although there is some slight

Table 4.3. *Departures of the galiotas from Macao to Japan, 1618–40.*

Year of departure	Number of vessels	Year of departure	Number of vessels	Year of departure	Number of vessels
1618	6	1626	6	1634	5
1619	8	1627	0	1635	3
1620	6	1628	5	1636	4
1621	6	1629	2	1637	6
1622	0	1630	2	1638	2
1623	7	1631	5	1639	4
1624	5	1632	4	1640	1
1625	5	1633	2		

Sources: ANTT, *GM*, and Boxer, *Great Ship.*

discrepancy in the data collated during the period of service of the não do trato, it is noted elsewhere and is minimal.[15] The frequency of service of Portuguese shipping establishes the number of years in which they exported silver from Japan.

The estimates and observed values of Portuguese exports of silver were obtained from a myriad of archival and secondary sources.[16] These estimates and observations represent our knowledge of silver exported by the Portuguese from Japan. Although they are far from perfect, this data is the result of lengthy and critical evaluation.

With the actual frequency of Portuguese shipping arrivals and departures and the estimates and reported volumes of silver exports by the Portuguese, it is possible to establish some global export volume figures. If a variable rate for respondencia and consignment could be computed, it would indicate the proportion of the amount of silver exported in Portuguese shipping that was borrowed by the Portuguese or consigned by Japanese or Chinese merchants. Unfortunately, these estimates are not available for the period.[17]

After the inception of their trade in the 1540s until a decline in Chinese competition c. 1562, Portuguese annual silver exports were highly profitable but did not reach the astronomical levels later associated with this voyage. Based upon Father Sebastião Gonsalves' contemporary calculations that the Portuguese exported an average value of 400 to 500,000 taels (15,000–18,700 kilograms) of silver bullion per annum and the knowledge of the number of Portuguese arrivals in Japan from 1546–79, it is estimated that the Portuguese exported from 12.4 to 15.5 million taels from Japan in those thirty-three years.

Throughout the last quarter of the sixteenth century and the initiation of go-shuin-sen activity, the total annual Portuguese export of silver bullion is estimated by Professor Kobata as having fluctuated between 500–600,000 taels (18,700–22,500 kilograms). From 1580 to 1597, relying upon Kobata's estimate, Father Alexandre Valignano's valuation for the 1593 voyage and the Portuguese failure to sail for Japan in 1592 and 1594, it is estimated that the Portuguese exported 7.5 to 8.9 million taels in those seventeen years.

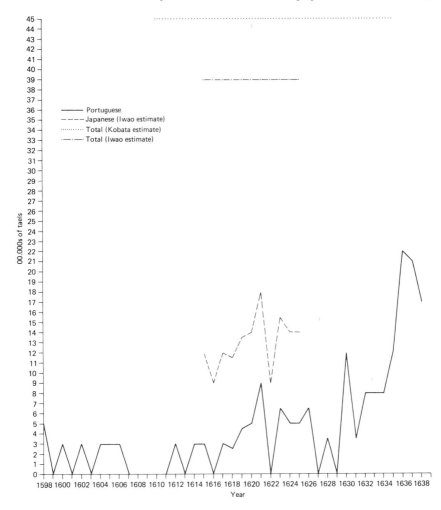

4.1 Silver exports from Japan, 1598–1638.

Data for the last forty-one years of Portuguese exports of silver bullion from Japan is far more precise than the previous years. Figure 4.1 demonstrates the fluctuations in Portuguese exports of Japanese silver bullion, 1598–1638. The minimum total value of Portuguese exports of silver over those forty-one years, it is conservatively estimated, were 16.7 million taels or an average of 417,500 taels (12,525 kilograms) per year. Over the entire period 1546–1638, the total Portuguese export of silver bullion from Japan to China, with its initial primary destination being Canton, is estimated between 36.6 to 41.1 million taels.

Professors Kobata and Iwao, respectively, estimate that the amount of silver annually exported from Japan over the period 1610–35 was 4 to 5 million taels

(150,000–187,000 kilograms) and 1615–25, 3.5 to 4.3 million taels (around 131,000–161,250 kilograms). In Figure 4.1, the average of each of these estimates is depicted. Iwao also claims that Japanese silver exports over the period 1615–25 averaged 0.8 to 1 million taels (30,000–37,500 kilograms) per year.[18] By comparing the average value of the two Iwao estimates with the minimum Portuguese participation in the export of silver bullion over this period as shown in Figure 4.1, it is possible to reconstruct the approximate relative market proportions by participants of silver exports from Japan for 1615–25.

Based on Iwao's estimate, the go-shuin-sen activity accounted for 23 per cent of the exports per year throughout the decade. The Portuguese fluctuated from having no participation in 1616 and 1622, to 6 per cent in 1618 and, their highest level in this period, 23 per cent, in 1621. It is suggested that there were greater fluctuations in the export of silver bullion by all trading competitors in this decade than the present data represents. The minimum estimates of Japanese and Portuguese market participation are either too conservative or the Chinese, Dutch, English and Spanish exported one-half to three-quarters of all silver exports from Japan in 1615–25. The second and, it is argued, most plausible alternative is that our present estimates for total Japanese, Portuguese and other trading competitors are too optimistic and are in need of revision.

Portuguese exports of silver bullion rose dramatically for most of the 1630s. One reason for such an expansion, was the gradual implementation of a Bakufu policy from 1634 which limited direct Japanese involvement in foreign trade and shipping and finally banned the go-shuin-sen trade in 1635–6 which stimulated Portuguese exports. Another reason and more immediate for the Portuguese was their requirement of large sums of silver in the attempt to service their debts caused by a liquidity crisis in the flows of New World silver into Manila, a tightening of credit supplies in Japan and the relentless financial losses caused by VOC naval activity against their shipping.

The vigour of Portuguese trade in Japan from 1632 to 1638 is startling. If the last year of go-shuin-sen participation, 1635, and Kobata's rather high annual total export of silver bullion estimate of 4.5 million taels is taken as the point for comparison with the Portuguese average annual totals, the relative minimum proportions of the Portuguese exports to the total was maintained at 18 per cent in 1632, rose to 49 per cent in 1636 and hovered at 37 per cent in 1638 just prior to their expulsion.

THE *PANCADA*, SILK AND SILVER

The Portuguese implemented four major innovations in their Japan trade in the seventeenth century either through their own initiative or in response to local and regional economic and political circumstances. Alterations in Japan's market environment by that state's political leadership with the imposition of a price-fixing system on the sale of raw silk prompted many of these innovations. The first was technological: the shift from the não do trato to galiotas in 1618. The second was economic: the evasion of the price-fixing system on raw silk by importing silks other than raw Chinese white and silk piecegoods on a scale that contributed to a change in the structure of Japan's foreign trade. The third was financial: the Portuguese attempted to lessen their dependence upon Japanese capital for their finances by arranging and shifting their reliance to the Chinese. The fourth was administrative and peculiar to Portuguese society: the Habsburg Crown implemented a policy of increasing its control over Macao's trade to Japan and securing an important source of revenue for the Estado da India with the appointment of an administrator of the voyage.

In 1604 the Bakufu ordered the organisation and imposition of the *Itowappu-nakama*. This was a guild of selected Japanese merchants from Sakai, Kyoto and Nagasaki, and later, Edo and Osaka, which was allowed to monopolise the purchase at a fixed rate and the distribution of Portuguese imported Chinese raw silk, after the Bakufu made its deductions. The *pancada*, as the Itowappu-nakama was known to the Portuguese, was a threat to high profit levels in the raw silk trade. The advantages for the Bakufu were that this guild controlled imports of Chinese raw silk and kept import prices low. By purchasing at this depressed price, the government controlled a significant portion of the market. With such control over the distribution and sale of raw silk, the Bakufu earned sizeable revenues.[19]

The immediate implication of the imposition of the pancada for the Portuguese trading in raw silk was readily apparent. Their shipping, the large não do trato, experienced a decline in the number and the frequency of their sailing from Macao for Japan. Caution, however, must be advocated in the use of such an elementary statistical indicator as the number of ships employed by the Portuguese, since such a depiction is potentially misleading, not all of the ships were the large twelve hundred ton plus carracks, whose size also fluctuated, but included Portuguese-purchased Chinese shipping of the ocean-going junk variety. Furthermore, such an indicator neglects to include Portuguese shipping from and participation in respondencia on Portuguese, Japanese and Chinese shipping from other areas of the South China Sea region.

Contemporary accounts support and suggest that there was a decrease in the availability and the desirability on the part of the Portuguese merchants at Macao to utilise carracks in the Japan trade. The concern of these merchants, which came to be shared by the Crown and the capitão-mor, intensified in the first decade of the seventeenth century. The arrival of the Dutch and the relative ease in which they captured richly laden Portuguese carracks demonstrated to Macao's merchants the necessity to employ smaller and more numerous vessels. The decision to use the galiotas in the Japan trade was taken and was quickly justifed in its first year of operation, 1618.[20]

The highly sensitive political and economic interrelationship between Japan and the South China Sea was demonstrated when Portuguese trade was embargoed as a result of the Spaniards indifferent attitude towards those relationships. In 1628 the governor of Manila dispatched Don Juan de Alcaraso to Siam to retaliate against the Siamese, who successfully attacked Don Fernando de Silva and his ship in 1624, and obtain restitution of the goods confiscated by them in 1625 from Andrés Lopes de Azaldegui's embassy. With the failure of his mission, Alcaraso and the Spanish shipping under his command stayed in the Gulf of Siam and seized and plundered several Siamese junks and a go-shuin-sen.

When the news of such treatment of a go-shuin-sen reached Japan, an embargo upon Portuguese trade was established; the Portuguese were unable to disassociate themselves from Manila's hostile acts and bore the brunt of Japanese anti-Iberian measures. This embargo coincided fortunately for the Portuguese with another placed upon the VOC from 1628 to early 1633 by the Japanese authorities on account of Dutch–Japanese altercations on Taiwan.

Portuguese commercial debts at this time were beginning to erode the confidence of their Japanese creditors. The Portuguese ambassador, Dom Gonçalo da Silveira, who was in Japan in the early 1630s trying to restore good political and commercial relations, stood bond for the repayment of these debts – a practice which became customary for the prominent Portuguese officials involved in the trade.[21] The total Portuguese indebtedness was estimated at between 200 to 600,000 taels. In general, when Crown administrators and local Portuguese merchants wrote of Macao's indebtedness, it was the city of Macao's that were meant unless otherwise stipulated.

Caught between the hammer and their shipping losses to the VOC and the anvil of high interest rate indebtedness to the Japanese, Portuguese institutions and individuals sought relief from higher trading profits and prevaricating on repaying their debts. The trading seasons of 1631 and 1632 revealed the Portuguese indecisive towards and finally opposed to the pancada in the attempt to increase their profit margins. The Japanese were equally insistent upon repayment of the outstanding Portuguese debts, some of which had been incurred over ten years or longer. Macao incurred in these two years an additional 216,000 taels of debt which brought the city's total to 300,000 taels. The Portuguese modified their previous position of prevaricating upon the immediate repayment of their entire private and public debt in Japan in 1632 by sending a number of individual Portuguese merchants to renegotiate and repudiate some of their debts – an action which met with some success and approval from Japanese authorities.

The following year, 1633, saw the revocation of the embargo on the VOC, a large volume of trade by the Japanese, Chinese and VOC and a subsequent decline in the price of raw silks and silk piecegoods. Faced with antagonistic Japanese officials at Nagasaki and being opposed to selling their raw, *boogy* (yellow) and *pool* (used in making velvet) silks at pancada prices, the Portuguese were ordered to either sell or depart. Pancada prices in 1633 were: raw Chinese white, first quality, 280 taels/picol, second 235, *boogy*, 170 and *pool*, 200.[22] The Portuguese as a result of this ultimatum and the local merchants knowledge of their predicament sold their silks at prices 70–80 taels less than those of the pancada.

For the Portuguese merchants, their dilemma was clear, if they faced no prospect of evading the pancada and the profitability of their trade did not increase to service let alone repay their debts, they would lose their position in that market. They supported political efforts for redress of their grievances from Japanese governmental authorities at Yedo. Relief was forthcoming from Yedo with orders to modify the pancada and allow the Portuguese to sell their *boogy* and *pool* silk varieties outside of the pancada but imports and the pricing of raw Chinese white silk remained within that system.

At Nagasaki the subsequent furor of the Japanese money lenders and merchants, after learning of Yedo's unfavourable decision to their interests, led them to demand payment of the outstanding debts from the Portuguese. Four, erstwhile prominent, Portuguese merchants with debts of 1.25 million taels declared bankruptcy as their Japanese creditors discovered the fragility of Portuguese finances.[23] Other Portuguese merchants had to promise that they would personally return to Japan the following year to make payments.

Despite their credit problems, the Portuguese initiated their policy of evading the pancada in 1634 by importing only 200 picols of raw Chinese white silk, and concentrated upon a large variety of other silks, silk piecegoods, and consignments of zinc and tin. The raw silk market reached high levels as a total of 4,040 picols were imported. Slightly over three-quarters of the total were imported by junks from the Fukien coast (1,000 picols), the Ryukyus (700), Cochinchina (500) and Tonkin (1,000), with the VOC importing only an additional 640 picols. The pancada prices for the Portuguese and the VOC (who had been obliged by Japanese authorities to participate in this price-fixing system in 1633) were low; prices for raw silk, first quality, were 260 taels/picol and, second, 215.[24] The Portuguese achieved dramatic results with their policy of evading the pancada; they departed, after repaying one-third the city of Macao's indebtedness, with more than 800,000 taels and a large consignment of copper.

In 1635, Portuguese galiotas from China arrived at Nagasaki carrying large quantities of merchandise which evaded the pancada, 200 picols of *boogy* and 150 picols of *pool* silks, 113,000 pieces of white and red *pansges*, along with 160,000 pieces of white and red *pelings* (both types of silk piecegoods), quantities of red woollens, *cangans* (cotton shawls from the Coromandel coast), mercury and zinc. The Portuguese imported only 160 picols of raw, Chinese white, silk, which were subject to the pancada. They exported silver bullion estimated as worth around 1.2 million taels, after deducting 73,000 taels used to pay the second of the city of Macao's instalments to eliminate its indebtedness and excluding approximately one-fourth of the total in Japanese respondencia.[25] While the city's indebtedness to Japanese creditors continued to be reduced, the private Portuguese merchants debt in Japan was estimated at 600,000 taels. Pressure for repayment and a tightening by Japanese creditors and officials on Portuguese access to credit indicated to Macao's merchants the necessity for them to contemplate alternative sources.

The Portuguese surpassed the VOC in 1636 by importing into Japan well over 3.5 million guilders worth of merchandise. The Portuguese followed their successful policy of evading the pancada by importing silk piecegoods; only a small quantity, 250 picols, of raw Chinese silk was imported, which fetched over 75,000

taels. With high prices, in part stimulated by reduced go-shuin-sen activity and
the Bakufu's edict prohibiting the departure of Japanese shipping and permission
for their merchants to reside overseas, the values of the Portuguese exports from
Japan soared to over 6.6 million guilders.[26] Although this edict released funds held
by Japanese money lenders to be loaned as respondencia, the VOC discovered that
the Portuguese paid the third and final instalment of the city of Macao's debt but
had not borrowed any significant amounts of capital.

It was not until 1637 that the VOC discovered where the Portuguese had
obtained alternative credit of an equal magnitude as had been provided in Japan:
this was from the *quevees* (Chinese merchant brokers) of Canton. The cost of money
and the ease of obtaining credit for the Portuguese in Japan as compared to China
for the Japan trade appears to have favoured Japan until the 1630s. Since Japanese
money lenders had ceased extending credit, the reason why the Portuguese
chose to avail themselves of credit facilities at Canton is that there was no other
choice except the quevees or their own resources. Portuguese capital resources
were insufficient; the Cantonese money lenders, as in the Manila trade,
could be convinced, if the interest rate was high enough, to loan money to the
Portuguese.

Portuguese competition in the raw silk market that year was to pose a serious
threat to VOC sales and profits. Six Portuguese galiotas arrived with enormous
amounts of silk piecegoods, including 300,000 pieces of white pansges. They
carried sufficient raw, white Chinese, silk, 373 picols, to disrupt the pancada. They
sold their raw silk at the Macao purchase price which resulted in the VOC receiving
a pancada price of 252 taels/picol for their 1,000 picols of imported, raw, Chinese
silk.[27] The arrival of an increased number of Chinese junks, sixty-four were
recorded, stimulated by the Bakufu's prohibition of the go-shuin-sen trade with
cargoes of raw silk, also contributed to keeping this market depressed. Portuguese
exports exceeded 2.1 million taels of silver bullion and with small amounts of
Japanese respondencia; the VOC hoped that the profitability of Portuguese trade
was low as a result of high interest rates on Chinese respondencia.

The Crown's creation of the *administrador*, and his imposition of control over
the Japan voyage in the mid 1630s was surprisingly successful in generating
revenue for the Estado da India. The fundamental difficulty from the Crown's point
of view was the safe transferal of these revenues to Goa from Macao. Sebastião
Soares Paes, a *dezembargador*, reported in 1635 that the Crown's participation in
the trade grossed 116,480 taels and after deductions of the operating expenses,
payment to the original grantee of the voyage and of Macao's garrison, a profit
to the Crown of 86,000 taels was realised.[28] In 1637, Romão de Lemos, the
administrador, reported that the Crown's gross receipts were 204,000 taels from
a 10 per cent duty on the freight imported into Macao from Japan; after deductions
for operating costs and the garrison, its profitability for the Crown was as high
as 160,000 taels.[29]

While the figures for Portuguese trade with Japan especially exports for 1636-7
are impressive, and apparently were never equalled by the VOC, the continuation
of this trade did not coincide with the Bakufu's politics which were emerging as

anti-Iberian and anti-Christian even prior to the Shimabara rebellion (a peasant, crypto-Christian, revolt in Arima and Amakusa) in 1637.[30] Afterwards, the Bakufu was galvanised to act against the Portuguese and the importation of Christianity into Japan. Bedevilled by a severe tightening of credit in Canton, exploited by local officials' extortionate demands and exacerbated by the collapse of significant silver imports from New Spain via the Portuguese trade with Manila, 1636–8, the Portuguese only despatched two galiotas for Nagasaki in 1638.[31] They were received with indifference but allowed to trade; they imported only 230 picols of raw, white Chinese, silk (150 picols of which the Japanese had the major participation according to the VOC) and the rest of their imports were sold outside of the pancada. Reports indicate that despair for their trade deepened, regardless of the fact that their exports amounted to a total of over 1.6 million taels including 400,000 taels of respondencia at 25–27 per cent.[32] The reason for this despair was the Bakufu's threat to destroy Portuguese trade if Catholic missionaries continued to arrive in Japan from the Philippines or China.

The end of the Portuguese trade to Japan was announced the following year, 1639, with the promulgation of the expulsion edict by Bakufu officials. Rich cargoes for four galiotas, despite credit problems at Canton, were forthcoming but their passage was a catastrophe. One galiota capsized, one returned to Macao in a sinking condition and the cargo ruined, two arrived safely with up to 500,000 taels of cargo on their Japanese creditors' account but were met by Bakufu officials and the exclusion edict was read. Returning to Macao, the Portuguese refused to accept the loss of this trade and despatched a special embassy in 1640 in the hope of reaching an accommodation with the Japanese; the ambassador, his entourage and crew were executed, the galiota burnt and an era of prosperity for Macao based on its trade to Japan was closed.

There was a major market in the South China Sea region in the early seventeenth century, created out of Iberian rivalry and supplied with New World silver, that also attracted Portuguese merchants' interest. Despite formal imperial prohibitions, the interest exhibited and cultivated by Portuguese merchants with the Spanish colony in the Philippines swept away such legal prohibitions. The trade that centred on Manila formed, for some vital and for others a profitable, market for Chinese, Indian and regional produce carried by Macao's and other Portuguese country traders from throughout the Estado da India.

MANILA

Early Iberian relations in the East were characterised by a mutual distrust of the other's intentions in regard to the security and the economic well being of the colonial settlements of both powers. Under the command of Miguel de Legaspi in 1565, the Spanish established themselves on the island of Cebu which elicited in response the deployment of a Portuguese squadron. This squadron, under the command of Gonçalo Pereira, was unsuccessful in its attempt to force the withdrawal of the fledgling Spanish colony in 1568. After their founding the city of Manila on the island of Luzon in 1571, the Spanish were in a stronger position

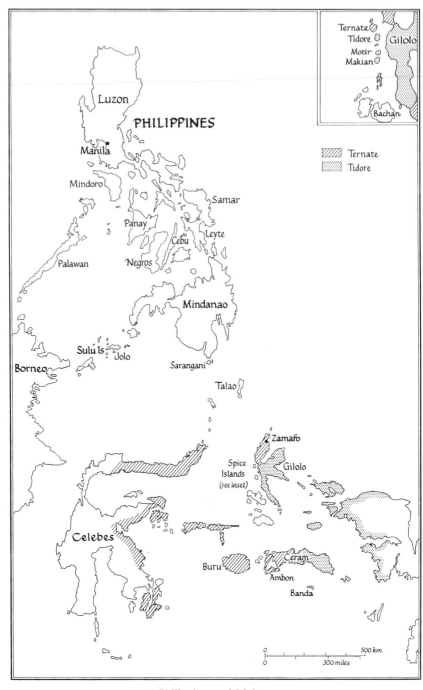

6 Philippines and Moluccas

to defend and to exploit the commercial possibilities of the region. Macao feared the potential damage to their trade by the Spanish presence.

The early trade between the Spanish and the Chinese in the first decade after Manila's founding was exploratory.[33] The Spanish had high expectations for the development of trade; a large commercialised cinnamon trade was illusory but gold was available in limited quantities.[34] The Chinese discovered that sugar, silk, porcelain and iron had a good market; by 1576, the Chinese were already profitably supplying Manila with pepper, cloves, and nutmeg from the centres of production of those spices immediately south of the Philippines in the Indonesian archipelago.[35]

The composition of imports into the Philippines was divided into local demand for agricultural produce, munitions, slaves, equipment for the outfitting of shipping, and certain types of low-cost cotton clothing, and external demand in New Spain and Peru for silks, porcelains, iron, copper and mercury. The stream of silver that had found its way across the Pacific from 1571–9 in order to purchase Chinese silks from Chinese and Portuguese merchants was by the late 1590s a roaring river in flood.[36] These sizeable purchases of silk by the Spanish in the Philippines coincided with increased silver bullion production in the New World mines of Zacatecas in Mexico and Potosi in Peru. Silver rapidly became almost the only commodity acceptable to the Chinese to pay for their produce; by 1582 Ming officials reported that Chinese merchants no longer bartered portions of their cargoes at Manila. By that date, Ming authorities had standardised the payment of customs duties by Portuguese and Chinese maritime traders in silver.[37]

Silk in various forms, raw and yarn, was present in the initial Sino-Spanish commercial transactions but it was not until Spanish merchants from New Spain arrived in Acapulco from Manila in 1579 with the first quantity shipment that the commercial relationship which dominated this early trans-Pacific trade was firmly established.[38] Chinese silk imports had an immediate impact upon the New Spain (Mexico) silk market which was detrimental for imported Spanish silks but beneficial for the Mexican manufacturers. The colonial Mexican market accommodated the massive introduction of Chinese silks but became dependent upon the supply of Chinese silk yarns which coincided with the decline of Mexican sericulture. The ruin of silk-raising in colonial Mexico may only in part be ascribed to the Philippines trade not because of direct competition with local production – in fact there was a tremendous expansion in market consumption of Chinese and Mexican silks in the 1580s at the cost of Spanish imports – but cheap Chinese silk yarn imports 'slashed the profits which could be gained from silk culture and further discouraged producers.'[39]

THE PORTUGUESE, THE PACIFIC AND THE *PARIAN*

The Portuguese had failed in their attempts to prevent Sino-Spanish trade. Macao learned of official and unofficial, Spanish Crown and resident-Manila religious, efforts to commence formal diplomatic contacts with China. The

Portuguese recognised that the Spanish emissaries' efforts at Fukien and Kwang-tung threatened their monopoly of direct access by a European trading power to the China, but specifically to the Canton, market. Seeking to protect their commercial position, Macao's inhabitants implemented a policy, through political and financial appeals to Ming officials in Kwangtung, of denying the Spanish direct access to the Canton market. The Portuguese course of action coincided with the prevalent unfavourable Chinese official attitude towards the Spanish but, the outcome of this Iberian diplomatic confrontation in China was further complicated by the arrival of the news of the death of the King of Portugal, Sebastião, at the battle of Alcazar.

After Sebastião's demise, King Philip II of Spain acceded to the throne of Portugal in 1580; the news of his accession reached Manila in 1581. The Spanish Governor, D. Gonzalo Ronquillo de Peñalosa, sent emissaries to the Portuguese capitão-mors of Macao, Ambon and the Moluccas informing them of the union of the two Crowns. A Spanish Jesuit, Alonso Sanchez, was chosen to go to Macao in 1582 where he was received and where the capitão-mor, the fidalgos, the religious and the people of the city swore their allegiance to King Philip II.[40]

Outwardly the transition of power was accomplished easily but caution was urged in letters from the capitão-mor of Macao, D. João de Albuquerque, and the Jesuit Alexandre Valignano. Peace, they argued, could only be guaranteed by Spanish assurances of the Portuguese independent political and commercial position at Macao. Recent Spanish diplomatic efforts with the Chinese had to be tabled because of the damage caused to the Portuguese by the political activities of Franciscans in China. D. João de Albuquerque also warned Manila that Portuguese fears for their trade must be lessened on account of the possible loss to the Crown of the profits it received through the collection of customs receipts and the monopoly of the Japan voyage. He informed Manila that Portuguese shipping from Macao paid 150,000 and 80,000 taels in duties to the Royal Treasury each year at Malacca and Goa, which sustained Malacca and made their trade one of the Crown's principal sources of revenue in the East.[41] This Iberian diplomatic confrontation in China was not resolved by such Portuguese representations to the Spanish Governor at Manila but by the failure that Father Sanchez met in his negotiations to regularise relations with Ming officials at Canton.

It was, however, a direct consequence of this Spanish diplomatic failure that certain Portuguese ship-owners and merchants at Macao sought to initiate trade with Manila.[42] Father Sanchez's ship was confiscated and sold by the Chinese authorities; he failed to return to Manila via Nagasaki. Consequently, a prominent Macao ship-owner, Bartolomeu Vaz Landeiro, outfitted one of his junks to return the Jesuit and to trade with Manila. The profits of this venture were such that Landeiro contemplated annual voyages; two of his junks traded at Manila in the subsequent year, 1584.[43] While at Manila, the Portuguese covetously observed the potential benefit if they could surreptitiously attract the Acapulco-bound galleon from Manila and induce the nascent direct communications from Peru with the Philippines to Macao. The frequency in which Portuguese, Chinese and Japanese shipping traded at Manila from 1577–1612 is presented in Table 4.4.

Table 4.4. *Portuguese, Chinese and Japanese shipping arrivals at Manila, 1577–1612. (Omitted years, records not available)*

Year	Chinese	Japanese	Portuguese
1577	9	1	
1578	9		
1580	19		2
1581	9		
1582	24		
1583			1
1584			2
1588	46		2
1591	21	1	
1596	40	1	
1597	14	2	
1599	19	10	
1600	25	5	
1601	29	4	1
1602	18	3	
1603	16	1	
1604	15	6	5
1605	18	3	2
1606	26	3	1
1607	39	3	
1608	39		
1609	41	3	1
1610	41		1
1611	21		
1612	46		7
Total	584	45	25

Sources: Chaunu, *Les Philippines*, AGI, Filipines, leg. 20 and *B&R*, XI and XVIII.

With the mutiny of the Spanish galleon, *San Martin*, after its departure from Manila and upon its arrival in Macao in mid 1583, Portuguese merchants were presented with an opportunity to ship goods across the Pacific. To quell the mutiny, Father Sanchez made his second visit to Macao, along with Juan Bautista Roman in May of 1584; the *San Martin* finally departed in that year for New Spain. That ship returned from Acapulco, not to Manila but to Macao in 1587, providing further evidence to the Bishop of Manila of Portuguese machinations and the tacit approval of this trade by the Viceroy of New Spain. Rumours of the outfitting of the *Santa Ana* in New Spain for Macao in the same year reached the Bishop and since the Chinese trade at Manila was increasing and providing the quantities and prices for profitable cargoes from Manila, the prelate could only advise and admonish the Crown that 'for ships to go from Mexico to Macao is to destroy both those kingdoms and these, since the Chinese raise the prices of their merchandise to such an extent that Portuguese and Castilians cannot live.'[44]

The possible inducement and redirection of direct voyages from Peru to the

Philippines to Macao, was still-born. The interested merchants in Macao either feared the possible official harassment of their trade or failed to obtain support of the Crown's representatives. This possibility receded, after Portuguese authorities seized the Spanish ship which the Marques de Canete, Viceroy of Peru, in league with other Crown officials and the merchants of Lima, had outfitted and despatched to the Far East in 1590.[45]

Possessing the technical ability and *roteiros* (rutters) of the trans-Pacific routes and ignoring Crown prohibition, the lure of the New World silver was too strong for the Portuguese not to attempt direct trade from Macao with Mexico.[46] Their initial trans-Pacific crossing was commanded by D. João da Gama, a fidalgo with a tarnished past; he along with a number of Portuguese and Spanish merchants departed Macao in 1589. The consternation that their arrival caused Spanish authorities was indicated by D. João da Gama's imprisonment, the confiscation of his goods, the lawsuit his inheritors brought against the Crown and the repercussions of such action on Macao–Manila relations.[47] The Crown had difficulties in determining D. João da Gama's exact participation in the ship's cargo. An early accounting estimated the sum to be 60,000 pesos but later, aided by the secreting and opening of his post and personal documents, this was revised to 140,000 pesos.

The other Portuguese merchants who were not imprisoned, carried out their transactions, and returned in their original ship via Manila to Macao with a substantial cargo of silver bullion. While at Manila in early 1592, those Portuguese merchants became embroiled in a confrontation between differing Iberian official and merchant viewpoints concerning their trading relations.

This confrontation had been brewing ever since newly appointed Crown authorities, some of whom actually intended to comply with and enforce their orders, began to arrive at Macao and Manila with instructions outlining further restrictions on trade between the Portuguese and the Spanish.[48] In 1589, the Crown ordered two revisions in Manila's trade; no duties were to be levied on provisions and ammunition and an investigation was to made into the advisability of the establishment of a price-fixing system on imports. The pancada, as this price-fixing system idea was known, was to limit the prices the Chinese, the Portuguese and others received for their imports, obliging them to sell at retail to a council under Crown orders at Manila. The Crown dreamed that silver bullion imports into the Philippines could be diminished and barter re-instituted when it ordered that the Governor would 'endeavour to give products of the islands in exchange for the said merchandise, so as to avoid, if possible, the introduction of so much coin into foreign kingdoms as has been customary.'[49]

The new Governor at Manila, who took office in May of 1590 and was to implement the Crown's orders, was Gomez Peres Dasmariñas.[50] An ambitious politician and soldier, Dasmariñas quickly eliminated the customs duties on provisions and ammunition but learned of the antipathy in which a pancada was held in the merchant community. He desisted in establishing import price-fixing on the Portuguese trade but did on the Chinese. Dasmariñas having been given wide discretionary powers by the Crown, received a petition from interested Manila merchants and, presumably, the agents of the powerful Mexican importers of Chinese wares resident in Manila to allow trade between the Spanish and the Portuguese.

After investigating their petition, the Governor decided to allow the Spanish and Portuguese to trade but only in various strategic items such as gunpowder, saltpetre and copper.[51] The Spanish despatched a *naveta* to Macao which carried substantial sums of money on the account of the Royal Treasury and private individuals in Manila.

At Macao, the Portuguese were less than pleased with the Governor's decision and the arrival of the Spanish naveta. The Portuguese were willing to go to great lengths to deny the Spanish direct access to the Canton market. Driving a lucrative trade at Manila, with selling prices at 60–65 per cent above cost, where they could double their investment with less trouble than other voyages in the region, the Portuguese country traders and inhabitants at Macao decided to embargo and confiscate the Spanish naveta. The merchandise, on the private *Manileños* account alone, amounted to more than 120,000 pesos.[52]

To cope with this Portuguese embargo and cavalier treatment of his envoys, Dasmariñas sought some leverage with these recalcitrant vassals of the Crown. His options were restricted, until the arrival in 1592 in Manila of the Portuguese ship and merchants that had gone with D. João da Gama to New Spain. Impounding the Portuguese merchants' silver and informing Macao of his actions, Dasmariñas had found the key by which he could get Macao's country traders to respond. On the first of March 1592, the Spanish naveta returned to Manila with a cargo of munitions; the Portuguese merchants' silver was subsequently restituted.[53]

Three significant results of this confrontation between Spanish officials and Portuguese merchants became apparent: first, Macao's ventures in direct trans-Pacific commerce ceased; the Portuguese found it preferable to make arrangements via Spanish or Portuguese inhabitants and agents to invest in the Manila galleon in the Philippines. Second, since the capitão-mor proved ineffectual in controlling the powerful Portuguese merchants of Macao, 'four or six powerful men who have the most wealth, supporters and servants do whatever they wish and have their hands in everything', Dasmariñas suggested to Madrid the necessity for a change in how Macao was governed; he proposed a permanently appointed Governor for three to six years as the solution.[54] Third, there was an apparent decline in overt Portuguese trading activity at Manila directly from Macao for nearly a decade. The Portuguese from Macao did not cease their trade with Manila but took advantage of sailing with and shipping their goods on Japanese trading ventures from Nagasaki to Manila which were in evidence as early as 1591 and were maintained on an annual basis until 1609.[55] Portuguese merchants from other parts of the Estado da India, the Moluccas, Malacca and India, some of whom may have been at one time residents of Macao, inaugurated trade between Manila and the Estado da India.

Despite Dasmariñas' *contretemps* with the Portuguese from Macao, trade at

Manila flourished. Chinese traders and merchants in the *parian* (the Chinese community's quarter near Manila) were responsible for the tremendous expansion in silk imports. The Governor attempted to staunch this outpouring of silver to pay for the silk but his measures as well as those in New Spain and Peru were a case of too little and too late.

Sumptuary regulations forbidding the Filipino and Indian populations to wear Chinese silk goods were at best after-the-fact recognition of the havoc that had been wreaked upon Filipino and Mexican textile manufacturers. In the Philippines, an investigation of the villages in the Pampanga (the hinterland behind Manila) region which was led by Juan de Alcega reported in 1591 that the importation of silk goods had reached such levels that Filipinos no longer weaved or wore local textile products in favour of Chinese silks and cottons. His report continued, the Chinese imported well over 200,000 pesos worth of silk goods which they had bartered for different items in the past and had departed with only 20,000 pesos in coin. By 1591, this was no longer the case and de Alcega's report confirmed that almost all of the Chinese exports were of bullion.[56]

Across the Pacific, the Crown, following its staunchly held mercantilist views, tried to protect the New World export markets for Spanish silk textiles by enacting a series of laws between 1587 and 1595 limiting the trade of the Philippines with New Spain to the exclusion of Peru. The Crown's officials also imposed a fiscal limit to the total official bullion export allowance to the Philippines of 250,000 pesos. This *situado* (aid) was later increased to 500,000 pesos per annum.[57] The failure of such enactments is fabled; by 1592, Chinese silk yarn imports from the Philippines replaced Mexican sericulture and became the major source of raw materials for Mexican silk manufacturers.[58] In Peru, according to the Marques de Canete, the smuggling trade in Chinese wares was endemic; he observed the pervasive penetration of Chinese textiles and reported 'that Indian caciques and even commoners were using them for clothing instead of cloth of local manufacture.'[59]

FEARS, CONTRACTS AND IBERIAN CO-OPERATION

Portuguese relations and trade with Manila from the 1590s to around 1620 underwent substantial revision. This revision, at first, was stimulated by the arrival and the progressive enlargement of the VOC's naval and military capabilities to threaten the Iberian colonial cities and trade in the South China Sea. Fear of the VOC, subsequently prompted the call by the Crown for the Catholic powers in the East to co-operate in joint naval and military activities against the Dutch.[60]

The enlistment of a Portuguese *pataxo* from Malacca in 1601 to aid the Spanish naval forces against the VOC, the financial support given to the Portuguese by the Spanish at Manila for the outfitting of Andre Furtado de Mendonça's squadron in 1602, and Macao's favourable reaction to the Governor of Manila's appeal for trade in urgently required munitions, after the Spaniards attack upon the parian in 1603, initiated a period of Spanish and Portuguese co-operation.[61] Macao despatched some nine ships directly to Manila to trade over the next several years. By 1610, overt trading relations between Macao and Manila were improving, if not intimate. The Crown despatched correspondence to the Governor of Manila suggesting close relations between the two cities and trade in munitions whenever required.[62] With tacit support of the Crown, the power of the Governor of the Philippines to expand trade with Macao was enhanced.

Mercury was one commodity that was desperately sought in the New World and which the Spanish Governor at Manila contemplated procuring in China. The development and expansion of the amalgamation process in the refining of silver in Habsburg lands brought about a reliance upon mercury, which was a vital raw material in the process. This reliance signified that the procurement of mercury was synonymous with the possession of silver. Mercury supplies were available worldwide; the Spanish purchased mercury from Almaden (Spain), Huancavelica (Peru) and, after 1620 to 1645, Idria (in present-day Yugoslavia) and knew of two alternative sources, Michoacán (Mexico) and China.

China, as an alternate source of mercury, was given immediate and intensive attention by Spanish officials, especially in the first two decades, and was used throughout the seventeenth century. Mexican deposits were late in being developed and efforts to mine them were made only after 1660. The official notion in the New World that China could supply mercury in enormous quantities was mentioned by the Viceroy of Peru in 1601; the Viceroy of New Spain in 1605 believed that no less than 100,000 *quintales* could be purchased at Canton! Monteclaros (the Viceroy of New Spain) hoped that 1,000 to 1,500 quintales could be imported into New Spain every year, at a cost price of 45 peso 5 reales/quintal which was one-half the cost of Spanish mercury in New Spain.

These estimates were excessively optimistic as proved by the attempts to procure mercury from China in late 1609 to 1615. Pedro de Baeza proposed in 1608 that the Portuguese from Macao should provide Manila with mercury.[63] His proposal aroused some Spanish officials to denounce it as inflicting yet another wound upon the body of Spain from which New World silver would flow. These Spanish officials fulminated against the Portuguese, who would take 'advantage of the "hidden means and trade" they had with merchants in the islands' and would doubtless bring other goods to New Spain along with the mercury, to the detriment of that colony and the Philippines.[64] Although such xenophobia was reciprocated by Portuguese officials and society, its existence did not impede the negotiation of a contract between Manila and Macao for the supply of mercury from Macao.

In 1609 the Governor of the Philippines sent Captains G. P. de Alcacar and H. Xison to Macao with letters to the Sanado da Camara, capitão-mor and the Bishop that requested an annual supply of 4,000 quintales of mercury. The Bishop of Macao arrived in Manila in 1610 to negotiate this contract with the Governor of the Philippines. Agreement was reached and the Bishop promised to supply whatever quantities that were available, the Spanish were to purchase them at the best market price, which the Bishop thought would approximate 50 pesos/quintal.

The Governor's representative, Pedro de Angulo Salazar, returned with the

Bishop to Macao with, at first, a capital of 25,000 pesos and an additional 25,000 pesos was sent shortly after. The contract was to be transacted between the Governor's representative and the Bishop and capitão-mor of Macao.[65] When the Marques de Salinas, Viceroy of New Spain, learnt of Governor D. Juan de Silva's contract with the Portuguese, he became its enthusiastic supporter. De Salinas requested that the Crown's situado to the Philippines be permitted to exceed 500,000 pesos; he noted that 72,000 pesos were already earmarked and despatched, for the purchase of mercury from the Portuguese and that New Spain required 2,000 quintales of mercury immediately and 4,200 quintales to be supplied annually without fail.[66]

This mercury contract between the Portuguese and Spanish existed for several years. Prior to its existence, in the 1608–9 trading season, the Manila galleon arrived in Acapulco with less than 20 quintales on board.[67] During its existence, in 1612, for example, a dramatic percentage increase in the amount of mercury purchased by the Spanish at Macao from the Portuguese and exported from China via Manila to the New World was recorded, 200 quintales arrived in New Spain. By 1615, the mercury contract between Macao and Manila was moribund as a little more than 36 quintales of mercury found its way, in official records, across the Pacific.[68] The contracting parties, the Governor of Manila, the Bishop of Macao, and the capitão-mor, had either been replaced or their policies had not met with sufficient economic and political success to warrant continuance. The Crown also thought, erroneously as it proved, that the Portuguese could be eliminated from the trade and the Chinese would carry mercury directly to Manila at lower selling prices.[69]

The reason for the Spanish failure to attract large exportable quantities of mercury to Manila from China centred on opposition from the Crown's colonial administrators prompted by their fear that New World silver would drain into China and not benefit Spain. The practical difficulties of procurement, although mentioned, on account of the insufficient knowledge of China's market and the regional demand for mercury, were not properly understood. This is understandable, our knowledge of China's production, internal consumption and exportation of mercury is less than extensive.

After Japanese silver mines introduced the amalgamation process, their productivity rose and the Portuguese initiated regular exports of mercury from China to Japan. The cost price of this mercury c. 1600 was approximately 40 taels/picol at Canton; it sold in Japan for around 91 taels. The volume of the Portuguese exports of mercury to Japan are estimated as being on the average of 150–300 picols (200–400 quintales) per annum for a total of 4,200–8,400 picols (5,600–11,200 quintales) for the period 1598–1638.

When compared with Spanish mercury imports and silver production in the New World, the exports of mercury by the Portuguese and others from China to Japan appear to be rather small, in twenty-eight years the Portuguese exported an amount near to New Spain's total requirement for three years. Chinese mercury production and exports, probably, never approached the magnitude of the Peruvian or

European sources; it is suggested mercury may have enjoyed strong internal demand and that legal restrictions may have been imposed on exports. Japan, certainly, was willing to pay higher prices for Chinese mercury in order to insure its supply and prevent large shipments across the Pacific.

Why then did the Portuguese agree to sell even modest amounts of mercury to the Spanish at a contract price of around 50 pesos/quintal from late 1609–15? Portuguese trade with Japan experienced some difficulties during those years on account of the VOC capture of the não do trato in 1607 and the hostile attitude of Japanese authorities, especially after the *Madre de Deos* affair in 1610. The simplest explanation is that the Portuguese or rather the capitão-mor and the Bishop, made, it is estimated, a minimum of 7 pesos/quintal profit on mercury purchased at Macao and re-sold to the Spanish in that city for consignment to Manila. The contract offered other economic opportunities as well for Macao since it enticed closer trading contacts with the Spanish paying in silver. By 1615, the Portuguese ceased to supply mercury to the Spanish in appreciable quantities. Afterwards the Spanish continued to trade at Macao, where Rios Coronel informed the Crown, the Portuguese monopolised the supplies of Chinese produce and sold some items to the Spanish at treble their cost.[70]

Other Iberian efforts towards co-operation in the defence field also encountered difficulties; a latent disagreement by Macao's inhabitants and the Crown's representatives in that city and in Manila over the question of security and its finance immediately surfaced in 1622 after the successful repulse by the Portuguese of the VOC attempt to conquer Macao. The Governor of the Philippines responded to the urgent Portuguese request for additional troops to garrison the city but soon learned that the Portuguese did not wish them there or to pay for their support.[71] When the VOC established itself on Taiwan, the Portuguese requested Spanish action but were reluctant to equal the Spanish military and naval aid.[72] Consequently, a combined Portuguese and Spanish squadron never confronted the VOC position on Taiwan.

The Spanish initiated a separate policy by establishing themselves at Keelung on Taiwan. From 1625 until 1629, the Governor of the Philippines also pursued a separate policy towards Siam which seriously jeopardised Portuguese trade to that state.[73] In the Taiwan case, contrary to repeated Crown requests and orders from Madrid and the Viceroy of India, Iberian military co-operation against the VOC never occurred. Macao's merchants, whose overwhelming priority was to execute as profitable trading operations as possible with the minimal Crown interference, were not interested in supporting the Crown's proposals for combined military operations. The Viceroy of the Estado da India urged the inhabitants of the city to act in their own interest and evict the VOC from Taiwan. The Crown ordered the Senado da Camara, the ouvidor, the capitão-geral, the Jesuits and prominent merchants to prepare armed shipping for the defence of Macao's trade and an attack on Taiwan. It was an order that the city did not respond to with any great vigour.

The Portuguese did attempt to elicit Ming officials' aid on the Fukien coast in disrupting Chinese supplies to the Dutch, and inquired at Manila for Spanish naval support. The Conde de Linhares, the Viceroy of the Estado da India, also desired to implement a convoy system from Macao to Manila and from Macao to Goa; he ordered penalties on Portuguese private traders who sailed without escort to pay additional duties from 2–4% on their cargoes.[74] There is no record that penalties were ever assessed.

Portuguese commercial activity at Manila from 1619 to 1644 is best explained by separating the trade by its geographical or market origin: the rest of the Estado da India and Macao. Geographical origin should not be misconstrued; Macao's country traders, who despatched their ships to Malacca, the west and east coast ports of India and returned via Malacca and Manila to Macao, were also participants in the trade at Manila from the Estado da India, as were the merchants and ship-owners at Goa, Cochin, Negapatnam and Malacca. It is impossible, on account of the absence of any substantial body of evidence, to assess or assign with any accuracy the degree to which Macao and other Portuguese communities benefited by this trade. This problem is absent in the assessment of Macao's direct trade to Manila since it primarily benefited the Portuguese merchants residing in south China and the Philippines.

Portuguese trade with the rest of the Estado da India at Manila was described by António de Morga in the first decade of the seventeenth century; this practice probably occurred sporadically throughout the 1590s as may be seen in the references to trade in the Moluccas. Spanish customs receipts records at Manila, however, cannot substantiate the practice as having occurred on a regular basis until 1620.

Between 1620 and 1640, as shown in Table 4.5, the largest number of Portuguese shipping arrivals from the rest of the Estado da India at Manila were recorded over the years 1620–32, barely maintained contact from 1633–9 and ceased altogether by 1640. Direct trade by the Portuguese from Macao to Manila, over the same period, from 1619, with the exceptions of 1634 and 1643, until 1644, when Iberian trading relations were eventually ruptured by the separation of the Crown of Spain and Portugal, was maintained on a regular basis with the annual arrival of at least one Portuguese ship from China.

The composition of the trading commodities imported and exported by the Portuguese from the Estado da India and China to Manila from 1619 until 1644 did not alter as those described by de Morga. Portuguese trade at Manila consisted of spices, slaves, cotton cloth, amber and ivory, amongst others, and were 'paid for in *reales* and in gold. These ships return with the January north-east monsoon winds, carrying to Maluco, rice, wine, crockery, and other items needed there. To Malacca they take only gold and money.'[75]

At Malacca, silver imported from Manila and the Estado da India, in conjunction with Indian cotton textiles, was disseminated throughout the archipelago to procure spices.[76] The expansion of the utilisation of silver bullion as a medium of exchange in certain markets in the South China Sea, such as Malacca and Bantam, was not exclusively an European initiative. The Portuguese at Malacca,

Table 4.5. *Portuguese arrivals at Manila, 1620–44.* (*Omitted years, records not available*)

Year	Macao	India[a]
1620	5	9
1621	2	
1627	6	2
1628	2	4
1629	2	5
1630	6	8
1631	3	6
1632	4	4
1633	3	1
1634	0	1
1635	4	1
1636	1	1
1637	3	1
1638	3	0
1639	3	1
1640	3	0
1641	2	0
1642	1	0
1643	0	0
1644	1	0
Total	54	44

[a] India = Malacca, Goa, Coromandel and Malabar coast ports.
Sources: Chaunu, *Les Philippines*, AGI, Filipinas, leg. 20 and *B&R*, XI and XVIII.

c. 1607, sold Indian textiles from Coromandel and Gujerat to Javanese inland traders who paid for them with reales. Subsequently, by using these textiles to purchase pepper and cloves from neighbouring centres of production, these inland traders sold spices to the VOC and EIC for silver.[77]

SALTPETRE, SLAVES AND COTTONS

By c. 1630 Portuguese country traders from the rest of the Estado da India intensified efforts at Manila as their trade in the Persian Gulf and northwestern India was being severely contracted by competition from the EIC and indigenous merchants. The VOC were also beginning to intensify their naval activities, especially off the Straits of Malacca, and Portuguese trade with Europe suffered as dwindling amounts of capital arrived from Portugal for the purchase of pepper. The silver and gold available at Manila offered some slight hope for these merchants to maintain themselves.[78] Demand in the Philippines for products from India centred upon three main commercial groupings: war materials, slaves and cotton textiles. Saltpetre and gunpowder were efficiently banned by Ming officials from being exported from China and there were other war materials which the Portuguese from Macao on account of their own requirements were not keen to sell.

Saltpetre and other war materials, described as gunpowder, iron, anchors and sail cloth were in desperate demand in the Philippines. By 1629, the Spanish Crown's representative, the Governor, D. Juan Niño de Tavora was so disgruntled by the excessive rates charged for these commodities by the Portuguese at Manila that he sought to supply the Philippines in Spanish Crown-operated shipping. He petitioned the Crown to order the imposition of a royal monopoly on the clove trade in the Moluccas and thereby lessen the Portuguese position in the clove trade in the South China Sea. With cargoes of this monopolised commodity, the Governor contemplated voyages to Cochin or Goa at the Crown's expense to purchase saltpetre and other necessities.[79]

Governor Tavora stressed that the fixed costs of the project would be lowered by the purchase of pataxos built in the Estado da India shipyards, especially at Cochin, where the cost was half that of the Philippines and the ships were more durable.[80] Cloves, available despite Dutch efforts in the Moluccas, were to be purchased either with silver or one-half the silver price in exchange for Indian textiles. His estimates on the operational costs, revenues and profits are summarised in Table 4.6. Although this proposal was not implemented, the Governor ordered one ship to be built at the Cochin dockyard on his personal account. The information that he prepared describing trading and market conditions at Manila, in the South China Sea and on the west coast of India permits a comparison of this data with what is known of the Portuguese country traders activities in those areas in the same time span.

The Portuguese country traders from Macao and Malacca sailed in pataxos and other ships built in India. They financed these operations with supplies of silver from Japan and Manila and Indian textiles; they centred trade for cloves at Macassar, which was a convenient location for the collection of that spice from local Macassar and Malay merchants and vessels from Banda and Ambon. Depending upon the individual ship-owner, the market and his concern for Dutch shipping, the Portuguese country trader decided whether to trade cloves in China, Manila, India or the intermediary market of Malacca. When the Portuguese country trader from Macao traded at Manila via the Estado da India, his outward cargo from China to Macassar comprised gold, Indian and Chinese cotton and silk textiles, and from Macassar to India, gold and cloves. Upon arrival at Cochin or Goa, his transactions paralleled those outlined by Governor Tavora, selling cloves and gold for saltpetre and gunpowder, purchasing slaves on the Malabar coast and Indian cotton piecegoods on the Coromandel coast.[81]

The Portuguese slave trade at Manila was not an innovation; there are recorded instances of early Portuguese traffic in the South China Sea region in the 1560s. By 1610, the Crown had promulgated a Royal order to the Governor of the Philippines to avoid damages to the colony caused by the expansion of slavery.[82]

Table 4.6. *Projected expenses, revenues and profits of one voyage from Manila via the Moluccas to Cochin or Goa to Manila, 1629.*

[ooo's of pesos]

	Expenses	Revenues	Profitability		
	ave. values			value	%
			Initial expenses	23	
(a) Fixed:			Revenue at Cochin/Goa	35	
(i) Ship: 1 pataxo, 150 ton	11		Profit	12	52
(ii) Armament: 8 pieces, 12–8 pounders	5		Investment at Cochin/Goa	35	
(iii) Crew: 56 sailors, soldiers	4		Revenue at Manila	95	
			Profit at Manila	60	
		ave. values			
(b) Cargo (Outward):			Total Profit	72	313
(i) Cloves: 50 bahars; 80–40 pesos/bahar in the Moluccas; lower price in exchange for Indian textiles	3	Sale of Cloves:			
		(i) Manila: 50 bahars @ 200 pesos/bahar — 10			
		(ii) Cochin/Goa: 50 bahars @ 700 pesos/bahar — 35			
(c) Cargo (Return):					
(i) Saltpetre: sale of 50 bahars of cloves, 100% re-invested in purchase of saltpetre at Cochin/Goa	35	Sale of Saltpetre:			
		(i) Manila — 95			

Source: B&R, XXIII, 30–3.

In 1617 as Rios Coronel reported to the Crown, Malacca served as a collection centre for slaves from the Indonesian archipelago and the Indian Ocean region.[83] The Portuguese continued to sell slaves to the Spanish at Manila as a result of the expansion in estate argiculture and the demand for the galleys. The participation in and the slave trade in general collapsed when they ceased trading in the Philippines in 1644.[84]

Indian cotton textiles, despite increased European competition, were an important commodity in the Portuguese trade to Manila from the Estado da India.[85] Portuguese merchants from Macao and Goa, Cochin and Negapatnam still had access to the Indian markets with large quantities of cotton cloth for sale in the 1620s and early 1630s. According to the VOC, who were established at Palicat on the Coromandel coast, the Portuguese bought up all available supplies of cotton textiles along this coast somewhat indiscriminately, a small margin of gross profit per unit being enough to cover their costs and leave a modest profit. In consequence, the Company was forced to buy poor quality cloth, just to maintain its hold on the buyer's market.

Indigenous manufacturers and middlemen also informed the Dutch that the Portuguese paid higher prices for all products. Unless the Company met this challenge, there was in the VOC's estimation a real danger of the Portuguese recapturing the Coromandel cotton cloth trade. In the local seller's market also, Portuguese activities undermined the prospects of the Dutch. Asian and Portuguese ships from Malacca, Aceh, Siam, Arakan and Bengal flocked to the ports on the coast with Portuguese communities; the large volume of their imports often adversely affected the demand for the Company's wares and caused sharp decline in prices.[86]

Although the number of recorded arrivals of Portuguese ships at Manila from Negapatnam is small, a portion, how large is impossible to reconstruct, of Portuguese cloth purchases on the Coromandel coast were destined for Manila and transhipment to New Spain. Whether the relative absence of quality seriously affected the sale price at Manila of these cotton textiles is unknown. Portuguese trade to Manila from Negapatnam stopped as a result of the *nayak* of Tanjore's attack on that city in 1632. The effectiveness of the VOC's cruising against Portuguese shipping, particularly between 1630–2, which had captured cargoes worth 24,851 guilders, was another factor in the Portuguese decision to desist from such voyages.[87]

SILK, SILVER AND QUEVEES

By 1619, Portuguese country traders from Macao were eager to re-establish direct commercial voyages to Manila. They tested their official reception in that year and found amenable conditions. From 1619 until 1644, with the exception of 1634 and 1643, one and often more Portuguese ships from Macao traded at Manila.[88] The Portuguese from Macao had established an important direct access to silver supplies which augmented those of Japan.

A common enemy and mutual economic benefit for the merchants of Macao and the Crown's representatives in Manila kept those two cities trading. The Crown had received a proposal from the Dominican Fray Diego Anduarte which recommended the destruction of Macao in order to prevent the continued loss of New World silver and the re-alignment of Macao's inter-Asian trade to Manila. Spanish trade to Japan, the Dominican argued, would replace the Portuguese; New World bullion imports into the Philippines would be substituted by Japanese silver and the Spanish would become the middleman in the supply of Chinese goods to Japan.[89] Crown support for such a radical plan, which could have ignited anti-Spanish feeling in Macao and through the Estado da India, was not in the style of the Spanish administration of Portugal and was not forthcoming.

Although the volume of trade at Manila according to Spanish customs receipts was declining in the period 1600–40, Portuguese direct trade from Macao to Manila expanded until the late 1630s. Action taken by the Portuguese at Macao with reference to their relations with the quevees of Canton account for this phenomenon. The decline in Chinese activity at Manila which permitted the Portuguese to improve their trade in the Philippines was, in part, a result of Dutch trading policies and naval activities along the Fukien coast and their establishment on Taiwan in the early 1630s.

The effect of Dutch vessels cruising against Chinese shipping, capturing and redirecting their trade to other ports, and the expansion of Dutch demand on silk for its trade to Japan and elsewhere caused modifications in the Fukien/Chekiang silk markets. These Dutch actions were accompanied by a re-invigoration of Chinese piracy along the south China coast and a weakening of the Ming dynasty's ability to respond to the VOC which was caused by the allocation of resources away from south China to the north-east and north-west to confront the Manchu challenge.[90] Ming decisions, such as the one-year ban on maritime trade in 1628 to force the Dutch to give up Taiwan, were ill-timed, poorly received and damaging amongst the Fukien/Chekiang silk producers, merchants and investors.

In the Kwangtung region, at Canton and at Macao, tension in Sino-Portuguese relations, around 1620, did not inhibit or impede Portuguese and Chinese merchants from perceiving a mutual benefit from and co-operating in the recently established Portuguese trade at Manila. It was this informal liaison between Chinese and Portuguese merchants of Canton and Macao that disturbed Spanish officials. Juan Grau y Monfalcon wrote to the Crown in 1635 and complained, a bit prematurely, that the decline of Chinese trade at Manila had set in as early as 1604, when silk prices had soared by at least two and one-half times per picol, and profits in trade at Manila were no longer that city's but Macao's.[91]

The Portuguese from Macao were successful in convincing Canton's quevees in desisting from sending their shipping to Manila. When Portuguese country traders from Macao were at the Canton fair, they persuaded some quevees to cease outfitting shipping for Manila altogether, those quevees being happy with a 25–30 per cent profit on the silk and other items sold to the Portuguese at the fair. The Portuguese used arguments that they facilitated the quevees trade by assuming all the risk, especially at a time when Dutch and Chinese piracy was on the increase, and the possibility of un-sold merchandise. The Portuguese merchants also convinced some Cantonese merchants to send their goods on consignment. A minimum of 150,000 pesos worth of goods were reported to be carried on consignment by the Portuguese from Canton to Manila in 1629–31; the Portuguese charged a 5 per cent commission. Failing to convince the quevees to sell to them in Canton or to consign merchandise on their ships bound for Manila, Macao's country traders resorted to piracy, as happened along the Ylocos coast in 1629 to two Chinese junks, one being sunk, the other escaping to Manila, to dissuade Cantonese quevees from despatching their junks to Manila.

At Manila, Captain José de Naveda, *regidor* of the city, complained of the damage the Portuguese caused by their evasion of the collection of the Crown's customs duties. One official estimated that the total average annual imports from Macao was around 1.5 million pesos and that duties were only collected on the average one-tenth of that amount. The Portuguese had refused to co–operate with these officials or accept an agreement fixing a 40 per cent profit for their trade with the inhabitants of Manila. The Portuguese were, in this official's opinion, causing the gradual impoverishment of Manila as they exported the silver that had come across the Pacific and increased their profit margins to 60 per cent or more by raising the price of silk and other items. This official also suggested that the agents of the Mexican importers of Chinese silk, because they received a commission of 8–10 per cent on the purchase price of silk, had become the tacit allies of the Portuguese merchants in the maintenance of high silk prices.[92]

Another major argument of the Naveda's against Macao's trade at Manila was based on the absence of any reciprocal treatment by the Portuguese of Spanish merchants at Macao. In Manila, the Portuguese had all of the city's facilities at their disposal; the Manileños continued, as discovered in 1631 with the loss of the galleon, *Santa Maria Magdelena*, to load Portuguese cargo destined for Mexico. When, however, the Crown or private Manila merchants sent a ship to Macao to purchase munitions or trade for Chinese produce, the Portuguese merchants did not allow the Spanish to buy directly from local Chinese merchants but only through Portuguese merchants who gained 25–30 per cent profits.

Embezzlement of the proceeds from the Spanish funds sent on board Portuguese shipping from Manila to be invested at Macao also caused ill-feeling between the two cities. When the Spanish located themselves at Keelung on Taiwan, it was in part as a response to the VOC at Zeelandia and a Spanish attempt to establish an independent access to China's produce from Fukien and Chekiang. The Portuguese at Macao, de Naveda bitterly observed, 'tried to obstruct that trade, by sending a religious of their nation to one of the commercial ports of China, in order that he might direct those Chinese not to take any merchandise to the said island [Taiwan]. They have persisted and are still persisting in those efforts.'[93]

Despite de Naveda's report, the Portuguese trade directly from Macao to Manila from 1619 until 1636 had the general support of the Governors and other Crown officials in the Philippines. There was one major exception to this generalisation in 1633 when the Governor extorted a 60,000 pesos loan from merchants from

Macao to pay the outstanding Portuguese commercial debts at Manila. Macao reacted by not despatching any shipping to Manila in 1634. The Portuguese at Macao were in the process of recovering from this minor disruption in their trade when a Spanish official with firm merchantilist views took action that tampered with the outflow of silver from New Spain to the Philippines.[94]

Empowered by the Crown to investigate and regulate the Manila galleon trade, Don Pedro de Quiroga y Moya found at Acapulco in 1636 that the arriving cargo from the Philippines had been registered at 800,000 pesos. Upon investigation, he discovered that the real value of the silks and other Chinese goods on board were worth closer to 4 million pesos. Seeking to dissuade such frauds and to diminish the export of silver on such a massive scale, Quiroga ordered an embargo on the arriving cargoes.[95]

His actions radically disrupted trade at Manila, where the Chinese and Portuguese had sold their cargoes on credit, and as a result of Quiroga's embargo only small amounts of New Spain silver arrived in the Philippines. The silver that arrived was insufficient to repay the Chinese and Portuguese merchants. For several years, from 1636 until 1639, conditions at Manila did not improve, although Quiroga died in 1637 as a result of illness in Mexico and his policies rescinded.[96] The damage to Sino-Spanish relations was devastating and contributed to Chinese discontent, which led to a Chinese uprising that the Spanish eventually suppressed between 20 November 1639 and 15 March 1640.[97]

The Portuguese trade from Macao suffered from the diminution of the amount of silver that was sent from New Spain but as Sino-Spanish relations deteriorated they quickly sought to improve their position. By 1642, two Portuguese ships from Macao had imported cargoes officially valued at 434,610 pesos and paid customs duties totalling 25,476 pesos.[98] But the benefit to Macao of poor Sino-Spanish relations was quickly lost by 1644. After the news of the revolt of the Crown of Portugal from Spain was received in the East, Manila and Macao took actions to cease their direct trade.

The Spanish Crown was interested in securing the allegiance of the Portuguese of Macao and gave orders to the Governor of Manila to secure this support; those orders resulted in the Governor, Don Sebastián Hurtado de Corquera, outfitting a ship on his own account and despatching it to Macao in 1644, under the command of Don Juan Claudio de Berastegui, to purchase munitions and secure Macao for the Spanish. The Portuguese at Macao confiscated the money that the Spanish carried and their treatment of this expedition contributed to poor Spanish Portuguese relations.[99]

JUNKS, GALIOTAS AND SPANISH OFFICIALS

The *almojarifazgo* (Crown's customs) receipts at Manila reveal the official version of the volume of revenue paid by Portuguese shipping, from Macao and the other cities in the Estado da India, Chinese and Japanese junks. These receipt figures, as Spanish officials were always careful to admonish, represented only the reported picture and did not take into account rampant smuggling and evasion of duties.

After the arrival and the anchoring of a Chinese, Japanese or Portuguese ship at Manila, royal officials inspected and established a landed value of the cargo; 'the worth of the goods' was established, 'according to Manila prices' and a 3 per cent duty was levied 'on everything to the royal exchequer.' Afterwards, according to António de Morga, 'the cargo of merchandise is unloaded by another official and placed on board sampans, and taken to the parian, or to other establishments and warehouses outside the city where it is sold freely.'[100]

Such procedures were not in themselves unique, the Portuguese at Macao, the VOC at Batavia, and some of the *shahbandars* in the trading states in the South China Sea employed similar systems of vigilance and collection of customs duties. Nor were the Spanish officials somehow inherently more susceptible to corruption than others; the geography of the islands and a natural human frailty when dealing with immense wealth permitted widespread smuggling operations. The tacit condonement, through the inaction and participation of the Crown's representatives, of the evasion of the prohibitions on the Macao–Manila trade and the importation of silver bullion established a climate of acceptance for such behaviour. That smuggling and corruption were rampant is without question but the exact magnitude may never accurately be reconstructed.[101]

In 1632, Capitan José de Naveda ordered the preparation of a certificate which would give an accurate accounting of the value of almojarifazgo revenues accruing to the Crown from Chinese and Portuguese imports. De Naveda outlined, as other officials had already written to Madrid, that the value and quantity of imports into Manila was declining. The decline in Crown revenues from the collection of import duties, he felt, was caused in part by the expansion in the Portuguese trade.

Based on the papers that de Naveda consulted, the total value of all official imports into Manila from 1606 until 1631 may be reconstructed.[102] The value of imports from 1606 to 1610 fluctuated from slightly over 1.8 million pesos in 1612, 88 per cent of which was collected from the Chinese, to the exceptionally low amount, a little over 120,000 pesos in 1618, 80 per cent of which was collected from Chinese shipping.[103]

In 1619, the Portuguese from Macao re-inaugurated a direct Macao to Manila trading relationship in military items, although other non-sanctioned commodities were traded. The data that de Naveda collected for his argument for the extermination of this trade must be used with caution since Portuguese smuggling and their importation of items exempt from customs, gunpowder and munitions, kept these figures on the low side.[104]

These figures do, however, indicate general trends and since the amount collected represented a 3 per cent *ad valorum* impost on imports until 1610 when it was increased to 6 per cent, a total minimum value of dutiable Chinese, Portuguese and others' imports may be computed. Table 4.7 represents the minimum total imports of Chinese, Portuguese (Macao) and others, which included receipts from Portuguese imports from the Estado da India, and all other

Table 4.7. *Annual total values and percentage of dutiable imports by carrier at Manila, 1619–31.*

			[000's of pesos] Portuguese					
	Chinese		(Macao)		Others		Total	
Year	Value	%	Value	%	Value	%	Value	
1619	186	61	19	6	99	33	304	
1620	463	54	148	17	246	29	857	
1621	111	25	161	36	172	39	444	
1622	134	32	123	30	161	38	418	
1623	29	13	71	31	128	56	228	
1624	50	30	90	54	27	16	167	
1625	182	41	115	26	143	33	440	
1626	376	52	171	24	178	24	725	
1627	340	66	135	26	39	8	514	
1628	49	21	151	63	39	16	239	
1629	66	28	11	5	158	67	235	
1630	105	19	194	35	258	46	557	
1631	344	51	125	18	214	31	683	
Total	2,435		1,514		1,862		5,811	

Source: AGI, Filipinas, leg. 27, 23/ix/1632.

traders from the South China Sea region into Manila over the period 1619–31. Unfortunately, de Naveda's data does not differentiate between duties paid by Portuguese shipping from the Estado da India in the 'Other' category which prohibits any exact comparison between total Chinese and Portuguese trading activity at Manila.

A comparison of the number of Portuguese arrivals from Macao and Estado da India with arrivals of foreign shipping from mainland China, Taiwan, Japan, Cochinchina, Cambodia, Macassar, and the Moluccas at Manila over the entire period, 1619–44, as shown in Table 4.8, indicates that the Portuguese dominated with the exception of those junks arriving from mainland China. Most of these were from the Fukien coast.[105] Portuguese imports from Macao alone in the years 1621, 1623, 1624, 1628 and 1630 surpassed the Chinese.[106]

If the data for Portuguese trade from India were available, it is suggested that the values of Portuguese annual imports at Manila in the 1620s would surpass those of the Chinese, with the possible exception of 1626–7. For the 1630s and first half of the 1640s, the almojarifazgo records indicate that Portuguese imports from Macao and the Estado da India continued to enter Manila in substantial volume and value but were declining. The Portuguese from Macao and India imported for 1631–5, 25 per cent; 1636–40, 14 per cent, and 1641–2, 50 per cent of the total for those years.[107]

To pay China for the silks and other goods that the Portuguese and Chinese imported into Manila for transhipment to New Spain, the Spanish required vast

Table 4.8. *Foreign shipping at Manila, by nationality and, in the case of the Chinese and the Portuguese, by geographical origin, 1620–44.*

	Portuguese		Chinese		Japanese		Undetermined		
Year	Macao	Estado da India	Mainland	Taiwan	Japan	Cochin-china	Cambodia	Macassar	Moluccas
1620	5	9	23	0	3	1	0	0	0
1621	2	na	na	na	na	na	na	na	na
1622–6	na	na	na	na	na	na	na	na	na
1627	6	2	21	1	0	0	1	1	1
1628	2	4	9	1	0	0	0	1	0
1629	2	5	2	2	2	1	1	0	0
1630	6	8	16	5	2	0	3	0	0
1631	3	6	33	3	0	1	0	0	0
1632	4	4	16	2	5	1	0	0	0
1633	3	1	30	1	0	0	1	0	0
1634	0	1	26	3	1	2	3	1	0
1635	4	1	40	3	0	1	0	0	0
1636	1	1	30	1	0	0	2	1	0
1637	3	1	50	1	0	0	1	0	1
1638	3	0	16	1	0	0	0	0	0
1639	3	1	30	4	0	0	0	1	0
1640	3	0	7	1	0	0	0	0	0
1641	2	0	8	1	0	0	2	3	0
1642	1	0	34	1	0	1	4	0	0
1643	0	0	30	0	0	0	1	1	0
1644	1	0	8	1	0	0	0	2	0

Source: Chaunu, *Les Philippines*, 156–7, and 160.

quantities of silver. The actual amounts of silver exported from the Philippines to China from 1590 until 1644 may never be precisely calculated. The estimates of the amount of silver imported into Manila from New Spain provide a rough calculation of the maximum amount of silver that could have possibly been available for export from Manila to China, the Estado da India and the rest of the South China Sea.

The final market for the largest proportion of this silver was China, whether brought in by Chinese junks or Portuguese galiotas to the Chekiang and Fukien ports, Canton or Macao. From 1590 to 1602, the total value of silver imported from New Spain into the Philippines approached 67 million pesos (2,010,000 kilograms), a sum computed by adding the estimates of an average of 5 million pesos per annum with the staggering amount of 12 million pesos in 1597.[108] From 1602 until 1636, the total value of silver imported into Manila was around 80 million pesos (2,400,000 kilograms), a sum computed by multiplying an annual average of 2.5 million pesos by the number of years that the galleon was in service.[109]

From 1636 until 1644, however, any attempt to estimate is made doubly difficult by the disruptive actions of Quiroga in Acapulco in 1636–7. Assuming a modest amount of silver being imported into the Philippines, such as the official sum of the situado, of 500,000 pesos per annum on the average for the years 1636–9 and a slightly higher figure of an annual average of 1 million pesos for the years 1640–4, based on the minimum amounts of silver that had to be available to pay for the declared values of foreign imports at Manila, an estimate of a total of 7 million pesos (210,000 kilograms) was imported into Manila from 1636 to 1644.

By converting these peso estimates to kilograms, we are confronted with figures, as in the case of Japanese silver exports, that are breathtaking. These estimates suggest that from 1590–1601, 167,500 kilograms, from 1602–35, 72,727 kilograms and from 1636–44, 26,250 kilograms of silver on an average yearly basis was exported from New Spain to the Philippines. From 1610–35, the Spanish yearly average was approximately 50–60 per cent less than one estimate of the total Japanese silver exports to China, primarily, of 150,000 to 187,000 kilograms. Taking another estimate of Japanese silver exports, the comparison of the percentage difference between the Spanish yearly average with the Japanese of roughly 45–55 per cent less is maintained for the period 1615–25.

When comparing just the annual average of Portuguese exports of Japanese silver to China from 1598–1636 with the Spanish imports of New World silver at Manila, the Portuguese kilogram volume was almost one-fifth less than the Spanish.[110] Examining and comparing these estimates and figures between Japanese exports and Manila New World imports of silver, suggests the possibility that both may be highly exaggerated. In the case of the Manila trade, there may be need of further research from Latin American silver-mining specialists to confirm those mines production capacities and to determine the availability and the feasibility of the silver volumes that are claimed to have crossed the Pacific.

Economic conditions in south China by the mid seventeenth century were severely depressed on account of the disruption and chaos caused by the struggle between the Ming and Manchu adherents for political and administrative control over the Middle Kingdom.[111] Insecurity, the absence of merchant confidence and imperial policies designed to eradicate Ming resistance, destroy piracy and intensify state control over maritime trade were a few of the conditions that engendered the severe market dislocations in the supply of export items at south China's ports.

The role of maritime trade in the transfer of gold and silver bullion between China and states in the South China Sea and Indian Ocean regions and the internal and external fluctuations in the circulation of silver in different areas of China emerged as major factors in the severity and the duration of this crisis. Evidence for the deterioration in south China's economic conditions, disruptions and fluctuation in its maritime trade can be found in the early 1620s. Its maritime trade, however, did not suffer any dramatic decline until the 1640s.

With the loss of the Japan and Manila markets, Portuguese influence upon the development of China's economy lessened and Portuguese trade and society in China ceased playing a major international role in the imperial struggle between the Estado da India and the VOC. Nevertheless, they retained an important role in the regional maritime trade of China and the South China Sea.

With south China's economy in crisis, Macao's continued existence was in peril.

The Portuguese faced an economic dilemma of gigantic dimensions. They retained, as a result of their truce with the VOC, tenuous trading contacts with the Estado da India. Complicated by the inconclusive struggle between the Ming and the Ch'ing, Portuguese supplies of Chinese produce were disrupted; in addition, they lacked silver to finance their purchase of Chinese export items. To obtain silver, they had to develop and trade in new markets in the South China Sea.

5

MERCHANTS AND MARKETS

Macao's merchants had neglected the markets of the South China Sea. Their neglect, with the exception of Manila and, to a lesser degree, the Lesser Sunda islands, is explained by the magnitude of their trading opportunities in other markets. There were, in addition, costs and difficulties of penetrating new markets which they, previously, saw no economic reason to incur.

In the Indonesian archipelago, the Portuguese from Macao encountered competition from their compatriots at Malacca and from the Estado da India, the Spanish, the VOC, EIC, other European Companies, Chinese, Indian and indigenous merchants. Malacca and the Estado da India's trade in the South China Sea was east–west in orientation. It was directed towards the purchase of spices in the Indonesian archipelago, to be shipped to Goa and Cochin for transhipment to Europe, silver and Indian cotton cloth sent in exchange.

The development of Macao's trade to mainland Southeast Asia was influenced by the activities of Japanese and Chinese merchants. By the early seventeenth century, trade in various ports in the South China Sea increased in the north–south direction; Japanese go-shuin-sen and Chinese ships frequented the Tonkin, Cochinchina, Manila, Siam and Cambodia markets, which provided the Chinese products and locally produced silks, gold, aromatic woods and skins in demand in Japan. After discovering that the Chinese and Japanese had substantially improved the trade at those ports, Portuguese country traders from Macao sought to establish or augment existing local Portuguese populations and increase the frequency of their trading visits to those states.[1] Catholic missionaries, especially the Jesuits, became active within those Portuguese and Japanese Christian communities.

Macao's immediate response to the loss of Portuguese trade to Japan in 1639 was to restrain its shipping to South China Sea ports in the mistaken belief that this initiative would seriously disturb the supply of Chinese goods in those markets and thereby disrupt the VOC purchases and, ultimately, Dutch trade in Japan.[2] Thereafter, Macao embarked upon a concerted diplomatic and commercial campaign to re-invigorate its trade, find shelter for its refugee population and improve its relations with the political representatives of the major non-VOC dominated markets in the South China Sea.

MACASSAR

Macassar was the primary market that the Portuguese from Macao turned to in the hopes of rejuvenating their trade. Located in the south-west Celebes, Macassar (the Kingdom of Goa) was at the height of its influence in the eastern Indonesian archipelago; 'Macassar was the name given by foreigners (and not by the Macassarese themselves) to the area between the Garassi river and Sambung Djawa. In this area, the Sultan of Goa, the senior ruler of the twin-sultanates of Goa and Tallo, had his palace-cum-castle, at Sombaopu... [he] was often taken by foreigners to be the (sole) ruler of the state.'[3]

Although the rulers and populace embraced the faith of the Crescent, Islam's relatively tardy arrival at Macassar in the late sixteenth–early seventeenth century did not displace certain regional, political, legal or commercial traditions.[4] The permanent antagonism and animosity of Islamic Aceh and Catholic Malacca was not evident in Portuguese relations with Macassar. Early Portuguese trade in the Celebes probably began on a small scale after the conquest of Malacca in 1511 but a regular Portuguese trading relationship can only be confirmed as happening after 1558.[5]

MACASSAR'S RISE AND THE PORTUGUESE RECOVERY

Macassar's rise as a commercial entrepôt in the early seventeenth century stemmed from the sultanates' favourable attitudes towards foreign merchants and maritime trade.[6] Macassar's rulers encouraged maritime trade by their support and fostering of conditions and facilities for trade, by participating in trade either in association with Malay and European merchants or on their own account and by dispatching trading vessels to Malacca and other ports in the western Indonesian archipelago.

One of the Sultan's policies, according to contemporary European accounts, made Macassar a free port with no customs duties being collected on foreign merchandise. There was no regulation or limitation of the exportation of gold or silver bullion and specie.[7] The expansion of maritime trade was not the outward objective in the extension of the Kingdom of Goa's political power, but the profits derived from maritime trade permitted Macassar's rulers and their supporters to maintain large households and a burgeoning military and naval establishment.

Macassar's early economic importance stemmed principally from its geographical location and the availability at that port of rice supplies. Its maritime trade in the late sixteenth century was dominated by Malay merchants from Johor, Patani and elsewhere, some Siamese, Chinese, Portuguese and Spanish, and the local rulers.[8] During the appropriate monsoon, foreign and indigenous merchants departed Macassar to trade rice, cloth, gold, silver, and jewelry in exchange for cloves, primarily, also nutmeg and mace throughout the Moluccas and for sandalwood on Solor and Timor. Returning to or purchasing their cargoes of cloth and rice at Macassar, merchants with varying capital resources departed for Malacca and the pepper port markets of Sumatra, Java and Borneo where they exchanged their cargoes of cloves and rice with Portuguese and Indian merchants for the Indian cotton cloth which was so highly sought after throughout the Indonesian archipelago. There they would also purchase the pepper which was sold at Macassar to shipping bound for China.

Macassar's rise is linked to the commercial opportunities offered to the Kingdom of Goa after the Portuguese expulsion from the Moluccas in the late sixteenth century and the favourable conditions thus created for Macassar and other merchants based at Macassar to increase their participation in the Molucca clove trade. Denied a direct presence in the Moluccas, Portuguese country traders were attracted to Macassar by its convenience and as a market where they could purchase all the major trading commodities of the eastern Indonesian archipelago.[9]

Macassar's rise also coincided with the expansion of its political power in the Celebes, the Moluccas, the Lesser Sunda islands and Borneo in the early seventeenth century. It established an overlord–subject relationship over many of the petty state systems that proliferated the south-west Celebes.[10] Within this system of loose vasalage, Macassar permitted and encouraged the retention of a high degree of control by the individual petty state over its internal affairs as long as it provided a portion of its food production and military manpower. Freed of any requirement for direct occupation and administration of neighbouring states. Macassar was able to preoccupy itself with plans for further expansion and the conduct of inter-state relations with neighbouring and distant state systems in the eastern and western Indonesian archipelago.

To the east, in the Moluccas, Macassar observed that the struggle for cloves continued as the Dutch occupied Ambon in 1605 and the Spanish effectively replaced the Portuguese by establishing themselves on parts of Ternate and Tidore in 1606.[11] The Sultan of Ternate continued to expand his claims to territory on west Ceram, Buru, Buton and coastal areas of the eastern and northern Celebes. Confronted with Ternate's political manoeuvres and territorial claims, Macassar's rulers, apparently, chose to ignore and not to recognise them. Macassar embarked upon acquiring access to suppliers of cloves.

The VOC agreement with Ambon in 1605 stipulated that no cloves were to be sold to any other trader and a contract price of 60 reals/bahar of cloves was fixed. By 1618 the VOD experienced difficulties in its relations with the Islamic areas on west Ceram and Hitu on Ambon. The Dutch were unable to interdict indigenous trade on Ambon and west Ceram with Javanese and Macassar merchants who paid 90–120 reals/bahar for cloves.[12] The VOC resorted to force but were frustrated when they found that the inland traders from Macassar did not concentrate their shipping near Hitu. Despite European agreements, the EIC discovered in 1623 as a result of the VOC execution of several English traders on Ambon, the 'Amboina Massacre', that the VOC would not permit competition in the clove trade. The EIC, subsequently, centred its commercial efforts in the eastern Indonesian archipelago at Macassar, where they had traded since 1613.[13]

At Macassar in the early seventeenth century, the Portuguese recovered from

7 Eastern Indonesian Archipelago

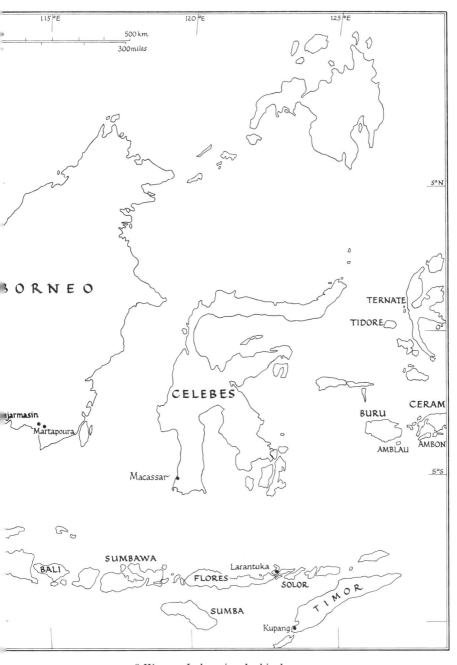

8 Western Indonesian Archipelago

their expulsion from the Moluccas and Portuguese country traders from Malacca occupied a predominant position in the Macassar market. In 1613, the English eyed the large Portuguese sales of Gujarati and Coromandel textiles covetously, John Jourdain wrote that Macassar 'would be a very profitable place for vent of Choremandell and Gujaratt commodities if the Portugall from Malacca did not furnish them.'[14] Cloves continued to be exported from the Moluccas via Macassar to Malacca; the Portuguese reported in 1610 that 4,000 bahars of goods arrived by Javanese shipping which probably carried quantities of cloves and in 1613 that the accounts of one galleon, *São João Baptista*, were slightly short of the 140 bahars of cloves that were loaded in the Moluccas.[15]

According to Jan Joosten's report in 1621, some twelve or more Portuguese ships and an additional unknown number of a variety of craft arrived at Macassar annually, where they purchased cloves and rice.[16] The price of cloves continued to rise as its cost was given as 150 to 160 reals/bahar. Joosten also indicated that the local Portuguese community numbered between twenty to thirty families with a reported capital of 40,000 reals, but its members swelled as did the capital employed during later trading seasons.

Joosten observed that Portuguese Indian cloth imports for 1621 did not saturate the Macassar market; this Portuguese commercial failure was noted by Joosten as a trading opportunity for the VOC. The Portuguese, joined by Spanish merchants who purchased rice for their garrisons on Tidore and Ternate and cloves for Manila, had established warm relations with the Sultan of Goa and various *Karaengs* and *Orang Kaya*'s (the Macassar nobility and men of power and standing).[17] The Portuguese encouraged the Sultan's profitable private trading operations at Malacca; they and the Spanish were also careful to bestow gifts upon him and his supporters.

The annual number of Portuguese shipping arrivals at Macassar in the early 1620s varied between ten to twenty-two ships. The frequency of Portuguese shipping at Macassar from 1627–67 is given in Table 5.1. In 1625, as reported to the VOC by the English merchant, Henry Short, the total annual value of the Portuguese trade on Macassar approximated 500 to 600,000 taels.[18] The Governor-General and the Council of the Indies at Batavia were staggered and alarmed at the dramatic intensification of Portuguese and Spanish trade at Macassar from the Coromandel coast (S. Thomé de Meliapor and Negapatnam), Malacca, Macao, Manila and the Moluccas. The Dutch believed that Macassar's more favourable geographical location, as compared with Malacca, was the reason for the strength of the Portuguese trade with the Kingdom of Goa. The VOC worried about Macassar's trade with Borneo, Java, Bali, Timor, Ambon and the Moluccas and declared its intention to limit Macassar's power.[19]

The VOC embarked upon a policy in the same year, 1625, in the Moluccas that they hoped would establish tighter control over the cloves trade and limit the growth of Macassar's growth and political influence. Dutch forces, under the command of van Speult, undertook a grandiose scheme that envisaged the total destruction of the clove culture on Ceram and portions of Ambon which were not controlled by the VOC. Since several mountainous clove growing areas were missed, the clove culture revived which was a bitter disappointment to the VOC.

At Macassar, the numbers of trading vessels arriving increased contrary to the VOC's hopes. Macassar merchants continued to pay high prices for cloves in the Moluccas with money, in the VOC's opinion, supplied by Portuguese, English and Danish merchants.[20] The Company's policy of destroying the clove culture in the Moluccas in areas not under VOC control was maintained and annual expeditions were similarly unsuccessful. Another measure, the despatch of two naval squadrons to cruise simultaneously off Malacca and the Celebes, was advocated within the VOC but it was only partially implemented since the shipping for two squadrons was unavailable and interdicting Portuguese shipping in the Straits of Malacca had a higher priority.

In 1629, a Macassar force left the Kingdom of Goa to attack Banda but it was recalled after reaching the islands of Amblau and Buru.[21] Learning of these preparations by Macassar, the Company recognised them as a potential threat to the VOC's spice trade; the Company worried that Macassar, with Portuguese support, would intervene and establish contact with indigenous anti-VOC populations in the Moluccas. The VOC promptly despatched a strong force to the Spice Islands in 1630; its leader, P. Lucaszoon, made a serious miscalculation by applying force against the local population in an attempt to eliminate the clove culture.

The Islamic anti-VOC resistance on Ceram and Ambon in the Moluccas grew as a result of the Dutch excesses in 1630; by 1634, they had retired from the coastal regions to the mountains in preparation for full-scale hostilities. These anti-VOC forces in the Moluccas, who appealed in 1629 for aid from Macassar, reiterated their request; the Kingdom of Goa initiated a policy of sending military aid to the Moluccas in 1635 with the arrival of forty-three junks and 2,000 troops on Ceram.[22]

MACASSAR, POLITICAL CHANGES IN THE MALAY WORLD AND THE ESTADO DA INDIA

Throughout the rest of the Malay world, in the western Indonesian archipelago, Aceh and Mataram experienced similar political and economic changes as Macassar in the early seventeenth century.[23] Aceh, the implacable foe of the Portuguese for commercial, political and religious reasons, maintained a consistent policy of attempting by diplomacy or force to dominate the state systems of north-western Sumatra and the Malay peninsula.[24] Sultan Ala ad-din Ri'ayat Syah al-Kahar (1539–71) implemented this policy and also revived Aceh's pepper trade to the Red Sea.[25] His successor was less fortunate in the struggle against the Portuguese and upon that ruler's death Aceh experienced a period of internal instability from 1579 until 1589. Two successive rulers re-established the sultan's claims of absolutist power. In 1593–4, the capitão of Malacca sent an emissary to Aceh, who advocated peace and improved commercial relations; the sultan contemplated but refused to

Table 5.1. *Portuguese shipping arrivals and departures at Macassar, 1622–67.*

Year	Arrivals										Departures								
	Macao	Manila	Batavia	Solor & Timor	Malacca	Coromandel[a]	Bengal	Goa	Unspecified	Total	Macao	Manila	Batavia	Solor & Timor	Malacca	Coromandel[a]	Goa	Unspecified	Total
1621										12+									
1625										10–22									
1629	1				1					11									
1630	2										1				1				
1631					1										1				
1634											2								
1637											1			1					
1638	2															2	2		
1639	1														1		1		
1640																			
1641																			
1642									1										
1643								2											
1644	5										5								
1645	2				1	1					2					1			
1646					1	1										2			

Year										
1647	3				1		3		2	
1648	2	1[b]			1		1		1	1
1649	3		1	2						1
1650			1[c]	1						
1651	1	1[b]	2	1	1		1[b]			1
1652	3	1[b]	3	1	1		1[b]	3		1
1653	3		1	1			2	1	2	
1654										
1655	1									
1656	5						4			1
1657						3	2			
1658	3			1			4			
1659				1			1			
1660	4				7					
1661	1						3	3		
1662								2		
1663							1			
1664	1	1					2	2		1
1665	1						2	1		
1666							2			
1667	1	1[c]					1	1[c]		

[a] Includes Negapatnam and Masulipatnam.
[b] Ship owned by João Gomes de Paiva, Portuguese country trader resident at Manila.
[c] Stopped at Batavia on diplomatic mission from Goa en route Macassar or Macassar en route Goa or Macao.

Sources: ARA, VOC 667/KA 569, VOC 1134/KA 1043; HAG, MR 26A, MR 26B; IOR, Celebes, Java 3; GM, DRB and Bouwstoffen.

sell Aceh's total pepper production to the Portuguese which, it was claimed, amounted to 15,000 bahars (51,316 picols).[26]

Aceh and the Portuguese were unable to accommodate each other's interests. By the 1620s Iskander Muda (1607–36) extended Aceh's control to the pepper-producing areas of west Sumatra; he controlled a large percentage of the pepper available for sale which caused frustration amongst the Muslim and European merchants. Foreign merchants subsequently encountered difficulties in coming to terms with the sultan for pepper and 'in 1620–22, the EIC and VOC were ejected altogether.'[27] To what extent Aceh's expansion on the west coast of Sumatra in the 1610s increased its supplies of and trade in pepper is not ascertainable.

The receipts from the sale of pepper helped finance Iskander Muda's successful expansion and raids to destroy and control Johor, Pahang, Kedah and Perak over 1613–20. These raids engendered greater long-term difficulties for those states. Raided in 1624, for example, Indragiri's pepper production had not recovered a decade later; 'the Achinese raids also impaired the movement of pepper from Kedah, Johor, Pahang, Indragiri and Kampar to Patani, on the east coast of the Malay Peninsula.'[28] Flushed with its successes, Aceh, disastrously chose to attack the Portuguese at Malacca in 1629.[29]

Mataram emerged in the early seventeenth century as the most powerful sultanate on the island of Java.[30] After usurping the throne of Pajang, just prior to the 1590s, Mataram seized every possible opportunity to extend its influence and control over a multitude of sultanates. Mataram's dramatic expansion stemmed from their policy of assuming from those conquered states their overlord–vassal relationships with other states, in a fashion similar to that of Macassar, which permitted the expansion of its power quite out of proportion to the time expended.

In some of these conquered states, a Mataram military governor assumed control, and in other states, Mataram left the internal government substantially unchanged, provided that Mataram was supplied with food and manpower. Distant states, such as Palembang and Jambi on the southwest Sumatra coast and Banjarmassin on Borneo, became vassals of Mataram on account of their previous suzerainty to Javanese states which had been absorbed by Mataram. Palembang's poor relations with a neighbouring power, Bantam, also contributed to its seeking the protection of Mataram. Another consideration in this calculus of power relationships for states like Palembang, Jambi and Banjarmasin was Mataram's perceived ability to extend its power by sea; after annexing Surabaya and Madura, Mataram obtained adequate numbers of ships 'to maintain its position as a maritime power at least on the coasts of Sumatra, Borneo and Celebes.'[31] Mataram's maritime capability was, however, unsuitable for any confrontation against European ships in fleet actions.

The initial contacts between the VOC and the Mataram developed as a result of Dutch commercial and Mataram political interest. Sultan Agung, the architect of Mataram's greatness, saw a potential utility in the Dutch presence in 1614 as an 'ally in his struggle with the rulers of the coastal states, especially the King of Surabaya.'[32] Subsequent Dutch actions, their occupation of Batavia (Jakarta) in 1619, alerted Agung to the necessity for caution. In 1622, Agung came to terms with the VOC in order to successfully conclude his war against Surabaya. After the fall of Surabaya in 1625, relations between Mataram and the VOC at Batavia deteriorated.[33] The VOC refused to support Mataram in its planned attack on Bantam, in west Java, and as a result Sultan Agung prepared and executed unsuccessful attacks upon the Dutch at Batavia in 1628 and 1629.

For the Estado da India, the events of 1629 in the South China Sea provided a respite from earlier gloomy reports of successes by the enemies of the Portuguese. Nuno Alvares Botelho's squadron won a dramatic victory over Acehenese forces in that year and the news of Mataram's attacks upon the Dutch at Batavia reached Goa.[34] Consequently, the new Viceroy of India, the Conde de Linhares, inaugurated diplomatic efforts to realign and strengthen the Estado da India's alliances in the South China Sea with the dual objective of maintaining an increasingly difficult position at Malacca and strengthening their interest on Macassar and Solor.

From 1629 until 1641 the Portuguese modified their previous alliances with Johor, Pahang and Patani. Although the Portuguese had previously derived some benefit, by the mid 1630s, the disadvantage of their two anti-alliances, anti-Aceh with Johor and Pahang and anti-Siam with Patani, outweighed any consideration for their maintenance. The desperate Portuguese position at Malacca forced the Estado da India to recognise that they had to obtain a truce with Aceh and Siam at the cost of their existing alliances in the western Indonesian archipelago or risk completely exhausting the Crown's resources in the attempt to maintain them.[35] The Portuguese, also, tried to establish an alliance with Mataram, but were unable to fulfil their promises of naval and military support on Java, and renewed diplomatic contact with Palembang. The Portuguese concluded an informal alliance with Macassar and supported its efforts in the Moluccas against the VOC.

These diplomatic shifts had important repercussions on the rulers of the Malay world states, their policies towards maritime trade and their opposition to the extension of the VOC's power throughout the South China Sea. Portuguese efforts to obtain peace with Aceh failed and the VOC, tired of trying to enlist Acehinese support for the siege of Malacca, contacted Johor and its allies. Aceh, as a result of the VOC-Johor alliance, was left diplomatically isolated after the conquest of Malacca. The failure of the Portuguese to conclude an alliance with Mataram and to provide naval support for Mataram's anti-VOC struggle led Sultan Agung to promote privateering and the temporary dislocation of maritime trade on the north coast of Java.[36] Ultimately, after Malacca's fall in 1641, it became incumbent upon Macao's country traders in south China and specially appointed envoys from the rest of the Estado da India to attempt to improve Portuguese relations with the indigenous states in the South China Sea.

In economic matters, by the late 1630s, the Portuguese at Malacca encountered supply difficulties; pepper, tin, cloves and other commodities, which the Portuguese Crown had been able to purchase in large quantities were no longer being sent to India.[37] The majority of Portuguese supplies of pepper were from the Kanara and Malabar coasts in south-west India. It has been assumed that the Portuguese were driven out of the pepper markets of the Indonesian archipelago soon after the arrival of the VOC and EIC. Recent research shows that the Portuguese Crown continued to send silver to Malacca for the purchase of pepper to be sent to Europe. In the 1610s the Crown, as Table 5.2 shows, successfully purchased and shipped pepper from Malacca to Europe. The Crown also tried to prohibit the transportation of pepper from Malacca to China, suggesting that Portuguese country traders participated in a minor shift of pepper sales away from India for Europe to China.[38]

The capitão of Malacca persisted in imposing short-sighted but lucrative restrictive practices which caused havoc in the indirect supplies by indigenous merchants and shippers of the major export commodities from the eastern Indonesian archipelago at Malacca. Written probably in 1636, the Senado da Camara of Malacca petitioned the new capitão, Dom Diego Coutinho Doçem, to restore the indigenous traders' confidence by eliminating those practices, price-fixing and defaulting in payments to traders. Coutinho was asked to write to the Sultans of Macassar and Pahang informing them of these remedial steps. The Sultan of Pahang was included because the traders from Macassar, after tiring of the capitão's mistreatment of them at Malacca, had established *bazars* (informal annual markets) under the patronage of the Sultan of Pahang at the small ports on the islands and the southern coast of the Malay peninsula.[39]

At Macassar, the Portuguese from Macao obtained supplies of pepper from indigenous traders who ventured into the markets in the western Indonesian archipelago that were closed or too risky for the Portuguese. Jambi was one of these markets; direct transactions with the pepper growers, the Minangkabau, were possible.[40] Pepper was also available in other markets frequented by indigenous traders from Macassar; those additional markets included some of the north Java ports and Banjarmassin and Martapoura on Borneo.

In the early 1630s, the informal alliance between Macassar and the Estado da India pursued military actions against the VOC's position in the Moluccas. It was as a result of one of the Macassar sorties with Portuguese support in the eastern Indonesian archipelago that a glimpse is recorded of the early career of the fidalgo, Francisco Vieira de Figueiredo, who figured so prominently in shaping Portuguese relations with Macassar.[41] He was captured in one of these actions by the VOC and his ransom at Batavia was arranged by Karaeng Pattingalloang in 1635.[42]

The VOC was concerned that this informal alliance between its two arch rivals, which was geographically restricted to the eastern region, would spread to the whole of the Indonesian archipelago with the conclusion of a tripartite pact between the Portuguese, Macassar and Mataram.[43] The spectra of Mataram joining and supporting Macassar and the Portuguese against the VOC quickly subsided on account of inconclusive Macassar–Mataram negotiations and Mataram's experience of the Portuguese inability to deliver military aid when promised. Although the Company was relieved when Mataram did not join Macassar and the Portuguese against them, by the mid 1630s the VOC position on Ambon continued to deteriorate.

In early 1637, the VOC concluded that it was necessary to launch a large-scale

Table 5.2. *The geographical origin and volume of*
Portuguese pepper shipments from Goa to Europe,
1612–18.

Year	Malacca	Malacca with others	Total (picols)
1612	1,956		9,295
1613	2,525		7,822
1614			6,258
1615		7,548[a]	10,121
1616		4,008[b]	15,484
1617			4,288
1618	1,464		11,330
	5,945	11,556	64,598

[a] Cochin with Malacca
[b] Cochin with Quilon and Malacca.
Source: Disney, *Twilight of Empire*, 162.

military action designed to subdue the indigenous uprising on Ambon and Ceram. This Dutch expedition proved to the VOC that their European military forces could only provide a temporary stability in the region. Although the VOC returned in 1638 with a large force, the Dutch sought to interpose the Sultan of Ternate through a treaty arrangement to guarantee the Company's monopoly of the region's cloves production. The Sultan of Ternate lacked sufficient forces to succeed in such an ambitious enterprise; he failed to stop the Macassar and Java traders from purchasing cloves and to interdict the anti-VOC elements receiving aid. By the mid 1640s, the VOC had lost confidence in the Sultan of Ternate and applied more repressive measures.[44]

MACAO, MACASSAR AND MANILA

During the 1630s, the Portuguese from Macao increased their interest in supporting the Estado da India's efforts on Macassar. Macao's support for Macassar's expansion and the thwarting of VOC efforts to stabilise their position in the Moluccas occurred at the same time as the importance of Macassar's market for Macao's country traders was in transition and shifting from an auxiliary to a primary market. From 1621 until 1643, the Portuguese of Macao sent on the average only one to two ships each year to that market. Over the years 1644 to 1660, as shown in Table 5.1, the Macao country traders concentrated between one and five ships at Macassar, the larger numbers represented approximately one-fourth to one-third of their entire fleet.[45] Between 1660 and 1667, Portuguese country traders from Macao sent an irregular and small number of vessels, which probably did not exceed one ship on an annual basis.

In the 1630s, António Bocarro, confirmed Henry Short's earlier description, added that the Portuguese from Macao also exported Chinese *cangas* and *nonos* (cotton and linen textiles) and traded in Crown-restricted export items, raw silk and silk piecegoods.[46] In 1634, the Viceroy of the Estado da India established Macao's trade to Macassar as a Crown monopoly and ordered this voyage to be regulated by an administrator. The Conde de Linhares ordered the numbers of Portuguese ships departing from Macao for Macassar be limited to two and prohibited each of them from carrying more than ten picols of Chinese raw silk and silk piecegoods, which he feared were sold at Macassar to the VOC, English and Danes. The Crown's authorities at Goa were also alarmed by the decline in Malacca's *alfandega* receipts and the Viceroy ordered the administrator of the Japan voyage, under whose jurisdiction the administrator of the Macassar voyage was to function, to collect the Crown's 6 per cent customs duties in gold from all arriving and departing country shipping from Macao via Manila or Macassar to Malacca.[47]

The Viceroy reversed his decision to establish a Crown monopoly of the Macassar voyage in part on account of Malacca's claims of jurisdiction over the customs receipts collected at Macao.[48] The administrator of the Japan voyage was ordered to despatch the Crown's customs duties collected at Macao in gold to Malacca. This system appears burdensome but functional; in 1639, the administrator of the Japan voyage, Romão de Lemos, while en route from Macao to Goa via Macassar, despatched a ship from Macassar to Malacca with a shipment of gold as payment of these collected duties.[49] Macao's country traders did not share the Crown's enthusiasm for the restriction of their trade in Chinese raw silk and piecegoods at Macassar nor the new regulations on the collection and disbursement of customs revenues. To what degree they evaded or complied with these orders is uncertain.

By the late 1630s and into the 1640s, Macassar's market was in the process of transformation because of VOC policies in the Moluccas and on Ambon which brought about falling supplies and increases in the cost of cloves. The economic interest of Portuguese country traders from Macao in the Macassar market had centred on their importing gold, raw silk, silk and cotton piecegoods, and ballast cargoes like zinc, radix China, candied ginger and porcelain to purchase or exchange for cloves and pepper at Macassar to return to China or to go on to India. Macassar was, furthermore, an ideal location for the Portuguese from Macao to stockpile sandalwood and sappanwood purchased in the Lesser Sunda islands.

By 1645, there were three market innovations in which the Portuguese from Macao participated and were involved at Macassar. The Portuguese participated in the resurgence of the Indian cotton cloth trade in which they were joined by English, Danes, Muslim and inland merchants to the detriment of the VOC's sales of Indian cloth throughout the Indonesian archipelago.[50] They were already and remained the primary market supplier of Chinese raw silk, silk and cotton piecegoods. Through the co-operation of Macassar's rulers and traders as intermediaries, the Portuguese acquired New World silver supplies from direct and indirect trade with the Spanish at Macassar, Ternate and Manila. Together with other foreign traders, they intensified the use of gold, in specie and bullion, as a trading and export commodity at Macassar.

The Portuguese practice of using their ships disguised as the property of, or ships owned by, the rulers and traders of Macassar was introduced by the Macao country traders in the 1630s for the sandalwood trade on Timor. The VOC reported that 'the Macao Portuguese that are residing in Macassar tried to ensure their trade with Timor in a very crafty way through the King Sultan of Macassar, Princes Pattingalloang, and ri-Boerane.' The method the Portuguese used in conjunction with their allies was 'by despatching their ships and cargoes under those names and pretend they are only factors of these same princes and administrators.' The VOC complained 'that if we came across them and damage their vessels they then claim damages on behalf of these princes.'[51]

The Portuguese used this same method and were, in part, if not wholly, responsible for arranging for the rulers and merchants of Macassar to trade with Manila. They involved themselves in similar arrangements with the *nawab* of Golconda and the indigenous merchants of the Coromandel coast to trade at Macassar.[52]

By the 1640s, Macao's country traders desperately required silver but were prohibited to trade directly with Manila. Encouraged by the Estado da India to open clandestine trading contacts with the Spanish, Macao's country traders were anxious to introduce this commercial practice at Manila. With the resurgence of the Indian cloth trade at Macassar, Macao's country traders had supplies of Indian and Chinese cloth and other trading items that were in demand at Manila.

The rulers of Macassar were involved, probably well before 1647, as participants and intermediaries for the Portuguese in the Manila trade. In 1647, Francisco Vieira de Figueiredo, as the Sultan of Macassar's factor, was already in the process of claiming compensation from the VOC for the capture of one of the Sultan's ships en route to Manila. Portuguese influence over the rulers and traders of Macassar can easily and understandably be over-estimated. Francisco Vieira de Figueiredo and Francisco Mendes held important diplomatic and advisory positions in the Kingdom of Goa, they acted, respectively, as the Sultan's diplomatic envoy and secretary. Macao's country traders supplied vital munitions and artillery to the Sultan that were required for Macassar's successful regional military campaigns.[53] The extensive mutual co-operation and working partnership between the Portuguese and the rulers of Macassar developed on the basis, which was readily accepted and perceived by both, of mutual benefit and reciprocal advantage for their economic and political requirements.

In 1648, the Spanish Governor at Manila professed *ex post facto* that he was opposed to Macao's proposals to introduce their trade via intermediaries from Macassar.[54] In the same year, a prominent Spanish Crown official, Pedro de la Mata, and a Portuguese country trader who resided at Manila, João Gomes de Paiva, expanded their trade at Macassar and encouraged Macao's country traders to trade with Manila.[55] Manila's trade continued to encounter difficulties

Table 5.3. *Macassar shipping arrivals at Manila, 1641–67.*

Year	Number of vessels	Year	Number of vessels	Year	Number of vessels
1641	3	1651	2	1660	3
1643	1	1653	2	1661	2
1644	2	1654	1	1662	2
1645	1	1655	1	1663	1
1646	1	1656	1	1664	2
1647	1	1657	3	1665	1
1649	2	1658	4	1666	2
1650	5	1659	2	1667	1
				Total	51

Sources: AGI, Filipinas, 64, and Chaunu, *Les Philippines*, 160–7.

exacerbated by the diminishing numbers of Chinese junks arriving from Amoy which the VOC were diverting to Taiwan and the prohibition of trade with the Portuguese.

Manila's market required imports of cloth, pepper, benzoin, and iron; pepper was being purchased at Manila for 18 to 20 reals/picol and sold for high profits in New Spain. The Spanish sailed to Macassar via the Moluccas and Cambodia with large amounts of silver, gold, and sugar.[56] In the Moluccas, where they retained a foothold, the Spanish purchased cloves; at Macassar, they sold their imports of cloves, silver and gold and purchased raw silk, silk and cotton piecegoods and iron from Portuguese country traders from Macao.[57] Other European merchants, the VOC, EIC and the Danes, tried to penetrate the Manila market but failed at this time.[58]

The number of ships arriving at Manila from Macassar, including those owned by Manila or Macao country traders, the Sultan, and different Karaengs of the Kingdom of Goa for 1641–67 is given in Table 5.3. The value of the almojarifazgo receipts collected by the Spanish authorities from the reported shipping over the same period totalled 12,536 pesos.[59] A large number of these receipts were collected at 3 per cent *ad valorem*, which if that rate and value are used only to approximate a potential figure, the total value of the imports from Macassar, in the same period, is estimated as approaching 417,867 pesos. These calculations suggest a modest trade when compared with Macao's direct trade with Manila in the 1620s.

Other records at Seville, which were incorporated into Table 5.3, indicate that additional ships arrived and traded at Manila from Macassar; these supplementary records provide the names of the *capitáns*, ships and cargo lists which, in the case of shipping from Macassar, mention what was considered to be the Sultan's or the Karaeng's.[60] The actual total value of imports from Macassar at Manila from 1641 through official trading and smuggling was unquantifiably larger than the figures suggested by relying only on the almojarifazgo records.

CLOVES, COTTONS AND THE *MAS*

Cloves from the Moluccas were the most procured export commodity at Macassar; the price and supply of this spice is a primary indicator of that market's condition. The price of cloves, as shown in Table 5.4, in the Moluccas rose dramatically from 105 reals/bahar (between 500–550 Dutch *ponds*) in 1618 to 390 in 1655; at Macassar, the price was 155 reals/bahar in 1621 and 750 in 1659. There was some price fluctuation at Macassar, as for example in 1641 when the cost price in the Moluccas declined on account of a particularly good harvest and supply at Spanish Ternate.[61]

The VOC's efforts to diminish output and maintain a low price for cloves in the inter-Asian markets, especially in the Indian Ocean, led the Portuguese country traders to complain of slender profit margins.[62] Macao's country traders tried to continue to traffic in this commodity but competition in general and from the English and Danes in particular intensified. By 1649, Macassar's market was so disrupted by the VOC's efforts that the English offer to pay 300 reals/bahar for cloves did not persuade indigenous traders to risk sending their shipping to the Moluccas and Ambon. Clove production was so reduced that in 1656 the VOC could no longer satisfy the European and Asian market demands with existing stocks and production. In 1659, only small amount of cloves were available on Macassar at the extremely high price of 750 reals/bahar.

During the Portuguese–Dutch truce (1644–52), the Portuguese participated, along with the English, Danes and Muslim merchants, in the resurgence in the Coromandel and Bengal cotton cloth trade at Macassar.[63] The benefit of this trade

Table 5.4. *Clove prices in the Moluccas*
(Ambon) and at Macassar, 1618–59.
(Prices in reals/bahar)

Year	Moluccas (Ambon)	Macassar
1618	105 (ave.)	
1621		155 (ave.)
1622	125 (ave.)	
1638		250
1641	100	
1645		260
1649		300 (offered)
1653		360
1655	390 (ave.)	475 (ave.)
1658		700
1659		750

Sources: IOR, Celebes, p. 111–13; Java, III, pt. 3, p. 475; *Bouwstoffen*, II, 351–2, 392–5; III, 12–13, and 238; Boxer, *Francisco Vieira de Figueiredo*, 21; and Ijzerman, 'Het schip *De Eendracht*,' 369–72.

for Macao's country traders was shortlived; in 1652, the VOC's naval forces quickly
made Portuguese voyages between Macassar and the Coromandel coast a difficult
and an extremely risky business venture. Macao's country traders also sought to
expand their sales of raw silk, silk and cotton piecegoods in order to purchase pepper
and sandalwood. By 1647, the Portuguese were frustrated in these attempts since
they had encountered supply difficulties in China.[64]

Gold and silver specie did not circulate as money in almost all of the economies
of the South China Sea region throughout the sixteenth century. Most economic
transactions were dominated by the circulation of primitive forms of money,
cowries, rice and cotton textiles and executed by barter.[65] The only commonly
accepted exception were those parts of the region where *caixas* (coins of copper,
tin or lead) of Chinese origin circulated. The Portuguese in an attempt to avoid
a drain upon their silver specie and bullion resources preferred to use Indian cotton
textiles and caixas.

By the late sixteenth century, although the Crown disapproved, the use of silver
specie crept into Portuguese commercial practices at Malacca, especially for the
purchase of pepper.[66] The South China Sea region apparently experienced an
increase in the indigenous production and use of gold in commodity transactions.
Certain states, Aceh and Macassar, either introduced or intensified the circulation
of gold in specie.

The *mas* (a gold coin) circulated in Macassar for the payment of large commercial
transactions. The caixa was used for smaller transactions such as the purchase of
food and payment for personal services. The exact age of the circulation of these
types of coins is imprecise but two hypothesis may be suggested. The first
suggestion is that the caixa antedated the mas, it was introduced in the mid
sixteenth century, prior to Islam's arrival on Macassar, and, similar to the
experience in the Moluccas, its use was linked to the spice trade.[67] The second
suggestion is that the mas antedated the caixa; this seems unlikely but it is
supported by an observation from Father Gervaise in the latter half of the
seventeenth century.[68] The dating of circulation of the different types of coin in
Macassar and the relative economic importance of each metal, gold and copper,
is important in providing data on Macassar's early economic and commercial
development.

Both coins, the mas and caixa, were in circulation by 1618 and all the Europeans
trading at Macassar utilised them as money. The EIC agents on Macassar
explained to their superiors at Bantam that it was their policy to keep the local
accounts in reals on paper but its capital was in mas; the VOC adhered to a similar
practice by quoting prices for goods at Macassar in mas or real, with the mas being
the dominant currency in circulation.[69] The mas was linked by a fluctuating
exchange-ratio to the real and caixa based on their intrinsic metallic values.

Little is known about the minting of the mas, which was presumably done
locally, regulated by a shahbander-like official. Any decision for any marked
debasement of its gold content with its impact on the real and the caixa, which
had internal political and external economic ramifications, probably came from the

court and in the name of the Sultan of Macassar. The size of the minted emissions and gold bullion movements in the Macassar market are difficult to answer with precision. Gold was available locally, primarily from alluvial deposits, imported from throughout the Indonesian archipelago, the Philippines and China.

By around 1610, the Macao Portuguese had ceased to export gold from China to Japan on any large scale. In the 1620s and 1630s, the Portuguese purchased and exported sizeable amounts of gold to the Estado da India. By the end of the latter decade, they also transported gold bullion from Macassar to Goa since the Estado da India desperately required gold to pay its expenditures and mint specie. In a letter captured by the VOC, Rui Dias da Cunha, the vedor da fazenda in Goa in 1640 reported to the capitão of Malacca that the Crown Treasury had minted gold specie from imports of that precious metal from Macassar.[70]

From the mid 1640s until the mid 1650s, with the resurgence of Coromandel cloth imports, gold was the major commodity used to pay for imported Indian textiles at Macassar. The Portuguese and other foreign traders, the EIC, VOC, Danes and Muslim merchants, profitably exported gold bullion and specie from Macassar to India on account of a favourable ratio between gold and silver and the preference in certain parts and ports of south India for payment in gold. The Portuguese over the same period attempted to enlarge the importation of gold bullion into Macassar from China and failed; they also, in conjunction with Macassar and Spanish country traders, imported gold from the Philippines. There was an increase in demand for gold at Macassar caused by a decline in its availability from internal and regional supplies and an intensification in the amounts of this metal that were exported in bullion and specie.

In 1632, the mas was valued at 0.87 reals.[71] It was used by the VOC, in conjunction with textiles and other items, to purchase cloves, slaves and other cargoes in the eastern Indonesian archipelago.[72] For Macassar's rulers, the ability to maintain the mas' intrinsic value was of interest on account of their direct involvement in maritime trade. By 1646, the Sultan and Karaengs of the Kingdom of Goa were concerned about the rapid depletion of their gold specie and bullion and their large outstanding trading debts to foreign merchants. Macassar's market was also disturbed by the decline in clove supplies and their price rise, the disturbingly high rate of imported Indian textiles that were paid for in gold and the dramatic dip in Chinese gold imports by Macao's country traders. The reason for the Sultan's and Karaengs concern about the depletion in gold supplies was related to the role of gold in the re-export trading network established at Macassar. For example, imported Indian cloth was paid for in gold and used in the purchase of cloves in the Moluccas. Cloves were sold in Macassar to Portuguese traders from Macao for gold from China.

The Sultan's reaction was to order the debasement of the mas in 1646 by one-quarter of its 1632 value in an effort to slow its export.[73] This devaluation was not warmly received by foreign traders and it did not seriously diminish the exportation of the mas and gold bullion. In 1647, the VOC complained of the profit margin in trading in the mas, but, in the absence of any other major export items, carried it to Batavia along with some tortoiseshell and sandalwood in the *Arneminden* for a total value of 71,717 guilders.[74]

The Manila trade, with its gold imports, temporarily stabilised the value of the mas and permitted the continued export of gold specie and bullion from Macassar to India. By 1655, after the resumption of Portuguese–Dutch hostilities and Macassar's expensive campaigns against the VOC and indigenous forces on Buton and throughout the Moluccas, Macassar ceased to receive cloth from Coromandel and Bengal.[75] Cloth, as a consequence, was not available for export to Manila and the amount of gold that was imported from Manila to Macassar declined and finally ceased.

The Sultan, in 1655, debased the mas once again but with the stipulation that the exchange rate for these new emissions be accepted by foreign traders at parity with the old mas; this new mas (the *checoe mas*) was devalued to a ratio of 12 old to 16 new mas. The Sultan attempted to keep the issues small in order to avoid its exportation. His decision was prompted, according to the EIC, in order to cheapen the Sultan's trading debts but it stimulated speculation and the importation of reals.[76]

Gold prices at Macassar rose as a result of the disruption of supplies, increase in demand and the speculation in the future valuation of the mas and of gold bullion. In 1648, the Portuguese sold their imported Chinese gold bullion for 25–26 mas/tael (of weight), imported gold sales reached an estimated value of 60,000 reals. In 1657, gold sold for 40–42 mas/tael. Just prior to the VOC's military activities against the Portuguese at Macassar in 1660, gold was still expensive at 37 mas/tael. This high price was maintained on account of the demand amongst the Muslim merchants from India and the failure of supplies of gold to arrive from Manila and China.[77]

After the VOC's naval victory over the Portuguese at Macassar in 1660, the Company negotiated a treaty with the Kingdom of Goa at Batavia, in which one of the provisions was the total exclusion of Portuguese merchants. The VOC flooded Macassar's market with Coromandel and Surat textiles. The Portuguese, who evaded expulsion with local support, English, Malay and Muslim traders sent twelve junks to Banjarmasin in 1662 for consignments of pepper and gold.[78]

Despite efforts to diversify their trade, Macassar's rulers were unable to maintain the value of the mas. By 1664, the mas had suffered a series of mini-debasements. The VOC blamed the Sultan and the Karaengs for those debasements; the Company recorded a profit of 129,903 guilders in 1664 on their sales of Surat and Coromandel cloth. The Dutch did not purchase any exports in the same year because the debasements had diminished the mas' value and caused an unsettled reaction in that market. The mas, which in the past was valued at two guilders, from 1664 was worth only thirty *stuivers*.[79]

MACASSAR, POLITICAL CHANGES IN THE MALAY WORLD AND MACAO

After the Estado da India's diplomatic efforts in the 1630s and Malacca's loss in 1641, the Senado da Camara of Macao and prominent Portuguese merchants assumed the responsibility for the maintenance of Portuguese diplomatic relations within the South China Sea region. Their initial contacts with the sultanates of Mataram, Palembang and Jambi, after the Portuguese–Dutch truce was announced, met with favourable response. The Portuguese also continued to support Macassar's territorial claims and operation in the eastern Indonesian archipelago. Macao's country traders, through their diplomatic, military and economic efforts in conjunction with Macassar made the VOC position in the Lesser Sunda islands very difficult and succeeded in temporarily excluding the VOC from any direct participation in that area's sandalwood trade during the truce and after the resumption of Dutch–Portuguese hostilities.

Many of the rulers in the Malay world publicly and repeatedly declared to the VOC that they opposed the continuation of the Portuguese presence in the Indonesian archipelago. The Viceroy of the Estado da India was of the opinion that in private, these rulers would reveal to Portuguese envoys their anxiety to find a counterbalance to the VOC and would be willing to discuss and to act upon a number of proposals to limit the growth of the Company.[80] The receptivity to Portuguese overtures by Palembang, Jambi and Mataram supported the Estado da India's perception of those rulers' attitudes. Fear of Portuguese success in its diplomacy with those rulers was a major reason why the VOC remained particularly eager to exclude the Portuguese from the eastern Indonesian archipelago and from south China.

In 1644 the Senado da Camara of Macao despatched a small ship under the command of their envoy, Feliciano Caetano de Souza, to negotiate an agreement with the *Pangeran* (Sultan) of Palembang to re-establish Portuguese relations and to obtain direct access to a major pepper market. Arriving at Palembang with a cargo of raw silk and Chinese textiles, the Portuguese discovered that the Pangeran had appointed a Portuguese mestiço from Macassar as that state's shahbandar.[81]

De Souza successfully negotiated an alliance agreement with Palembang that granted the use of that port to supply a Portuguese Crown fleet, should it appear in the South China Sea, and discounts to Portuguese merchants on customs duties on goods excluding pepper.[82] The Portuguese acquired a cargo of pepper which the VOC captured along with the ship after its departure. The Dutch argued that no restitution of the ship or its cargo would be forthcoming, although the truce had been declared, on account that Palembang was a prohibited area for the Portuguese according to the Hague Treaty.[83] The Portuguese were deterred from procuring directly at Palembang as a result of the VOC's actions in 1644. The trading activities of Javan and Macassar merchants, and that sultanate's status as a vassal of Mataram insured that pepper from Palembang was available to the Portuguese at Japara on Java and at Macassar.

After the announcement of the Portuguese–Dutch truce, there was also a marked improvement in Portuguese relations with Mataram. Portuguese ships from India, especially the Coromandel coast, began to make Japara a port of call en route to and from Macassar. The improvement in Mataram's relations with the Portuguese may simply be ascribed to that state's, and the Mataram governor of Japara's interest in benefiting from foreign trade but this explanation would neglect the impact of the major changes in Mataram's government. With the death of Sultan Agung in 1646 and the accession by his son, Mataram's paramount position in the central Indonesian archipelago deteriorated as a result of Mangku Rat's weak diplomatic, military and economic policies towards his vassal states on Sumatra, Borneo and neighbours on Java.[84]

In 1647, the Portuguese at Macao were informed by the Crown to relinquish the responsibility for direct negotiations with the sultanates of the Indonesian archipelago to the Estado da India's appointee, Francisco Vieira de Figueiredo.[85] Figueiredo was ordered to keep Macao well-informed; based on Macassar, he had established contact by visiting or corresponding with the rulers of Palembang, Jambi, Bantam and Mataram just prior to and during his visit to Batavia in 1648.[86] He was involved as a major ship-owner in making Japara a port of call for Portuguese shipping from India and supported the introduction of a Jesuit mission on Macassar.[87]

A Portuguese ship from Macao called at Japara in 1653 and received a free pass from the Pangeran of Jambi to trade at that port. Despite VOC opposition, the Portuguese loaded 6–700 picols of pepper at Jambi in the same year and departed for Macao.[88] The potential danger of a tripartite alliance between Macassar, Mataram and its vassals, with the Portuguese against the VOC led the Company, towards the end of the truce, to concentrate their naval forces to interdict Portuguese shipping on the Java coast and in the South China Sea.[89]

The Portuguese continued to support Macassar's claims in the eastern archipelago to the extent of their capability. Macassar wanted portions of Ambon, Butung, Buru and Ceram to be recognised as vassals or areas of paramount political interest by the VOC and Ternate and was willing to support groups in the Moluccas rebelling against the control of the VOC and Ternate. In the early 1650s, the VOC captured several Portuguese ships carrying cargoes in which large consignments were owned by the Sultan and several Karaengs of Macassar. This incident and the VOC's slow response to their demands for restitution was seized upon by the Sultan and the Karaengs as sufficient justification for Macassar to renew its support of indigenous rebel activities in the Ambon area. The decision by Macassar's rulers to despatch a large Macassar force in November of 1652 to the Ambon area and to re-enforce it in 1653 led to the Macassar–Dutch war of 1653–5.

Although the Estado da India and Portuguese country traders from Macao promised support with men, arms and munitions, the Portuguese were not directly involved in hostilities in the Ambon theatre. They confined their support to penetrating the Dutch blockade and mounting successful counter-attacks against the Company in the Lesser Sunda islands. The Dutch successfully utilised indigenous troops in the Ambon area to counter-balance the arrival of troops and aid from Macassar. Although the VOC blockade of Macassar was incomplete, the Dutch were able to eliminate the arrival of Indian cloth shipments; the company's envoys, while unable to restore peace, obtained assurances from the Sultan that the war would not spread outside the Ambon area. With the death of the most pro-Portuguese, anti-VOC elements within Macassar's leadership, the Sultan Mohamad Said in November 1653 and the Karaeng Pattingalloang in September 1654, disheartened by the absence of logistical support from the Estado da India and their losses in trade as well as against the Dutch, Macassar made a separate peace with the VOC in 1655.[90] Macao's country traders and the Portuguese communities throughout the Lesser Sunda islands continued their struggle alone against the VOC.

THE PORTUGUESE IN THE LESSER SUNDA ISLANDS

The Portuguese positions in the Lesser Sunda islands, Flores, Solor and Timor were, in reality, isolated communities surrounded by small states that were vassals, antagonists or so insignificant as to be treated indifferently. These Portuguese communities had certain outward manifestations of Portuguese society in operation, such as a Crown appointed capitão and a Santa Casa da Misericordia. They were established primarily through the efforts of Catholic missionary activity, which was entirely operated by the Dominican order. They served as modest collection centres and markets for the exchange of merchandise brought by Portuguese country traders from China and Macassar: Indian and Chinese textiles, primitive forms of money and small amounts of Chinese gold for the purchase of sandalwood, wax, slaves and gold from indigenous and Portuguese merchants who resided and traded in those islands.

In the 1630s, Portuguese country traders interest in the sandalwood trade in the Lesser Sunda islands increased as high profit levels for the sale of this commodity were recorded in south China. The total annual sandalwood trade on Timor in the late 1620s was reported as 1,500–2,000 bahars (or 5,851 to 7,802 picols). Macao's country traders had increased the number of their visits and based on a conversation with Macao country trader, in 1629, the usual profits on the sale of sandalwood from Timor at Macao were 150 per cent and in that year had been 200 per cent.[91] Macassar traders were also involved in the sandalwood, wax and slave traders in the Lesser Sunda islands. They, along with Muslim preachers, had established several villages on Timor which acted as base camps for their trading and missionary activities.[92]

In the early 1640s, conflict between Macassar and the Portuguese appeared and their informal alliance in shambles, when the Portuguese believed that Macassar's expansionist tendencies were focused on the petty states to the south of the Kingdom of Goa on Sumbawa, Flores, Solor and Timor in the Lesser Sunda islands.

The Sultan of Tolo, the uncontrolled ally and father-in-law of the Sultan of Macassar, laid claim to the Portuguese position on Flores at Larantuca in 1642.

Tolo's attack on Larantuca was executed after the death of the *Sumbanco* (the Sultan of Macassar) which leads to speculation that there was, in actual fact, some question amongst the Karaengs and vassals of Macassar about the continuation of their alliance with the Portuguese. The Portuguese and their indigenous forces refused to acknowledge Tolo's claim, and retreated to the mountainous hinterland from where they successfully counter-attacked. Within the next few years, by appealing and receiving forces from the pro-Catholic rulers on Timor, the Portuguese castigated and pacified the Belos region (on Timor), whose leader, Behale, had supported Tolo's attack.[93]

On Macassar, the Portuguese received with relief the reassurances of the new Sultan of the Kingdom of Goa that this incident had not represented a change in their alliance. The Estado da India remained concerned and stipulated in Francisco Vieira de Figueiredo's orders in 1648 that one of his responsibilities was to prevail upon the rulers of Macassar not to attack the Portuguese positions in the Lesser Sunda islands.[94] The strengthening and the re-enforcement by the Dominicans and the Portuguese country traders of their position on Solor, just prior to and immediately after the implementation of the Portuguese–Dutch truce, prompted Batavia to respond by re-occupying in 1646 Fort Henricus on Solor, which the Company had abandoned in 1615.[95]

During the truce, the Portuguese, VOC and Macassar merchants were all active in the sandalwood trade throughout the Lesser Sunda islands. There were a number of market opportunities offered to Macao's country traders by the sandalwood trade; they purchased this commodity directly in those islands, transshipped and sold it on Macassar to other Portuguese, VOC, EIC, Danish or indigenous merchants, sold it at Batavia to the VOC or carried it to Macao. Figueiredo figured prominently in arranging contracts with the VOC but the resumption of hostilities in 1652 and the VOC occupation of Cupang on Timor disrupted this type of trading.[96]

The VOC–Portuguese conflict for supremacy throughout these islands was particularly intense; each adversary employed the troops of indigenous allies which exacerbated rivalries between various petty states and the social cleavages between and within different communities in the islands.[97] By 1656, the VOC had not been expelled from the region, but the low profit margins, the high cost of maintenance, the Portuguese-led resistance and commercial competition forced Batavia to decide to abandon its direct participation in the sandalwood trade.[98] By 1658, the success of the Portuguese and their indigenous confederates in hampering and harassing the Company in the Lesser Sunda islands coupled with Macassar's military prowess and resentment of the VOC led the Governor-General and the Council of the Indies to express fears of collusion between the Portuguese and the rulers of the Kingdom of Goa in preparing an attack on the VOC's shipping at Macassar.[99]

The VOC was anxious to remove this threat, especially when the Company's resources were concentrated off south-west India. The VOC also wished to re-establish its direct access to large supplies of sandalwood. In 1659, the Company, through its emissary, Hendrike ter Horst, offered the Portuguese communities and the country traders operating on Flores, Solor and Timor a localised truce.[100] The Portuguese immediately rejected this offer which influenced the VOC's decision to attack the Portuguese at Macassar in 1660. The Company attacked in order to eliminate Portuguese commercial competition and to weaken Macao's attempts to recoup its commercial position in China from its trade at Macassar and in the Lesser Sunda islands.[101]

The VOC's successful attack on the Portuguese in 1660 left the Company in a position of strength in negotiating with Macassar. Although one of the principal stipulations of the Macassar–Dutch treaty of 1660 was the expulsion of all foreign traders, by prevarication and diplomatic support from a number of Karaengs, a small group of Portuguese traders remained in Macassar. The Portuguese participated in a number of joint efforts with those supporters in the attempt to stabilise their rapidly declining maritime trade. Tired of the prevaricating and anti-VOC attitudes and actions of some of Macassar's leaders, the Company forces with support from staunchly anti-Macassar allies, the Bugis, under the leadership of C. Speelman conquered Macassar in 1667. For the Portuguese from Macao, who were immobilised by Chinese officials threats to their very existence, a strong ally, a loyal friend and an important market in the South China Sea was lost.

Portuguese trade at Macassar, via Macassar with Manila and India, and in the Lesser Sunda islands from the 1640s into the 1660s helped Macao to adjust to the loss of the Japan trade. The volume and value of this trade did not approximate that of Japan and cannot be estimated owing to deficient archival records. The vitality of Macassar's market and the apparent buoyancy of the sandalwood trade from Timor in the China market, however, based on Dutch and Portuguese records, contributed to the maintenance of the Portuguese position in China.

The Portuguese from Macao in the 1640s also attempted to maintain and expand their trade with the mainland Southeast Asia states. These efforts met with some success but were quickly countered by the VOC and the demands made upon their resources by the rulers and merchants residing in those states. Small Portuguese communities already existed in Siam, Cambodia, Tonkin and Cochinchina. It is beyond the scope of this study to examine Portuguese country traders' activities in all of the markets of mainland Southeast Asia nor is it possible to elaborate at any length upon internal political and economic developments within those states. Consequently, their activities in one market, Tonkin, are examined over the period 1644 to 1669.

TONKIN

Portuguese country traders from Macao developed a commercial interest in mainland Southeast Asia, in part, as a result of the expansion of the Padroado's missionary efforts. In the 1630s the Jesuits and the Macao country traders shared and responded to similar trading opportunities offered in those markets for the provision of raw silk for the Japan trade. In the early 1640s, their primary aim was to maintain access to Japanese silver supplies; from 1644 until the 1660s, they sought to extract silver from those markets to finance their trade in China and missionary activities.

In theory, the rulers of Tonkin and Cochinchina disdained merchants and commerce but, in practice, were keenly aware of the fiscal benefits from controlling and administering foreign trade. The ruling family of Tonkin, the Trinh, and of Cochinchina, the Nguyen, were engaged for nearly fifty years in a bitter civil war in the seventeenth century which meant that revenues had to be found to finance large military forces. For the Trinh, who had usurped power but maintained the façade of supporting the Le emperor, the secession of Cochinchina from Tonkin by the Nguyen was intolerable and required every effort to re-incorporate that territory. The Nguyen adopted a strategy of defence against the Trinh's offensive thrusts in order to maintain their independence and expanded their control to the south.[102]

Tonkin's foreign trade as Cochinchina's, was based upon three main types of transactions: those between visiting foreign merchants trading among themselves, those between foreign merchants trading with the local rulers and influential court officials and those between visiting foreign merchants trading with resident foreign merchants in a Vietnamese port. In the sixteenth century, Vietnam offered few products which inherently interested foreign merchants. Towards the end of that century, Chinese and Japanese merchants, who were barred from trading with each other by Ming edicts, began to frequent the ports of Cochinchina, Fai-fo (Hoi-an), and Tonkin, Ke-cho (Hanoi) and Pho-Hien (Hung Yen) to exchange Chinese raw silk, silk piecegoods and other products for Japanese silver.

Within, perhaps, less than three decades, Chinese and Japanese communities expanded and formed residential trading quarters in several of Vietnam's ports. For some of these merchants their commercial position changed from 'external' to 'internal' traders. This change occurred contemporaneously with an intensification in the attempts by the Trinh and Nguyen monarchies and influential court officials to participate in the sale and to monopolise the sale of certain export commodities.

Between 1604 and 1616, prior to the commencement of Trinh–Nguyen hostilities in 1627, some 42 Japanese red-seal passports were issued for trade from Japan to Cochinchina and 11 to Tonkin.[103] By the late 1630s, Chinese Portuguese and VOC merchants competed in the Tonkin market.[104] The Tokugawa edicts of 1635 which restricted the residence of Japanese merchants and prohibited the sailing of any Japanese vessel overseas, eliminated Japanese competition in Tonkin and the South China Sea.

By 1644, Portuguese efforts to trade in Japan via Chinese and indigenous merchant intermediaries from Tonkin and other mainland South China Sea markets had failed. The Portuguese capabilities to compete against the VOC and the Chinese in Tonkin were also limited by foreign competition, Trinh monopoly policies, exactions on foreign traders from the *capados* (Trinh eunuch bureaucrats who were involved in the regulation of foreign trade) and other highly placed bureaucrats, an alarming number of shipwrecks and captures of their ships by Chinese pirates. Despite these unfavourable conditions, the Portuguese continued to trade in the Tonkin market – why and, perhaps most interesting, how?

The Jesuits, who initiated their missionary efforts in Cochinchina (1615), Cambodia (1616), and Siam (1626), established a mission in Tonkin in 1626.[105] Their visit inaugurated regular Portuguese trading contacts with Tonkin. From the inception, the Trinh decision to permit Catholic missionaries to propagate their faith was consciously linked, by the ruler and the Jesuits, as a method of insuring regular trade from Macao.[106] The Portuguese country traders were initially reluctant to participate in the high risk of piracy or shipwreck on this voyage and their involvement in other trading ventures. The Jesuit mission was persecuted and placed in jeopardy in 1628–9 when Macao shipowners did not consent to despatch vessels to that market. After presenting gifts to and negotiating with the Trinh in 1630, Father António Francisco Cardim was able to secure the continuation of the mission.[107]

From 1626 until 1660, one Portuguese vessel usually departed Macao each year to trade at Tonkin, as shown in Table 5.5. The erratic arrival of their shipping between 1660 and 1669 stemmed primarily from Chinese officials' interference at Macao and VOC and Chinese competition. When more than one ship arrived, it was unplanned, as in 1638 when two ships en route to India arrived on account of poor weather in the South China Sea. The Portuguese also employed ships of Chinese origin, described as *chos* (large ocean-going junk-type vessels). The most probable explanation for the use of Chinese ship types is linked to the lower purchase and operating cost of a junk for the short voyage from south China to Tonkin.

A number of the Portuguese vessels were owned or loaded primarily with Jesuit merchandise and capital. In 1645, the Jesuits owned and operated one ship for the Tonkin and Cochinchina missions and were in the process of building a second.[108] Jesuit annual reports add that many of the vessels were actually owned and operated by Macao country traders; in others, an individual or group of Portuguese country traders were part owners with the Jesuits. Both the Jesuits and the country traders, freighted or consigned goods on each other's ships for that market.

From 1626 until 1640, in the early years of their trade, the Portuguese and Jesuits from Macao exported the same type of cargoes as the Chinese and the VOC from China and Japan to Tonkin. Silver was the principal item that was imported, along with gold, Chinese raw silk, silk and cotton piecegoods and, in the Chinese case, ballast cargoes such as porcelain and iron pans. Tonkin raw silk, silk piecegoods, were the principal items that were exported from Tonkin, along with the Chinese silks, for the Japan market.[109] Exports for the China market, carried by Portuguese country traders after 1640, consisted primarily of silver.

By 1642, the VOC reported that the Portuguese exports from China to Tonkin, which had consisted of silver, were now of gold and Chinese ballast cargoes (iron, porcelain and other items).[110] The Jesuit annual letters are clear that, although they and the Portuguese country traders from Macao had ceased to send large quantities

Table 5.5 *Portuguese shipping at Tonkin, 1626–69.*

Year	Number of ships	Comments
1626	1	Pataxo, owner: Gaspar Borges da Fonseca.
1627	1	
1628	0	
1629	0	
1630	1	
1631	1	Cargo: caixas.
1632	1	
1633	1	
1634	1	
1635	1	
1636	3	Arrive with silver, gold, damask, velvets and cloth; depart with 965 picols Tonkin raw silk, about 1/3 of Tonkin's total annual production; one cho, owned by Jesuits, one junk and one galiota, owned by Manoel de Moraes, which shipwrecked off Hainan island.
1637	1	
1638	3	Two accidental, forced into Tonkin on account of bad weather; one trading is the *paters jonk* (Jesuits).
1639	1	
1640	1	
1641	1[a]	One junk, owner: Japanese resident, Risemondonne; departed from Japan, cargo worth 50,000 taels with Portuguese participation in silk goods.
1642	1	One junk carrying Jesuit annual capital; cargo previously consisted of silver; this junk imported iron pans, gold, pearls; VOC estimated value at 10,000 taels.
1645	1	
1646	1	One cho shipwrecked off Hainan, cargo valued at 30,000 taels.
1647	1	Pataxo, owner: Salvador Coelho Mourão.
1648	1	One junk, departs with rice.
1649	1	
1650	0	
1651	1	One ship shipwrecked off Hainan; two other ships, chos, owners Tonkinese residents, shipwrecked en route from Macao to Tonkin with Jesuit investment of silk and silver worth 22,000 taels.
1652	1	Pataxo, owner: Vasco Barbosa de Mello; cargo: caixas; departs with 20,000 taels.
1653	1	Naveta.
1654	1	Naveta; cargo: gold, porcelain, iron pans.
1655	1	Captain: António da Costa Benuchio.
1656	2	One en route from Macao to Cambodia; the other, the regular caixa trader, carried a cargo worth 30,000 taels; both lost by shipwreck after departure.
1657	1	Shipwrecked.
1658	1	Captured by Chinese pirates.
1659	1	Naveta.
1660	1	Naveta, attacked and crew killed by pirate, named Thun, near Hainan.
1661	1[a]	Junk, owner: Bastien Brouwer, from Macao for Macao; imported: silk piecegoods, Chinese wares, caixas and iron pans; exported: silver and salt.
1663	0	
1665	1	
1669	1	

[a] Non-Portuguese ship, with Portuguese participation recorded

Sources: Ajuda, JA, 49–IV–61, 49–V–6, 49–V–9, 49–V–15, 49–V–31, 49–V–32; Cardim, *Batalhas*; and Buch, 'La Compagnie des Indes Néerlandaises.'

of silver to Tonkin, they usually exported cargoes of caixas.[111] The ability of the Portuguese to continue to trade in Tonkin is directly attributable to their participation in the supply of caixas and the knowledge of their trading importance.

CAIXAS, SILK AND SILVER

Caixas circulated throughout China, Japan, and almost all of the economies of the South China Sea and the Indian sub-continent.[112] In Tonkin, caixas were known as *dong* and consisted primarily of copper. They were a form of currency adapted to Tonkin's trading requirements and market environment.

In the seventeenth century, the Trinh failed to mine and mint the copper deposits in the provinces of Tuyen-Quang, Hung-Hoa and Thai-Nguyen. In the absence of textual archival references to the contrary, Tonkin relied entirely upon the importation of supplies of caixas from China and Japan.[113] According to the VOC, the minting of this coin in Tonkin was prohibited by the Trinh to all upon pain of death.[114] The Trinh did not establish mints or methods to supervise the control of emissions of this coin until the active exploitation of their copper deposits in the mid eighteenth century.[115]

In the last sixteenth century, caixas circulated along with a system of trading by weight of bullion and barter. With the arrival of Japanese merchants and ships, they appear to have imported large quantities of caixas as well as silver from Japan which radically modified and monetarised sectors of the local economy. The importance of barter diminished as caixas, not the real nor any silver or gold specie or bullion, were used as payments for small everyday transactions by all groups in Tonkinese society. Caixas were tied on strings which meant that they could be easily counted and larger monetary units transacted.

Caixas, it may be imagined, were rather cumbersome on account of their weight; they possessed deceptive similarities with 'cowries in Africa,' since 'their most important use may always have been as market currencies, to facilitate exchange within the market rather than to carry from one market to another.'[116] There is one important exception to that comparison. Caixas acted as a market currency in Tonkin but were also the currency which established a monetary circuit between Tonkin's economic and political centres and its silk producing hinterland.

Caixas were converted on a seasonal and fluctuating basis to weight of silver bullion. The system of trading in Tonkin, by weight of bullion for large transactions, was similar to that employed in China, although silver bullion was more commonly utilised than gold. In China, according to the Jesuit Father Gabriel de Magalhães, 'pieces of gold and silver are not coined, but cast into ingots in the form of a small boat.' He described further that at Macao, the ingots were 'called *paes* or loaves of gold and silver'; they were 'cut with steel scissors, which the people carry about with them for that purpose.' The pieces of gold or silver were 'weighed in a balance which is called *dachem*.'[117] This system had little efficacy in Tonkin's hinterland where trading transactions scarcely attained the magnitude to warrant its use.

An increase in the sale and circulation of Japanese and New World silver in

Tonkin accompanied the expansion of its foreign trade. Strong demand for silver emanated from the major commercial and political participants in Tonkin's economy: the Trinh monarchy and bureaucracy and foreign merchant communities, especially the Portuguese, who from the 1640s onwards purchased and exported this bullion to China. Silver circulated primarily in the ports and principal markets but were unsuitable for small-scale negotiations with silk producers.

Caixas, not silver, were used to establish a monetary circuit between the political and economic centres of Tonkin, Ke-cho and Pho Hien, with the silk-raising villages. Caixas were the medium of commercial exchange used to arrange purchases of raw silk among its producers. At the ports, the visiting Japanese and Chinese merchants, in addition to transactions among themselves for Chinese raw silk and silk piecegoods, were interested in acquiring supplies of Tonkin raw silk to export to Japan. Aware of this demand for locally produced raw silk, the resident Japanese and Chinese merchant communities began to act as intermediaries between the producers in the hinterland and the purchaser at Pho Hien and other port/markets.

These resident Japanese and Chinese merchants bought raw silk in the hinterland with caixas at a lower price in advance of its production. The silk farmer succumbed to those merchants' offer of credit and obligated his production. With regular supplies of caixas, these intermediaries sustained this practice each year and carefully attempted to balance the supply of those coins to the demand in the silk-producing hinterland. By this method, Tonkin's port markets were supplied with raw silk; market prices depended upon supply and demand, the quantity of caixas available and the velocity of their circulation.

The Portuguese arranged the manufacture of caixas amongst the Chinese residents at Macao.[118] Copper was available from Japan, which the Portuguese imported until their expulsion and afterwards purchased at Canton or Macao from Chinese merchants who had imported it. By 1688, after the Ch'ing established tighter controls over Portuguese trade with the establishment of the *hoppo*, this practice of minting caixas at Macao was extinguished. The hoppo influenced the Senado da Camara in that year to prohibit the rental of any house or property by Macao's Portuguese inhabitants to any of the city's Chinese residents for the purpose of manufacturing caixas.[119]

The Portuguese country traders and the Jesuits purchased or contracted the manufacture of caixas in China to trade in Tonkin as any other commodity. Caixas on account of their weight were, as most of the Chinese commodities the Portuguese could afford, a ballast cargo. Loaded first near the keel the caixas helped maintain the ship's stability and formed a bed upon which the more expensive and more perishable items could be loaded. Caution in loading was maintained since shifting of the cargo could cause sailing problems and result in shipwreck. The VOC and Chinese supplies of caixas were not manufactured or purchased in China, largely because of their scarcity and the control over their export, but in Japan with its plentiful copper supplies, and the relative ease of contracting the manufacture and arranging the exports of caixas.

Tonkin produced an estimated total of 3,000 picols of raw silk in the 1630s and approximately one-third was exported to Japan. The Portuguese, according to the VOC, were active in its export; in 1636–7, they had exported 965 picols of Tonkin raw silk in the direction of Macao for transhipment to Japan.[120] The Portuguese lost, by shipwreck, one of their three ships en route from Tonkin to Macao with 350 picols of raw silk on board. The other two reached Macao safely and the Tonkin silk was sold profitably in Japan in 1637. After their expulsion from Japan and disappointment in their arrangements with resident foreign merchants in Tonkin, such as the Japanese merchant Risemondonne in 1641, for the sale of Portuguese consignments of that silk in Japan, the Portuguese from Macao ceased to compete in the purchase of Tonkin raw silk and silk piecegoods.

The Tonkin market transactions of the Portuguese, VOC, Chinese and Spanish from 1636 to 1669 demonstrate the relationship of the caixas trade to the supply of silk. With the Portuguese withdrawal in the 1640s from competing for the purchase of Tonkin's raw silk and silk piecegoods, the VOC, the Chinese, and later the Spanish were the remaining major traders. Despite efforts by the VOC to market Tonkin silk in the Netherlands and Spanish marketing attempts in Manila, Japan continued to be the principal export market for Tonkin silk.

Tonkin's raw-silk production and exports fluctuated in an erratic fashion. A high percentage appears to have been exported: throughout the 1640s, the VOC exported an annual average of a little over 500 picols with the Chinese annual average fluctuating from 300 to 820 picols of raw silk. Total annual exports oscillated from amounts as low as 200 picols to the average good year of around 1,000 picols and an exceptional year such as 1650 with 1,415 picols.[121]

The Chinese, Spanish, and earlier the Portuguese, purchased their silk from the market intermediaries, Chinese and Japanese resident merchants. The VOC's trading methods differed from their competitors in that they experimented in purchasing from both the foreign resident communities and the Trinh. In 1644, for example, the VOC purchased a total of 645 picols of silk, only 138 picols of which were supplied by the Trinh and the rest, 507 picols, from private merchants, who were probably resident Chinese. The VOC later changed its methods to contracting silk from Tonkin's rulers and paying for it in silver. The VOC desire to secure large quantities of silk supplies in this manner encouraged the Trinh bureaucrats towards imposing a monopoly over the sale of this commodity to foreign traders. The conflict over the imposition of a state monopoly over the sale of silk to foreign traders did not extend to the production of silk or the sale of that production to intermediaries.

Silk production in Tonkin, as elsewhere, was influenced by fluctuations in mulberry production caused by poor weather conditions (floods, heavy rains, unusual cold spells and drought) and disease afflicting the silk worms. Whenever mulberry production was low in Tonkin, as in 1646, the VOC recorded price rises in raw silk and silk piecegoods and lower trading profits in those commodities in Japan.[122] Mulberry production recovered in 1647 and a rich silk harvest in Tonkin was reported by the VOC. Several Chinese junks arrived early in the 1647 trading season with 80,000 taels of silver; the Chinese purchased some 400 picols of silk despite the attempt to monopolise the sale price by the capados. This Chinese competition and the capados monopoly attempt increased the price of raw silk and limited the VOC purchases to 643 picols of raw silk and piecegoods with 100,000 guilders left unspent.[123]

Portuguese commercial competition in other commodities in the 1640s was curtailed not by the VOC or Chinese commercial transactions but by shipwreck, as in 1646 when one cho en route from Macao to Tonkin was lost near Hainan island with a cargo valued at 30,000 taels.[124] Portuguese demands upon the Tonkin market also fluctuated; with famine at Macao and in Kwantung province, the Portuguese purchased rice in Tonkin and other markets in the South China Sea in 1648. Rice sold for 20 reals/picol in China and was worth more than silver to the starving Portuguese and Chinese populations. Adverse conditions in the Canton market limited the degree of compliance by the Portuguese to the demands of the Trinh for produce from south China; the Portuguese country traders and Jesuits had been unable to comply in 1648 with Trinh import requests of gold, pearls, and other items which resulted in the Trinh confiscation of one-half of the Portuguese cargo.[125]

Demand for caixas in Tonkin grew in the 1650s; in 1652 the VOC reported that these coins were very scarce and that the Portuguese enjoyed high profits by importing them. In that year, one Portuguese naveta arrived with a cargo of caixas which sold for 20,000 taels. The VOC also learned that the Portuguese trade in caixas was not limited to Tonkin. In 1651 the Portuguese claimed they had exported 120,000 taels worth of caixas to Cochinchina where that cargo sold for 180,000 taels. Impressed by the market opportunities in Tonkin to sell caixas and by the high profits, one VOC merchant suggested to the Company's administrators on Java that Chinese residents at Batavia be employed in minting these coins.[126]

The minting of copper coinage at Batavia, even if it benefited the Company's trade in silk in Tonkin for Japan, was a practice which the *Heeren XVII* in Amsterdam would never have permitted.[127] The VOC was aware of the caixas importance in Tonkin as a medium of commercial exchange and its profitability as a trading commodity. The Company also knew that these coins were available in Japan, but, as Jacob de Keyser described, in 1653 the VOC did not act to secure regular supplies for their trade in Tonkin on account of the Company's capital deficiency.[128]

The VOC complained of variable profits from their Tonkin silk trade in 1652 and for most of the decade. The stabilisation of silk prices in that market was one of the Company's objectives but silver became more plentiful and caixas became scarcer. Prices for silk or any other commodity paid for in silver were subject to strong inflationary pressures on Tonkin in the 1650s.[129] During the months prior to silk being traded at the ports, the exchange rate of caixas to 10 taels of silver in the 1650s was 20,000 caixas to 10 taels; while trading took place, that exchange rate gradually dropped to between 6 and 7,000 caixas to 10 taels.

The demand for and the scarcity of the caixa during the trading seasons kept the price of raw silk high with an adverse impact upon silk piecegoods production;

in 1654, for example, weavers, presumably Chinese but possibly Vietnamese, ceased operations and departed Pho Hien and other markets on account of the high cost of raw silk.[130] Raw silk was contracted in caixas not taels in the countryside; consequently, during the trading season caixas became dearer *vis-à-vis* taels in order to pay for contracted raw silk. When natural disasters occurred in the silk-growing areas, caixas devalued *vis-à-vis* taels in the ports. The fluctuation of the exchange rate of caixas to taels, the VOC maintained in 1656, caused the high price for raw silk and silk piecegoods.[131] In a year with a poor silk harvest, as reported in the trading season of 1660–1, the VOC recorded a 30 per cent devaluation in the caixa to tael exchange rate from 5,700 to 8,500 caixas to 10 taels of silver.[132]

The Portuguese imported caixas into Tonkin in the 1650s. In the five trading seasons between 1656 and 1660, the Jesuits reported that only one out of the six ships returned to Macao safely. Three of these ships were shipwrecked and two captured by Chinese pirates.[133] In 1660, the VOC as a result of the insistence of the resident Japanese merchant Risemondonne, who advised the Company in Tonkin, finally requested a consignment of caixas from Japan.[134] The VOC recorded profits in 1662 of 40 per cent on the sale of caixas in Tonkin.[135] Subsequently, in the late 1660s, the VOC and the Chinese purchased and imported substantial quantities of caixas into Tonkin and glutted that market. The profitability of selling caixas as a commodity was destroyed by VOC and Chinese imports by the early 1670s.[136] The VOC continued to import them in order to keep the purchase price of Tonkin silk low and negotiated in 1675 a proposal with the Trinh that the Company monopolise the importation of caixas.[137]

The Portuguese from Macao ceased to trade at Tonkin on an annual basis in the 1660s. Chinese and VOC competition in the sale of caixas and other ballast commodities had narrowed Portuguese profit margins which contributed to their leaving that market. Conditions at Macao, with the Ch'ing coastal evacuation policy and the official exactions upon the Portuguese community, so incapacitated Portuguese trading capabilities that their voyages to Tonkin became sporadic. After 1673, Portuguese trade at Tonkin from Macao almost totally ceased for the remainder of the seventeenth century.

When surveying their maritime trading opportunities in the South China Sea in the early 1670s, the Portuguese country traders at Macao recognised that their capabilities were limited and restricted by their continued capital impoverishment. After the destruction of almost one-half of their entire fleet at Macao on the orders of Chinese officials in 1667, the Macao-based Portuguese country trading fleet concentrated upon the most profitable markets for the type of commercial activities their capabilities permitted. There were only five major markets in the South China Sea and the Indian Ocean, Siam, Batavia, the Lesser Sunda islands, Bantam and Goa, where the Portuguese from Macao maintained active and regular maritime trading efforts in the 1670s and early 1680s. Other markets, such as Manila and Banjarmassin, were visited by Portuguese country traders shipping from Macao on a sporadic basis.

From Macao's perspective, Portuguese trade at Siam, Batavia, the Lesser Sunda islands, and Goa was restricted by various political and economic factors. At Siam, the Portuguese from Macao were encumbered by the necessity to make repayments to the Siamese Crown for the loan that had been given to Macao in the 1660s for Saldanha's embassy. At Batavia, friction in the relations between the Portuguese at Macao and the VOC clouded their commercial transactions; the Company, to the annoyance of the Portuguese at Macao, permitted Dutch *vrij-burgers* to trade in south China by despatching their ships to the Macao islands and continued to demand Portuguese payment of an inequable toll system at Malacca.

In the Lesser Sunda islands, and at Goa, the Portuguese country traders from Macao confronted the Crown's and other country traders' interests to limit and gain advantage over their trade. For almost the entire 1670s, Portuguese country traders nullified the Crown's attempts to monopolise the sandalwood trade on Solor and Timor. Crown officials at Goa resented the Macao country traders attitudes towards the Crown's authority over trade in the Lesser Sunda islands. Portuguese country traders at Goa were also uncomfortable about the Macao country traders activities on the west coast of India. This resentment and discomfort did not immediately disturb the commercial activities of the Macao country traders at Goa but contributed towards the creation of tension between Goa and Macao that eventually led to restrictions upon Macao's trade on the west coast of India.

BANTAM

Bantam, west of Batavia on Java, offered the best commercial opportunity for the Portuguese country traders from Macao on account of the relative absence of political restrictions to their trade. Bantam offered export commodities at prices and in quantities on which the Portuguese from Macao probably realised higher profits than, for example, the sandalwood from the Lesser Sunda islands and the salt from Goa that was imported into China. Portuguese imports from China found ready purchasers on account of Bantam's policy of attracting all European and Asian merchants to its market – a policy which the VOC resented. The Portuguese not only found purchasers but investors in Macao's trade.

Bantam was the market where for under a dozen years Macao's country traders tried to re-coup their fortunes and entered into trading and freighting arrangements with other European merchants. The acceptance and scale of goods freighted on board the Portuguese country traders ships suggests a new and novel economic role for them in the South China Sea. Based on the available data, the Portuguese country traders from Macao arrived at Bantam in nine out of twelve years from 1670 to 1682. The frequency of Portuguese shipping at Bantam is presented in Table 5.6. Portuguese arrivals from Coromandel, Porto Novo via Madras, belonged to the Portuguese mestiço and Sephardic Jewish communities on that coast.

The Sultan of Bantam and the English ship captain on loan to him from the EIC were responsible for attracting the interest of Portuguese country traders from Macao into this market. After the EIC was expelled from trading at Macassar, the English regrouped at Bantam where they had traded since the early seventeenth

Table 5.6. *Portuguese shipping at Bantam, 1670–82.*

	Arrivals					Departures			
Year	Macao	Timor	Siam	Coromandel (Porto Novo via Madras)	Rimbangh (Java)	Macao	Timor	Batavia	Coromandel (Madras)
1670	2					1			
1673	2					2			
1675	1			2		1	1		
1676	1				1	2			1
1677	2		1			1		1	
1678	3	1				1			
1679		2							
1680	1	1		1					
1681	3	1				3			1
1682	1						1	2	

Source: DRB.

century.[138] In the late 1660s, the EIC supplied the Sultan with some of its employees to man and captain his small merchant fleet. From 1667 to 1672, in particular, the Sultan and other local officials such as the shahbandar were involved in despatching a series of trading ventures to Macao, Manila and Tonkin in order to dispose of the surplus of pepper at Bantam.[139]

The transactions by the Sultan's ships, trading *sub-rosa* with the Chinese, Portuguese and other Europeans near Macao, were substantial if the amounts of pepper traded is used as an indicator. Their arrival and activities as well as those by the Dutch vrij-burgers, stimulated and re-enforced Chinese merchants and officials at Canton to arrange for supplies and participate in this illegal trade. By 1671, probably through the official influence of Shang K'o-hsi at Canton, Chinese export commodities were in plentiful supply and modestly priced for the traders active in the Macao islands.[140]

With the supply of Chinese export commodities restored to the Portuguese country traders at Macao, one of the limitations upon the expansion of their trade was the amount of finance and credit they could arrange. The absence of large amounts of capital at Macao also influenced the types of commodities from the Canton market available to the Portuguese country traders to purchase and export on a large scale in the South China Sea and the Indian Ocean. The arriving Portuguese ships from Macao at Bantam were laden with large consignments of ballast cargoes along with reduced amounts of the more expensive and, generally, more profitable items. The Portuguese country traders from Macao exported the more profitable items such as raw silk, silk piecegoods, musk and gold, along with the different ballast cargoes such as radix China and Chinese household items like iron pans. Three unusual Chinese export commodities aided Portuguese trade at Bantam, zinc and porcelain as ballast cargoes and, more controversial, tea which was to dominate Europe's direct trade with China in the eighteenth and nineteenth centuries.

In 1676 and 1678, two out of four Portuguese country traders' ships from Macao arrived at Bantam with cargoes including a total of 12,664 pounds (avoirdupois) of tea.[141]

That amount of tea was double the quantity of tea that was imported by the EIC into England from China in six years from 1669–82 and slightly larger than the amount imported by the EIC in 1685.[142] The Portuguese from Macao were obviously involved in the early dissemination of tea as a commercial commodity throughout the South China Sea. The Portuguese were overtaken as suppliers of that commodity to the South China Sea and Indian Ocean markets by the Companies and other European country traders, as sizeable markets for the tea were created in Europe in the late seventeenth and early eighteenth centuries.

The Portuguese from Macao, at Bantam and elsewhere, Batavia, Malacca and various ports in the Indian Ocean, were involved in selling sizeable quantities of Chinese zinc and porcelain to supply demand in India for these commodities. The zinc they sold was purchased to be used directly and as an alloy in the minting of non-precious coinage, such as the *bazaruco* in the Estado da India. It was also employed in the manufacture of bullets, cooking utensils, and certain types of statuary.[143]

Chinese porcelain, coarse and fine, was found at certain ports in India in sizeable quantities for use by the European and indigenous communities; the Portuguese had supplied small amounts of fine China to aristocratic families and a tiny market in Portugal since the sixteenth century. From the 1670s onwards, after the resumption of large-scale supplies, the Portuguese exported fine and coarse porcelain from China to various South China Sea and Indian Ocean markets. Although coarse porcelain was purchased by the Chinese, European and indigenous populations at Bantam, the export of fine porcelain to Europe from supplies acquired in India and, more commonly, directly in China grew in the late seventeenth and, particularly, in the eighteenth century.

At Bantam, the Portuguese from Macao sold those Chinese commodities and purchased, primarily, pepper, silver, salt and *arreca*. The total amounts and values of these purchases were unquantified in the VOC's records. Pepper, salt and arreca were ballast cargoes; pepper and silver were the commodities that were in greater demand by the Portuguese on account of their necessity for capital and the better market for pepper in south China. Salt and arreca were purchased in quantity; the actual purpose arreca served in China is unascertainable but it appears that it was not of any great importance. Salt, in the sizeable quantities the Portuguese country traders imported into Macao in the last quarter of the seventeenth century from Bantam and Goa, probably had a reasonable but small profit margin in China. The Portuguese, it is speculated, were involved in an arrangement, legal or otherwise, formal or informal, with Chinese salt officials for its importation.

The Portuguese country traders from Macao had entered into trading and freighting arrangements with other European merchants at Bantam. The extent to which these arrangements arose, and when, is impossible to calculate or date with precision. Later, in the eighteenth century, the Portuguese country traders from Macao also participated in this practice in their relations with European Company and country traders in the Indian Ocean. The specific evidence to support this assertion rests upon the VOC's investigation of one of its servants' involvement with the Sultan of Bantam in the piracy of a Portuguese country trader ship from Macao, the *Santo António*, at Bantam in early 1682.[144]

The VOC was implicated in this incident on account of the Dutch nationality of Jacob Jansz de Roy and in Europe as a result of French, English and Portuguese protests. While in the service of the Sultan of Bantam in early 1682, de Roy pirated the *Santo António*; he transferred part of the confiscated cargo to Bantam and the rest on board the VOC ship, *Roemerswael*, to Batavia. The cargo consisted of gold, silk, silver, diamonds, pearls and other items, divided into consignments to Portuguese, English and French merchants. The French continued for quite some years afterwards to demand the restitution of 18,000 guilders, their estimate of the value of their consignment, from the VOC. The VOC rejected responsibility for restitution, imprisoned de Roy for a short time, and then re-instated him into the Company.

The VOC for other more important economic and administrative reasons, sought to find an excuse to exclude the Portuguese from Macao, and other Europeans from trading at Bantam. The Portuguese and other foreign merchants' presence unsettled the VOC's dominant commercial position throughout the Indonesian archipelago. In 1682, the Sultan Aboe'l Nassar appealed for VOC aid and intervention in Bantam's internal politics; the Company quickly responded and provided the requested aid. In return, the Sultan ordered the Portuguese, the EIC and all other foreign merchants to leave Bantam.[145]

With the closure of Bantam's market, only one non-VOC controlled pepper market remained in the Indonesian archipelago. There were portions of the South China Sea that were administered or influenced by the VOC and had their primary commercial crops engrossed by the Company. In contrast, with the establishment of a Manchu peace, south China entered on the first half of the eighteenth century a period of unparalleled prosperity in its early modern history.

Chinese junks came to dominate the inter-regional maritime trade and the VOC as a result of its political control over the major centres of production dominated the supply of produce from the South China Sea for the China market. Macao did not enjoy the prosperity brought about by the Manchu peace. The Portuguese from Macao were left in the quandary of determining in which markets to compete and which commodities to trade in order to survive.

6

COUNTRY TRADERS
AND THE SEARCH FOR MARKETS

The Portuguese country traders' search for markets focused, in the late seventeenth century, on the few non-VOC-controlled markets in the South China Sea. Manila's market offered some opportunity but the Portuguese could not displace the Chinese junks. Portuguese trade on Timor in the early eighteenth century suffered from the over-cutting and depletion of sandalwood stocks, Chinese competition and the Batavia market becoming a centre for the sale of sandalwood to Chinese junks. Chinese maritime trading competition became more intense after 1684, which was related to the revival of, and stability provided by, the Ch'ing for seaborne trade in south China.

BANJARMASIN

Banjarmasin in the late seventeenth century temporarily offered some enterprising Portuguese Crown officials and country traders the opportunity to monopolise pepper supplies in quantities that were large enough to command significant portions of the market and compete against the European and Chinese suppliers of that spice in south China.

The sultanate of Banjarmasin was located in the south-east of Borneo. Two main groups lived in the area claimed by the Sultan (or *Panambahan*) of Banjarmasin, the valley or lowland people, the *Banjarese*; and upland people, the *Biajus* or *Njadjus*.[1] Banjarese society was part of the Malay world and they claimed to be the descendants of the original Javanese inhabitants and foreign immigrants on Borneo; Biajus were the aboriginal Dayak tribes of south-east Borneo whose mobile village life co-existed with the extension of Banjarese political control. The Banjarese settled in the early seventeenth century on the banks of the Barito river and extended their political power to areas between the Barito and the Antassankween rivers and neighbouring districts.

By the mid seventeenth century, Banjarese settlements and power extended to areas of the Upper Negara to Kota Waringin and Sampit. Although the Banjarese were not inclined to any great activity in agriculture, the sultanate cultivated pepper on a sizeable basis for commercial purposes in Palau Laut and Molukko. Pepper was also available to the Banjarese from the Biajus, who participated in pepper cultivation as *ladang* (shifting dry cultivating) planters. Pepper was the basis for the prosperity of the sultanate.

In theory, the sultan was the supreme ruler of the land, supported by *pengerans* (princes or chieftains) who ruled over territorial units normally granted to them by the sultan. There were other social levels: officials, and slaves. At the harbours, where trade was transacted, there were small groups of foreigners from which a shahbandar was selected to collect port duties. In practice, the sultan often had to contend with rival pengerans who sought to depose him and support other members of the sultan's family or others in that quest. Fundamental for the maintenance of Banjarese society was its control of all internal and external commercial transactions with the Biajus.

From 1637 until 1659, Banjarmasin's relations with its neighbours were dominated by Mataram, which the sultanate recognised as its suzerain and paid tribute. Attempts to recover Mataram's control over Banjarmasin were made and failed in the 1660s; the threat to Banjarmasin disintegrated with the rapid decline in the power of that Javan state in the 1670s.[2]

Not all of the threats to the sovereignty of the sultanate were removed; the VOC had demonstrated an earlier interest in monopolising the pepper trade at Banjarmasin but were evicted in 1638 by a pro-Mataram faction among the sultan's advisers and pengerans who envisaged greater economic benefit by an open pepper market than an exclusive arrangement with the Company. Despite demand for pepper by foreign and indigenous traders at Macassar, Banjarmasin's pepper cultivation appears to have expanded slowly throughout the early seventeenth century because of limitations on its cultivation caused by indigenous political and commercial uncertainties. By 1660, the Company faced increased demand in Europe and the amounts of pepper from Palembang and west Sumatra were reduced which meant that they had to find additional supplies.

The VOC returned to Banjarmasin in 1660 to secure the sultanate's pepper production by a monopoly contract. Although the Dutch became embroiled in an internal political struggle over the succession of Sultan Ratu by Sultan Dipati Anom, they negotiated the contract.[3] But, the Company was unable to secure the pepper as the Biajus proved reluctant to supply pepper to the Banjarese and the pengerans became involved in a smuggling trade with Macassar and Portuguese country traders as a result of the VOC refusal to advance money to them. In 1667, the VOC once again abandoned its trading efforts at Banjarmasin.

The interest of the Portuguese country traders from Macao in Banjarmasin stemmed from their involvement in the pepper trade in the Indonesian archipelago for the China market. To supply that market, Macassar and other indigenous traders succeeded in locating and transporting pepper to Macassar where it was purchased by the Portuguese and exported to Macao. Chinese junks at Batavia also supplied China's demand for pepper in the late 1650s and very early 1660s.[4]

Portuguese country traders from Macao obtained pepper from Banjarmasin through other merchants and by trading directly at Martapoura in 1659 and 1660.[5] After the VOC's successful attack on Macassar in 1660 and the expulsion of most of the Portuguese community, the Portuguese country traders from Macao regrouped and in 1662 despatched a naveta from that city with the captain as the Senado da Camara's envoy to the Sultan of Banjarmasin.[6] No reference to the explicit objectives of this mission survive but the Portuguese were probably in search of improving relations and expanding their 'smuggling' trade with the pengerans. Whether the city of Macao's emissary was rebuked or not is not recorded in VOC sources; Ch'ing officials in south China initiated implementation of their coastal evaluation policy at this time and Portuguese efforts at Banjarmasin from Macao suffered from the Ch'ing officials' inadvertent disruption of their activities.

The recovery of Macao's interest in Banjarmasin occurred in the mid 1670s as the Dutch vrij-burgers', Chinese and other foreign merchants' trade in the Macao islands heralded a modest upturn in maritime trade for Kwantung province. The Portuguese required a source of pepper that would be capable of supplying relatively large quantities of that commodity which would permit Portuguese merchants to compete against the intrusion by foreign and Chinese merchants upon their economic position in south China. Macao's country traders re-initiated their trade at Banjarmasin with annual trading voyages; by 1677, the VOC began to report their arrival and activity at Banjarmasin.[7]

Banjarmasin produced around 3,000 picols of pepper annually in the late 1670s and early 1680.[8] In 1678, the VOC reported that the Canton market's annual demand for pepper was 5,000 picols; the Dutch also reported to the Heeren XVII that in order to secure enough additional pepper for the China trade, since Jambi's production was down, the Company decided to re-establish its trade at Banjarmassin.[9] The Portuguese from Macao were already trading when the VOC arrived at Banjarmasin in 1679 intent upon securing that trade and ousting Macao's country traders from that market.

The ambitions of the Portuguese country traders involved in this market were greater than the VOC at first imagined. The Company learnt that on account of an internal power struggle, Sultan Dipati Anom was challenged by his nephews, Sultan Ratu's two sons, Suria Angsa and Suria Negara, and Portuguese aid had been enlisted by the insurgents against Sultan Dipati Anom.[10] The Portuguese from Macao were embarked upon their first attempt to establish their monopoly over Banjarmasin's pepper production.

The Portuguese policy of intervention and supporting Sultan Dipati Anom's overthrow was eventually successful with Suria Angsa becoming Sultan and the Portuguese obtaining commercial privileges. These commercial privileges did not amount to a monopoly but sufficiently upset the VOC, which was already displeased with Banjarmasin's interminable political unrest, that the Company ceased to trade at Banjarmasin in 1681; the VOC was convinced that it could secure additional pepper stocks from increased production at Palembang and Bantam.[11]

The Estado da India and some Portuguese country traders at Macao were not satisfied with the commercial privileges they had acquired at Banjarmasin. During the administration of D. Rodrigo da Costa as Viceroy of the Estado da India (1686–90), the Crown proposed to administer a factory and establish a fortress in that sultanate. Two Crown appointees to establish this factory, José Pinheiro and Bernardo da Silva, arrived at Macao from the Estado da India by late 1689; this

Crown attempt to participate in the pepper trade came at a very inopportune moment in the judgement of the Portuguese country traders within the Senado da Camara.

Demand for pepper in China was growing as sales at Batavia to the Portuguese and Chinese in 1685 averaged an estimated 5,500 picols and in 1692 totalled 13,561 picols as shown in Table 6.12. Banjarmasin's production at the same time was around 10,000 picols per year.[12] For the Portuguese country traders, the customs duties collected from their ships from Banjarmasin financed Macao's fragile cash flow and the trade itself was considered vital to the survival of the city.[13] Any attempt to interfere with their trade by the Crown, Chinese junk traders, or Spanish merchants were resented and some vigorously resisted for a short time in the early 1690s.

From 1688 to 1689, a group including the city of Macao's capitão-geral, Andre Coelho Vieira, and several Portuguese country traders who had experience in trading at Banjarmasin, Manoel de Araujo Garces and others, supported a project to stabilise and to circumvent the sultan's and Banjarese control over the supply of pepper by contacting and dealing directly with the Biajus. De Araujo Garces was successful in arranging such an agreement with the Biajus; his group had supported the establishment of a Catholic missionary presence led by Father António Ventimiglia as a ploy in order to facilitate his negotiations.[14] By 1690, that group had reconsidered its programme and initiated its support of the Crown's monopoly project.

In 1690, as a result of negotiations between Manoel de Araujo Garces and the Sultan of Banjarmasin, the Portuguese Crown and country traders believed that a contract existed in practice which acknowledged their monopoly over the sultanates pepper.[15] Both the Crown and different groups of country traders were anxious to implement a monopoly but differed as to the necessity for the establishment of an actual fortress and a physical presence on a permanent basis. As the Senado da Camara records reveal, passive resistance to the Crown administrators' plans for a fortress was focused at Macao.[16] From 1690 to 1692, the Portuguese Crown and Macao's country traders tried to enforce the monopoly on Banjarmasin.

The Portuguese monopoly was quickly tested; in 1691–2, several Chinese junks and two Spanish ships from Manila sailed to Banjarmasin. The Portuguese had sent four ships from Macao and were upset with the Sultan's and the pengerans attitudes towards the monopoly. After failing to secure their compliance with the contract, the Portuguese attacked the Chinese junks, and, later, the Spanish ships under the command of General António Nieto.[17] The repercussions of the heavy-handed Portuguese actions were felt in their trade in 1692 as the Sultan and his supporters stopped the Portuguese loading their pepper.

Without resources at Macao or political leverage in Banjarmasin, in the early 1690s, the Portuguese Crown and country traders from Macao were prevented from trading for pepper at the only major non-VOC-controlled port in the Indonesian archipelago. Banjarmasin continued to court different traders, Chinese junks,

English Company and country traders as well as the VOC. Its average annual pepper production rose to 19–25,000 picols in the early 1700s and hovered below 20,000 picols in the late 1710s to 1720s.[18] The English followed the Portuguese monopoly experience with an attempt of their own in the early 1700s with a similar lack of success.[19] The VOC returned to trade for pepper at Banjarmasin in 1711–12 in order to enlarge exports to Europe; by the late 1720s, the Company once again returned to trade as Bantam's and Palembang's pepper production failed to meet European demand.[20] From 1726 to 1747, the VOC retired from the Banjarmasin market on account of overwhelming competition from Chinese junks which the Chinese maintained until the Company finally and firmly established its monopoly in 1747.[21]

Denied a monopoly on Banjarmasin's pepper production by indigenous political and military hostility, the Portuguese from Macao lost the one commercial opportunity in the South China Sea that, in theory, offered them some prospect of relief and modest prosperity in south China. After their failure at Banjarmasin, the Portuguese country traders at Macao reverted to using commercial practices that would keep their ships sailing but only offered low returns on their invested capital. The freighting and consignment of foreign merchants' goods on board a Portuguese country trader's ship was one such commercial practice. Although they employed that practice in their trade with the English, French, Armenians and other merchants in the Indian Ocean, the Portuguese had particularly startling and successful results with it with Cantonese quevees in their trade at Batavia.

BATAVIA

The interest of Portuguese country traders from Macao in the Batavia market developed gradually; some of the traders were related to those merchants who in the mid seventeenth century had traded with the Dutch on Java and since the late 1660s had sent one ship on an annual basis to trade. Macao's interest in the Batavia market was to become one of near dependence as other markets in the South China Sea were closed to the Portuguese.

Yet the Portuguese involvement in the Batavia market had an additional significance in the development of China's maritime trade. The growth of regional economies and provincial cities in south China, which in the early Ch'ing thrived on maritime trade, was concentrated on the Fukien and Chekiang coast at Amoy and Ning-po. The Portuguese from Macao, as compared with the Chinese, were also fundamental participants in the Batavia trade. The Portuguese at Macao, by acting as carriers of Chinese merchants' cargo and whose trade itself was an adjunct of the Canton market, along with Canton's participation in the Batavia market, demonstrate that claims of Amoy or Ning-po maritime trading and commercial superiority are dubious in one major market in the South China Sea in the early decades of the eighteenth century.

Portuguese trade at Batavia from Macao and the rest of the Estado da India was influenced by three factors. The first was the resolution or diminution of outstanding friction points in the political and economic relations between the Portuguese and the VOC. The second was the result of the revolution of and the fluctuation in Sino-Portuguese commercial relations. The third was the decline of Portuguese and Chinese trade at Batavia towards 1730 as a result of two VOC policies, the re-inauguration of direct VOC trade with China and the Company's controlling the purchase and selling price on imports from and exports destined for China.

Friction between the Portuguese and the VOC existed over a wide variety of issues and incidents in their political and economic relations from 1684 until 1693. Although the Portuguese from Macao traded at Batavia, the VOC's expulsion of foreign traders at Bantam in 1682, the promotion of its and Dutch vrij-burgers' trade on the south China coast through the 1680s and the last diplomatic attempt to improve Sino-VOC relations with the embassy of Vincent Paats to Peking in 1685 to 1687 irritated the Portuguese at Macao; they worked surreptitiously with the aid of the Jesuits to thwart and limit the growth of Dutch trade.[22]

The Portuguese were not blameless in the creation of friction between Macao and Batavia; based on correspondence and Dutch reports the capitão-geral, António Coehlho Vieira, and the Senado da Camara incited Chinese officials to take harsher attitudes towards the Dutch vrij-burger trade and their evasion of paying tolls to the hoppo at Macao.[23] Those Portuguese officials, also, refused to restitute either monies advanced for the payment of a Portuguese country traders' ransom, as with the Senado da Camara emissary to Johor in 1685, or amounts loaned at Batavia to Portuguese merchants from Macao but reneged on repayment. The Portuguese treatment of Chinese shipping and the whole concept of the Macao country traders' attempt to establish a monopoly at Banjarmasin in 1691 was anathema to the Company.[24]

In 1690, the Governor-General and the Council of the Indies suggested in their letters to the Heeren XVII a modification in the policy of trading directly with China by Company or vrij-burger shipping. The reason for their reconsideration was the failure in their recent diplomatic initiative at Peking to obtain favourable trading conditions for the VOC. The Company also experienced a shortage of ships to maintain the China trade and argued that they could buy Chinese produce more profitably from the Portuguese from Macao and the Chinese at Batavia than by sending Dutch ships to China; the VOC also argued that it could control the prices on the goods sold to the Portuguese and Chinese at Batavia and would be able to charge as much as they sold for in China.[25] By 1693, the Heeren XVII agreed with the Company's modification in its trade with China; the outstanding minor incidents that marred Portuguese–Dutch relations were pursued with less vigour by Batavia's authorities as the Portuguese and Chinese trade was the VOC's mainstay for the supply of Chinese produce for the inter-Asian and European markets.[26]

With the VOC's dependence upon Portuguese and Chinese ships for Chinese supplies at Batavia, the Portuguese at Macao and the rest of the Estado da India regained lost confidence and expressed their displeasure with the Company's policy

Table 6.1. *Tolls paid by Portuguese shipping at Malacca, 1684–1704.*
(All values in rijksdaalers)

Year	Value	Year	Value	Year	Value
1684 }	3,225	1691	2,215	1698	655
1685 }		1692	1,415	1699	180
1686	2,350	1693	915	1700	1,190
1687	2,425	1694	1,450	1701	680
1688	1,820	1695	1,450	1702	790
1689	1,190	1696	885	1703	250
1690	1,975	1697	910	1704	210
				Total	26,180

Sources: ARA, VOC 1403/KA 1292 to VOC 2570/KA 2462 and *GM.*

of charging tolls and duties on their shipping at Malacca at higher rates than other European shipping. The initiative for this Portuguese protest came from the Estado da India in 1695, as suggested in a letter from the Viceroy to the Governor of Malacca which requested the exemption of Portuguese Crown ships from the payment of anchorage fees.[27] Table 6.1 reveals the tolls paid by Portuguese shipping at Malacca 1684–1704.

All Portuguese shipping continued to pay these tolls but by early 1708, the Portuguese Crown and country traders successfully refused to pay the Company's passage and anchorage fees.[28] In 1715, the VOC had to explain to the Heeren XVII that the Portuguese from Macao and the rest of the Estado da India were avoiding Malacca in protest of the VOC's fee policy; in 1725, Batavia requested that the Senado da Camara accept responsibility for payment of anchorage and passage fees that the Company had been unable to collect from Portuguese shipping from 1708 until 1724.[29] The Senado da Camara rejected the VOC's claim.

The Macao country traders' practice of carrying freight on their ships from Canton's merchants for the Manila trade was common in the early seventeenth century. By the end of the century, this practice was growing between the Portuguese country traders at Macao and Canton's quevees, but only for the Batavia trade. The manipulation of the rates on Macao's customs duties in 1689 by Cantonese merchants was not an isolated occurrence but handled as the individual circumstances warranted.

In 1689, a prominent Portuguese country trader and ship-owner at Macao, Pero Vaz de Siqueira, agreed to lend two of his ships to trade in freight at Batavia to two Chinese merchants known to the Portuguese as Guia and Lingua residing at Canton.[30] After the freight contract was agreed upon and apparently after the departure of the two ships, one of which was *São Pedro e São Paulo*, the two Chinese merchants visited Macao and requested reductions in the city's customs rates from the Senado da Camara and threatened that unless they received them they would advise their agent in Batavia to transfer their purchased merchandise to a Chinese junk for the return voyage to China. They wanted reduction in Macao's customs rates from 10 to 6 per cent on coarse goods, from 8 to 4 per cent on fine goods, and from 3 to 2 per cent on silver. The Senado da Camara, in the absence of any option except for Macaos ships to return without cargo and for the city not to receive any revenue at all from customs duties on two empty ships, agreed to reduce its customs duties rates.[31]

Sino-Portuguese commercial relations continued to evolve on a basis of inequality as Canton's quevees and Chinese officials recognised the Portuguese country traders reliance upon Chinese credit and investment. In 1705, several Cantonese merchants intended to freight their goods on board the *Jesus, Maria e José*, which was owned by the Macao country trader, Francisco Loureiro de Carvalho. In this instance, the Senado da Camara conceded to these Cantonese merchants a reduction of its customs duties rates from 2 to 1 per cent on silver; and for the coarse and fine goods, the Portuguese owner and other Macao investors were to arrange the rate independently in negotiations together with the Chinese. De Carvalho was informed that with this concession the Senado da Camara was not abrogating its intention to collect customs from this voyage at the usual rates for the Portuguese-owned merchandise.[32]

With the imposition of the Ch'ing ban on overseas trade in 1717 until its official retraction in 1727, Macao's trade at Batavia experienced a major change with regard to the Portuguese country traders' ability to extract favourable and preferred treatment from Canton's merchants. The reason for the change in the treatment of the Portuguese by Canton's merchants was on account of their newly developed total reliance upon Macao's country traders to carry their freight to Batavia. Dutch records reveal that Chinese junk activity at Batavia was never totally extinguished; in 1721, for example, one junk sailed from Shanghai after bribing local officials and after the death of the K'ang-hsi emperor, the number of junks returning to trade rose. Chinese junk-owning residents at Batavia as well as Chinese merchants from Canton, Amoy and Ning-po were involved in evading the ban by trading via Tonkin and Cochinchina, locations in addition to Japan that were excluded in the original edict. Canton's merchants, it appears as a result of Ch'ing official surveillance, did not avail themselves to any significant degree of these opportunities for the evasion of the ban. The Dutch were also dependent upon the Portuguese for their supplies of tea from China for the European market.[33]

These were heady years for Macao's country traders as they flocked to Batavia where they purchased ships to expand their fleet's total cargo capacity. At Canton, they demanded and received exorbitant freight rates from Chinese merchants. The purchase of some of the ships by the Portuguese was made possible, it was claimed, by capital advanced by Cantonese merchants, some of whom had moved to Macao.

In 1721, the city of Macao set freight rates, in particular those for tea, for Chinese merchants and the VOC at nine *pardãos*/picol. Through the intervention of the VOC, an attempt by the Chinese to force the Portuguese to lower their rates to four paradãos/picol was met by an icy refusal at Macao. The EIC supercargoes reported in 1721–2 that the Chinese merchants at Canton were complaining of having losses in their tea trade and that the losses would continue even if the Portuguese freighted their tea free to Batavia. Despite some attempt to fix these rates, the Chinese were subject to price discrimination by the Portuguese country traders regardless of Crown and Senado da Camara orders for them not to charge the Chinese a higher rate than that paid by Portuguese inhabitants of Macao.

During the last few years of the ban, the system of selecting Macao's country traders' shipping for the Batavia trade permitted too many Portuguese ships into this market especially after the Chinese merchants evasion efforts proved successful. With the revival of fully fledged Chinese competition in the Batavia trade, relations between Macao's country traders and Canton's merchants returned to the *status quo ante*. Without Chinese investment and freighting arrangements and although they despatched more ships, the fortunes of Macao's country traders, as one Portuguese account described, reverted to having only sufficient capital to outfit and invest in cargoes for two ships.[34]

SHIPS, JUNKS, *CHALUPAS* AND *WANKANS*

An accurate reconstruction of the numbers, frequency, ship types and their tonnage employed by all foreign, including Portuguese and Chinese, shipping calling and trading at Batavia is possible through the careful compilation and its inclusion in annual reports to the Heeren XVII by the Governor-General and the Council of the Indies of the VOC. The VOC's records provide a rare insight into the shipping and commercial movements in one of the South China Sea's major markets in the late seventeenth and throughout the entire eighteenth century.

Prior to 1716, the Company's administrators recorded the arrival, departure and other pertinent reports and letters concerning foreign shipping in a regular fashion with some inconsistencies in the amount of detail included in the *generale missieven* (an annual report of the Company's trade) and in various *dagh-registers* (day registers). Tables 6.2 and 6.3. reveal the frequency of Portuguese and Chinese shipping at Batavia, from 1684–1714 using these sources. From 1715 until 1792, the VOC compiled detailed lists of all recorded foreign shipping movement at Batavia almost without interruption.[35]

Similar Portuguese records for Macao no longer exist and as a consequence the Dutch materials are of an added importance as they identify Portuguese country traders' ships from Macao, their captains, sometimes their owners, their size, complement, armament, sailing time and movement from a previous port of embarkation. Comparable information in Chinese records at Canton, Amoy or Ning-po no longer survive.

The Portuguese employed two major ship types in their trade. The most commonly used ship type among the Portuguese country traders from Macao were ships generally and poorly described only as *barcos* or *navios*; these ships ranged in size from around 150 or 200 to 400 tons. The second ship type was the *chalupa* (sloop); these sloops were from around 50 to 150 tons. The Chinese employed three general ship types. The junk was by far the most important; a junk variety, the *wankan*, and curiously, a ship type cryptically noted as a sloop were also mentioned. The junks usually ranged in size from 120 to 220 tons with a few of 300, 360 and 500 tons. Sloop sizes were highly variable with many of the smaller ones being 50 to 60 tons but the larger and more frequently used were 120 to 200 tons; wankans ranged from a mere 30 to 150 tons.

The VOC did not specifically list the total foreign shipping activity at Batavia until 1715; by integrating information on the number of Chinese arrivals, a composite list was constructed of the total foreign shipping activity at Batavia from 1715 until 1754 and is presented in Table 6.4. By foreign shipping the VOC included all of the European Company shipping that called at Batavia, en route from Europe to China. The EIC dominated with a few French, Ostend and Swedish ships being registered. The English Crown also sent a few warships but the numbers of English country traders shipping were more numerous than the Crown's, but not the Company's ships. The size of the English country trader vessel also tended to be smaller than the Company's, whose ships reached 500 tons at this time, but compared equally to the Portuguese country traders vessels.

The foreign shipping that traded at Batavia from China and the South China Sea were, in the order of the magnitude of the number of vessels registered over the period 1715 to 1754, Chinese (499), Portuguese (255), Spanish (29), Armenian (16), Muslim (11) and Siamese (3). The Spanish and Armenian vessels were primarily employed in trade between Manila and Batavia. By Muslim vessels, there is some confusion as to what the VOC meant; most of these were indigenous Indian owned and operated ships from the Coromandel coast and Surat to whom the Company had given passes to trade, and were involved, it appears, in trade from India via Malacca and Batavia to Manila. The few Siamese Crown trading vessels that frequented Batavia carried diplomatic envoys or made exploratory commercial forays which they did not maintain.

The Portuguese and the Chinese were easily the two most active trading groups at Batavia from 1684 until 1754; the frequency of the arrivals and departures of both groups by port of embarkation and intended debarkation was reconstructed for 1684 to 1714 in Table 6.2 and 6.3 and reproduced from 1715 to 1754 in Table 6.5 and 6.6. The vast majority of the Portuguese ships were owned and based at Macao. They arrived at Batavia from Macao, traded and returned to south China; a few sailed on from Batavia to Timor, where they traded and returned via Batavia to Macao. There were instances of Portuguese Crown ships calling at Batavia en route to Timor from the Estado da India and returning before leaving for Goa in the late 1710s to the late 1720s, which was connected to the suppression of anti-Portuguese disturbances in the Lesser Sunda islands. A few Portuguese Company East Indiamen stopped at Batavia en route to China; some small Portuguese mestiço-owned ships from Timor along with a few indigenous Indian owned ships flying the Portuguese flag from Surat also frequented Batavia.

One of the most important exceptions to the general pattern of Macao country-trader shipping dominating Portuguese trade at Batavia was the arrival of Portuguese country-trader shipping from Siam via Manila and return in the late

The Survival of Empire

Table 6.2. *Portuguese shipping arrivals*

Year	Macao	Canton	Manila	Siam	Timor	Borneo	Banjar-masin	Malacca	Junk-ceylon	Pegu	S. Thomé	Goa	Surat	Lisbon	Na	Annual total
							Arrivals									
1684	3															3
1685	1														1	2
1686	1			1												2
1687	3															3
1688	3				1		1	2								7
1689	2															2
1690	2															2
1691	2															2
1692	1															1
1693	1															1
1694	1															1
1695																—
1696																—
1697																—
1698	1		1	2												4
1699																—
1700	2		1	4												7
1701				4												4
1702	1			4	1											6
1703																—
1704	1		1		1											3
1705	3			1	1										1	6
1706	2															2
1707	4			1	2							1				8
1708	4		2	1	1							1				9
1709	2		1									1				4
1710	1		1	1	3							1			1	8
1711	2			2	2							1		1	1	9
1712	2		1	2	1											6
1713	2			3	3							1				9
1714					2											2
Total	47		8	26	18		1	2				6		1	4	113

Symbols: [*] for ships that record this port as port of call with * as final destination.
Sources: GM, and ARA, VOC 1409/KA 1298 to VOC 1848/KA 1740.

1690s and the 1710s. There is evidence to suggest that those ship-owners were Portuguese residents or former residents at Macao who were temporarily living as expatriates in Siam that had joined other ship-owners from the long-established Portuguese community which had not been expelled in 1688.[36] The other exception was Macao-based Portuguese country traders shipping which arrived at Batavia from China via Manila and returned to China via Manila in the mid 1710s to the late 1730s.

and departures at Batavia, 1684–1714.

	Departures											
Macao	Canton	Manila	Siam	Timor	Borneo & Banjarmasin	Pegu	S. Thomé	Porto Novo	Madras	Goa	Lisbon	Annual total
1		1										2
1												1
3												3
3												3
1												1
	[1*]	2*										2
	[1*]	4*										4
		4										4
		5										5
2			1				1					4
1												1
1			1		2				1			5
3			1		3				1			8
2			1									3
4			1	1					2			8
2	[2*]	4*	3									9
2	[1*]	3*							1			6
3	[3*]	3*	1	1					1			9
29	[8*]	29	11	2			1		6			78

Chinese maritime trading activity at Batavia from 1684 until 1754 was dominated by the shipping which arrived from and departed for Amoy, Canton and Ning-po. The total available number of arrivals were 853, Amoy (385), Canton (127) and Ning-po (119). Some 14 junks from Shanghai also traded there but their voyages were concentrated over 1722 to 1724 during the Ch'ing ban on foreign trade. Ships from several non-Chinese ports augmented these numbers; Chinese vessels arrived from Tonkin (68) on a regular basis from 1701 until 1741. Chinese junks from Japan (11), some of which were owned by Chinese residents at Batavia, arrived irregularly from 1686 until 1714; Chinese arrivals from Manila (9) were very erratic but

Table 6.3. *Chinese shipping at Batavia, 1684–1714. (No data available for departures)*

Year											Arrivals										
	Canton	Amoy	Ning-po	Shanghai	Hocksiew	Foochow	Munsoe	Toansiew	Tsiantsia	Tsansiew	Tangtsiao	Panhaii	Japan	Manila	Tonkin	Cochinchina	Cambodia	Riow	Samarang	N.a.	Annual Total
1684													2	2							4
1685		6											2								8
1686		9											1		1						11
1687	1	8			1										2					2	14
1688	1	9													4						14
1689	1	9				1														1	12
1690																				10	10
1691																					—
1692																				16	16
1693	3																			18	21
1694																				4	4
1695																					—
1696																					—
1697	3	8	1																	2	14
1698	2	3																		1	6
1699	2	10	5																		17
1700	2		5																	3	10
1701															2					17	19
1702	1	4	4										1		2						12
1703	3	7	5											3	3					3	24
1704	3	2	5												1					3	14
1705	3			3																3	9
1706	4	7	1										1	1	3					3	20
1707	1	4	2										1	1							9
1708	1	1	4											1							7
1709	4	5					1								1					1	12
1710		5	1																	2	8
1711	2	5	2										1		1						11
1712	4	3	3										1		2	1				3	17
1713	3	5	4										1		1					1	15
1714	2	3	4												2					5	16
Total	46	113	46	3	1	1	1						11	8	25	1				98	354

Sources: GM and ARA, VOC 1311/KA 1329, VOC 1337/KA 1355 and VOC 1414/KA 1432 and VOC 1444/KA 1222

Table 6.4. *Foreign shipping arrivals at Batavia, 1715–54.*

Year	Chinese	Siamese	Armenian	Muslim	Portuguese	Spanish	English	French	Ostend	Swedish	Annual total
1715	18	1			9		6	1			35
1716	15		1		5		9	1	1		32
1717	16		1		9		2	2	1		31
1718			2		8	1	5	1			17
1719	2		1		13		10		1		27
1720	1		1		8	1	4				15
1721	3		1		13	1	15				33
1722	11		2		15	1	14		2		45
1723	24		1		10		6				41
1724	17				10		7				34
1725	13			1	12		8				34
1726	16		1		9		5	1			32
1727	19				13		3				35
1728	18				9		6				33
1729	18		2	1	8		4				33
1730	23		1		10		6	1			41
1731	20				10	1	7				38
1732	20				4		7	1			32
1733	17				8		1				26
1734	14				6		3				23
1735	21		2	1	4		4				32
1736	15				4	1	6				26
1737	19				2	2	7				30
1738	24				3	3	7				37
1739	14				3	3	4				24
1740	14				5	2	7				28
1741	13				5	3	5				26
1742	na				3	3	6	1			13
1743	5				6	1	6				18
1744	14			1	7	1	10			1	34
1745	9			1	4		18				32
1746	12			1	5		7				25
1747	8				3		18				29
1748	14			1	2		7				24
1749	10				2		11				23
1750	na	1		1	2	1	6				11
1751	8				2	1	9				20
1752	na	1		1			4				6
1753	7			1	2	1	11	1			23
1754	7			1	2	2	11	1			24
Total	499	3	16	11	255	29	292	11	5	1	1,122

Sources: ARA, VOC 1860/KA 1752 to VOC 2828/KA 2720.

Table 6.5. *Portuguese shipping arrivals*

Year	Macao	Canton	Manila	Siam	Timor	Borneo	Banjarmasin	Malacca	Junkceylon	Pegu	S. Thomé	Goa	Surat	Lisbon	Na	Annual total
1715	3		1		3							1	1			9
1716	2		2		1											5
1717	1		1		5							1		1		9
1718	4		1		2							1				8
1719	9		1		3											13
1720	6				1									1		8
1721	6	1	3		3											13
1722	13				1							1				15
1723	5		1		2	1	1									10
1724	7		1		1				1							10
1725	9		1		1			1								12
1726	6	1										1		1		9
1727	9		1		1			1					1			13
1728	5		1		1					1	1					9
1729	7		1													8
1730	6		3		1											10
1731	7		1		1					1						10
1732	3				1											4
1733	6		1		1											8
1734	3		2		1											6
1735	3				1											4
1736	2		1		1											4
1737	2															2
1738	2				1											3
1739	3															3
1740	4				1											5
1741	5															5
1742	3															3
1743	5				1											6
1744	6				1											7
1745	3				1											4
1746	3	1			1											5
1747	2				1											3
1748	1				1											2
1749	1				1											2
1750	1				1											2
1751	1				1											2
1752																
1753	1				1											2
1754	1				1											2
Total	166	3	23		45	1	1	2	1	2	1	5	2	3		255

Sources: ARA, VOC 1860/KA 1752 to VOC 2828/KA 2720.

and departures at Batavia, 1715–54.

	Departures											
Macao	Canton	Manila	Siam	Timor	Borneo	Pegu	S. Thomé	Porto Novo	Madras	Goa	Lisbon	Annual total
2		1		1	1	1						6
1				2								3
2												2
5		1		1						1		8
14				2								16
9												9
7		1		2							1	11
11		1	1	1		1						15
7		2								1		10
8		1		1								10
10		1								1		12
6	1			1					1			9
8	1	2							1			12
6		1	1							2		10
4		1	1	1								7
5		2		1				2				10
4		1		2	1					1		9
2				1					1			4
6		1		1								8
3		2		1								6
3				1								4
2		1		1								4
2												2
1				1								2
3												3
4				1								5
4				1								5
3												3
5				1								6
6				1								7
3				1								4
3				1								4
2				1								3
1				1								2
1				1								2
1				1								2
1				1								2
1				1								2
1				1								2
167	2	19	3	34	1	2	1	2	3	6	1	241

Table 6.6. Chinese shipping arrivals

Year	Canton	Amoy	Ning-po	Shanghai	Hocksiew	Foochow	Munsoe	Tsoantsiew	Tsiantsia	Tsansiew	Tangtsioa	Panhaii	Japan	Manila	Tonkin	Cochinchina	Cambodia	Riow	Samarang	Na	Annual total
																				Arrivals	
1715	2	9	4												3						18
1716	3	4	5												2	1					15
1717	4	6	4												1					1	16
1718																					0
1719														1						1	2
1720															1						1
1721												1			2						3
1722		2	3	4											2						11
1723		13	2	6				1							1	1					24
1724	1	3	5	1				1	2						3	1					17
1725	1	5	4							2	1										13
1726	1	8	3					2							2						16
1727	2	9	3												3		1	1			19
1728	2	9	3												3					1	18
1729	2	12	4																		18
1730	4	12	4												3						23
1731	3	12	4												1						20
1732	7	9	3												1						20
1733	5	8	2												2						17
1734	4	9	1																		14
1735	5	11	2												3						21
1736	3	10	2																		15
1737	3	13	1												2						19
1738	4	15	2												3						24
1739	3	10													1						14
1740	4	8	1												1						14
1741	4	6	1												2						13
1742																					
1743		5																			5
1744	3	10	1																		14
1745	1	6	2																		9
1746	3	7	1												1						12
1747		7	1																		8
1748	3	10	1																		14
1749	2	7	1																		10
1750																					
1751	2	5	1																		8
1752																					
1753		6	1																		7
1754		6	1																		7
Total	81	272	73	11				4	2	2	1	1		1	43	3	1	1		3	499

Sources: ARA, VOC 1860/KA 1752 to VOC 2828/KA 2720.

and departures at Batavia, 1715–54.

															Departures
Canton	Amoy	Ning-po	Shanghai	Tsoantsiew	Siantan	Panhaii	Siam	Tonkin	Cochinchina	Timor	Samarang	Malacca	Kedah	Trengganu	Annual total
3	4	8						2							17
4	5	4						1				1			15
															0
						1		1							2
					1							1			2
	2	2	5					1		1					11
1	10	4	6	1				1							23
1	3	5	3	1				1	1		1	3			19
1	7	3	1	2				2							16
2	9	5						1					1		18
2	9	4						3							18
2	11	4												1	18
4	12	4						2							22
3	12	4						1							20
6	9	4						1							20
5	7	2						2							16
3	9	2													14
4	9	4						2				1			20
3	10	2													15
3	13	1						2							19
4	13	3			2			2							24
3	9	1						1							14
4	8	1													13
4	6	1						1							12
	4	1													5
3	9	2													14
1	6	2													9
2	7	2													11
	7	1													8
3	10	1													14
2	7	1													10
2	5	1													8
	6	1													7
	6	1													7
75	244	81	15	4	2	1	1	27	1	1	1	6	1	1	461

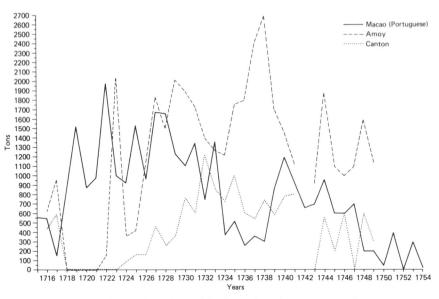

6.1 Total annual tonnage of arriving shipping at Batavia, Portuguese from Macao
compared with Chinese from Amoy and Canton, 1715–54.

important for the VOC's trade over the few years, 1704 to 1708, that a regular
trading trend developed.

A comparison of the numbers and frequency of Portuguese and Chinese ships
at Batavia suggests that the Portuguese were intimately involved in that trade. The
counting of ships has obvious restrictions; the discrepancy in size of the vessels,
the individual cargoes and the value of the individual cargoes are three important
limitations. Although the Dutch kept records of the total purchases and sales of
goods imported and exported at Batavia by the Portuguese and the Chinese from
China, Macao and Manila, those purchases and sales are not readily or easily
differentiated by supplier or purchaser. The VOC records rectify one limitation,
the discrepancy of the size of the vessels, and permit a comparison of the total
tonnage of the arriving Portuguese shipping from Macao and the Chinese junks
from Amoy and Canton, as depicted in Figure 6.1. Amoy's predominant market
position at Batavia began in the 1730s as shown in the figure of the total annual
tonnage of shipping which arrived at that port.

When the size of Macao and Canton ships and junks are combined and then
compared with the tonnage of the arriving Amoy and Ning-po junks, as depicted
in Figure 6.2, the Portuguese and Cantonese tonnage surpassed that of Ning-po
over the entire period and closely approximated, equalled or surpassed Amoy from
1715 until 1735. The dramatic domination by Amoy's shipping of the Batavia trade
was established from 1736 to 1740 but was lost as a result of the massacre of the
Chinese population at Batavia in 1740 and the Ch'ing official reaction and

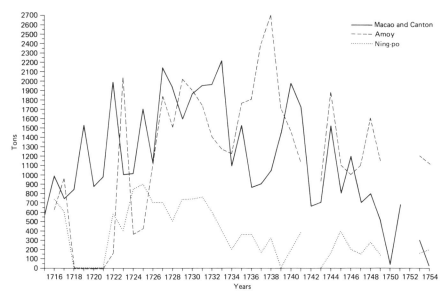

6.2 Total annual tonnage of arriving shipping at Batavia, Portuguese from Macao and Chinese from Canton compared with Chinese from Amoy and Ningpo, 1715–54.

temporary prohibition of trade for one year in 1742. Amoy's ships recovered their position in that market in 1743 and maintained it until 1754.

The efficacy of comparing the tonnage of competing merchant's shipping is a questionable exercise in the attempt to determine the position occupied by the Portuguese and the Cantonese and the importance of their trade at Batavia. Some question may also be raised about combining Macao and Canton's shipping to compare with those of Amoy and Ning-po. Yet, there is a strong case to be made in this instance that the comparison of tonnage is a good indicator.

First, Macao acted as an adjunct of the Canton market; the produce which the Portuguese sold at Batavia was purchased at Canton and the Chinese goods freighted on the Portuguese ships were on the accounts of Cantonese quevees. Second, a comparison of tonnage may actually underestimate the value and quantities of Chinese imports at and exports from Batavia carried by the Portuguese. In a few instances, where the VOC records compared or permit a comparison of the quantities and values imported or exported by the Portuguese ships from Macao and by the Chinese, Portuguese trade is shown to be influential.

In two trading seasons in the 1680s, Portuguese ships departed with around one half or more of the pepper purchased from the VOC at Batavia for China. In 1684, three Portuguese country trader ships from Macao arrived with Chinese merchants on board; their cargoes comprised porcelain, tea, radix China, alum, and 2,793 picols of zinc. The zinc was sold to the VOC for 27,930 *rsd*; the proceeds of that sale were used to purchase around 3,103 picols of pepper from the Company. Four

Table 6.7. Portuguese and Chinese sales at Batavia, 1688–1743. (Quantities in picols, values in rijksdaalders)

| | Tea | | Silks | | | | Silver | Gold | Zinc | | Other commod.[a] | Total |
| | | | China | | | Tonkin | Sp. Reals | | | | | |
Year	Quantity	Value	Raw quantity	Raw value	Pcegds value	value	value	value	Quantity	Value	value	value
1688			129	26,657					2,794	72,500[b]		109,923
1693	752	33,767	49	10,922					3,467	34,638	48,628	108,511
1694											63,822	355,158[c]
1700												
1704		—										
1707	52											
1708			—	16,000							82,789	98,789
1709	575						68,839					85,560
1710	573	31,345									59,089	160,173
1711	575	31,710									26,890	58,600
1712	561	35,176					37,556				27,138	99,870
1713	580	37,945					126,513				23,384	187,842
1714	619	45,008				22,734			2,057	35,162	17,803	120,707
1715	531	33,657							1,461	20,388	19,694	73,739
1716	627	26,755									31,825	58,580
1717												52,794
1718	446	35,040			435						7,940	42,980
1719	764	43,836			390						2,339	46,610
1720	2,000	126,812									3,272	130,474
1721	2,753	248,891							204	3,063	5,435	257,389
1722	2,847	96,279	43	9,947	3,572			46,831	375	4,670	5,460	116,356
1723	3,041	101,954	118	27,068	20,585			90,994	750	9,373	3,926	192,724
1724	1,699	62,489	82	17,729	2,735			89,982	202	2,354	6,240	200,391
1728	2,519	146,886			3,351				569	8,527	465	248,595
1729	4,795	256,295	293	66,194	5,555				47	709	1,958	262,313
1730	10,762	564,294			3,375						1,396	637,439
1731	8,145	201,970									12,470	217,815
1733	6,542	97,836			2,940				97	1,642	1,670	104,088
1735	6,079	125,560			4,546				881	14,981	8,620	153,707
1737	5,431	181,531			930				190	3,230	9,087	194,778
1742	1,737	43,415									10,587	43,415
1743	76	1,819										12,406

[a] Amalgamation of different commodities such as alum, radix China, various woods and copper.   [b] Average.

Chinese junks traded in the same year and exported 2,429 picols of pepper.[37] The following trading season the Portuguese arrived with two ships and sold 2,000 picols of zinc to the VOC for the same amount of pepper. Seven Chinese vessels traded but they exported only a total of 2,550 picols of pepper purchased from the Company.[38]

The quantities and values of the commodities imported at and exported from Batavia by the Portuguese and the Chinese were recorded as the goods sold or purchased by the VOC from 1684 to 1754. Prior to 1719 the VOC collated and included this information and incorporated it into the text of the generale missieven; from 1719 onwards it was presented in a tabular format as a supporting document attached to the annual letter. Table 6.7 details the commodities, quantities and values of the Portuguese and Chinese sales at Batavia, 1688–1743. This serial data did not, unfortunately, differentiate between the quantities or values carried by the Portuguese or Chinese. During the years that trade between Batavia and Manila was carried on by the Portuguese, Chinese and other merchants, such as the Spanish and Armenians, the date that the VOC recorded and sent to the Heeren XVII included those transactions; those values did not significantly alter the characteristic trends in China's trade with the VOC. The Company's methodology of record keeping for the sale of maritime trade imports at Batavia was modified in 1748 to include VOC transactions for inland produce from Java.[39]

The Chinese commodities which the Portuguese and Chinese sold to the VOC at Batavia from 1684 to 1754 reflect a major change in the structure of the Dutch Company's trade in the South China Sea. The VOC's interest in raw silk and silk piecegoods from China and Tonkin, which had dominated for most of the seventeenth century, was curtailed as the market for two Asian beverages, coffee and tea, grew in Europe. Tea, at this time, was available exclusively from China and coffee primarily from Yemen at Mocha.

The sale of Chinese raw silk and silk piecegoods at Batavia did not cease completely but the quantities seldom rose above 100 picols with an exceptional year in 1730 when 293 picols were purchased by the Company. During the early years of the eighteenth century, there was a dramatic increase in the amount of reals sold at Batavia to the VOC by Portuguese, Chinese, Spanish and Armenian markets that traded there from Manila. In the mid 1720s, the Company recorded their purchase of significant values of Chinese gold. Zinc was the primary ballast cargo commodity sold to the VOC; alum, radix China and copper were also carried as ballast cargoes and sold at Batavia.

TEA

Tea was the most important commodity by volume and value traded by the Portuguese and Chinese at Batavia. The quantity of tea they carried from China hovered around an average of 5–600 picols per annum from the 1690s to 1719. With the imposition of the Ch'ing ban on foreign trade and its creation of the

Company's near-total reliance upon the Portuguese to carry that commodity to Batavia, the Macao country traders ships supplied the Dutch demand for tea which had increased dramatically; the Portuguese exported 2–3,000 picols of tea per annum to Java to be transhipped to the Netherlands in 1720–3.

Purchase of tea at Batavia from 1724 until 1729, when the Dutch returned to trade directly at Canton, fluctuated from a little over 1,500 to 4,000 picols of tea per year. Perhaps as a result of a continued increase in demand and an attempt by Portuguese and Chinese merchants to convince the VOC to cease direct voyages to Canton, purchases of tea rose to a high of over 10,000 picols in 1730 and accompanied the decline in the Batavia trade. Only 1,737 picols of tea were bought by the Company in that city in 1742, and a mere 76 in 1743. Although the quantities of tea carried by the Portuguese and Chinese to Batavia were large and significant, as were the VOC's sales of that commodity in Europe, a comparison as shown in Table 6.8 with the EIC's imports into Europe at the same time reveals the strength and superiority of the European Company competition that traded directly in China *vis-à-vis* the VOC's reliance on the Portuguese and the Chinese.

The total values paid by the VOC for tea were substantial; from the 1690s to 1719, the Company paid slightly over 26–45,000 rsd for that commodity which represented one-fifth to one-half of the total value of the goods purchased from the Portuguese and Chinese. In the four trading seasons in which the Portuguese supplied almost all of the tea to Batavia, 1720–3, the VOC paid a little over 96–248,000 rsd which amounted from, approximately, over 50 to 90 per cent of the total value of VOC purchases. This dominating trend of the value of tea to the total value of the VOC purchases at Batavia was maintained.

With the growth and the VOC's anticipation of even greater demand for tea in Europe in the 1710s, the Company implemented a policy of fixing prices paid for tea. On 2 March 1717 the Governor-General and the Council of the Indies announced to the foreign traders that the VOC would pay only 40 rsd for ordinary green (Singlo), 60 rsd for green (Bing or Imperial) and 80 rsd for black (*Bohea*, first quality) per picol. Compared with prices the VOC had paid previously, the Company offered the Portuguese and Chinese merchants very low prices for their tea and, adding insult to injury, suggested that they return with that commodity to China.

The Chinese merchants indicated that as a result of the high cost of freighting their green tea, in particular, from China, they could not sell it for less than 60 rsd per picol. The VOC would not rescind their fixed prices and the Chinese and Portuguese sold their tea but the Chinese 'in return promised that they would never more go to Batavia.'[40] This confrontation over tea prices and the mistreatment of Chinese merchants at Batavia contributed to the Ch'ing imposition of a ban on Chinese foreign trade.

For the Portuguese at Macao, their opportunity to recoup their fortunes had arrived, they refused to accept any VOC price-fixing idea on tea at Batavia and forced the price of black (Bohea, all grades) up from 80 rsd in 1717 to 115–125 rsd per picol in 1718. Although Macao's country traders increased the quantity

Table 6.8. *Tea purchased at Batavia for Europe compared with actual EIC imports from China, 1704–43. (All quantities in picols)*

Year	VOC purchases	EIC imports	Year	VOC purchases	EIC imports
1704	52	150	1728	2,519	1,972
1713	580	1,186	1729	4,795	10,897
1714	619	1,602	1730	10,762	12,832
1718	446	4,069	1731	8,145	13,587
1719	764	3,872	1733	6,542	6,155
1720	2,000	2,389	1735	6,079	4,265
1721	2,753	9,315	1737	5,431	12,337
1722	2,847	10,171	1742	1,737	13,219
1723	3,041	4,976	1743	76	12,347
1724	1,699	8,092			

Sources: Chaudhuri, *Trading World*, 538–9, *GM*, and ARA, VOC 1904/KA 1796 to VOC 2590/KA 2482.

Table 6.9. *Different varieties of black and green teas exported from China to Batavia by the Portuguese and Chinese, 1719–43. (All quantities in picols)*

Year	Black				Green	
	Bohea	Congo	Souchon	Pekoe	Singlo	Bing (Imperial)
1719	280				474	10
1720	903				1,097	
1721	1,367				1,320	66
1722	153				1,955	739
1723	1,819				1,122	100
1724	263				1,196	241
1728	2,519					
1729	4,604				165	25
1730	9,618				908	236
1731	7,482				663	
1733	4,524	5			1,654	359
1735	3,155	1,643		141	1,056	83
1737	1,769	3,591	13	58		
1742	1,737					
1743	76					

Source: ARA, VOC 1916/KA 1808 to VOC 2590/KA 2482.

of tea they supplied to the VOC in 1718 from 446 to 2,000, and to 2,753 picols in 1720 and 1721, the Portuguese did not allow the price to fall and the Company paid an equivalent average price per picol for black tea as in 1718. When the Amoy and Ning-po junks returned to Batavia in 1722, tea prices fell sharply.[41]

The different tea varieties available in China, which the Portuguese and Chinese

Table 6.10. *Portuguese and Chinese purchases at Batavia,*

	Pepper		Cinnamon value	Cloves value	Nutmeg value	Silver value
Year	Quantity	Value				
1685	5–6,000[b]	44,000				
1686	4,332	34,656				
1692	13,561	125,047				
1693	13,960	128,729				
1694	18,590	176,185		25,150		
1700	26,280					
1703	20,680	155,100				
1704	23,550	176,625	33,660			
1706			52,345			
1707	10,308	87,618	31,875			
1708	12,210	103,782	59,850	46,275	5,719	
1709	9,775	87,975				
1710	16,000	144,000				
1711	13,000	141,956	71,440			
1712	15,100	162,100	63,600			
1713	6,400	60,981	141,780			
1714	11,000	99,062				
1715	11,800	107,062				
1716	26,010	255,724				
1717	1,948	19,480				
1718	19,734	197,370	114,320	32,630		
1719	11,195	111,945	560	15,950	2,250	
1720	560	5,600	49,440	1,355	750	
1721	500	5,000	64,000	1,564	281	
1722	8,370	83,700	35,600	2,127	188	
1723	23,529	235,290	56,400	6,672	3,376	
1724	13,680	136,800	46,400	8,173	2,147	
1728	13,850	138,500	17,200	5,317	610	
1729	16,530	165,300	140,000	4,379	188	30,281
1730	17,640	176,400	108,000	22,518	2,625	1,434
1731	19,200	192,000	94,080	3,336	750	
1733	4,300	43,000	95,200	15,012	0	
1735	10,310	103,100	80,485	21,163	2,063	
1737	2,160	25,920	73,840	3,794	563	
1742	1,850	22,200	101,840	2,293	938	
1743	275	3,300	70,400	417		
1744	3,500	42,000	92,000	11,259	1,313	
1746	6,065	72,780		4,427	3,375	
1747	6,986	83,836	6,400			
1748	4,520	54,210	76,380	22,005	5,252	
1749	7,768	93,240	56,000	1,200	293	
1750	4,106	49,029		14,010	12,396	
1752	900	10,800	16,650	1,302		
1754	1,685	22,660	19,333	22,396	1,750	

[a] Amalgamation of different commodities such as Dutch textiles (woollens) and manufactures, copper and various woods.
[b] Estimate.
[c] Conversion of 1,630,273 guilders to rsd. (3 rsd/fl).
Sources: GM, and ARA, VOC 1904/KA 1796 to VOC 2848/KA 2740.

1685–1754. (*quantities in picols, values in rijksdaalders*)

Gold value	Tin		Lead		Other commod:[a] value	Total value
	Quantity	Value	Quantity	Value		
						—
						—
						—
						194,891
						230,532
						543,424[c]
			6,862	36,889		—
			6,923	38,078		—
					177,051	229,396
					95,691	215,184
			6,323	34,777	65,399	315,802
			5,587	30,729	48,556	167,260
			3,140	17,270	58,936	220,206
					75,511	288,907
					68,513	294,213
					79,466	282,227
					116,718	215,780
					72,215	179,277
					113,150	368,874
					315,233	334,713
					113,857	458,177
			40	220	44,112	175,037
			75	413	44,497	102,055
					28,558	99,403
					90,666	212,281
			3,476	19,118	51,233	372,089
	1,060	15,983	730	4,015	94,369	307,887
	4,000	60,000	1,366	7,513	30,098	259,238
	3,000	49,950	2,100	11,550	61,598	463,246
141,394	5,160	82,180	5,250	34,125	153,978	722,654
	4,640	75,140	95	621	116,446	482,373
204,080	2,000	34,000	770	5,005	73,187	469,484
	2,490	39,840	2,460	15,990	54,814	317,375
13,308	4,063	73,134	1,481	9,627	105,043	305,229
			19	124	17,284	144,679
	1,227	28,508	500	3,250	62,892	168,767
123,381	1,173	25,202	931	6,051	72,024	373,230
35,722	2,290	48,090	1,500	9,750	33,378	207,522
	1,400	30,015	500	3,250	84,962	208,463
	3,460	74,390	1,780	11,570	212,412	456,219
	3,918	81,211			119,184	351,128
	4,147	89,146	810	5,124	124,485	294,190
	3,300	70,950	400	2,600	106,689	208,991
	325	6,988	232	1,805	182,874	257,806

supplied the VOC in the early eighteenth century, were divided into two broad categories, black and green, with a number of types and gradings within each of the categories.[42] The availability of tea supplies in China and the Chinese port/market relationships with the internal and external demand for different teas are difficult to isolate with precision or to quantify. The European Companies, European country traders and Chinese merchants at Canton and the Chinese merchants at Amoy and Ning-po, obviously, had different capabilities and market strategies when purchasing and selling tea.

After 1720, the European Companies' market preferences were the ordinary and cheaper varieties of black or green teas. In the late 1720s and early 1730s, the EIC concentrated upon purchasing teas of the green variety.[43] The VOC followed a diametrically opposite course and bought large quantities of black tea. The precise policy of the VOC was to purchase the greatest possible amounts of tea, regardless whether black or green, in an effort to damage the Ostend Company's trade in Europe.[44] The Portuguese and Chinese, but more particularly the junks from Amoy and Ning-po, responded to the VOC's encouragement and sent large quantities of tea to Batavia.

The VOC purchases of different varieties of black and green teas at Batavia from 1719 to 1743 are depicted in Table 6.9. During the years of the Portuguese dominating the shipping activity from China, 1719–24, large and regular imports of green tea varieties, which were readily available at the Canton market, were recorded. But, with the commercial supremacy of junks from Amoy and Ning-po between 1729 and 1743, where black tea varieties especially Bohea were plentiful, and the EIC's implementation of its strategy to concentrate upon purchasing green tea varieties at Canton in the late 1720s and early 1730s, the VOC's tea purchases at Batavia from 1729 to 1743 were dominated by those of the black variety.

The commodities that the Portuguese and Chinese purchased at Batavia from 1685 to 1754, as shown in Table 6.10, consisted of merchandise that the Company obtained from throughout the Indonesian archipelago, Ceylon and Europe. Large-scale purchases of pepper from the VOC were not an innovation in the pattern of trade in the South China Sea but an intensification of an existing commercial relationship. Before the Company's arrival in the Indonesian archipelago, Chinese junks bought pepper; after the VOC centralised the pepper trade at Batavia, the Chinese junks frequented that port on an annual basis throughout the seventeenth and eighteenth centuries.

The Portuguese and the Chinese purchased other spices, cloves and nutmeg, in particular, which suggests their return, on a small scale, to the south China markets. The Portuguese from Macao had exported some cloves to Macassar in the 1630s but that trade had been disrupted by the 1640s with the imposition of the VOC spice monopoly on Ambon and throughout the Moluccas. The values of such spices were high but the volumes were small; for example, in 1730, the Portuguese and Chinese purchased some 108 picols of cloves for 22,158 rsd and 14 picols of nutmeg for 2,125 rsd.

Cinnamon was supplied to the Company at Batavia from Ceylon; its purchase was not linked to the China but to the Manila trade carried on by Portuguese, Chinese, Spanish and Armenian merchants. Dutch woollens and manufactures, along with a multitude of other commodities, such as aromatic woods and copper, were also purchased. The two primary ballast-cargo commodities that the Portuguese and the Chinese bought were lead and tin. The lead was usually brought out to Batavia from Europe, although the Company records indicate some stocks came from Siam. Tin was available from the Malay peninsula but purchases at Batavia were dominated by supplies from the island of Banka in the Indonesian archipelago where overseas Chinese were involved in its exploitation.[45]

PEPPER

Pepper was a particularly popular commodity that the Portuguese and Chinese purchased at Batavia. Its use in China in flavouring food was similar to that in Europe. According to one Dutch writer, the Chinese also believed in its medicinal value and drank it with water to warm the stomach. In Ming times, in the late sixteenth century before the dramatic growth of silver in the economy, certain types of payments to officials were made with pepper, which indicates that commodity's intrinsic value in that society.

The quantity of the pepper purchased by the Portuguese and the Chinese at Batavia suggest that annual supplies in the port/markets of south China, barring significant losses by shipwreck, rose from around 4–7,000 picols in the 1680s to 13–18,000 picols in the 1690s. Trends in the purchase of pepper at Batavia reveal a sustained rise at the very beginning of the eighteenth century to quantities rarely reached again, 20–26,000 picols per year. From 1707 until 1716, there was a dip in purchases with an average of 10–15,000 picols per annum; in 1713 and 1716, they fluctuated wildly from two extremes, a low 6,400 to a high 26,010 picols. Between 1717 and 1722, during the VOC's confrontation with the Chinese merchants on fixing tea prices and the years of the Ch'ing ban when Chinese ships were not recorded as having arrived at Batavia, the Portuguese purchased large quantities of pepper (around 20 and 11,000 picols) in 1718 and 1719 but the total for 1720 was barely over 1,000 picols. For the next fourteen trading seasons, between 1722 and 1735, the Portuguese and the Chinese bought quantities of pepper that ranged from 10–23,000 picols with only two years in which the amounts fell below the lower figure, 8,370 picols in 1732 and 4,300 picols in 1733. The decline in Batavia's trade and the Portuguese and Chinese participation in that market in the 1730s to 1754 was also reflected in pepper purchases by those merchants. After the Dutch massacre of the Chinese community in 1740, small purchases of pepper by the Portuguese and the Chinese were recorded in 1742 and 1743 of 150 and 275 picols; average annual purchases of pepper in those years were low and fluctuated from around 1 to 7,000 picols.

China's demand for pepper from the South China Sea in the early eighteenth century had important implications on the trade in that commodity carried by the EIC and the VOC. Although there was a general stability in the supply of pepper

Table 6.11. *Pepper purchased at Batavia by
the Portuguese and Chinese for China compared with the total recorded amounts of
pepper arriving in Europe carried by the EIC
and the VOC, 1715–32. (All quantities in
picols)*

Year	Portuguese and Chinese	EIC	VOC
1715	11,800	11,442	24,040
1716	26,010	9,991	41,040
1717	1,948	14,193	34,720
1718	19,734	10,171	38,880
1719	11,195	25,817	34,720
1720	560	24,415	51,360
1721	500	309	46,560
1722	8,370	8,920	72,400
1723	23,529	10,841	37,760
1724	13,680	9,737	63,360
1728	13,850	9,311	46,960
1729	16,530	3,998	66,480
1730	17,640	6,352	48,080
1731	19,200	17,232	37,920
1732	4,300	7,059	31,280

Sources: ARA, VOC 1916/KA 1808 to VOC 2172/KA
2064, Chaudhuri, *Trading World*, 529–30 and Glam-
mann, *Dutch Asiatic Trade*, 297.

to the Companies in this period, the total exports to Europe were not exclusively
dependent upon European demand but fluctuated from instability of supply among
producers in the South China Sea and Indian Ocean, European Company
difficulties in obtaining capital for the purchase of these supplies and, of primary
importance, demand from the China market. For the Portuguese and the Chinese,
pepper was available at Batavia from the major producers in the Indonesian
archipelago, Palembang, Jambi and Bantam; Banjarmasin was a large secondary
supplier with an annual production which grew from 10,000 to around 20,000 picols
in the late 1680s to the 1710s. After Bantam's closure to foreign traders in 1682,
the EIC relied upon supplies available from west Sumatra at their settlement at
Bencoolen and from their trade and factories on the Malabar coast in south
and west India.[46] The VOC was also dependent upon the same pepper suppliers
in the Indonesian archipelago as the Portuguese and Chinese; in addition, their
settlement at Cochin in the Malabar coast supplied quantities of pepper.[47]

The quantities of pepper that the two major European Companies and the
Portuguese and the Chinese carried to supply the European and Chinese demand
for that commodity from 1715 to 1732 are depicted in Table 6.11. The VOC's
dominant position in the pepper trade is re-iterated in this table. But the

Table 6.12. *Total EIC pepper imports into Europe and the total VOC sales to the Portuguese and Chinese at Batavia for China, 1692–1714 and 1734–54. (All quantities in picols)*

Year	Portuguese and Chinese	EIC	Year	Portuguese and Chinese	EIC
1692	13,561	3,461	1734	10,310	17,640
1693	13,960	2,468	1736	2,160	16,423
1694	18,590	0	1741	1,850	14,976
1700	26,280	13,968	1742	275	35,766
1703	20,680	14,559	1743	3,500	31,622
1704	23,550	5,601	1745	6,065	25,513
1707	10,308	10,952	1746	6,986	25,150
1708	12,210	14,838	1747	4,520	11,202
1709	9,775	2,944	1748	7,768	6,466
1710	16,000	6,068	1750	4,106	13,568
1711	13,000	7,260	1751	900	11,743
1712	15,100	3,098	1753	1,685	17,133
1713	6,400	13,014	1754	200	16,913
1714	11,000	10,003			

Sources: ARA, VOC 2262/KA 2154 to VOC 2826/KA 2718, Chaudhuri, *Trading World*, 529–30.

comparison of the EIC import totals to Europe with those of the Portuguese and Chinese to China is quite startling. A trend suggesting an equality, if not a slight overall advantage, in the quantities of pepper supplied by the Portuguese and Chinese to China as contrasted with the EIC's to Europe is evident.

A further comparison of the quantities of pepper supplied to Europe by the EIC and to China by the Portuguese and Chinese as shown in Table 6.12 over an earlier period, 1692 to 1714 supports the same conclusion and suggests that this trend was longstanding and a permanent feature in the demand for pepper between West and East. Between 1734 and 1754, the EIC stabilised its access to pepper supplies primarily from India and this is reflected in the amounts they imported into Europe; in comparison, the Portuguese and Chinese were unable to sustain their previous trend in the large-scale purchase of pepper at Batavia over the same period.

The VOC policy of concentrating foreign trade at Batavia involved the Company in the sale of pepper to the Portuguese and the Chinese in order to avoid those foreign traders penetrating or, in the VOC's eyes, smuggling in markets where the Company claimed its control.[48] In the early 1700s, the VOC sold large quantities of pepper to the Portuguese and the Chinese at low prices and profit margins on account of excess in supplies from Bantam and Palembang. The Company, subsequently, fixed a minimum price of 7 1/2 rsd per picol that rose on the orders from the Heeren XVII to 10 rsd per picol in 1715.[49]

The Company found that it was not always possible to maintain sufficient supplies of pepper to Europe when faced with a strong demand for that commodity from the Portuguese and in particular, the Chinese for China. During the trading seasons, 1716 to 1722, when there was an expansion in production and purchases by the Company at Palembang and Jambi, an increase in demand in Europe and some fluctuation in Portuguese purchases of pepper at Batavia, the VOC's exports grew and registered their highest quantity, 72,400 picols in 1722. When the Chinese, and to a lesser degree, the Portuguese, traded at Batavia in 1723, they demanded and purchased a large quantity of pepper, 23,529 picols. The Company, as a result, complained of a shortage of pepper supplies to export and in 1723 only despatched to Europe around half of the amount sent in 1722.

At Batavia, the value of the pepper purchased by the Portuguese and the Chinese from the VOC did not dominate the total value of purchases as did the value of tea to the total value of their sales to the Company. The trends in the values of pepper follow those described for the amounts of that commodity that were purchased. The relationship of pepper to the total values of purchases by the Portuguese and the Chinese fluctuated from as low as around 5 per cent in 1720, 1721 and 1752 to as high as 60 to 75 per cent in 1694, 1710, 1715, 1716, and 1723. Cinnamon and other commodities (in which Dutch textiles, woollens primarily, and manufactures figured prominently) were two areas in which the values of the transactions compared favourably with those for pepper.

CINNAMON AND SILVER

The purchase of Ceylonese cinnamon in large quantities by the Portuguese from Macao and Siam, Spanish, Armenians and some Chinese merchants, from the VOC is one intriguing facet of the trade between Batavia and Manila in the early eighteenth century. The cinnamon sold to those merchants was destined for sale at Manila for transhipment across the Pacific via the Manila galleon to New Spain. This spice was sold in *fardeelen* (bales) of eighty *ponds*, and the number of bales sold from 1704–54 is given in Table 6.13. The purchase of cinnamon, by its value, trailed that of pepper from the late seventeenth century when it was first recorded, until 1713. After that trading season, purchases of cinnamon fluctuated erratically but the overall trend was their equalling and surpassing those of pepper. From 1733 to 1754, in the years that cinnamon was purchased at Batavia, that spice usually outsold pepper.

Towards the late seventeenth and in the early eighteenth century, Manila's market modestly revived with the arrival of New World silver, the return of Portuguese ships and Chinese junks from China, and the country trade from the west and east Indian coasts.[50] Although the VOC failed to trade with Batavia directly, the Company sought to establish a commercial link with Manila by the end of the seventeenth century. They tried to negotiate a contract with the Portuguese country trader, Manoel d'Abreu, to trade between Siam, Manila and Batavia and return. Their negotiations with d'Abreu were a failure but the Portuguese country traders initiated this triangular trade in 1697–8.[51]

The Portuguese country traders, on their first voyages from Siam and Macao via Manila to Batavia, did not purchase any quantities of cinnamon. Significant

Table 6.13. *Cinnamon bales sold by the VOC to the Manila traders at Batavia,* *1704–54.* (*Each bale* = 80 *ponds*)

Year	Number of bales	Year	Number of bales	Year	Number of bales
1704	396	1721	800	1737	923
1706	695	1722	445	1742	1,273
1707	425	1723	705	1743	880
1708	798	1724	580	1744	1,150
1711	893	1728	215	1747	80
1712	795	1729	1,715	1748	918
1713	1,772	1730	1,350	1749	700
1718	1,429	1731	1,176	1752	100
1719	7	1733	1,190	1754	145
1720	618	1735	1,000		

Sources: GM, and ARA, VOC 1904/KA 1796 to VOC 2848/KA 2740.

purchases of cinnamon by the Manila traders at Batavia were registered in 1704 and from that date onwards, depending upon the safe arrival of the Manila galleon and New World silver from Acapulco to the Philippines, Ceylonese cinnamon was traded at Batavia for reals. The early Portuguese country traders' role as the intermediaries in this trade was challenged by the Chinese but was successfully countered. Portuguese ships and those flying Portuguese colours were joined by Armenian and Spanish-owned vessels; after 1736, Portuguese ships ceased to trade at Batavia from Manila. The cinnamon for silver trade was entirely in the control of the Spanish merchants, in the years that shipping activity between the two ports was recorded, from the late 1730s until the 1750s.

The importance of this trade between Batavia and Manila for the VOC's commercial and financial position in the Indonesian archipelago in the early eighteenth century was crucial in supplying capital to pay for the Company's increased purchases of pepper and coffee for the European market, and Mexican reals in particular, owing to the South China Sea's preference for this currency over the Peruvian pillar real which had developed in the past on account of a series of debasements and fluctuations in the amount of silver in the coin.[52] The Company at Batavia received much of its capital and silver from the New World via the Netherlands and Europe. By 1714, however, Batavia required 200 to 250,000 Mexican reals for pepper purchases and 60 to 80,000 reals of any type in order to buy coffee in Arabia where there was no marked preference for the Mexican real.[53] Access to quantities of Mexican reals was available at Manila and it was from Mexico via the Philippines and carried on board Portuguese, Chinese, Armenian and Spanish ships that they came to the VOC on Java.

Despite Portuguese Crown and country traders' attempts at Macao to organise their trade in order to avoid sending too many ships in the same year, the Portuguese encountered severe difficulties in maintaining their position in the

Batavia market in the late 1720s with the return of the Chinese junks and the revocation of the Ch'ing ban on foreign trade. By the mid 1730s, the Chinese junk traders faced problems in the Batavia market as a result of the VOC's resumption of direct trade to China. The Portuguese and Chinese trade at Batavia was in decline. Their tea sales to the VOC were diminishing; pepper purchases were down and surpassed by cinnamon. Tin was the only commodity in which they increased their purchases and exports to China. Resentment over the economic conditions in that market and VOC policies towards the overseas Chinese community burst in 1740; the VOC quickly and brutally repressed that community. Ch'ing officials did not react as the VOC feared; Chinese merchants were permitted to trade with the VOC at Batavia.[54] The junks continued to frequent that port.

By the late 1720s, Batavia ceased to offer the same commercial opportunities for the Portuguese from Macao as it had in the late 1710s and early 1720s. Once again, Macao's country traders were confronted with developing markets that would maintain their trade. Earlier, in the first decade of the eighteenth century, they had tried to trade at Surat, but Portuguese Crown and country trader interests at Goa had stopped this promising initiative. Macao's country traders had developed some modest experience at trading in some ports, like Madras, in the Indian Ocean. By the early 1730s, the Portuguese from Macao concentrated almost all of their meagre resources in the search for markets in the Indian Ocean.

MALABAR

The Portuguese from Macao frequented the various Malabar coast ports throughout the early decades of the eighteenth century in an effort to develop new markets for Chinese produce and to purchase Indian commodities that could be sold profitably in south China. They sailed to the Malabar ports dominated by the VOC at Cochin, the French at Mahe, the EIC at Tellicherry and Anjengo, but even more important to those ports still in the control of Indian merchants and the indigenous states along the coast such as Calicut. These were challenging times for the Portuguese at Macao and these were desperate men that sailed in the Indian Ocean in the late 1720s.

Economic conditions on the Malabar coast favoured their arrival and their willingness to trade openly with the Companies and Indian merchants or furtively with Company servants, country traders and indigenous merchants and officials trying to impose a state monopoly on the sale of pepper.[55] By the late 1720s and early 1730s, the Malabar coast experienced 'a commercial boom which hit the port of Calicut' and infused 'new life as shoals of vessels from the north came looking for pepper, sugar and spices.'[56] The boom was prompted by a favourable local political situation and the increasing demand by foreign traders, in particular, the French, for goods available on that coast. Asian traders, primarily Gujeratis and Arabs, also increased their activities at Calicut and other Malabar coast ports after having been displaced from trading in the Persian Gulf.

The Portuguese and the Asian traders were both after the same major

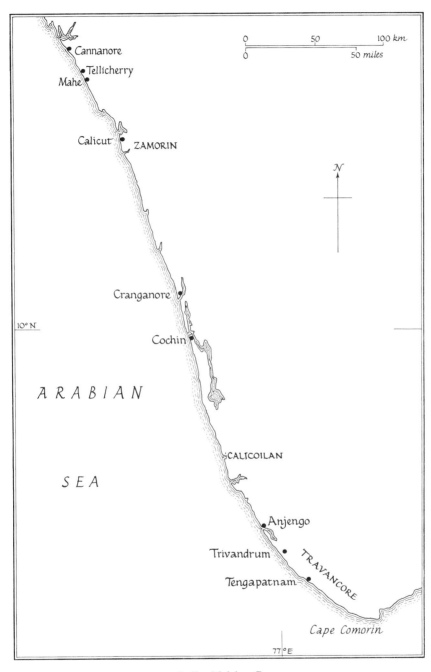

9 India: Malabar Coast

commodity produced on the Malabar coast, pepper. The Macao country traders also purchased sizeable quantities of different varieties of woods, sandalwood in particular, on account of their difficulties in procuring sufficient stocks and competition in the Lesser Sunda islands and the strong demand for that wood in China. The Portuguese country traders supplied sugar and other ballast cargo produce, zinc, radix China, alum and porcelain from China in a market where the exportation of pepper dominated and the goods imported from China were re-exported to the north or further west and not consumed on a large scale at the local level.

Demand for sugar in western India by the Asian traders was strong; Portuguese exports of that commodity from China to India were aided by a buoyant phase, if not an expansion, in the cultivation of sugar in Kwangtung and other provinces in the 1740s. The amounts of sugar recorded as exported by Portuguese country traders from China to India at Malacca in the early 1740s as shown in Table 6.16 indicates an upturn and later in Cochin and Malacca in the 1760s to the 1780s the volumes are impressive.[57] They were also aided by disruption in sugar production on Java as a result of the overseas Chinese revolt in 1740 and subsequent Dutch policies.[58] The Portuguese had found a niche in that market. Slightly later, in 1763, the VOC encountered difficulties confronting the Portuguese competition in the supply of sugar on the Malabar coast; 'it was impossible to raise the price as the Portuguese had imported a great quantity from China and were selling at a lower price' and 'the import from China rose spectacularly in 1767.'[59]

With the establishment of the VOC on the Malabar coast, by expelling the Portuguese from Cochin in 1663, the Company claimed and attempted to exercise a pepper monopoly. By the 1690s, the EIC had established factories on the northern and southern flanks of the area of the VOC's monopoly, at Tellicherry and Anjengo. The Dutch eventually retired from trying to impose a monopoly and competing against European and Asian merchants in northern Malabar; in 1725, the French settled at Mahe in an area relatively free from VOC interference. By the late 1720s, the VOC not only faced a panoply of European competitors, a bevy of small principalities whose loyalties to the Company were contractual and binding only in proportion to the VOC's strength, but also confronted an unexpected rise in the power of one of the most important indigenous principalities in southern Malabar with the accession of Martanda Varma to the throne of Travancore. Martanda Varma's rule over Travancore led to the creation of a bureaucratic state and the transformation of political and economic conditions on the Malabar coast. Travancore expanded largely at the expense of the small principalities along the coast financed by its intervention in the pepper trade to the detriment of the VOC.

Although the Macao country traders were engaged in exporting sugar and other ballast-cargo produce from China to the Malabar coast ports and others in the Indian Ocean and importing pepper and sandalwood from India to China in the 1730s and into the 1750s, it is difficult to quantify the extent of their trading activities on account of the absence of Portuguese and Indian country-traders' records. The frequency and the numbers of Portuguese ships at selected ports in

Table 6.14. *Portuguese and Macao country shipping arrivals at selected ports in the Indian Ocean, 1719–54.*

| | Malabar Coast | | | | | | | Coromandel Coast | | |
| | Surat | | Cochin | | | | | | | |
Year	Total	Macao	Total	Macao	Tellicherry total	Anjengo total	Ceylon total	Madras total	Negapatnam total	Bengal total
1719							1	1		
1720	1						1	1		
1721	0						0	1		
1722							1	1		
1723	0		2				3	4		
1724	1		4	1			2	2		
1725	0		4	2			6	1		
1726	0		4	3			1	2		
1727			3	1	1		1	2		1
1728	2	1	3	2			3	2		
1729	2		5	1			5	3		
1730			4	1			2	1		
1731			5	2	2		3	3		
1732	0		5	3			2	1		
1733	0						0	1		
1734			2	2			1			1
1735	0		5	3			3	1		1
1736	0		6	3			2	2		1
1737	2		4	2			1	2		
1738	3	1	4	3			1	2		1
1739	2		5	2	1		1	5	2	1
1740	2		4	2	2		2	1		
1741	1		5	4	2		1		1	
1742			3	3	3		2	2	1	
1743					2		1	3		
1744					2	1	1	3		
1745						1	0	4		
1746					6	1	0	2		
1747					6	3	4			
1748					6	3	0			2
1749					8	3	0			1
1750					4	2	1	5		1
1751							1	3		
1752							1	1		
1753							0	4		
1754							2			

Sources: Surat: ARA, VOC 1963/KA 1855 to VOC 2582/KA 2474;
Cochin: ARA, VOC 2015/KA 1907 to VOC 2580/KA 2472;
Tellicherry: *Tellicherry, Letters Tellicherry* and *Tellicherry Letters*;
Anjengo: *Anjengo*;
Ceylon: ARA, VOC 1963/KA 1855 to VOC 2833/KA 2725;
Madras: *Madras*;
Negapatnam: ARA, VOC 2471/KA 2363 to VOC 2539/KA 2431;
Bengal: *Ft. St. David*.

The Survival of Empire

Table 6.15. *Portuguese shipping arrivals*

Year	Macao	Manila	Siam	Timor	Aceh & Kedah	Batavia	Goa	Surat	Bombay	Cochin (Malabar)	Mangalor	Madras	Pulicat	Total
							Arrivals							
1684	2						3							
1685														17
1686														12
1687														10
1688	2													8
1689	1						2							6
1690	2						1							10
1691														10
1692	1				1									5
1693	2						1							6
1694	2						4					1		8
1695														9
1696												1		6
1697	3													7
1698	2						1							5
1699							1							1
1700	3											1		9
1701	4											1		5
1702														5
1703														2
1704														2
1705	1													
1706	3		1				1			1		1		
1707	4		1				2	1				1		
1708	5	1	2						1			1		
1709	1			1										
1712							1							
1717	2													
1724	1					1	2							
1725	2						2			1		1		
1726	2					1	1					1		
1727	4						2					1		
1728	2											1		
1729	1				1				1			2		
1730	1											2		
1733						1	2							
1735	1		1		1						2	1		
1736	2						3						1	
1741	3				1		1			1		4		
1742	4				1					3		1		

Sources: ARA, VOC 1403/KA 1292 to VOC 2570/KA 2462 and *GM*.

and departures at Malacca, 1684–1742.

					Departures								
Macao	Manila	Siam	Acch & Kedah	Batavia	Banjarmasin	Ligor	Pegu	Goa	Surat	Cochin (Malabar)	Mangalor	Madras	Total
3								2					
													17
													12
													10
								2					8
2													6
1	1							1					10
													10
								1					5
1					1			1					6
5								1				1	8
													9
1													6
								2				1	7
1								1				1	5
1													1
1								1				2	9
1								2				2	5
													5
													2
													2
								1					
3								2				2	
5								2				3	
2	2	1							2	1		3	
								2					
1													
												2	
2							1	1					
3	1							1				1	
2												3	
3			1					1	1		1		
2					1								
2		1							1			1	
2								1					
2												1	
4		1							1				
4								1				1	
6		1										3	
5		2									1	1	

the Indian Ocean from 1719 to 1754 has been reconstructed based on VOC and EIC records, as shown in Table 6.14.

Those Companies' reports indicate that at Surat the Portuguese ships were in reality divided into Asian-owned vessels flying and using the Portuguese flag for convenience and a few Macao-owned ships. At Ceylon, almost all of the recorded Portuguese arrivals were Macao-owned and operated vessels, and the same appears to be true at Madras but cannot be distinguished in the Dutch records at Negapatnam and Bengal.

On the Malabar coast, at the English factories of Tellicherry and Anjengo, the EIC servants recorded the vast majority of the Portuguese shipping as being 'Macao men' which was substantiated by a comparison of the name of the vessel and captain with the known names of Macao country traders' ships and captains from Macao and Batavia archival materials. At Cochin, the VOC kept shipping lists of foreign arrivals from 1720 to 1742 which corroborate that Macao country traders' vessels dominated the Portuguese trading activity on the Malabar coast with the other Portuguese ships belonging to the Crown from Goa under orders to convoy the Macao ships or to operate against the Angria and other pirates along the coast. Both the VOC and EIC records substantiate that the Macao ships visited Calicut, Mahe, Mangalor and other ports but their activity in those ports was impossible to reconstruct.

The VOC's dagh-register at Malacca also provided fragmentary supplementary evidence of Portuguese shipping activity and frequency in the Indian Ocean. Table 6.15 demonstrates the sailings of Portuguese Crown and country shipping at Malacca, 1684–1742. Used in conjunction with the VOC and EIC information found in Table 6.14 a more complete composite picture of Portuguese trading activities is possible.

Portuguese country traders' records of their exports and imports to and from China and India are even more elusive. Fortunately, the VOC records at Malacca of the cargoes carried by the Portuguese country-trader ships to and from Macao, establish the basic data from which certain observations can be made. The VOC's records of these cargoes indicate the import and export trends from China, as shown in Tables 6.16 and 6.17. Occasionally, the actual individual ship sales and purchases emerge in other reports of commercial activities of the Portuguese at the ports in which the VOC or the EIC were present or capable of obtaining information.

The record of Portuguese trading efforts on the Malabar coast from Macao in the 1730s to the 1750s was modest on account of several factors. First, the type of cargo that was exported and imported; their trade was primarily in ballast cargoes. Sugar was exported in large volume and had a low unit cost in China and pepper was being imported in significant volumes, although at the same time its unit cost was rising as a result of increased demand on the Malabar coast.[60] Second, competition in the importation of pepper and sandalwood intensified at Canton by English country traders from India and the Chinese junks from the South China Sea. Third, the Macao country traders' activities were hampered by their commercial rivalry with Goa and the Crown's insistence on their payment of customs duties even if they did not sail to the capital of the Estado da India. The fourth was their apparent over-dependence on Asian and European merchants to act as agents in procuring pepper.

By the late 1720s and early 1730s, the news of Macao country traders' activities on the Malabar coast, some of whose ships had not called at Goa, came to the attention of the Crown's authorities. The Estado da India attempted to hold the purchaser of the Goa custom duty *renda* responsible for the collection of duties from transactions of Macao's country traders on the Malabar coast as well as those at Goa. The Crown reiterated its orders requiring that all of Macao's shipping call and pay duties at the capital of the Estado da India. The hapless purchaser of the Goa custom duty renda remained accountable to the Crown's officials for the transactions carried out by Macao's country traders in all of the ports south of Goa to Cape Comorin.[61] Since their trade on the Malabar coast was less susceptible to Portuguese Crown surveillance and control as compared with that of Surat, Macao's country traders were more successful in evading the Crown's orders to call and pay customs duties at Goa.

The Estado da India's relations with the Zamorin of Calicut and the French at Mahe also influenced the Macao country traders' activities. By despatching Crown warships and establishing a factory at Calicut, the Portuguese at Goa sought to collect revenue from the sale of *cartazes* (sea passes). This policy was well-established and expressed in peace treaties between the Zamorin and the Estado da India on various occasions in the late seventeenth and early eighteenth centuries.[62] By the early 1740s, as a result of Calicut's commercial resurgence, this Estado da India's political and commercial interference was tiresome and antedated; hostilities occurred on a small scale between a Portuguese frigate and the Zamorin's troops in 1743.[63]

Friction between the Estado da India and the Zamorin of Calicut was hardly the most efficacious policy that Goa could follow to support the Macao country traders' activities. But, the Estado da India's cordial relations with the French aided the Portuguese shipowners and merchants from China. According to the EIC, in 1746, six Portuguese ships, the majority owned and operated from Macao, appeared on the Malabar coast and two sailed into Mahe, where the French had been assiduously purchasing the available pepper in the northern portion of the region; the Macao country traders sailed from Mahe for China with 4,000 picols of pepper, 1,680 picols of sandalwood and 21 picols of cardamon.[64] Although the actual annual transactions are less than well-documented these instances of Portuguese commercial activity influenced the availability of pepper and sandalwood stocks and prices on the Malabar coast, and were not isolated events but had regularly been noted in EIC records from the early 1740s.[65]

Further south on the Malabar coast, at Travancore, after Martanda Varma established his pepper monopoly, the Portuguese from Macao evinced a notable interest in trading with that state. By 1747, the English at Anjengo were active in trying to impede the Macao ship-owners and merchants from trading; in 1748, the EIC's merchants noted in one of their consultations the Portuguese efforts,

Table 6.16. *Portuguese*

Year	Number of recorded cargoes	Tea	Silk	Sugar Powdered	Sugar Unspecified	Zinc
1684	2	10	4 (pk) 2 (ch)			3,700
1688	2		4 (ch)			2,500
1689	1	10	10 (ch)		600	1,200
1692	1	5	6	15		1,000
1693	2	10	1.5 8 (ch)	400		2,800
1694	2	3 (b)	6 (ch)	750		
1697	2	12	20 (ch)	320		
1698	2	20 6 (b)				
1700	3	10		514		2,300
1701	3			1,400	200	2,500
1705	1	10		25		200
1706	2	25		400		400
1707	3			2,800		
1708	4		20 (ch)	5,000		
1709	1		10 (ch)	1,500		
1724	1			50		
1725	2	15 (b)			100	300
1726	2			150 150 (c)	120	110
1727	4				1,800	
1728	2					
1729	1	200			300	200
1730	1	180				
*1733	1			400	250	300
1735	1	200				150
1736	2				450	3,000
1741	3					
1742	4				1,400	350

Cargoes reported by the VOC at Malacca of those Portuguese arrivals from Macao only, with one exception * a Macao owned and operated ship from Batavia; all quantities in picols unless otherwise indicated. (b) = bales, (c) = canisters, (ch) = chests, and (pk) = packs.
Sources: ARA, VOC 1403/KA 1292 to VOC 2570/KA 2462 and *GM*.

exports from China, 1684–1742.

Radix China	Alum	Porcelain	Others
140	30	120 (b) tea cups, 7–8,000 cups, 1,200 (b) plates, 3,000 plates, 2,000 bowls	
100	50	10 (b) cups and plates, 110,000 plates	36 (ch) of gold thread
30			
3		95 (b), 10,000 plates	
60	200		
200	20	35 (b) cups	40 lacquered chests
	1,400	250 (b)	
	1,400	145 (b), 1,000 bowls	50 picols copper
	262	110 (b), 12 (ch)	300 picols sappanwood
50	200	50 (b)	1/4 picol gold, 250 picols copper
30		50 (b)	25 picols copper
100		80 (b), 30,000 pieces	2 lasten wheat
260		40 (b), 10 (ch)	
140	100	40 (b)	300 picols harpuys 200 picols copper
	60	100 (ch)	
200		30 (ch)	50 picols cowries
150		30 (b)	
	950	235 (b)	15 bahar harpuys, 2,400 bundles of cane 200 picols mercury
	200	3,400 pieces	300 nests of iron pans, 150 picols mercury
		150 (b)	35 bahar harpuys, 4,300 bundles of cane
		150 (ch)	
			146 bahar harpuys 700 bundles of cane
		80 (ch)	250 picols copper
	1,300	50 (b)	800 picols camphor
500	770	130 (ch), 2,000 pieces	2,600 nests of iron pans
150	1,200	200 (ch), 5,000 pieces	3,800 nests of iron pans

Table 6.17. *Portuguese*

Year	Number of recorded cargoes	Cloth	Cotton	Slaves	Poetsjock	Incense
1684	2	15 (pk)			30	15
1689	2			200		
*1690	2	70 (pk)		100*	40	30
1693	1				60	85
1694	4				40	50
1699	1				30	20
1700	1					
1701	1					
1706	1	insignificant report; carrying ballast				
1707	5		100 (pk)		68	
1708	2					
1724	1		20 (pk)			
1725	3					
1726	2				50(ba)	
1727	3					
1728	1					
1729	2					
1730	2					
1733	1					
1735	4					
1736	3		50 (b)		150	
1741	6	150 (pk)				
1742	4					

Cargoes reported by the VOC at Malacca of those Portuguese departures for Macao only; with one exception * a Macao owned and operated ship bound for Manila; all quantities in picols unless otherwise indicated. (b) = bales; (ba) = bahar; (pk) = packs; (c) = caliatour; (e) = ebony; (s) = sappanwood. *Sources:* ARA, VOC 1403/KA 1292 to VOC 2570/KA 2462 and *GM*.

and that they were encouraged by officials in the employ of the King of Travancore.[66] Despite EIC attempts to prevent the loading of pepper on Macao ships along the southern Malabar coast, the Portuguese continued to obtain supplies. In 1750, the English reported that the supercargoes from one Macao ship had visited the King of Travancore and presented him with various gifts from China with the immediate result of settling a contract for pepper at 95 *rupees* per *candy* (560 lbs. avoirdupois); the Macao merchants obtained 400 *candys* or 1,680 picols of pepper. The pepper was loaded immediately from Travancore stocks *imports into China, 1684–1742.*

Pepper	Sandalwood	Other woods	Salt	Lead	Others
			1,815		
			975		
			2,017		
			538		700 bundles cane
			3,000		
		100 (c)	700		
		700 (c)	200	200	70 picols unprepared laquer
		530 (c)	1,150	700	2.5 lasten of rice
		200 (c)	1,949	600	
200					
	200	300 (c)		822	200 picols of sugar
	250		300		
	40 (ba)				
350			1,075		150 casks of arrack; 3,500 bundles of cane; 150 picols mercury; 4,000 bundles of cane
450		1,100 (s)			
	900	1,800 (s)	504		
			1,344		
	1,500	1,400 (s)		300	300 picols of tin, 300 of alum, 500 of iron; 50 lasten of rice; 4,000 bundles of cane
500	1,500	500 (s)	1,344		25 half casks of arrack; 800 picols of areca
	2,500	1,750 (s)	840		880 picols of iron
1,200	800	800 (e)			50 (ba) of tin, 2,000 picols of areca
		2,400 (s)			

previously supplied to but removed from the VOC warehouse at Calicoilan on the orders of the King, and from supplies sent from ports further south.[67]

The geographical focus of the search for markets by Portuguese country traders from Macao shifted in the 1730s away from the South China Sea to the Indian Ocean. As the distance to the markets in which they operated grew, the type of cargo they carried changed and the profit margins they enjoyed they officially claimed diminished, the Macao country traders were able to maintain their trade but incapable of sizeable expansion. As individual entrepreneurs with consummate knowledge of local conditions and access to Asian capital as well as from Portuguese society in China and throughout the Estado da India, they were able to identify market opportunities and exploit them on a modest but fascinating scale. Their trade produced sufficient revenue to meet the city of Macao's expenses. But the consequence of the shift was that their survival continued to be threatened as the ascendancy of the English Company and country traders as major competitors in the Indian Ocean and the South China Sea emerged in the late eighteenth century.

The fortunes of the Portuguese merchants at Macao adjusted to this shift of market dependence from the South China Sea to the Indian Ocean. Their economic adjustment was difficult just as the political and social costs were high. Portuguese society in China had developed a resilient capacity to face economic and political change in its environment.

7

IMPERIAL RELATIONS: MACAO AND THE ESTADO DA INDIA

Macao's imperial relationship within the Estado da India over the seventeenth and into the eighteenth centuries was characterised by conflict and conspiracy. These manifestations of societal tensions revolved around the fundamental issues of economics and defence. Portuguese country traders, the Crown and the Church clashed within each group, and over which group would derive the maximum benefit from participating in maritime trade. These same groups had serious differences of opinion on Crown and communal defence decisions with reference to external threats to the survival of Macao.

Portuguese country traders at Macao actively protected their involvement in inter-Asian trade at two different levels. The first was external with the Senado da Camara, their collective representative embodiment, defending their political and economic interests against the Crown and other Portuguese municipalities. The second was internal, between different individual country traders and the representatives of the Crown and the Church at Macao. Varying degrees of competition, conflict and mutual co-operation were apparent within and between Macao, the Crown and the commercial elites of the various cities of the Estado da India. Crown administration, at the best of times, led these disparate communal and commercial interests in the direction of policies which were not always seen as being beneficial by local Portuguese societies.

Although conflict and tension were frequently present, there was general acquiescence by Portuguese communal groups *vis-à-vis* Crown authority and Goa interests on issues that did not threaten Macao's economic position. An example of the Senado da Camara of Macao's compliance towards the Crown and Goa's interests within the Estado da India concerned Cochin in the late sixteenth century. At that time, a fledgling commercial rivalry existed between Goa and Cochin. The Portuguese Crown administered the Estado da India from Goa but relied upon Malabar pepper from Cochin for its finance. Through their Senado da Camara, Cochin's Portuguese merchants made repeated attempts to redress this political and commercial imbalance without noticeable success.[1]

Macao's commercial interests were drawn into this rivalry. In the late sixteenth century, over several years, Portuguese shipping from China arrived at Cochin and sold Chinese silk and gold for silver and, perhaps, pepper; they paid local customs duties without sailing on to Goa. Crown authorities at Goa ordered Portuguese shipping from Macao to cease this practice. The Crown's decision was influenced by the nexus of Crown and country interests at Goa who saw that practice as a threat to Goa's commercial primacy which would also cause a decline in the collection to the Crown's customs receipts. Portuguese country traders at Macao chose not to support Cochin and to follow the Crown's orders on this occasion.

The characterisation that the Crown monopoly system limited the growth of Portuguese maritime and commercial development in Asia is directly linked to the question of who benefited from Macao's maritime trade.[2] Portuguese country traders at Macao were involved in the Crown's system of monopolising various voyages but whether such a monopoly seriously curtailed their activities and the development of the individual Portuguese entrepreneur may be examined by briefly comparing Portuguese trade to Japan, Macassar, Solor and Timor.

The Japan trade was a Crown monopoly. It offered, however, tremendous investment opportunities for the individual country trader and institutions of local Portuguese societies. After his appointment, the capitão-mor had to secure a vessel and arrange its outfitting. This process of preparing to sail depended on the capital available and the freight items to be carried on the voyage. With the outfitting of the vessel complete and the loading of freighted goods on the account of the Crown, local municipality or other institution or individual Portuguese and, on occasion, Asian merchants, the ship would depart Goa and repeat this procedure at the various ports of call en route to and in China and Japan.

The Crown's monopoly only involved the sale as opposed to Crown officials actually administering the voyage, consequently, it did not hamper the development of spectacular capital accumulation by a few Portuguese country traders. Crown administration of a trading route was in practice a different problem for the country trader to confront than the Crown's monopoly. With the Crown's administration of the Japan and Manila voyage in the 1630s, the previous investment opportunities for and the evasion of Crown customs duties by the country traders were curtailed.

The Portuguese trade at Macassar was not a Crown monopoly voyage so country traders were free to trade there without paying the Crown for the voyage. The Portuguese country traders at Macao were of the opinion that if the Crown administered the Macassar trade, as was ordered in 1634, they would lose access to a market where they could re-coup their financial losses without Crown supervision and their profit margins would fall to levels where the individual country trader would be in financial jeopardy. When the Crown attempted to administer the Macassar voyage Portuguese country traders at Macao and Goa were able to persuade the Viceroy, the Conde de Linhares, to revoke this order in 1635.

After the loss of the Japan and Manila trades, the Crown's monopoly of voyages from Macao ceased and its interest in the administration of Macao's trade to other parts of the South China Sea waned, in part, because it sought to husband its resources for the struggle against the VOC for Ceylon and the Malabar coast, and the voyages could not compensate the Crown sufficiently for its effort in capital and manpower. The Crown continued to despatch its ships from Goa to Macao and other ports in the region.

It was not until 1672 that the Crown sought again to administer a trading route in the South China Sea for its benefit. From 1672 to 1678, the Portuguese Crown tried to monopolise the sandalwood trade of Solor and Timor to China.[3] This policy encountered bitter resentment from local Portuguese society on Solor, Timor and Macao, and the Crown's administrators discovered that they could not rely upon the Portuguese country traders at Macao for support. The Senado da Camara of Macao obtained a reversal of this policy in 1678. Afterwards, and until 1784, a *pauta–bague* system was devised (the *pauta* being the method of selecting Macao's ships for voyages from sealed lists and on a rotating basis, the *bague* being the possibility of participation in the cargo space by all of the city's citizens through certificates of ownership). In theory, this would insure sufficient income for the poorer segments of Macao's population through the purchase of bagues in the sandalwood trade carried on the Solor and Timor voyages.[4]

PORTUGUESE CROWN AND COUNTRY TRADE IN ASIA: VALUES AND LOSSES

The working capital invested annually by the Portuguese Crown and country traders in the inter-Asian trade of the Estado da India, according to one exaggerated VOC estimate in 1622, approximated 50 million guilders. This figure, the report went on, excluded several million guilders-worth of trade carried on from Portugal to India by the Cape and the value of the Portuguese ships, fortresses, munitions and provisions in the East.[5] This particular report was an exaggeration in order to obtain larger amounts of capital from the Netherlands. The comparison of the estimated value of the Portuguese inter-Asian trades and of Macao in particular with that of the VOC establishes some fixed points to determine the extent of Portuguese commercial difficulties.

The VOC's original capitalisation was only 6.5 million guilders and its annual working capital for all of its operation at this time came to 1.25 to 1.50 million guilders.[6] The value of captured Macao goods sold by the VOC at Amsterdam in 1608 was over one-half of the total initial capitalisation of the VOC.[7] In 1622, Portuguese traders from Macao, on the trading route to India alone, were carrying cargoes worth 5 to 7.5 million guilders because of the large amount of gold being shipped.[8] By 1630, the annual capital invested in inter-Asian maritime trade at Goa was fifteen times the value of Portuguese exports to Europe and the equivalent of 6.6 million guilders.[9]

The Portuguese country traders in the Estado da India were threatened by impoverishment and collapse through their and the Crown's maritime and territorial losses to European and Asian foes. Macao and other Portuguese country traders disadvantageously encountered the superior armed and manned vessels of the VOC, Dutch vrij-burgers (the non-Company Dutch merchants), the EIC, and they also fell victim to the resurgence of Chinese, Indian and Malay piracy in the South China Sea and Indian Ocean. The number of Portuguese country traders' ships that were lost by shipwreck was on the increase; their owners were keeping the ships in service for a longer period than previously on account of rising costs for a replacement and refitting; ships were also overloaded and sailed by inadequate or less than skilled crews.

Several estimates may be attempted to quantify the extent of Portuguese country traders' shipping losses at the height of the VOC naval and military campaigns to destroy Portuguese trade throughout the Estado da India. Over the years 1629 to 1636, one Portuguese source estimated their total losses at some 155 ships destroyed or captured and, including the fall of Hugli in 1632, placed the value of their losses at 7.5 million xerafines.[10] It is possible from this same source to delineate forty Portuguese ships destined for Malacca and on to Manila and Macao, which probably contained cargoes in which Portuguese country traders from Macao participated, that were either captured or destroyed by the VOC or shipwrecked, for a total estimated value of 2.54 million xerafines (the equivalent of 5.9 million guilders).[11]

Based on the available archival and secondary accounts describing captures, losses and shipwrecks of Portuguese shipping which identifiably were owned by Portuguese country traders from Macao or were Crown or privately owned and traded at Macao, it is possible to tabulate a more precise picture of the magnitude of their losses. The results of such a tabulation cannot claim to be comprehensive but do enhance our knowledge of the role that the VOC, piracy, Chinese administrative policies and shipwreck had in Macao's maritime trading difficulties. There are some 245 recorded losses over the years 1601–83 of Portuguese ships sailing to or from Macao or with the investments of Portuguese country traders from Macao on board. The cargo value on 59 of the 245 losses is calculated as having been approximately 13.3 million guilders.[12]

The method by which Portuguese country traders sought to defend their economic interests *vis-à-vis* those of the Crown was a combination of intransigent individual and communal behaviour re-enforced by a consensus of communal support within the Senado da Camara of Macao. When support for such a position was expressed in local society, the Senado da Camara would lobby the Crown, as it did in the case of avoiding Malacca in preference of Macassar, by appealing to and writing for support from the Viceroy. They would also elicit as much support from other municipal institutions in Macao and in Goa, whose members were also country traders, and on many separate issues their interests coincided.

PORTUGUESE COUNTRY TRADING AND FINANCIAL METHODS

Portuguese trading methods and sailing techniques were relatively sophisticated in the early seventeenth century.[13] It was common practice for Portuguese merchants to make freight contracts between the owner/operator of a vessel and the major investors of freighted goods. Rates and conditions were clearly established in the contract. In one such contract, the capitão-mor of the Japan voyage of 1617, Lopo Sarmento de Carvalho, went into a limited partnership with a group of Portuguese merchants from Macao. The contract established the mutual liabilities of the two parties and the various exemptions for the capitão-mor and his partners for specified quantities of goods from the freight charges they were to receive from other merchants.[14]

In another such contract concluded in April of 1616 in Goa, two Portuguese traders, Vicente Rodrigues and Fernão de Araujo, agreed with the owner of the galiota, *S. José*, Francisco Mendes Maroco, to freight their goods on board his ship to Malacca and on to Macao. The freight rates for goods to be sold at Malacca fluctuated for the various qualities of Indian textiles between two xerafines and eight *tangas/corje*; spices, especially pepper, were fixed to the rate paid over the past five years, and silver was at 6 per cent.[15] Contracts between Portuguese country traders in China were probably common; after the loss of the investment opportunities in the Japan voyage, the freight rates for Portuguese country traders' goods to the major South China Sea ports were no longer established by individual merchants but by the Senado da Camara of Macao.

The Portuguese rapidly adapted to the idiosyncracies of obtaining local capital from Indian, Chinese and Japanese sources. By the early seventeenth century, the Portuguese country trader was more dependent upon Asian capital than European on account of the enormous sums required to maintain his trade.[16] These loans, which existed with striking similarities in medieval Asia and Europe, were known as respondencia and were utilised for the purchase of freight goods at variable rates of interest. Within Portuguese society, these loans were made available from local institutions such as the Society of Jesus, the Santa Casa da Misericordia, and prominent individuals with sufficient capital resources.

The Portuguese country traders used whatever shipping was available and viable. Large Chinese sea-going junks were used in the Japan and other trades in the South China Sea and occasionally in the Indian Ocean. On the west coast of India, a plethora of types of local coastal craft were employed in evading the VOC blockade to bring foodstuffs to Goa. In the restricted and sometimes shallow waters of the Straits of Malacca and parts of the Indonesian archipelago, they used *armada de remo* (oared galley craft) to good effect against European shipping.

The ship that the Portuguese used to carry on their trade with Japan was the famous *não do trato* (*carrack*), which was 'a large merchant vessel, broad in the beam, with high poop and forecastle, lightly gunned and an indifferent sailer.'[17] The career of this type of vessel lasted from initial contacts with Japan until its removal from service in 1617. The size of these ships was truly impressive; it is estimated that they ranged from 800 to 1200 tons and some even larger, but they proved unsuitable on account of being too unwieldy, susceptible to shipwreck, and lacking manoeuvrability and speed to outrun the faster, smaller, better-sailing Dutch and English shipping in the early seventeenth century.

The shift from the lumbering, towering carrack to a more manoeuvrable ship type occurred in 1618 and permitted the Portuguese to maintain their trading position in Japan. From that year until the end of Portuguese trade with Japan, the *galiota* (galliot), a swift dispatch vessel of 200 to 400 tons, was the predominant ship employed on account of its suitable size, cargo capacity, cost of operation and other specifications. It also became the primary ship type used to carry the

Portuguese inter-Asian trade for most of the seventeenth century and throughout the eighteenth century. In addition to the galiota, the country traders employed well known ship types, the *pataxo* (pinnance), between 100 and 300 tons, the *naveta* (galliot-type of ship), as large as 600 tons but usually the size of a galliot, and the *chalupa* (sloop), the smallest European-styled shipping used by the Portuguese which ranged from 50 to 150 tons.[18]

The size and other performance capabilities of the galiota, naveta, pataxo and chalupa compared favourably in functional design with the equivalent vessels utilised by the EIC and VOC as is testified by the number of captured Portuguese ships being incorporated into the VOC fleet.[19] The performance of the Portuguese country trader ships was deficient in the areas of armament and manning.[20] The cost of armament, its security, despite a Crown gun foundry in Macao, and merchant and Crown reluctance to outfit such a costly item on their respective shipping were factors in the under-armament of Portuguese shipping.

The Crown was extremely alarmed by the light armament of Portuguese country trader and Crown freighted shipping. The Crown did attempt with little success to entice Portuguese country traders to arm their ships more heavily.[21] It was not until Portuguese inter-Asian shipping losses reached critical levels in the decade from 1628–37 that the Crown and the Viceroy of the Estado da India inundated themselves with proposals and counter-proposals on how to resolve this crisis. Convoys, Crown squadrons and aid from the Spanish in the Philippines were all mentioned and most were rejected on account of the prohibitive cost.[22]

A comparison of ship-building, armament and operating costs between different Portuguese and European Company ship types is difficult to establish. There are several reports that suggest the value of and the operational cost of a Portuguese galleon and pataxo in the period 1621 to 1661. The fundamental operational cost, excluding the actual construction of the hull, masts and sails, for any European shipping was its ordnance. In 1640, the most important Crown Treasury official at Goa appealed by letter to the Senado da Camara of Macao for a substantial contribution for the preparation of one galleon to leave India for Europe; three-quarters of the necessary sum, slightly over 430,000 xerafines, was for seventy pieces of large calibre bronze artillery with the average price per piece being 4,600 xerafines.[23]

The pataxo, the favourite country trader ship type, rarely carried ten pieces of small-calibre ordnance. One Spanish estimate of the cost of building a 150 ton pataxo in either the Cochin or Goa shipyards in 1621 was around 5,000 reals (5,350 xerafines), eight pieces of artillery cost another 5,000 reals (5,530 xerafines) and the operational cost for a crew of fifty-six sailors and soldiers on one return voyage from Manila to India was another 4,000 reals (4,280 xerafines). In 1661, the Senado da Camara of Macao purchased at the Crown's shipyard at Goa for 25,749 xerafines a completely outfitted pataxo, the *Nossa Senhora dos Remedios do Cassabe*, of 300 tons.[24]

The Portuguese, as the defensive imperial power, may have felt the restrictions of the relative absence of manpower more acutely but the EIC and VOC experienced similar problems. The northern European companies, however, had recourse to greater resources for their remedy.[25] A century and a quarter had already elapsed since the establishment of the Estado da India and local Portuguese populations helped alleviate the manpower shortage, but the maintenance of the Empire acted as an endless drain on continental Portuguese manpower. This was aggravated by losses caused by the conditions of passage to the East, acclimatisation, disease, epidemics, and the naval and military actions against hostile European and Asian powers.[26] The failure of the Crown to improve the conditions of the passage to the East was coupled with a high desertion rate from the Crown's ships and fortresses to more lucrative pastimes as traders, mercenaries, dacoits and pirates.

This manpower shortage led the Crown and private merchants to outfit their shipping with only a minimum number of continental and mostly racially mixed Portuguese and the rest of the crew a combination of various European, Indian and Southeast Asian sailors and slaves. The consequence of this manning policy did not adversely affect their sailing skills but damaged their martial capabilities. When facing EIC and VOC squadrons or individual yachts manned by highly motivated crews on account of their participation in prize money from captured shipping, the Portuguese country traders preferred to run or beach and destroy their vessels and escape overland instead of giving battle.[27] This Portuguese country trader practice so upset the VOC, their squadron commander threatened keel-hauling as a punishment to captured Portuguese captains in an effort to halt the destruction of cargoes and ships.

The utilisation of smaller ship types, normally constructed by the Portuguese in the South China Sea or in the Indian Ocean and purchased from English or Danish merchants, increased the demands upon the fiscal and manpower resources of the local Portuguese communities in Asia.[28] The provision of increased numbers of smaller ship types was met primarily by the country traders and the Jesuits within local society, not by the Crown. The substantial losses inflicted upon Portuguese shipping in the South China Sea, by the VOC naval actions in and near the Straits of Malacca, brought about a serious and seemingly relentless drain upon financial and physical resources within local societies in Macao and in Goa, the two major foci of Portuguese private ship-owning and merchant interests.

The tension caused by the magnitude of the losses of and the threat to the fortunes of Portuguese country traders at Macao prompted those merchants to be increasingly reluctant to support the Crown's defence projects. They also turned upon each other in rage over failure to support certain political factions or policies aimed at obligating the community to repay individual financial failures. In 1623 the Senado da Camara, in its search for the finances to fortify Macao, explained its position concerning the Crown's demand that the city pay for its defences. The city claimed that it had expended, since its foundation, a sum approaching one and three-quarter million taels for the development of its trade with Japan and China, and since 1602 had regularly paid for the cost of repairs to the Crown's warships that visited Macao, which excluded the city's normal operating expenses.[29] A temporary palliative was found to pay for the city's fortifications by the Crown and the Senado da Camara by nominating the city a recipient of a Japan voyage.

The Portuguese country traders were faced with serious personal financial problems and the Crown's chronic demand for greater municipal contributions for defence projects aggravated the situation. The Crown had already discovered and tried to prohibit heavily indebted or bankrupt merchants in Macao from holding positions in the Senado da Camara.[30] By the date of the departure of the first capitão-geral from Macao in 1626, the communal leadership of Macao, which inherently had been based upon the occasional individual or more commonly the extended group economic interests, began to disengage from thinly veiled political alliances to open conflict in the attempt to control local municipal institutions.

Rival factions employed whatever means necessary including murder and enlisted the support of Crown officials in the pursuit of their own political and economic advantage. Municipal elections became subject to open attempts to suborn the electorate.[31] The scale and frequency of disruptive incidents was serious and regular enough to hamper some of Macao's more promising maritime trading initiatives.

After the losses of the cinnamon and pepper trades of Ceylon and the Malabar coast, golden Goa had been stripped of its last vestiges of gilt. The Estado da India's maritime trade, excluding Macao's contribution, consisted of the annual arrival of a Crown ship from Portugal, a few Goa country trader-operated ships from that port and the ports of the *Provincia do Norte* (the Province of the North, Diu, Bassein, Daman, and Chaul) via east Africa, the Persian Gulf and the Red Sea regions, and a plethora of indigenously owned and operated coastal craft with Portuguese participation from Cambay and the Malabar coast.[32] In addition, the Crown maintained a small squadron of war ships at Goa to be used to convoy and protect Portuguese country shipping in wartime and from European and indigenous pirates, collect revenue whenever possible from reluctant indigenous merchants who had not purchased a Portuguese sea pass and protect Portuguese political influence amongst the smaller state systems along the south-west coast of India. Goa's country traders were insulating themselves from Macao's competition in and operators as opposed to freight investors and contractors, were jealous of Macao's penetration of the markets on the west coast of India. By the late 1720s, Goa's country traders were insulating themselves from Macao'a competition in maritime trade on the west coast of India, in part, by ceasing to operate their shipping to the same ports as those of Macao. They modified the type of investment in which they participated by acting as freight investors, contractors and agents for Macao and European shipping. They also diversified their economic interests by expanding their investments in the agricultural sector.

The Estado da India was dependent upon the sale of rendas to generate sufficient revenue for the Crown. *Renda* was a term used collectively for the sale or farming out to the highest bidder of most sources of Crown revenue in the Estado da India. The financial dependence of the Crown on this method of obtaining revenue was already developed by the seventeenth century; 'the usual term of the sale was three years. The holder had to have a guarantor, and deposit a surety before taking up his contract. If no satisfactory bid was received the *renda* was run by Crown officials – as frequently happened with the Goa and Cochin customs duties.'[33]

By the early eighteenth century, the Crown's dependence upon the renda system deepened. The office of collecting Goa's maritime trade customs duties was incorporated into this system. The Crown was interested in securing the highest price for the Goa customs duties renda. Consequently, in the Crown's view, the activities of the Portuguese country traders from Macao threatened to diminish the amount of duty collected and the sale price of this renda. In order to prevent this decline in their revenue, the Crown became involved in the commercial rivalry between Goa and Macao.

Portuguese country traders from Macao lacked Goa's options for the diversification of their economic activities and their fortunes remained entirely dependent upon maritime trade. They encountered difficulties in maintaining their trade at several ports in the South China Sea. Those difficulties occurred, in part, on account of Chinese and European competition, internal political disruptions at those ports and the adverse impact of European wars and alliance upon their trade.

MACAO COUNTRY TRADERS AND THE ESTADO DA INDIA: SURAT

Commercial rivalry between Goa and Macao emerged in the early eighteenth century as Macao's country traders continued to despatch one or more of their vessels to Goa on an annual basis. According to the records of the Senado da Camara of Macao, these merchants became increasingly reluctant to trade at Goa on account of the low profits at that market and the changing of customs rates on goods destined for the ports on the west coast of India. They preferred to avoid Goa and trade north of that city at Surat. Unfortunately, the records of their trading activity, the composition, volumes and values at Goa and Surat have not survived. Although in the late seventeenth century the Portuguese from Goa and Macao were involved in an incipient pepper-smuggling trade on the Malabar coast, it was the activities of the Macao traders at Surat that engendered this rivalry.[34]

The Viceroy, Caetano de Melo de Castro, learnt of the transactions by a Macao country trader's ship, the *Boas Novas*, at Surat in 1706-7. The Viceroy ordered the Senado da Camara of Macao in 1707 to collect the Estado da India's customs duties from the local ship-owner and participating investors. The Senado da Camara called a public town meeting where the Macao country traders declared that on account of Timor almost being lost to them and the rest of their trade to neighbouring markets in the South China Sea being in jeopardy, they intended to send their ships to the ports on the west coast of India. Unless ordered from Lisbon to the contrary, they refused to collect the Estado da India's customs duties from Macao shipping that passed the Cape of Camorin (southern tip of India) and did not stop at Goa.[35]

The Senado da Camara immediately sought redress of the Viceroy's decision by appealing to the *Conselho Ultramarino* (the Overseas Council, the Lisbon-based Crown deliberative body which was empowered to investigate and regulate colonial affairs).[36] The Portuguese country traders received exemption from the Conselho Ultramarino for payment of duties at Goa for their shipping to Surat for the duration of the War of the Spanish Succession.[37] Although Portugal concluded an armistice in 1712 and separate peace treaties with France and Spain in 1713 and 1715, the Viceroy of India's decision in 1715 to reissue his order that Macao shipping stop at Goa en route to Surat was prompted not only by the termination of the war but also by the dangerous maritime conditions of the region and losses to Macao shipping inflicted by hostile Arab craft.[38]

The members of the Senado da Camara and the more important Macao country traders that were interested in the Surat trade were aware of the Viceroy's intention to reimpose this order. They had already filed their petition for an extension of the Crown's exemption from the payment of fees in Goa to the Conselho Ultramaraino in late 1714. This petition and the conflicting opinions of the major judicial and commercial figures of Goa and Macao outlined these two communities' differences of view on this issue.[39] Their arguments centred on whether the non-payment of duties and the commodities carried by Macao's shipping to Surat were competitive and harmful to the Estado da India's interests.

Those against the Macao petition are represented by opinions from one dezembargador and two prominent Goa merchants. They argued that Macao's trade and shipping at Surat damaged the collection of the customs duties of the Estado da India. The commodities carried by the Portuguese shipping to that port competed with each other directly and the Macao shipping was a security hazard on account of the recent captures by Arab shipping. Finally, they felt that the Macao country traders should be satisfied with their trade with a restricted number of markets in the South China Sea and Indian Ocean without any further expansion or diversification.

Supporting Macao's request, one dezembargador and two prominent Macao merchants, Francisco Xavier Doutel and Luis Sanches de Casares, argued that Macao's trade at Goa was becoming less viable. The absence of Macao shipping at Goa was not detrimental to the finances of the Estado da India and the products that the Macao ships sold (zinc, porcelain, sugar and copper) did not compete with Goa's trade in pepper and agricultural produce at Surat. Finally, in their opinion, it was of paramount importance for the Portuguese country trader in China to have additional markets as they had recently ceased trading with Banjarmasin, Siam and Cochinchina, and faced disturbed trading relations with Manila on account of the War of the Spanish Succession.

The Conselho Ultramarino despatched its decision in 1716. This body was temporarily in favour of Macao's petition and ordered that all of Macao's ships that passed Cape Comorin had to stop and pay customs duties at Goa but only on those items sold. One Macao ship was allowed to go on to Surat on an annual basis but this concession was only granted for a three-year period.[40] After the three-year Crown concession terminated, the Viceroy of the Estado da India reissued the prohibition of trade from Macao to Surat. In one of the Senado da Camara's letters to their Lisbon representatives in 1735, they ordered that the city's case for the revocation of this order be placed before the Crown. Since trade at Surat was free to all except Macao's country traders, and Muslim and English competitors from that port were successfully trading at Canton, the Portuguese at Macao felt their commercial interests were being sacrificed on account of unjust interference from Goa.[41]

The Crown's decision to require that Macao's shipping stop at Goa was detrimental to those Portuguese country traders from the mid 1710s onwards because, as they claimed, it allocated some of the city's trading resources to a market with declining profitability. It also forced their shipping to have customs duties collected on all of their cargo whether sold at Goa or destined for the Malabar coast. The account books for the revenues and expenditures of the Estado da India for the years 1719–22 suggest that around 4 per cent of Goa's receipts came from revenues generated by Macao's trade and the Crown's trade from Macao at Goa. The value of Macao's trade at Goa in relation to the total revenue of the Estado da India was proportionally smaller as Goa's receipts formed roughly one-third of the total revenue collected in those years.[42] From 1719 to 1722, the Estado da India collected revenues totalling approximately 5,561,000 xerafines, of which Goa contributed 1,824,000 xerafines and 74,000 xerafines of that amount was generated from trade and commercial transactions with Macao. In the mid 1720s, Goa's market offered Macao's country traders so few incentives that the Viceroy had to order the Senado da Camara to despatch shipping to that city.[43] Later, as their trade to the Malabar coast improved, Macao's ship-owners became less reluctant to despatch their ships in the direction of Goa but remained resentful of the Estado da India's policies on the payment of customs duties.

Macao's trade with Goa had a disastrous impact upon the Estado da India's monetary policies. Zinc was one of south China's principal export commodities that was profitably exported from Macao and sold at Goa. The Crown allowed zinc to be employed in the minting of the Estado da India's copper coinage by the purchaser of the Goa mint renda. These debasements occurred during a period which coincided with an increase in the price and demand for copper in India. The mixing of zinc with the Estado da India's copper coinage and the instability of Goa's mint may, it is speculated, have influenced the EIC's decision to cease accepting payment with Portuguese coinage in their territories in western India.[44]

A number of other issues also caused controversy between the Crown and the Portuguese at Macao and centred upon whether in fact the Portuguese country trader in China derived any economic benefit in passive acquiescence or active support of the Crown's orders. Those other issues concerned, for example, the organisation and the financing of protection for shipping belonging to the Portuguese Crown and different Portuguese Companies from Europe, along with Macao's country trade to India from China and to Timor.

In the 1690s, the Portuguese crown initiated discussions within the Estado da India and the Senado da Camara of Macao towards discovering their receptivity to its idea of establishing a company, the *Companhia do Comercio*, similar in purpose to the defunct *Companhia das Indias* of the 1630s, for the modernisation and renovation of Portuguese trade from Europe to Asia based on the successful northern European company models.[45] Macao, as in the 1630s, was opposed to its inclusion in such a company for a number of reasons, the most important being that the Companhia do Comercio would claim the monopoly of trade from Macao to the Estado da India, which would place the interests of Macao's country traders in jeopardy and their economic control over the China trade subject to outside interference. In this instance, Macao was successful in deflecting Crown efforts for its inclusion.[46]

The Crown sporadically despatched its own ships directly to Macao, and supported the formation of companies in Lisbon which were granted at different intervals the exclusive right to trade with China from Portugal. The financial success of these companies in Europe still awaits further research. The *Companhia de Macao* operated in the 1710s into the early 1720s; the *Companhia da Fabrica Real da Seda* in the 1740s; Felix von Oldenburg in the 1750s and one of the Marquis de Pombal's creations, the *Companhia Geral do Grão Pará e Maranhão* in the late 1750s onwards.[47]

The Crown's efforts to establish the Solor and Timor voyage as a monopoly and its interest in maintaining a fiscal official at Macao in the 1680s fuelled the fears of Macao's country traders as to the nature of the Crown's intentions. The Crown sent a *feitor* (factor) to Macao for the years 1689 to 1698; the feitor collected and administered an extra duty of 5 per cent instituted in 1685 on sandalwood brought by Macao's shipping from Timor for the payment of the salaries of the capitão-geral and the garrison of Macao.[48] There is a report which provides the partial accounts of the revenue actually collected by the feitor between 1702 to 1704 which suggests that this fiscal position was extinguished quite soon after 1704.[49]

The Senado da Camara complained bitterly to the Conselho Ultramarino of the Crown's imposition upon the limited economic resources of the country traders and specifically requested through the personal representation of Father Miguel de Amaral that the feitor be replaced by the *procurador* (authorised financial agent) of the Senado da Camara which was refused in 1695.[50] The Crown in 1709, while re-issuing its *alvara* of 1689 which had established the pauta/bague system, described that the Timor voyage prior to 1689 had been administered by a capitão-mor. The capitão-mor functioned for a period of three years, he was granted one-third of the total cargo space and the rest was to be freighted to the rest of Macao's citizenry. The first and last capitão-mor had been Fructuoso Gomes Leite, a prominent country trader, who in 1684–5 had been Macao's ambassador to Tonkin, Cochinchina and Cambodia.[51]

Macao's fears of direct Crown encroachment upon their trade was realised over the years 1698 to 1714. As a result of the losses suffered by Macao shipping en route to India at the hands of indigenous and European pirates and with the increased difficulties facing Macao's ship-owners during the War of the Spanish Succession, the Estado da India decided to provide a naval escort and convoy between India and China.[52] Although welcome for security reasons, the Crown's escort was resented as it was allowed to accept freight from merchants at Goa or Macao, a practice which directly competed in a previously profitable area of Macao's trade with Goa.[53]

Despite Macao's protestations and the partial dismantlement of the escort system which came at the end of the War of the Spanish Succession in 1715, the Estado da India continued to provide this system along the west coast of India from Calicut to Goa and permit the Crown's ships to sail to China from India carrying freight goods on private merchants' accounts.[54] The continuation of such practices exacerbated Macao's disenchantment with Goa's market opportunities which, as we have seen, cannot be commented upon further because of the absence of sufficient data. Macao's country traders, who were already embarked in search of markets elsewhere in the Indian Ocean, only reluctantly decided to return to trade at that port.

The Crown in Lisbon and the Estado da India's interest in trade to Macao, however, did not lessen but was stimulated in the 1730s on account of their hopes for China as an export market for their Brazilian tobacco production.[55] With the deterioration of the Estado da India's defensive capabilities and the successful conquest of the Provincia do Norte by the Marathas in the late 1730s, these efforts to market tobacco in China were severely disrupted. After receiving Goa's appeal for aid in 1740, the Senado da Camara had to reply that Macao's country traders were unable to send any significant aid on account of the city's economic difficulties.[56] The security threat posed by the Marathas on Goa and the rest of the Estado da India remained in the forefront of the Crown's attentions and neither Goa's nor Macao's interest in the trading prospects to China or to the remaining ports of the Estado da India was significantly revived for the remainder of the period.

CROWN AND COUNTRY TRADERS ON TIMOR

Towards the end of the seventeenth and into the early years of the eighteenth century, the relief of the Crown's position on Timor is yet another illustration of the degree of difficulty of obtaining co-operation between the Crown and the Portuguese country traders from Macao. After the loss of the Bantam market in 1682, Timor was the only remaining profitable South China Sea market in which the Portuguese Crown could hope to monopolise the local trade, with the short-term exception of Bajarmasin on Borneo.[57] The Crown's vision of enforcing a monopoly on Timor was far removed from the reality of its capabilities in the late seventeenth and early eighteenth centuries.

The Portuguese country traders from Macao, however, had successfully minimised the VOC and Chinese penetration of the Timor market throughout the 1670s and into the 1690s.[58] During the same period, the chronic friction created by the Crown's attempts to impose its authority upon the indigenous and mestiço population on Timor had not seriously disturbed the preferential supply of sandalwood to Portuguese country-trader shipping from Macao. In the mid 1680s, there was an incipient intensification, especially by Chinese junks from Batavia, of foreign competition for sandalwood supplies on Timor. From 1692 to 1694 and in 1697, the numbers of Chinese junks from Batavia at the principal port of Timor,

Lifão were 5, 4, 5, and 7 per annum respectively; the quality of their purchases of sandalwood was inferior in comparison with those of the Portuguese.[59]

Although sandalwood stocks were being depleted, the Portuguese country traders from Macao, according to a VOC report in 1690, were still able at this time to purchase the best qualities and quantities of sandalwood which were destined for the Chinese market. In the same report, one of the prominent mestiço community leaders with whom the VOC were dealing, António Hornay, confirmed that the quality and quantity of sandalwood available on Timor was declining. In 1692, only 500 picols of sandalwood, as compared with earlier levels of double and occasionally triple that amount, were exported from Timor by the Portuguese to Macao.[60]

By the early eighteenth century, segments of the indigenous and mestiço community on Timor were in revolt against Portuguese Crown authority. The Crown became involved in a desperate attempt to maintain its political influence with the numerous minor state systems and the indigenous populations on that island. It sought to enlist support from the Portuguese country traders from Macao whose sandalwood trade on Timor was now threatened by VOC and Chinese competition and where sandalwood stocks were in danger of being exhausted as a consequence of overcutting to supply all the competitors and finance the island's rebellion.[61]

The Crown appointed António Coleho Guerriero capitão-geral of Timor in the hope that he could reverse the declining position of the Estado da India in the Lesser Sunda islands.[62] Arriving in China from Goa in June of 1701, Guerreiro was able to convince the Portuguese country traders to aid the Crown. He freighted two of Macao's ships, and requested and received volunteers from the local population in order to have sufficient manpower for his military operation on Timor.

Aid from Macao, in particular from Pero Vaz de Siqueira, one of the city's major ship-owners and capitão-geral for 1702–3, was forthcoming. In return, Macao's country traders sought to benefit from the Crown's implementation of a vigorous naval patrolling policy aimed at restricting the access of Batavia-owned Chinese shipping to the Timor market. This alliance of Crown and Portuguese country-trader interests on Timor was short-lived, as Guerreiro's personal and Crown trading operations incensed his supporters from Macao whose aid immediately diminished.[63]

The Crown was satisfied to return the rebellion to the *status quo ante* by accepting the submission of Domingo da Costa, the most important rebel leader on Timor, in 1708 and re-incorporating him into the Crown administration of the island.[64] The Portuguese country traders did not receive any benefit from the Crown's intervention, since the forces for a properly operated naval patrol were either not present or utilised in trading activities that were in direct competition with those of Macao.

Temporary support for the Crown's position on Timor by Macao's country traders had failed to reverse the growth in Chinese competition on that island. By

1711, Chinese junks were not only active on Timor but the Portuguese country traders from Macao were encountering tremendous difficulties in acquiring sandalwood cargoes on Timor. Slightly earlier, around 1705, António Coelho Guerreiro reported to the Crown that he had failed to stop the over-cutting of sandalwood but had secured larger quantities for Macao's ships. He recommended that only 4,000 picols of the wood be cut each year, but he estimated that an annual total of 10–12,000 picols was being cut. The Macao Portuguese, although they were exporting 2–3,000 picols, were experiencing a fall in the price for sandalwood in China on account of the remainder of the wood was being exported by 12–16 Chinese junks or sloops to Batavia and from there on board junks to China.[65] By the 1710s, the Batavia market had assumed a greater importance for Macao's country traders and the Portuguese had started to import Malabar coast sandalwood into China; the Portuguese country traders from Macao, as a consequence, lessened their interest in trading on Timor.

In the 1720s, the Crown was faced with another rebellion of the indigenous and mestiço populations on Timor and appealed for aid from Macao. The Senado da Camara, who had already complained in 1724 of the deterioration of Timor's trade as a result of Crown administrative mismanagement, the charging of exorbitant export duties on sandalwood and the high rises in rates on imports of gold and iron, replied in 1727, that owing to the commitment of Macao's resources to financing the embassy of Alexandre Metello de Souza e Menezes to Peking, it was only able to contribute a token amount of aid to the Crown for the subjugation of Timor. In addition to citing the poverty of Macao's country traders on account of losses in the Manila trade and the expense of the de Souza embassy, the Senado da Camara explained why it would not order Macao's country traders to invest large amounts of capital in any ship going to Timor; the selling price of sandalwood on the China coast was only 6 pardãos/picol and the Crown's customs duties charges made that trade unprofitable.[66] Macao upon the insistence of the Crown continued to send one of its ships on an annual basis to Timor for the remainder of this period.

COUNTRY-TRADER AND MUNICIPAL FINANCES IN CHINA

Throughout the late seventeenth and into the eighteenth century, Portuguese country traders at Macao experienced difficulty in financing the expenses of the municipality and in making their obligatory contribution towards the maintenance of the Crown's administrators and the local garrison. The revenue to pay for these expenses had to be generated from the collection of customs duties on goods imported into Macao on their shipping and, only upon rare occasions, on other European country traders and Asian shipping.

The Senado da Camara met each year in a meeting open to all of the voting inhabitants, before their shipping departed China for South China Sea and Indian Ocean markets. At that meeting, the Senado da Camara set the customs duties rates on the various types of commodities that were to be imported. The commodities were placed into three major groups: coarse, fine and those weighed by a set of calibrated weights and measures.

The coarse goods, which were roughly the equivalent of ballast cargoes, included pepper, sandalwood, cloves, opium, birds' nest, rattan, areca nuts, sugar, lead and tin. There was a certain amount of controversy concerning the collection of the coarse goods rate – in the case of sugar, when this commodity was being imported into Macao for transshipment to India; pepper, when the selling price in China was depressed and this rate threatened the profit margins of the merchants trafficking in this commodity; lead and tin, which were permitted lower rates on the basis of arguments similar to those for pepper. Fine goods consisted of textiles, a large portion of which were woollens from Europe purchased at Batavia, Madras and Goa; this category may have included Indian textiles and perhaps Surat cotton. Those goods which were weighed were subdivided into silver and other items; all types of silver, whether as specie or bullion, were weighed. Other weighed goods included coral, amber and pearls.

At the same meeting, the inhabitants of Macao, in addition to deliberating upon the annual customs duties rate to be levied on imported goods, also decided how the collected revenues were to be spent in the succeeding fiscal year. The city's expenses were allocated the lion's share of the revenue, normally from 70 to 80 per cent, with smaller amounts, the equivalent of 10 per cent each, being contributed to the Santa Casa da Misericordia, the convent of Santa Clara at Goa, and set aside for the repayment of the city's debt to the King of Siam which remained from the 1660s until the 1720s.

Although the amounts of revenue the Senado da Camara collected from these customs duties for most of this period are unknown, the Senado da Camara records outlining the annual rate structure and the reasons for its modification exist and are summarised in Table 7.1. The customs duties rates and revenues that were charged and collected by the Senado da Camara were designed and maintained at the absolute minimum required to make payments to the capitão-geral and the garrison, the Bishop, the Chinese authorities for Macao's ground rent and any extraordinary charges. The Senado da Camara's financial records as reported to the Crown for 1740–5, indicated that Macao's trade in general, and this method in particular, could only hope to produce the minimum revenue to maintain the city. Over these six trading seasons, the Senado da Camara collected a total of 77,888 taels worth of customs receipts from seventy-seven ship and sloop arrivals at Macao; the city's coffers held a reported cash balance of a little over one hundred taels.[67]

Shipwrecks, piracies and captures also drained the finances of Portuguese country traders.[68] While the magnitude of these losses is difficult to tabulate, let alone calculate, an accurate image of their impact upon local Portuguese society may be outlined. On an annual average in the early eighteenth century, the Macao country traders and ship-owners despatched some fifteen ships and sloops to different ports in the South China Sea and the Indian Ocean. When, for example, in the 1697–8 trading seasons, four of Macao's ships were taken by pirates, although

Table 7.1. *The Senado da Camara of Macao customs duties rate schedule on imports, 1681–1741. (All figures as % of total value of amount imported)*

	Commodity grouping			
Year	Coarse	Fine	Silver	Other
1681	17	—	—	—
1686	10	5	2	2
1687–8	10	5	2	—
1689	10	8	3	—
1690	12	8	4	4
1691	10	5	2	2
1692	11	5	3	—
1693	8	5	2	—
6/1693	10	5	2	—
1694	12	10	5	5
1695	10	5	2	2
1696	12	8	2	5
1697–9	10	10	2	2
1700	12	12	2	—
1701–3	10	5	2	2
1704	10	5	3	2
1705	12	5	2	2
1706–10	11	5	2	2
1714	$12\frac{1}{2}$	6	$2\frac{1}{2}$	$2\frac{1}{2}$
1715	11	5	2	2
1719–26	8	4	2	2
1729–30	9	4	2	2
1731–2	7	—	—	—
1733–41	8	4	$2\frac{1}{2}$	$2\frac{1}{2}$

Source: AM.

one ship was retaken by its original crew, the disastrous impact upon the capital resources of the Portuguese country traders was reported by Crown officials.[69] With the numerical loss of one fifth of Macao's entire fleet in two years, the Portuguese country traders had to compete with the Senado da Camara for finance from the local sources of capital to cover their losses and re-capitalise their trade.

Within local Portuguese society at Macao, there were two major internal sources of capital – institutional and private. Capital was continuously competed for by the Senado da Camara and Macao's country traders, who were paradoxically the group that formed the leaders of these institutions. The institutional capital sources were the Santa Casa da Misericordia and the Jesuits of the Province of Japan and the Vice-Province of China. Private sources came either from prominent Portuguese country traders or, in rare circumstances, Chinese merchants residing at Macao. An accurate estimation of the real magnitude of the internal sources of capital available to the Portuguese country traders at Macao is impossible from the available records. Depending upon the actual date chosen, in the early eighteenth century, a maximum estimate of around 100,000 taels from the Santa Casa de Misericordia may be sustainable with an equivalent figure, or sometimes only half, from the Society of Jesus. Private Portuguese sources could raise, it is estimated, around 10–15 per cent of this total institutional figure.

The Santa Casa da Misericordia's administrative expenses were supposed to be defrayed by an annual stipend from the Senado da Camara's customs duties receipts. Its capital was generated by their administration of estates and legacies for widows and orphans. The brotherhood invested in the limited amounts of the city's real estate and made respondencia loans to country traders at a fluctuating interest rate. This rate depended upon the ship's final destination and the danger involved in the contemplated voyage. Surat was 25 per cent, Cochinchina and Tonkin were 15 per cent, and the remaining ports were 20 per cent. These loans were used in the preparation of shipping and the purchase of cargoes upon the provision of a suitable financial guarantor from the community. The brotherhood also made substantial loans to the Senado da Camara for the payment of the city's expenses and to local inhabitants to be used in investments on land, hence their name *ganhos da terra*, at fixed interest rates of 7 and 10 per cent. The Jesuits' financial activities functioned in a similar fashion in the provision of respondencia loans but on a slightly smaller scale than the Santa Casa da Misericordia.

The reliance of the Senado da Camara of Macao upon the Santa Casa da Misericordia for financial support was slight in the late 1680s but by the 1750s had evolved into a pernicious dependence. In 1688, towards the end of the Senado da Camara's fiscal year, Macao's expenses had exceeded its customs duties revenue which left the city's leaders without any other recourse but to request that the capitão-geral order the release of sufficient funds from the Crown's collection of a 5 per cent duty on sandalwood imported from Timor to cover the city's deficit. With the capitão-geral's refusal to release these funds, the Senado da Camara decided in that year to borrow a small amount from the funds administered by the Santa Casa da Misericordia for the benefit of orphans and widows.[70] By 1691 the Senado da Camara had borrowed a little over two thousand taels from the brotherhood and was obligated to pay 7 per cent interest.[71]

The Senado da Camara accounts for 1696–1718 and 1726–44 reveal that these civic leaders continued to be burdened by these borrowings from the Santa Casa da Misericordia. The city's repayments were irregular and in small amounts; the interest on the principal accumulated at an alarming rate. In addition, the city was committed to contributions to the brotherhood on an annual basis of all the city's customs receipts.

By 1711, the Senado da Camara had borrowed a little over 4,000 taels from the Santa Casa da Misericordia but had been unable to pay any of the principal and owed 3,000 taels of interest. By 1718 the city had made no repayment on the principal and the total outstanding debt to the brotherhood was 12,293 taels. From 1706 to 1718 the Senado da Camara made repayments to service the accumulated interest on this loan to the total amount of a little over 2,700 taels excluding the city's contribution to the brotherhood of a little over 3,300 taels over 1710–18 from customs receipts.[72]

In 1726, on account of the expense associated with Macao's usual expenditures and its support for the embassy of Alexandre Metello de Souza e Menezes to Peking, the Senado da Camara borrowed an additional amount from the Santa Casa da Misericordia that brought the principal of the loan to a total of 6,000 taels. By 1744, the total outstanding debt, interest and principal of the city to the brotherhood that accumulated over 1726–44 was 14,252 taels. At the same time, the Senado da Camara decided that in order to service this debt the customs duties collected from all ships arriving from Manila at Macao would be allocated towards its repayment.[73]

The Senado da Camara's dependence upon the financial resources of the Santa Casa da Misericordia had a special significance for Macao's country traders. With the city's inability to diminish significantly the outstanding debt to Macao's major local lending institution, the Santa Casa da Misericordia remained dangerously undercapitalised which weakened its ability to finance the activities of the city's country traders. The Crown received reports in the 1680s that the Santa Casa da Misericordia's funds deposited with it for the benefit of orphans and widows were being misused by improperly loaning them as respondencia without adequate security and financial guarantors to Portuguese country traders. The Crown, as a consequence, ordered the *juiz dos orfãos* (a municipal appointed magistrate in charge of orphan welfare) to regulate and investigate these improprieties in the administration of the brotherhood's funds.[74]

The practice itself was not improper but the failure to provide adequate security, guarantees and the subsequent inability to repay the interest let alone the principal of the loan seriously threatened to impoverish this institution and the widows and orphans that relied upon the correct administration of their inheritance. In an attempt to assuage the fears of the community, the Crown and the Church, the Santa Casa da Misericordia leadership sought the opinion of the Bishop of Macao on the legality and propriety of appropriating all of the orphans' funds, whether stipulated or not, as the capital for respondencia loans. After receiving a series of opinions from theologians within the different Catholic orders at Macao, the Bishop informed the brotherhood in 1699 that it was permissible to appropriate all of the orphans' funds if one half the amount left with the brotherhood was loaned at a fixed rate of interest as ganhos da terra which would protect the legacy from extinction. The second half could be applied towards respondencia loans, if those loans were available to only and all of Macao's qualified shipping investors. The qualification for those shipping investors was that they had to present a financial guarantor who would agree to obligate himself to repay the loan.[75]

These excessive practices did not disappear, the Crown reiterated its orders prohibiting the misuse of these funds in 1709 and also ordered the Santa Casa da Misericordia in 1716 to desist from using them for loans to Macao's country traders.[76] The brotherhood did not desist from making respondencia loans.[77] By 1728 reports of the misappropriation of these funds reached Lisbon, and the Conselho Ultramarino ordered the ouvidor in Macao to investigate and to ensure that the juiz dos orfãos actually executed his duty.[78] These orders were issued but were easily and openly defied by Portuguese country traders at Macao who were the brotherhood's leaders and whose personal requirements for capital could not be deterred by the Crown's orders.

The capitão-geral at Macao in 1735, Coseme Damião Pereira Pinto, informed the Crown that out of a total accumulated capital of 50,000 taels in the orphans' coffers, the Santa Casa da Misericordia had 6,000 taels stopped by its loan to the Senado da Camara, 15,000 were outstanding and the rest lost in non-collectible loans. In the capitão-geral's opinion, the brotherhood's finances were so exhausted by the mismanagement that it was temporarily unable to make respondencia loans. He recommended that the Jesuits of the Province of Japan be nominated by the Crown as the administrators of the Santa Casa da Misericordia of Macao.[79]

The capitão-geral's drastic recommendation for the fiscal reform of the Santa Casa da Misericordia was not implemented but this institution benefited from his election as *provedor* of the brotherhood from 1736 to 1738. The deliberations of the *Mesa* (governing board of the brotherhood) for those years in which he was provedor demonstrate that he advocated and the brotherhood adopted a very stringent attitude towards the repayment of outstanding and non-collectible loans with moral persuasion and threats of legal action at Goa.

The Santa Casa da Misericordia never reconstituted the total accumulated capital of 50,000 taels in the orphan's coffers; it was, however, able to continue under Coseme Damião Pereira Pinto's leadership and afterwards to make respondencia loans.[80] The Senado da Camara agreed in 1744 to earmark the customs duties receipts of ships arriving from Manila for the repayment of the interest on the brotherhood's loan to the city. The brotherhood's records indicate that those revenues were utilised for a modest expansion in the provision of respondencia loans. Without administrators of Pinto's stature and despite his return to Macao as capitão-geral between 1743 and 1747 and as provedor from 1744 until 1746, by 1753 the Santa Casa da Misericordia's revenues faced severe contraction from a failure by some Macao country traders to make repayments and by others in the leadership of this institution to force their collection.[81]

THE PADROADO AND COUNTRY-TRADER FINANCES

The suggestion made to the Crown by the capitão-geral in 1735 that the Jesuits be employed in the administration of the Santa Casa da Misericordia is only one instance in which the Padroado was considered by the Crown and Macao's country traders as not only an integral, but a fundamental contributor towards the maintenance of Portuguese society in China and the South China Sea. The Padroado played an important political role in justifying the Portuguese Crown's continued imperial claims in Asia long after the reality of their debility in relation to other European powers was apparent. The Padroado's actual missionary role in China became subject to question by French and Spanish missionary activities, and various Catholic doctrinal controversies ensued in the late seventeenth and early eighteenth centuries.

In the early eighteenth century, the Jesuits increased their political influence throughout the Estado da India. The Crown deepened its reliance upon the Jesuit order for financial and administrative support. The relief of Mombasa was financed largely by loans from this order; the Jesuits loaned the Estado da India in 1727 and 1728 a total of 139,000 xerafines for the reconquest of Mombasa at 8 per cent interest with the income from Crown lands on several islands near Goa as a guarantee of repayment.[82] In various locations in the Provincia do Norte, the Jesuits acted not only in a pastoral role but as administrators for the Crown.[83]

Although the heyday of Catholic missionary activity as supported by the Portuguese Crown was over, the Jesuits of the Province of Japan and the Vice-Province of China continued their missionary activities in China and the South China Sea from Macao as their logistical base and Peking where they occupied a privileged position at the Imperial Court. Chinese official acceptance and permission for the propagation of the Catholic faith was subject to periodic revision and recension with the subsequent adverse impact upon the convert, missionary and Portuguese communities. The extent of their success in China as missionaries was negligible, but as technical advisers they met with a startling degree of receptivity by Ch'ing officials and scholars.[84] The political influence of these Padroado-supported Jesuits in northern China was greatly enhanced in the late 1680s with participation in negotiations for the Ch'ing with the Russians which resulted in the signing of the Treaty of Nerchinsk.[85]

At Macao, the diplomatic and economic talents of the Jesuits were both admired and resented by different Crown administrators and country traders. A principal reason for this resentment stemmed from the lay perception of their economic power. Although the Macao traders' idea of Jesuit economic power was correct in the context of local Portuguese society, the funds the Society of Jesus actually administered in the late seventeenth and into the first half of the eighteenth century were modest relative to Asian merchant capital resources. Based upon partial records of different available revenue sources, as described below, over the period, the Society of Jesus appears to have administered a minimum of, perhaps, 50-100,000 taels of silver.

The Jesuits financed their missionary activities by virtue of grants and donations from the Crown, prominent individual Portuguese, friendly indigenous officials and converts. They administered legacies left to them on a similar basis as the Santa Casa da Misericordia and invested in maritime trade by involving themselves as an institution through their procurador in bullion and merchandise transactions on ships that were owned wholly or in part by the Jesuits or on Crown or Portuguese country shipping.

During the halcyon days of the Japan mission and voyage, the Jesuit involvement in maritime trade was bitterly resented and condemned by the Crown, some Portuguese country traders, and other religious orders. The Crown's chronic inability to provide sufficient funds to support the mission left the Jesuits with little alternative, as they argued, than to utilise the commercial activity which would derive the maximum political and economic benefit for the order and would permit them to attain their spiritual objectives. Prior to the loss of the Japan trade the

Jesuits of the Province of Japan relied primarily upon their direct involvement in maritime trade for their support. The Crown's payments, capital transfers from their rental and agricultural property in India and the administration of donations and legacies from Macao's inhabitants were the principal additional sources of revenues.[86]

The finances of the Jesuits in China, from the 1640s up to the 1680s, mirrored the difficulties that surrounded Macao's trade. According to Father Luis da Gama in 1664, the Jesuit missions in the South China Sea that were initiated – in Cochinchina (1610s), Tonkin (1620s) and later in Macassar (1650s) – by the Province of Japan involved the finances of that Province in extraordinarily heavy expenditure and losses in maritime trade to the total of 22,000 xerafines. Da Gama also was pleased with the Province in their past selection of a procurador to handle the Jesuit investments and finances at a time when the structure of Macao's maritime trade was in the process of modification. He approved of the concentration of the Province's investments in the specific Chinese export commodities of silk, gold and zinc which were purchased on a contractual basis with Portuguese country traders at Macao. By 1664, at the height of and despite Macao's troubles with the Ch'ing officials at Canton, the Province had made a series of payments on its outstanding debts and had accumulated sufficient capital to approach the Crown for permission to purchase agricultural property in India. Despite the promise of expansion in their ownership of land in India, da Gama was adamant that the Province's finances should remain dependent upon revenue from maritime trade.[87]

In Lisbon in 1666, while engaged in negotiations with the Crown, the *procurador geral* of the Province, Father Phillippe Marini, received news of da Gama's observations and recommendations for the Province's fiscal reforms. A portion of the Province's indebtedness, a sum of 10,000 xerafines, had been incurred when the Jesuits had previously made two loans to the Estado da India for its finances. The first loan was made in 1642 and the Province was subsequently frustrated in their attempts to receive repayment. Marini negotiated a method of repayment that was a major concession of the Crown's prerogatives. On account of the absence of liquidity in the Estado da India's finance, the Crown conceded a tax exemption on the Province's landed property, until the debt was repaid.

Although Lisbon supported the strengthening of the Province's finances, the Viceroy of the Estado da India took a decision in order to avoid compliance of these orders which he viewed as detrimental to the Crown. The Viceroy, the Conde de São Vicente, João Nunes da Cunha, ordered the transfer of a small number of properties owned by the Jesuit College of Rachol, which was part of the Province of Goa and whose right of possession of this property had never been confirmed by the Crown, to the Province of Japan in 1667. He also requested the Crown's confirmation of the Province of Japan's purchase of the village of Morosi in the Provincia do Norte.[88] In this manner, the Viceroy was able to avoid having to execute the tax exemption granted by the Crown to the Jesuits.

By the early 1680s, with the modest revival of Macao's trade, several prominent Portuguese country traders at Macao had taken notice of the Jesuits' expertise in the administration of legacies and donations at a time when the Santa Casa da Misericordia's funds were diminishing by mismanagement and fraud. The Jesuits of the Province of Japan, as a result, received several rather large legacies and donations. The Jesuits' administration of these funds became for some of Macao's country traders an important alternative source of finance and for others – those denied access to this finance – a practice that was bitterly resented. There were two donations and one legacy, in particular, that provided substantial capital for Jesuit investment and finance.

The first donation was that of Father Paulo dos Santos for 12,000 taels in 1636 for the foundation of a seminary for Japanese for that mission. The dos Santos donation was invested in rental properties in Macao with the purpose of supporting twelve seminarists. In 1699 it was decided that the principal and interest from this donation were to be employed in financing the expenses of the Tonkin mission which was done from 1700 to 1711. After an inquiry of the misuse of these funds, Father Miguel de Amaral ordered the restitution of 3,503 taels to the dos Santos donation's account in 1713. That capital was then loaned and invested by the Jesuit procurador until the total original amount of the donation was replaced in 1748. By 1762, however, there were only 3,062 taels credited to this account as a result of losses in Jesuit respondencia investments.[89]

The second donation was that of Francisco Vieira de Figueredo and his widow, Dona Catherina de Noronha, of 11,728 taels in 1680 for the foundation of a college within the jurisdiction of the Province of Japan. These funds were invested in the purchase of additional rental and agricultural property in northern India in 1721, the profits of which were used in the support of their missionary activities in China. These properties with their vital incomes were extinguished after the Maratha conquest of most of the Provincia do Norte in the 1730s.[90]

The legacy was that of Nicolão Fuimes and his widow, Antonia Correa, for 10,000 taels in the form of a contract between his widow and the Jesuits. They administered this sum under the obligation to pay Antonia Correa an annual stipend of 500 taels. These funds were vigorously employed and the contract complied with by the Jesuits from 1737 until 1761. They were used in making profitable respondencia loans and freight contracts between 1737 and 1748. On account of the trading difficulties encountered by the ships of Luis Coelho, a Macao-based country trader, with whom the Jesuits had concentrated their loans, these investments began to suffer substantial losses. By 1761, the capital of this legacy was nearly exhausted as the Jesuits had allocated them to pay for deficits in their operating expenses. Their contractual arrangement with Antonia Correa was retained until their expulsion in 1762, with the continued payment of the stipend from this and other Jesuit financial sources.[91]

The most dramatic change in the Province of Japan's financing of its regular operating expenses over the period to 1684 to 1754 was the shift from its nearly total dependence upon revenues generated from maritime trading loans and investments to a greater reliance upon the transfer of silver specie purchased in Goa from the proceeds of the rents from villages and sales of agricultural commodities and lands owned by the Jesuits in northern India. The Province did not cease to generate revenues from maritime trading loans and investments. Since the Jesuits kept their accounts by each separate administrative entity, the Province of Japan in this instance is used to encompass the accounts of the Province, the Vice-Province of China, the College of Macao, the Tonkin Mission as well as a few minor entries which globally represents the total Padroado-supported Jesuit missionary activity in China.

The Province of Japan administered these villages, farms and other property, in an identical manner to all of their other investments in Portugal and China, through a procurador. He was one of their order and a member of the Province selected on the basis of his commercial acumen. He also oversaw the collection of rents, sales of agricultural produce, and the payment of their land taxes to the Crown's treasurer at the local fortress, depending upon the location, either at Bassein or Goa. The number of villages, farms and palm groves over which the procurador in the Provincia do Norte and at Goa acted as an overseer expanded throughout the sixteenth, seventeenth and eighteenth centuries; in 1730 they totalled fifteen and one-third.[92] These fifteen and one-third villages and other properties ownership and locations were distributed as follows: the Province of Japan, nine (Morol, Mulgão, Condolim, Ponvem, Borbata, Quirol, Moroci, the cassabe of Caranja and a farm, Taleigão, near Goa); the College of Macao, four (Arem, Mirem, Malvara, and the collarias of Tanna); and the Tonkin Mission, two and one-third (Moroci, Sar, and one-third of Maljaca). His most important responsibility, as far as this study is concerned, was his despatching to Goa all of the disposable annual income from these properties.[93]

The disposable annual income from the Provincia do Norte arrived at Goa in letters of exchange, acceptable currencies (*larins* and *pagodas*) and merchandise, where it was converted into silver specie or bullion and sent via Macao's country traders or Crown shipping to China.[94] Table 7.2. reveals the amount of revenue generated and remitted to Goa.

In the last forty-five years of the Jesuits' ownership, these properties remitted a total of 1,202,039 xerafines to Goa. At Macao, these revenues provided on the average the equivalent of well over one-half of the annual amount of funds used to pay the operating expenses of the Padroado supported Jesuits in China.[95]

With the loss of the revenues from these villages in the late 1730s, the Province's finances returned to a precarious state with having to rely for its finance from maritime-trading investments. These revenues were substantially augmented by utilising funds administered from legacies and donations. From the extant accounts, the Province was able to generate adequate revenues for their finance from these investments until the late 1740s and early 1750s when they encountered severe losses, which were not recovered by the date of their expulsion from Macao in 1762.

Resentment of the Jesuits' wealth and power, whether justified or not, continued to exist amongst the Portuguese community at Macao. The Jesuits, for example, refused a Senado da Camara petition for a contribution towards meeting the city

Table 7.2. *Remittances from the Provincia do Norte to Goa for the financing of the Jesuit Province of Japan, 1691–1735. (All values in xerafines)*

Year	Value	Year	Value	Year	Value
1691	20,300	1706	40,678	1721	28,227
1692	6,358	1707	33,425	1722	25,101
1693	17,186	1708	35,713	1723	29,569
1694	16,423	1709	39,769	1724	29,419
1695	5,915	1710	37,118	1725	27,275
1696	18,066	1711	24,562	1726	27,237
1697	19,328	1712	33,919	1727	31,375
1698	21,001	1713	31,856	1728	22,633
1699	23,080	1714	33,323	1729	21,814
1700	18,884	1715	16,277	1730	28,807
1701	17,891	1716	34,542	1731	19,050
1702	30,162	1717	36,714	1732	18,931
1703	46,781	1718	37,471	1733	16,919
1704	42,058	1719	30,836	1734	12,877
1705	40,572	1720	29,886	1735	14,711

Sources: Ajuda, JA, 49–IV–65, fols. 365v–74 and HAG, Macao, 1497.

of Macao's expenses in 1703. Father Miguel de Amaral replied to the city's request that Goa's remittances from the northern Indian villages were less than anticipated and that their respondencia and investments on Macao's ships trading at Manila had yet to return. Some Portuguese country traders at Macao were upset by what they considered as the Jesuits harbouring their relative wealth to the detriment of themselves and of the community.[96] Despite the Jesuits' unique position at Peking and their financial and political contribution towards ensuring Macao's survival, by 1762 at Macao and throughout the Empire, communal resentment against the Society was endemic and the Jesuits were expelled by the order of the Marquis de Pombal.

Portuguese society at Macao was weakened by the conflicts and conspiracies that characterised this community in China, and its imperial relationship within the Estado da India. Economic opportunities that evolved, especially those such as the Portuguese companies' trade to China which called for the amalgamation and *sublimation* of familial or group interest in favour of a corporate structure, were rejected since control over the enterprise did not reside in Macao.

Portuguese society in Macao was structured to defend local economic interests and it was successful in that defence. It was not involved in the development of other structures that could return Macao to its previous prosperity. Never free from these tensions, the ingenuity of Portuguese society at Macao was tested further in their relations with the Chinese empire of the Ming and Ch'ing.

8

IMPERIAL SURVIVAL: SINO-PORTUGUESE RELATIONS FROM MING TO CH'ING

The survival of Portuguese society in China was seriously in question during the decline of the Ming and the establishment of the Ch'ing dynasty. Although the municipality was administered by the Portuguese, by the mid eighteenth century, Macao was incorporated through the implementation of a number of economic and administrative procedures into Ch'ing China. Elements of this process of incorporation had been present from the beginning of Sino-Portuguese relations, others evolved as a result of Chinese strength and Portuguese pragmatism.

Towards the 1620s, Portuguese commercial and political relations with Ming officials and Canton's merchant community began to deteriorate. A system had evolved in Sino-Portuguese commercial contact which regulated Portuguese access to China's production. Portuguese merchants were restricted to visits to two annual fairs held at Canton. These fairs occurred several months prior to the departure in different monsoon seasons of Portuguese shipping from Macao for India and Japan. A small number of rich and influential Portuguese merchants departed Macao for Canton where they could stay as long as four or five months to contract, to attend the fair and to supervise the loading of their purchases of raw silk, silk piecegoods, gold and other items. The Portuguese travelled up the Pearl river and arrived at a small island in mid-river opposite Canton, where they would wait until received by the Viceroy of the Two Kwang (the provinces of Kwantung and Kwangsi) or in his absence by the Governor. The Portuguese would submit a substantial present to either official in order to obtain permission for free trade.[1]

The Portuguese country traders, after obtaining permission to trade, initiated their negotiations with the major Chinese quevees (*k'uai*: merchants/brokers) to establish the price and to order the desired quantity and quality of silk cloth and other trade items. With agreement on such contracts, the Portuguese advanced substantial portions of their capital to the Chinese merchants who contracted the requisite number of weavers and looms to supply these orders. The Portuguese obtained credit from these quevees and received merchandise on consignment.[2]

These commercial contracts were not without risk to both sides; one Portuguese report, whose ethnocentric bias is obvious, stated that 'there are many [Chinese merchant/brokers] who entrust great sums of money and goods with the Portuguese, and consequently the Portuguese with them, but it has been and still is frequently seen that these *quevees* embezzle the money of the Portuguese and flee without returning it to them.'[3] Although embezzlement was evident for both groups of merchants, it appears that the Chinese authorities were not greatly interested in involving themselves in obtaining redress for such sharp practices, nor were Macao officials capable of obtaining redress in cases which were in favour of Portuguese merchants. Since Chinese officials appeared to be indifferent, the Portuguese ignored similar petitions from Chinese merchants with relative impunity.

Once contracts for Chinese produce were agreed, the Portuguese had to petition the same Chinese authorities for the fair or open market to be announced, and this was accomplished only after another substantial gift was presented. After this announcement, any Chinese merchant could contact the Portuguese and offer his merchandise. When all significant transactions were completed, the Portuguese purchases and consigned goods were loaded upon, usually, two *lanteas* (large riverine broad-beamed lighters, lading 600 to 800 tons of cargo).[4] To depart, the Portuguese country traders had to request permission from the Chinese authorities, which required the payment of a gift. After obtaining this permission, the lanteas departed Canton, paid official duties at Ansao (the district capital of Hsiang-shan) and completed their journey to Macao in a convoy of a dozen or so *choas* (armed, oared vessels with a complement of soldiers for protection from pirates).[5]

The deterioration of Sino-Portuguese official relations towards the 1620s, according to Gabriel de Matos, the Jesuit Rector of the College of the *Madre de Deus*, was caused by the persistence of ill-conceived commercial practices.[6] De Matos ennumerated five such practices: the Portuguese traffic in Chinese children; the reception of Japanese go-shuin-sen and Christians at Macao; the delivery to and sale in Macao of non-taxed Chinese merchandise by *lorchas do risco* (ships of the Chinese owners' responsibility without any offical sanction or pass and carrying raw silk and gold which evaded customs – in the 1620s these visits averaged three to five per year and they continued into the 1630s); the building of houses on sites in the city without official permission; and the non-payment of Chinese measurage duties on some arriving Portuguese shipping.[7] The Portuguese paid a *foro do chão* (annual land rent) to the Emperor in recompense for his permission to utilise the land upon which the city was situated; this rent was paid at the Canton fair.

The Portuguese traffic in Chinese children and perhaps domestic servants was an impediment of a singular nature to better Sino-Portuguese relations. By arrangement, the Portuguese would meet Chinese merchants somewhere in the Pearl River estuary or the islands south of Macao to purchase human cargo that would fetch 10 pardãos/child, according to the ouvidor Manuel Luiz Coelho, in Manila. The capitão-geral of Macao, D. Francisco Mascarenhas, and the Viceroy had tremendous difficulties in effectively outlawing and extinguishing this practice.[8]

The Portuguese recorded changes in the treatment they received from Ming officials at Canton. *Chapas* (official passes or communiqués) which in the past had been readily available to Portuguese envoys or merchants travelling to the fairs were no longer free but subject to payment. Ming officials in verbal and written communications were using harsher language towards the Portuguese and in public these officials ceased treating the Portuguese with deference.[9] The Portuguese by

1628 had lost the privileges of entry, contact and the right to sell merchandise to the Chinese in the new and old parts of Canton.

One of the reasons for these changes was the intervention of the merchants from the Fukien coast ports (*Chincheo*) at Canton. Those merchants, who competed against the Portuguese in the Japan and Manila markets, encountered at this time problems in their maritime trade as a result of the VOC's position on Taiwan with its policy of curbing Chinese trade and Ming official interference. These merchants wanted to influence Ming officials at Canton to dampen Portuguese commercial efforts. Another, and probably more important reason was the failure of the Portuguese country traders to half their flagrant evasion of the orders of Ming officials to cease offensive commercial practices.

Accompanying these changes was a rise in the incidence of Chinese piracy upon Portuguese ships off the south China coast. The Portuguese believed that this piracy was committed with Chinese official connivance or through official indifference. Prior to 1621, five ships (two after departing from Macao for Japan and Cambodia, three while attempting to arrive at Macao from Tonkin, the Luzon area and India) were lost to pirates with the crews killed or captured. The Portuguese claimed that 300,000 taels worth of silver was on board the ship from India and the female captives from the ship destined for Cambodia were sold at Canton.

The Portuguese felt this gradual shift in Sino-Portuguese relations most significantly in the area of commercial practices. Prior to 1582, the Portuguese paid their Chinese customs duties in merchandise, usually spices. After that date, silver became the only acceptable method of payment. Chinese customs duties on imports were levied on the size of the measurage of the arriving vessel. The measurage duties, for example, on a pataxo (pinnace) of approximately 100–120 tons were 375–450 taels regardless of cargo.[10] Crown warships in escort of merchantmen were granted exemption. By 1620, the measurage of ships, once fixed, became subject to fluctuation and required the subornation of Chinese officials.

Export duties rose and new ones were created at Canton and Ansao. The Portuguese paid a surcharge of 800 taels/lantea for permission to export gold. Passage duties for each lantea to and from Canton sky-rocketed from 15 to 150 taels. Duties on raw silk, which the Chinese sailors had customarily absorbed in the past, were now levied on the Portuguese at 1.5 tael/picol. The imposition of these duties on the Portuguese country traders annual purchases of raw silk, which fluctuated between 2,000 and 4,000 picols, resulted in a substantial increase in their costs. Permission from Chinese officials to open the fairs and permit free trade became linked to political and commercial demands such as the expulsion of the Jesuits from *Ilha Verde* (a small island adjacent to Macao) and the payment by the Portuguese of outstanding measurage duties.[11]

The Jesuit Rector, Gabriel de Matos, also believed that the Chinese authorities in Canton were in violation of the legal concept of royal security. The Rector argued that traders who were already accepted at Canton or any other port and conformed to local political and commercial practices were guaranteed some type of security. This concept was violated in 1620, when the Chinese official granted the

Portuguese permission to trade but then denied them food and water and made them pay all duties in advance. This incident forced the Portuguese to cancel their voyages in that year on account of the lateness of their return to Macao and the treatment received at Canton.[12]

The Rector argued that the deterioration in Sino-Portuguese commercial and political relations could be resolved by the Portuguese refusal to attend the Canton fairs and to hold them at Macao. Macao, in his opinion, would receive abundant and cheaper goods because this policy would be in the best commercial interest of Canton's quevees and local Ming officials. The Chinese merchant/brokers, who were concurrently risking their own capital, merchandise and shipping in trading ventures to Manila, Japan, Cochinchina and many other ports, would divert some, if not all, of their merchandise to Macao. By shifting their merchandise to Macao the Chinese merchants would avoid risk and in an easy transaction earn a guaranteed return on their investment by selling to the Portuguese.

The local Ming officials, because of the profit they derived in their dealings with the Portuguese, would not prohibit the quevees dealing with Macao if they were convinced of the Portuguese resolution to end trade at Canton and they could be persuaded it was the Portuguese intention to continue to pay all Chinese customs duties. Other economic conditions favoured the plan; de Matos did not believe that the economic interests from the interior of China, the merchants, farmers and miners who supplied the quevees at Canton with raw silk, silk and cotton piecegoods and gold, if faced with a substantial decline in demand for their products, could be effectively prohibited from arranging or pressuring for some type of deal with Macao. In addition to the lanteas sent by Cantonese quevees there would be an intensification of the existing illicit, non-taxed, Chinese trade brought in lorchas do risco to Macao.

Based on previous experience, when the Portuguese did not trade at Canton, as happened in 1602 when Don Paulo de Portugal was capitão-mor of the Japan voyage, the Chinese supplied merchandise to Macao. Once the Chinese delivered merchandise, it was argued that the Portuguese could bargain more sharply over prices. The Chinese merchants would not wish to return to Canton with their merchandise on account of potential losses caused by transport costs and customs duties which would be applied twice. What entered Macao as contraband would have to be sold there because it was not registered as exported at Canton.

The benefits for the Portuguese at Macao would continue with the existing Chinese merchant community enlarging and adding new establishments to sell the more desirable Chinese products. The enlargement of the Chinese commercial presence at Macao would help insure the regular supply of foodstuffs to the city. The saving to Portuguese merchants of such a plan was advanced as a major factor for its acceptance. The annual costs of going to Canton were estimated at 10 to 15,000 taels, a figure that excluded the savings on the embezzlement of Portuguese funds by the quevees which was mentioned as worsening.

The proposal also offered something for the less powerful within Portuguese society. But not going to Canton, the existing system of representation by thirty or so rich merchants within Macao and their control over the entire investment capital of the city would be weakened. The less privileged could improve their economic position in trade by direct supervision over the investment of their capital, the acceptance of Chinese goods on consignment and greater access to loans from Chinese merchants.[13]

The actual course of action taken by Portuguese society to resolve the deterioration in Sino-Portuguese relations was substantially different from the proposals of the Rector of Macao. The Portuguese attempted to maintain their position by political initiatives at the regional level to the Chinese officials at Canton and through the good offices of the Jesuits to enlist Ming official support at the national level. Local Ming administrators increasingly exploited their power over the Portuguese settlement and its trade as Macao became an obvious source of wealth which could be pressured by the individual administrators for personal or imperial gain. Macao was repeatedly called upon by Ming officials for contributions.

The Senado da Camara and Crown authorities made repeated attempts to eliminate the commercial abuses that were the source of complaints by Ming officials. A dangerous imbalance in Sino-Portuguese commercial relations at Canton developed when Portuguese country traders were faced with alarming debts in their Japan trade and manifested a desperate demand for Chinese credit facilities. This dependence upon capital and Chinese goodwill forced the Portuguese country traders towards a policy of accommodation to various Chinese demands at the local and national levels.

During the years associated with the rapid decline and fall of the Ming dynasty, 1620–44, the major Portuguese initiative, which must be seen for its political significance as an attempt to stabilise any further deterioration in Portuguese relations with the Ming, was to send military aid and auxiliaries to the Ming dynastic forces.[14] The Portuguese were jeopardised by their adherence to this policy with the arrival of Manchu forces in south China, in particular the Kwangtung province, and the continued resistance of the Ming adherents.[15] In 1645, the Jesuit father, Francisco Sambiasi arrived at Macao from Nanking with new Ming concessions, and with further requests for aid. The Portuguese were tempted by the Ming proposal, since it offered the cancellation of outstanding Portuguese customs duties debts at Canton, guarantees for the free flow of Chinese food stuffs and the right of free construction of any structure at Macao, and grants of several islands.[16]

The Portuguese response to these proposals from Yung-li, 'the last, and for a time the most successful pretender to the Ming Throne,' was positive and in 1646 a Portuguese contingent of 300 men under the command of Nicolão Ferreira departed Macao. Yung-li had raised the standard of rebellion against the Manchu in 1646 and was successful in gaining control of Kwangtung and Kwangsi; the Manchu counter-attack saw their forces entering Canton in January 1647. Yung-li and the Portuguese contingent retired to Kweilin, the provincial capital of Kwangsi, where they were besieged by the Manchu for five months in 1647. The

Portuguese contingent played a crucial role in the defence of Kweilin and the repulse of the Manchu in July 1647 'was the signal for a general revolt in South China, and not only Kwangtung but seven provinces in all rallied to the banner of Yung Li.'[17]

The inevitability of the military success of the Manchu against the Ming forces in south China convinced the Portuguese of the necessity of reversing their policy and shifting their allegiance to the Ch'ing dynasty. The Viceroy of the Estado da India reported to the Crown that in 1647, in Macao's opinion, despite Ming resistance rallying to Yung-li, the Manchu controlled the most important provinces of China, and Canton was peacefully obeying its new rulers; trade in food stuffs between Macao and Canton was resumed. Regardless of Yung-li's repulse of the Manchu before Kweilin, by 1648 his position was desperate.

In coming to terms with the Ch'ing dynasty, the Portuguese were not severely hampered by their previous policy of aid to the Ming. Portuguese reports of their initial attempts to establish a rapport with the Manchu indicated ambivalent, although seemingly friendly, attitudes. Portuguese–Manchu relations remained distant as Manchu–Ming confrontations in south China continued but without Portuguese participation and brought famine to the region and the city of Macao by the late 1640s. This famine was particularly severe in 1648 and these conditions persisted after the sack of Canton by Manchu forces in November 1650. According to an eyewitness report by Jesuit Father Pedro Canevari in 1651, the reasons for this calamitous famine were linked to Canton and Kwangtung's dependence upon the importation of basic food stuffs from Kwangsi and Hainan island.[18] Since Kwangsi and Hainan were in the hands of Ming adherents and Kwangtung was controlled by the Manchu, the arrival of foodstuffs at Canton was disrupted. Kwangsi's population, agricultural labourers in particular, had been hard hit by the wartime and famine conditions. The military demand for manpower also had a disastrous effect on agricultural production.

The Portuguese country traders, as a direct result of these adverse conditions, could not find their usual export cargoes of Chinese commodities, silk, piecegoods or gold except a little zinc and lower-price handicrafts. They did not import much silver or pepper in 1651 but concentrated upon markets where they could purchase rice and other foodstuffs.[19] The price of one picol of rice at Macao rose from two to eighteen taels with other foodstuffs accompanying its rise; despite prices being high, produce still became scarce. The Portuguese, especially the orphans and widows, suffered deprivation as did all of the population of Kwangtung. With such disturbing economic and political conditions, the recruitment of Chinese personnel for pirate bands was on the increase. These pirates infested the South China Sea from their bases in the Pearl River estuary. Their existence and the problem of eradication was shared by the Portuguese at Macao and the Ch'ing officials at Canton.

The activities of one pirate band operating in the Pearl River estuary came to the attention of the Manchu and the Portuguese authorities in 1651–2. The destruction of this pirate band, known to the Portuguese as the *ladrão da bandeira vermelha* (the thief of the red banner), was seized upon by Macao's leaders as a method of improving their relations with the Manchu at Canton. The Portuguese mounted a successful attack upon this pirate band's haven, described by the Jesuit Simão da Cunha, capturing a large number of ships and pirates. Their efforts were rewarded at Canton by Manchu officials.

The Manchu and their Chinese supporters were favourably inclined towards the Portuguese initiative to improve relations but on account of their involvement in eliminating Ming resistance in Kwangtung and on Hainan island, they were unable to respond immediately. After clearing the Luchow peninsula, and despite suffering losses in naval actions to Ming forces, the Manchu occupied and pacified Hainan island in 1652.[20] By 1654–5, if not slightly earlier, economic conditions at Macao began to improve too as a result of the Manchu's success in establishing and consolidating their power in Kwangtung. This improvement in Macao's trade and relations with the Manchu came late because some of its inhabitants had departed to live and trade in Cambodia, Siam and Macassar, as a result of the famine conditions and high cost of food-goods and merchandise in south China.

Although some of the Portuguese population had migrated, trade in Macao improved modestly for a few years in the latter half of the 1650s as Canton's merchants purchased Portuguese imports with silver instead of exchanging them for Chinese products for export. Payment in silver replenished the almost exhausted capital reserves of the Portuguese country traders. Prices for Chinese exports, however, had risen and various products, porcelain and silk for example, were still not in abundance. With the advances obtained by the Manchu in establishing a *pax Sinica*, Macao's relations with the Ch'ing dynasty at the regional and national level were closer than they had ever been.

By the late 1650s, when the VOC attempted to establish direct trading contacts at Canton, the Portuguese and the Jesuits had already established methods of obtaining audiences and sought to develop their influence within the Chinese bureaucracy at Canton and Peking.[21] Portuguese attempts to frustrate the VOC encountered some success but the Dutch failure was primarily on account of their attitudes and the Chinese perception of them.[22]

The south-eastern coast of China during the mid 1650s remained in the hands of forces hostile to the Ch'ing dynasty. In the early 1660s the Manchu–Ming confrontation was far from over but entering a phase of conflict between the Ch'ing and Cheng forces which threatened Macao's existence. Since 1646, Cheng Ch'eng-kung and his family had continued their resistance to the Ch'ing from their outposts on the Fukien coast; 'the Cheng family was also allowed to maintain its commercial network within the empire, an accommodation that fitted well into the negotiation strategy and also into the partial reversion to late Ming corruption characteristic of this period. But after the negotiations broke down in 1655, large Ch'ing forces pushed Cheng Ch'eng-kung out of most of his conquests on the Fukien mainland, maritime trade was prohibited, and there were more prosecutions of individuals accused of trading with the Cheng regime.'[23] After the Cheng siege of Nanking in 1659, the Ch'ing implemented a policy of evacuating the coastal population of south China inland and prohibiting maritime trade with greater force and purpose in Kwangtung province with alarming results for Macao.[24]

The Ch'ing authorities at Canton, who had previously permitted trade at Macao, seized seven Portuguese country traders' vessels in 1663 and 1664 and destroyed another six in 1666.[25] For the next decade the Portuguese sought to regularise their trade in south China with the Chinese authorities at Peking through the efforts of two ambassadors, Manuel de Saldanha (1667–70) and Bento Pereira de Faria (1678). Prior to Saldanha's arrival at Peking, the Ch'ing had already appointed a new viceroy, Chou Yu-te, at Canton, who petitioned for a relaxation of the edicts prohibiting maritime trade. At the same time an imperial commission led by Tu Chin investigated conditions in Kwangtung and made recommendations which were acted upon to reassure coastal populations.

The Rebellion of the Three Feudatories (the rebellion of the three great feudatory princedoms of south China in Yunnan, Fukien and Kwangtung which had allied themselves to, aided the Manchu to come to power, and revolted when the Ch'ing tried to abolish them) raged from 1674 until 1680.[26] Parts of Kwangtung were involved, and prolonged and disrupted political and economic conditions in south China were inimical to the economic interests of the Portuguese at Macao. The Portuguese were worried, perhaps, that their association with Shang Chih-hsin, who was granted extensive powers in Kwangtung by 1671 and led his feudatory princedom against the Ch'ing in 1676, would come to the attention of Peking.[27] They also feared, as a consequence, that their efforts to reconstitute their trade would be nullified. Macao hoped, in addition, that it could obtain Imperial support for the exclusion of VOC trade to China; towards that purpose Bento Pereira de Faria's embassy was sent to Peking in 1678. The possibility of this mission being successful was complicated by the Ch'ing's ambivalent attitudes towards accommodating or attacking the Cheng forces at their bases along the Fukien coast and on Taiwan.

By 1678, the Portuguese were convinced that the Ch'ing would eventually find the means and resolve to pacify south China. By sending this embassy, they declared their loyalty and support to the Ch'ing dynasty. This embassy did not achieve any immediate results, but it gained important political support at Peking for future Portuguese relations with the Ch'ing. In fact, in early 1680, the Senado da Camara had to vote customs duties on imports of 17 per cent, a figure almost double that collected on an annual basis for most of the seventeenth century, to finance the extraordinary expenses with which the city found itself encumbered.[28]

Economic relief for the Portuguese country traders at Macao and a modest expansion in their trade occurred several years after the Bento de Faria embassy but through the efforts of local Ch'ing officials and Canton's merchants, not those ordered by Peking. This modest stimulation of Kwangtung's foreign trade antedated the recession of the official ban. The overland trade from Canton to Macao was regularized in late 1680; substantial tax receipts of 12,200 and 18,076 taels were collected by Chinese officials on food and export produce traded at Macao in 1681 and 1682.[29]

By 1683, the disruption of the illicit non-controlled foreign trade on the south China coast and the reluctance on the part of the Portuguese at Macao to co-operate with the overland trade proved to be a source of disturbance to the high ranking Ch'ing officials at Canton; previously, these officials had benefited lucratively from the provision of guarantees for the security and direct participation in this illegal trade near the Macao islands.[30] With the establishment of peaceful conditions along all of the south China coast in 1683 as a result of the efforts of Shin Lang and Yao Ch'i-shêng in the destruction of the remainder of the Cheng family forces and the capture of Taiwan, it became apparent to Ch'ing officials at Canton that orders for the lifting of the ban on maritime trade were about to arrive from Peking.[31]

Although orders did arrive lifting the ban, south China did not command the attention at the centre in the late seventeenth and early eighteenth century. The K'ang-hsi emperor devoted much of his personal and the state's attention to the pacification of China's north-west frontiers through diplomacy with the Russians and successful military campaigns against the Western Monguls. He attached a great deal of importance in safeguarding China's periphery.[32]

Ch'ing officials, at the provincial level, sought from 1684 to the early 1710s to create stable conditions and to enhance their administration of the south China coast. They embarked upon the administrative and economic integration of Taiwan and presided over the expansion of China's foreign trade on their terms with European Companies and country traders. With the lifting of the official ban on overseas trade by 1684, Ch'ing officials established a series of customs posts and Peking created positions of customs superintendents, popularly known as *hoppos*, in the provinces of Kwangtung, Fukien, Chekiang and Shantung. Other Peking appointees, the Viceroy and the local military commander, also played an influential role in the development of foreign trade.[33]

Canton's foreign trade began to expand slowly without, apparently, any immediate major changes in the collection of imperial customs and any radical attempts to control merchant activities in maritime trade. By 1686, Ch'ing officials at Canton had separated the collection of customs duties from maritime and terrestrial trading transactions. These officials categorised different merchants and groups by the extent of their trade and the products they handled. In an attempt to establish greater control over the involvement of Canton's merchants in the supply of export produce traders, Ch'ing officials addressed a series of requirements to those merchants and their merchant associations.

The Ch'ing officials wanted the *hongs* (merchant associations) to act as agents of the government rather than as individuals and to assume the full responsibility for managing trade with foreigners. Any merchant interested in dealing with foreigners was required to request a government certificate to that effect at Canton. Any merchant groups that had previously been involved in foreign trade were informed that they could voluntarily regularise their position with the local government. Merchants who wished to trade within China in gold and silk were also allowed to participate in foreign trade provided they held separate certificates and each certified business occupied different premises. The Ch'ing officials wanted all merchants, foreign or indigenous, upon arrival at Canton to declare their products and sell them according to the nature of the product to the appropriate hong which it was hoped would prevent a monopoly of the market. Those merchants dealing with foreign trade were responsible to the government for the collection and payment of all import and export taxes.

Between the time of K'ang-hsi's sixth and seventh tours of south China, 1705–7, serious latent threats to the security of the Ch'ing dynasty re-emerged and Peking's interest, when not absorbed in the court politics of deciding an heir to the throne, was focused southwards. The reason for this renewed interest in the southern periphery by the 1710s was the popular support for the Ming pretender by the name of Chu Tz-u-huan, who was known as the *Chu San T'ai-tzu* (the third Heir Apparent of the Ming royal house); the *I-nien* revolt (an insurrection led by a Buddhist monk of the same name in the Ta-lan mountain area near Ning-po); and the dramatic increase in bandit bands operating in the Ssu-ming mountains (also near Ning-po).[34] The news of local unrest in the south evoked fear in Peking that Heaven, perhaps, was considering the withdrawal of its mandate to the Ch'ing.

The impact upon Portuguese society at Macao of the complex amalgam of Ch'ing administrative and Cantonese merchant interest and involvement in maritime trade from 1684 to the 1710s was ambivalent. Portuguese country traders at Macao derived an immediate economic benefit from the renewed Chinese interest in maritime trade in that export commodities were in plentiful supply. But, the cost of such benefits, the sharing of Portuguese administrative and economic control over Macao with Ch'ing officials and intensified Chinese commercial competition, caused concern.

Several years after the establishment of the Chinese customs post at Macao, in 1686, according to the hoppo, I-er-ko-t'u, the Senado da Camara requested that he write a memorial to Peking and petition that all foreign ships engaged in trade no longer be permitted to anchor near Macao but at Whampoa near Canton.[35] Although any explicit request for this petition is absent from Macao's archival records, the Senado da Camara's desire for such a prohibition of the Dutch Company and vrij-burger, the English Company and country, the Siamese Crown and Chinese trade in the Macao islands was an objective prior to the Imperial edict legitimising foreign trade. With foreign ships anchoring at Whampoa, the Portuguese hoped that any responsibility for the control over foreign traders would pass to Ch'ing officials or to Canton's merchants. It is also not clear from the existing archival records whether this petition was granted or not by the Ch'ing authorities. The evasion of any accountability to Ch'ing officials for the behaviour of foreign traders was, from Macao's view, in order to protect the Portuguese from having to finance any failure by foreign traders to pay measurage customs duties or any other fiscal charges.

In the same year, the Senado da Camara and the hoppo were involved in discussions over the new measurage and custom duties that he had imposed upon Macao's ships. As a general rule in the past, all arriving Portuguese ships except the Crown's had to pay a graduated tax, based on the size or measurage of the ship involved, and Chinese customs duties. The Senado da Camara met in late 1685 with the country traders who owned Macao's ships to inform them that the Senado da Camara had been told by Chinese officials that the previous informal method of payment of measurage duties by the individual Portuguese merchant was no longer acceptable and that the Senado da Camara was henceforward responsible for the payment.

The procurador of the Senado da Camara was selected to represent the city and Macao's ship-owners in talks with the Chinese officials. He was empowered, if necessary, to suborn those officials in order to secure measurage and customs duty rates that Macao could afford. The cost of the bribe would be divided and paid by the city's ship-owners.

The procurador, José Vieira da Silva, met with Chinese officials in early 1686; a measurage and customs duty rate formula was announced and the Senado da Camara assumed responsibility for payment. Although the Senado da Camara attempted to counter-offer and lower the rates, the hoppo was adamant and the new rates (excluding the bribe of four hundred taels) of five hundred taels per ship, regardless of size, and 20 per cent *ad valorem* were implemented. In case of default, as with two country traders' ships in 1686, merchandise or other property owned by the shipowners and participants in those voyages was confiscated in order to make payment.[36]

These new rates were highly unfavourable and prejudicial to Macao's trade. In a meeting with Macao's shipowners in late 1692, the Senado da Camara received a proposal from one of its officials and a ship-owner, João Garcia de Luares. Based on the Jesuit success in north China, after the Treaty of Nerchinsk and with their favour at K'ang-hsi's court, de Luares advocated that the city petition the Emperor through the good offices of Father Thomas Perreira in Peking for the reduction of measurage duties on a *pro rata* basis.

Macao's ship-owners wanted their shipping to be charged at a rate of 100 taels per 1,000 picols (roughly $66\frac{2}{3}$ tons). The relief of this plan for Macao's smaller ship-owners was obvious, which were already paying on the new scale the rate only ships of 5,000 picols (approximately $333\frac{1}{3}$ tons) or larger paid.[37] The size of most of Macao's country trader ships was usually slightly smaller than that figure, ranging anywhere from 65 to around 400 tons. Records of Jesuit intercession on Macao's behalf on this occasion have not been found; but, by 1698, Peking ordered the reduction of the collection of Kwangtung maritime customs duties and, 'the following year the duty on Portuguese ships from Macao, but not other European ships, was further reduced. The Portuguese ships from Macao were taxed according to the rate for Chinese ocean-going ships which was much lower than that for Eastern Ocean ships, therefore the reduction was an extraordinary favour to the Portuguese at Macao.'[38]

Although the Portuguese began to receive some preferential treatment on measurage duties with the Ch'ing officials at Macao, Canton and Peking, they were not as fortunate in other financial obligations to the Chinese. In 1691, the Senado da Camara had to accept an arbitrary increase of 100 taels in its *foro do chão* (land rent) payment which brought the total amount to 600 taels. Since the increase was by Imperial order, the Senado da Camara was advised by the Jesuits that the increase be accepted without protest.[39]

Portuguese resentment over the treatment that they received from Ch'ing officials and Canton's merchants grew in the 1710s as peaceful and stable economic conditions in south China began to fray. Ch'ing official control over Canton's maritime trade demonstrated that with such powers Chinese, Portuguese and other European merchants were obliged to seek advantages by offering or having bribes extorted from them. The corruption of Chinese officials by Chinese merchants for economic advantages in Canton's foreign trade by 1704 reached as far as Peking and as high as one of the Emperor K'ang-hsi's sons, Yin-jeng.[40]

Macao's country traders persisted, on account of their capital and investment requirements, in making contracts with Chinese officials and Cantonese merchants for the delivery of export goods. The incidence of Chinese embezzlement of capital advanced by the Portuguese was reported as being on the rise in 1709 when the Portuguese Crown ordered this practice terminated. The Portuguese Crown demonstrated that it was powerless in its attempts to recover such losses through legal action since such action was not recognised by the Chinese. The Crown warned that the responsibility for such a contract and its payment was with the individual Portuguese merchant.[41] Although in Lisbon the Crown's order of 1709 was comprehensible, at Macao the possibility of the city voluntarily divorcing itself from Cantonese capital was nonsensical.

Piratical activity, both Chinese and European, worried Macao's country traders, Ch'ing officials and Chinese merchants from Canton to Ning-po. Although the English pirates of the late 1690s had largely disappeared in the South China Sea, the War of the Spanish Succession brought French naval units and privateers into this region.[42] Banditry and piracy along the lower Yangtze and down the south China coast which had been hit by severe drought was on the rise.[43] By 1713, Macao's country traders had become so alarmed with the threat of attack from Chinese pirates as well as French privateers that the proposal, by Macao's capitão-geral, António de Siqueira de Noronha, to assign municipal funds to outfit a ship to advise arriving shipping of danger and to convoy them into port, was accepted by the Senado da Camara.[44]

Although the Portuguese could claim that they had cause for their growing resentment of Ch'ing officials and Canton's merchants, their own actions were not above reproach. Repeated Portuguese Crown and Chinese officials prohibitions of the Portuguese country trader traffic in Chinese slaves (the *muitsai* who were 'limited to household and domestic servants...took the form of impoverished parents selling their unwanted female children into domestic service for a fixed number of years [usually forty] or for the term of their natural lives') suggest that this practice was maintained.[45] The markets for the muitsai, in addition to their widespread employment in Macao, ranged as far afield as east Africa and India but, it is suspected that this traffic became involved with the Portuguese illegally carrying Chinese emigrants to Manila and Batavia. The size of the traffic in muitsai and the number of emigrants carried by Portuguese ships to Manila and Batavia is not quantifiable.

Macao's country traders were culpable of embezzling capital from local Chinese merchants and gravely mistreating the city's Chinese population. Although the Portuguese never attacked and murdered the Chinese on the scale of the Spanish at Manila and the Dutch at Batavia, one incident in 1710 is illustrative of the haughty behaviour of certain powerful Portuguese traders at Macao. In an attempt to recover a trading debt from a Portuguese country trader, a Chinese merchant from Chincheo was murdered by the Portuguese. When the leaders of Macao's Chinese community requested the arrest of the culprit from the capitão-geral and ouvidor, they were referred to the procurador of the Senado da Camara, Manuel Vicente Roza. At their meeting with Roza, the Chinese leaders were abused, injured in sword play and claimed they would have been killed if prominent former Crown officials had not intervened.

The Chinese community at Macao reacted by closing their shops and homes but were convinced by the capitão-geral to reconsider and send their petition to the Viceroy of the Estado da India for justice. Macao's prominent Chinese inhabitants threatened that if they did not succeed with their petition, they would leave the city. Although Roza was not expelled from Macao, communal tensions were assuaged after this particular incident.[46]

In the late 1710s and into the late 1720s, in the few years prior to the death of the K'ang-hsi and in the intervening years after the accession of the Yung-Cheng Emperor, Ch'ing official maritime trade policy oscillated from fully fledged support to prohibition back to support with tighter official controls. Chinese contacts with foreign traders, although they were not prohibited, were also the target of tighter official controls. With Peking in the midst of a succession crisis, unease about the deteriorating security conditions and the potential Western threat on the periphery of the Empire was commented upon in a memorial written by the K'ang-hsi Emperor in 1716. There were additional reasons for the Ch'ing concern for conditions in south China and the South China Sea. These included Ch'ing opposition to the real or perceived threat of large-scale exportation of rice, an official distrust of the political sympathies of those engaged in overseas trade and those who had emigrated, and the belief that China's resources – its ships and ship-building materials – were being sold overseas on a scale that endangered the Empire's strength.[47]

The promulgation of an edict in 1717 that banned the participation of Chinese merchants and ships in overseas trade was the direct manifestation of the extent of the Ch'ing's concern for the perpetuation of its reign. The implementation of this edict upon the south China ports was swift and effective. The degree to which it intensified the popular discontent felt for the Ch'ing regime on the south China coast cannot be determined.

The expanding numbers of foreign traders and the activities of Catholic missionaries disturbed Ch'ing officials at Canton and Peking. Several memorials of Ch'en Mao, a former military commander in Kwangtung, that advocated the prohibition of the propagation of Catholicism and the tightening of controls over foreign traders were favourably received at Peking in 1717 and 1718.[48] In late 1720, as the English East India Company's supercargo (shipboard Company factor) reported, some of the wealthiest Cantonese merchants and their merchant associations or guilds with the support of the Ch'ing officials, the hoppo in particular, had formed an enlarged merchant association. The objective of this enlarged association were 'to check abuses, to foster foreign trade, and to protect foreigners from the malpractices of the unworthy among the merchants of Canton.'[49]

The formation of an enlarged merchant association was also intended by Ch'ing officials to insure the use of Chinese merchants for greater control over foreign traders as well as being a method for Chinese officials and merchants in the association to fix prices. This initiative met with a considerable degree of controversy that involved the Viceroy, Yang Lin, through the instigation of the English Company's supercargoes in a test of wills with the merchants and other Ch'ing officials. In this instance, the Viceroy prevailed upon the merchants to withdraw their agreement.[50] Other methods of tightening official controls on the activities of foreign traders were employed such as the inspection of ships and the continuation of the practice of off-loading foreign traders' cannon upon arrival. At Ning-po, in the province of Chekiang, shortly after the ban on Chinese participation in foreign trade was rescinded in 1728, that region's trade to Japan was reorganised with eight merchants selected to carry it out in an association which was possibly similar in its objectives to the one established at Canton in 1720.[51]

Rebellion erupted on Taiwan in the spring of 1721 led by Chu I-kuei on account of the latent anti-Manchu feelings held by the population in south China and the inflexible Ch'ing administrative policies towards the aborigines and the Chinese migrants on that island. The initial success of this rebellion stemmed in part from Chu I-kuei's claim to be a descendant of the Ming Imperial House, By late May, his forces were in control of the entire island. Unable to control the ambitions of some of his supporters, a rival faction to his rule formed. At the same time, Ch'ing officials on the south China coast were assembling their forces to quash the insurrection.

Learning of the insurgents' success, two Ch'ing naval and military officials in Fukien province, Shih Shi-p'iao and his subordinate, Lan T'ing-chen, took immediate measures to prevent Chu I-kuei's forces crossing from Taiwan to the mainland. They raised a large force, which was reported to have totalled 18,000 men and 600 ships, for the re-occupation of the island. Chu I-keui and his rivals were involved in altercations when the Ch'ing re-occupation force arrived near An-p'ing, the capital of Taiwan. The Ch'ing forces successfully attacked that city in mid July and by the end of that month had captured Chu I-kuei. The complete pacification of Taiwan was reported in 1723.[52]

Between the arrival at Peking of the news of rebellion and the announcement to the Emperor of the total pacification of Taiwan in 1723, the succession crisis was resolved with the accession of the Yung-Cheng Emperor after the death of

K'ang-hsi in late 1722. Yung-Cheng and his supporters were convinced that Catholic missionaries, in particular the Jesuit Father João Mourão, had opposed his accession and ordered them from Peking to Macao in 1724. Absorbed in strengthening his position, the Emperor maintained the ban on overseas trade, although there was increasing evidence of its wholesale evasion, sought tighter controls over foreigners trading with China and in 1726 had Father Mourão executed.[53] Unable to react, the Jesuits stoically accepted the loss of one of their number and sought to re-gain access to the Emperor and Peking.

By 1727, the new Emperor and his followers evinced a greater confidence in their position. The purpose of the Portuguese embassy of A. M. de Souza e Menezes (1726–7), in the Chinese view, was to pay tribute to the new Emperor. For the Portuguese, this embassy was to assuage the Chinese fears of the intentions of the Catholic missionaries and to further improve Macao's trading position. An edict lifting the prohibition of Chinese adherence to Catholicism was promulgated but there was no further improvement in Macao's trade. It was in fact at this time (1727) that the Yung-Cheng Emperor lifted the ban on Chinese participation in overseas trade.[54]

Portuguese relations with Ch'ing officials from the late 1710s to the late 1720s, demonstrated that Macao's country traders desired to be excluded from the ban on overseas trade and were worried about the possibility of tighter controls on their trade and about Peking's opinion of their involvement in the support of Catholic missionary activity. After Macao's country traders were certain that they were not to be included in the ban, Portuguese relations with Canton's merchants altered radically from 1717 to 1727 on account of the Chinese dependence upon Macao's ships to carry their freight to Batavia.

The Portuguese at Macao were informed of the ban on overseas trade in the spring of 1717 by a *chapa* (an official communiqué) that ordered, as Macao's country shipping was abroad trading, a list of those ships, captains, pilots and other particulars be prepared and delivered to the appropriate official. The Senado da Camara, after taking the advice of the Jesuits as to the most appropriate manner to respond to this communiqué, conformed with the chapa's request without referring to the ban. Within a month after the receipt of this chapa, Yang Lin, the Viceroy of the Two Kwang (Kwangtung and Kwangsi), made an official visit to Macao where, Portuguese records attest, he learnt of the potentially disastrous consequences of its inclusion in this ban, heard complaints by the inhabitants of official maltreatment and a Portuguese proposal to outfit a small naval force that would go on the offensive to eliminate the immediate vicinity from Chinese pirates.[55] The proposal to outfit a naval force to eliminate Chinese pirate bands in the Pearl River estuary was advanced, if the Emperor would agree to pardon Macao's land rent and measurage duties payments. This proposal was not agreed upon by Yang Lin.

Yang Lin's memorial for Macao's exclusion from the ban was approved by the Emperor and the Board of War in early 1718 possibly as a result of influence exerted by Macao's inhabitants but more probably through his independent appreciation of the situation and advocacy for this position with Jesuit support at Peking.[56]

Macao, whose trade had not been disrupted during Yang Lin's trip to Peking, responded to the confirmation of their exclusion by sending several letters acknowledging the Emperor's concession and gifts.[57]

After the accession of Yung-Cheng, Ch'ing official concern at Peking and Kwangtung grew over the expansion of European trade at Canton (where they found the European Companies and country traders difficult) and Macao. In 1725, an edict to limit the number of Macao country trader ships to twenty-five was promulgated and with minor variations and instances of evasion remained applicable to Portuguese shipping until 1849. The Portuguese, who knew of Yung-Chen's unfavourable attitudes towards Catholic missionaries (although official permission for the missionaries to stay at Canton in 1725, instead of their retiring from Peking to Macao as ordered in 1724, indicated that only specific missionaries and not the entire body were in disfavour) and were aware that their trade would be jeopardised by noncompliance, accepted the imposition of the quota system.[58] The liberal provision within this system for the re-fitting and replacement of the quota ships were also factors that ameliorated any Portuguese despair at this Chinese official initiative to control their shipping.[59]

The Portuguese Crown's decision to send A. M. de Souza e Menezes as its ambassador to China came after Lisbon learned of the death of the K'ang-hsi Emperor and the Crown received repeated requests from Macao and Goa over the years for such support. Upon his arrival in China in 1726, de Souza e Menezes received a series of representations and appraisals of the position of Macao and the Padroado from Portuguese country traders and Catholic missionaries. The letter from the King of Portugal to the Emperor Yung-Cheng contained little of a substantive nature to dissuade the Ch'ing interpretation that this was a tribute embassy. Even in its Portuguese version, the question of China's attitude towards Catholicism was omitted by design and the King of Portugal's hopes for the maintenance of close Sino-Portuguese commercial relations was mentioned only obliquely. De Souza e Menezes was to mention to the Emperor that the Portuguese hoped to maintain their trade as they had during K'ang-hsi's reign and that both countries would continue to derive mutual benefit from it.

The Embassy was well received by Ch'ing officials at Canton and Peking but, once again as with Saldanha, the ambassador's expenses were exceedingly high. The Senado da Camara, the Province of Japan, the Vice-Province of China, and a number of Macao's country traders, were obliged to contribute 18,500 taels to defray its cost. The benefits were negligible but the position of Catholic missionary activity was improved. Negotiations for concessions for Macao's commercial position, either in the elimination of the quota system or the continuation of the ban on overseas trade, were beyond the scope of this mission. Macao was left in debt, with only the hope that de Souza e Menezes would convince the Viceroy of the Estado da India to eliminate the practice of Goa charging customs duties on Macao's trade along the Malabar coast. The final result of this embassy was depressing for Macao's leaders as there was no substantial improvement in their economic or political position *vis-à-vis* China or the Estado da India.[60]

After the lifting of the ban on overseas trade in 1727 until just prior to the imposition of trading regulations for the control of the European Company and country trade at Kwangtung in 1754, Ch'ing policies towards maritime trade evinced a continued pattern of regulation without seeking to diminish its growth. Yung-Cheng's and Ch'ing officials' desire for control over China's foreign trade and internal security on the periphery were immovable fixtures of this reign. Anti-Manchu dissidents, for the Ch'ing most of the overseas Chinese in Java and the Philippines, were banned from returning to China in an effort to ensure continued stability on the periphery. Although excesses by Ch'ing officials at Canton were reported, Peking retained its implicit faith in their methods of administration over foreign trade. Discussions between Ch'ing officials at Canton and the Portuguese at Macao explored the possibility of the European Company trade being removed from Whampoa to Macao and the responsibility for its control being transferred to the Portuguese. The first edict banning the use of opium was promulgated and towards the end of Yung-Cheng's reign, Catholic missionaries on the Fukien coast were arrested and banished.[61]

In 1736, upon the accession of Ch'ien Lung, whose succession was a tranquil affair, China was prosperous and felt complacent in its internal security: a complacency which was again spoilt by the discovery of Catholic missionary successes in southern provinces which brought about the renewal of a policy of religious persecution. Foreign trade benefited from imperial orders for the reduction of taxes and the granting of permission to the Spanish to trade on the Fukien coast. At Canton, the English and French Company trade grew especially over the years 1739 to 1745. The Dutch massacre of the overseas Chinese population at Batavia in 1741 did not, as most feared, seriously disrupt China's overseas trade to Java, nor the VOC's activities at Canton. The decision for further Chinese initiatives towards the incorporation of Macao emanated from the belief on the part of Ch'ing officials of its necessity on account of the influx of foreign trade; the issue of extra-territoriality aroused these officials to action.

By 1754, Ch'ing officials at Canton were inclining towards the conclusion that the trade of the European Company and country traders had to be regulated through an intensification of their utilisation of the existing *hongs* of Canton. In 1755, these officials announced to the Europeans that a co-hong was to be responsible for their trade. The co-hong was an initial step in developing a control model over China's foreign trade that became known as the Canton system. The Canton system refers to the Ch'ing bureaucratic efforts towards the re-organisation of the methods of controlling foreigners trading with China. The establishment of this system took place from 1755 to 1761. Specifically, it was the formula implemented in 1761 which was maintained into the nineteenth century. The formula stemmed from a decision taken in 1757 for the centralisation of all trade in which foreigners participated from different ports to Canton. In 1760, in an effort to tighten bureaucratic controls, while permitting the monopolisation of trade, hong merchants were permitted by Ch'ing officials to consolidate their control over transactions with foreigners with the establishment of an enlarged co-hong. This co-hong was subsequently subsumed in 1761 with the formation of the co-hong entitled *Wai-yang hong*, and became the merchant association that controlled China's trade with Europeans.[62]

Along the south China coast, Chinese merchants involved in overseas trade found their activities under greater scrutiny by Ch'ing officials. These merchants, and at Canton many of them were from Fukien, were organised along basic historical antecedents. Around 1727, there were several major groupings of merchants distinguished on geographical and dialectical bases, and known as *pang*; 'at Fukien there were notably the Ch'uan-Chang (Ch'uan-chou and Chang-chou) and Fu-chou (Foo-chow) *pang*, at Chekiang the Ningpo *pang* and at Kwangtung the Kuang-Chao and Ch'ao-chou *pang*, all of which were established actual trading bodies or guilds known as *hang* (hong) denoting both the ship and the organisation (*hui-kuan*, a collective organisation of ships and concerns bound together for mutual purposes).'[63] They relied upon joint investment on account of the risk and the large capital expenditure involved in keeping a junk trading. In their efforts to regulate this trade. Ch'ing officials along the coast required, for example, that junks departing Canton could only return to Canton. In 1731, it was ordered that for the purposes of verification the identification markings of these ships were to be standardised. The owners and participating merchants had to establish their bonafide trading intentions by the use of a mutual guarantee system (the *lien-huan-pao*), in this instance described as, 'for every ship putting to sea, three more owned by related concerns were to be presented as a guarantee for the sailing ship's return.'[64] They had to adhere in theory to a fixed sailing schedule.

Sino-Portuguese relations from 1727 to 1754 followed a general pattern of accommodation by Macao's inhabitants. The preoccupation of Ch'ing officials towards control over Macao's trade continued as the Portuguese were prohibited from exporting gold from China in 1731.[65] There is evidence that the Ch'ing officials were uneasy over the influx of European Company and country traders at Whampoa and the difficulty in regulating their activities.

Although the Portuguese accommodated the Chinese on most issues, there were a few instances in which Macao's country traders were able to reverse basic Ch'ing decisions that were antithetical to their interest by threatening to abandon the city. One such major incident occurred in late 1743 and early 1744. Peking received various reports from Kwantung officials advocating a tightening of internal administrative control over Macao; an Imperial edict was promulgated in 1743 to place a Chinese district magistrate in that city to 'take particular charge of the lawsuits between the Chinese and the barbarians.'[66] Advance warning of the edict's promulgation came from Father Andre Pereira at Peking. When this Chinese official arrived and tried to enter the city in April and May of 1744, the Portuguese not only advised him that they would depart if he attempted to establish himself but that they would resist if he contemplated the use of force. This incident of the Emperor wanting to establish a mandarin at Macao ended in failure for the Ch'ing.[67]

There were other instances in which the attitudes and actions of the capitão-geral forced the city's inhabitants to confront Ch'ing officials over the question of extraterritoriality. This confrontation arose as a result of the decision made in 1748 by the capitão-geral, António José Telles de Menezes, not to deliver to Chinese officials Portuguese soldiers who had killed several Chinese. Macao defended the actions of its soldiers through negotiation between the Senado da Camara, with Jesuit support, and local Ch'ing officials. The incident did not recede into obscurity. When Peking received reports of Macao's actions in 1749, extraterritorial privileges enjoyed by the Portuguese were revoked by imperial edict. This edict ordered that in the case of murder of Chinese by Europeans, the Ch'ing juridicial system was to have jurisdiction and officials were to insure that this occurred.[68]

The ill-feelings that this incident engendered between the Portuguese and Ch'ing officials lingered. When the embassy of Francisco de Assiz Pacheco de Sampaio arrived in China in 1752, one of its objectives was to mollify and improve Macao's relations with Ch'ing officials. The ambassador was also instructed, as with A. M. de Souza e Menezes, to discuss the future of the Padroado-supported Catholic missionary activities. At Macao, he conducted an inquiry into the commercial and financial status of the city for the Portuguese Crown.

Although the Crown made its inquiries, there was little within its power that it could do to alleviate their financial burdens without remitting capital from Portugal for investment in country as well as Company trade. The embassy was received cordially by the Emperor, and Macao's recalcitrance over the question of extraterritoriality was set aside during the visit.[69] By 1754, Portuguese country traders, cognisant of their diminished economic and political power, had permitted the near-total incorporation of Macao, a fact which was not lost upon Ch'ing officials whilst they searched for methods to control the maritime trade of foreigners with China.

Sino-Portuguese relations did influence Ch'ing officials views on how to control foreigners and maritime trade, as the other Europeans that came to China discovered. Those Europeans had come to trade and also to attack and destroy the Estado da India. Macao's confrontation and survival against the onslaughts of these other Europeans attacks brought the conflicts of Europe to China.

9

MACAO, COMPANIES AND COUNTRY TRADERS: THE OTHER EUROPEANS IN CHINA

Portugal's incorporation into the Habsburg Empire in the late sixteenth century involved the Estado da India in a world-wide imperial contest between the Habsburgs and the Protestant powers. The Netherlands, as the north Atlantic's premier naval and commercial power, lead the Protestant powers' attack upon the Portuguese in the East. Although the Dutch threat to Macao receded, the Portuguese were replaced in the pre-dominant commercial position in China by the European Companies and country traders.

Intrepid individuals employed by companies sailed from Holland for the Indonesian archipelago in search of obtaining spice supplies direct from Asian producers. These early Dutch companies encountered obstacles and conditions that led to the establishment of the VOC in the Netherlands in 1602. Almost immediately after the Dutch arrived in the East, Portuguese shipping en route from Macao to India and throughout the Indian Ocean and the South China Sea became the prey for superior Dutch naval forces. The isolated Portuguese outposts in the Spice islands were occupied by VOC forces in 1605. The Dutch were successful in their attack on Tidore and Ambon but were surprised by the subsequent Spanish counter-attack on Tidore and portions of Ternate, which the Spanish captured and held until their recall to the Philippines in 1662.

After their occupation of the Spice islands in 1605 and until their establishment at Batavia (Jakarta) on the island of Java in 1619, the VOC naval and land forces were superior in numbers to the Portuguese in the South China Sea and, possibly, in the entire Estado da India. These Dutch forces were diffusely employed consolidating their position in the Indonesian archipelago. In the late 1610s with the Company under the leadership of J. P. Coen, the conflict between the Portuguese and the Dutch intensified to such an extent that it began to threaten Macao. Portuguese country traders, who earlier demonstrated that they had contemplated accommodating the Dutch became victims to the Company's classic implementation of naval power for the control of the sea lanes between China and India.[1]

By the early 1620s, participation in the China and Japan trades was a high-priority company objective. Although the VOC had frequented ports in the South China Sea where they could obtain Chinese produce and had traded in Japan on a very minor scale for almost a decade, they had been frustrated in acquiring large quantities of silver and silk, the fundamental pillars of trade between those two states. The Company decided to eradicate one of the reasons for the difficulties they were experiencing in their trade in the East by attacking the Portuguese at Macao in 1622. This attack failed on account of unusually fortunate circumstances for the Portuguese, the accuracy of their artillery and the resolution of the religious and slave populations to repel the Dutch. The VOC, as a result, briefly occupied the Pescadores islands before establishing themselves on Taiwan.

The VOC was successful on Taiwan. They occupied portions of that island from 1624 until 1662 and pursued policies that had a long-term adverse impact on the maritime trade of south China and Macao. Secure in their base at Fort Zeelandia, the VOC disrupted Japanese trade to Taiwan, Sino-Spanish trade at Manila and Portuguese trade with Japan and Manila. From Batavia and Zeelandia in the 1630s, the VOC expanded its trade in Tonkin, Cochinchina, Cambodia, Siam and Macassar and, in instances where it was rebuffed, went to war against the recalcitrant state. The Dutch efforts in the South China Sea were linked to their expansion into the Japan market and occurred at the same time that Portuguese country traders from Macao were increasing their reliance on those same markets.

The failure of Portuguese Crown attempts to modernise its trade with India by establishing a Company modelled on the VOC and EIC, along with EIC concern for the rapid ascendancy of the VOC, prompted the signing of the Anglo-Portuguese Truce at Goa in 1635.[2] By administering the Japan and Manila voyages until the Portuguese were expelled from those locations in 1638 and 1644 respectively, the Crown secured a lucrative source of desperately required revenue to aid the finances and defences of the Estado da India but had to find a secure method of transporting those revenues from China to India. One of the immediate benefits of the Anglo-Portuguese Truce was that it permitted the utilisation of EIC shipping to carry freighted goods from Macao to Goa. Despite protests from Macao, where fears of adverse Chinese administrative reactions prevailed, the Crown employed the EIC and the Courteen Company for over a decade on such voyages.[3] Difficulties between the Portuguese and English at Macao, Goa and Surat arose over these freighting agreements and the VOC also demonstrated that it seriously objected to such activities. This practice ceased after the implementation of the ten-year truce between Portugal and the Netherlands in Asia in November 1644.

In early 1641, prior to the occupation of Malacca by the VOC, the Governor-General and the Council of the Indies at Batavia had to determine whether to continue the Company's economic and military strategy. At that time, the Company's strategy was to concentrate their commercial efforts upon expanding their penetration of the Japan and China markets. Their military forces were utilised in the destruction of Portuguese power at Malacca and in the South China Sea and in the maintenance of the blockade at Goa. The question in their minds was whether to shift to a strategy of using those forces to wrest the centres of cinnamon and pepper production on Ceylon and the Malabar coast from the Portuguese. António van Diemen and the Council of the Indies decided to maintain the VOC's strategic focus in the South China Sea region and informed the Heeren XVII (the directors of the VOC in the Netherlands) that it was their intention to pursue their claims against Cochinchina and at the earliest possible date to occupy Macao.[4]

Van Diemen's plans to attack the Portuguese in south China were reversed after the arrival of the Macao-based fidalgo and country trader, António Fialho Ferreira, from Europe at Batavia with news of Portugal's revolt from Spain and the accession of João IV. The VOC transported Ferreira to Macao in order to announce the new Portuguese monarch and assure his acclamation. The Company administrators at Batavia declared as a result of the news from Europe that the conquest of Ceylon now took precedence over that of Macao. In their opinion, the VOC's manpower and ships would be better utilised trying to secure cinnamon than eliminating the Portuguese in China. The VOC's penetration of the market for Chinese goods on Taiwan had increased to the maximum level that the Company's capital resources would allow, and permitting the Portuguese to stay in China, so they wrote, would not seriously damage their trade.[5]

There was an additional reason for the Company to reconsider attacking Macao. The Portuguese country traders of south China, which included António Fialho Ferreira's family, contemporaneously proposed to the Company that they be permitted to trade at Batavia, an offer which would benefit the Dutch and revitalise the economic situation at Macao. This group delivered their proposal to the Governor-General at Batavia, when Ferreira returned there to obtain passage for Europe. The proposal received the Company's tacit approval in the same year, 1642.[6] In the following year, after Macao's warm reception of several storm-battered Company ships and despite complaints of Portuguese mistreatment of Dutch prisoners in Cochinchina, trade continued between the Portuguese and Dutch at Batavia.[7] The Portuguese country traders offered coloured Chinese silk piecegoods for sale at very advantageous prices to the VOC. The Company estimated that, on an annual basis, the Portuguese were capable of supplying silk worth 3–400,000 guilders to Batavia. In return, these Portuguese country traders purchased large quantities of pepper for the Chinese market.[8]

After four trading seasons and as a result in part of complications in the implementation of the ten-year truce agreement arising over the demarcation of control on Ceylon, the VOC lost interest in continuing to trade with the Portuguese from Macao at Batavia. The VOC had delayed the implementation of the truce for its own benefit.[9] When Batavia learned of the detention of one of the Company's richly laden ships, the *Pauw*, at Goa, its retaliation was swift and injurious to Macao's trade to India. The Portuguese direct trade from China at Batavia was not immediately disrupted. Portuguese shipping en route from Macao to India was diverted and held at Batavia where the cargoes were purchased by the Company with the provision that payment be made at some future date after the restitution of the *Pauw*.[10]

The Company decided that it was not in their interest to continue to rely upon the Portuguese to deliver Chinese silk to Batavia when they learned that Sino-Portuguese relations were deteriorating and that south China was experiencing disruption in the supply of silk to its ports.[11] Amidst these events of 1644, António

Table 9.1. *Portuguese shipping arrivals and departures at Batavia, 1643–83.*

Year	Arrivals					Departures			
	Macao	Goa	Macassar	Timor	Siam	Macao	Goa	Macassar	Timor
1643	1								
1644	1					1			
1645	2					2			
1648		1						2	
1650			1				1		
1651		2						3	
1661						1			
1664		1				1			
1665	1					1			
1667	1					1			
1669	1					1			
1670	1			1	1	2			
1671	3					2			
1672	1								
1678	1								
1679	1			2		2			
1680	1			2		2			1
1681	1								
1682	1								
1683	1								

Sources: GM, DRB and van Dam, *Beschrijvinge.*

Fialho Ferreira arrived at Batavia en route from Europe in the company of the Portuguese ambassador to Japan, Gonçalo Siqueira de Souza, in need of VOC assistance to continue their journey to Macao.[12] Based upon the belief that this Portuguese embassy to Japan would fail, the VOC came to this mission's aid.

Despite Ferreira's presence, the VOC was adamant in their decision to bar any further direct trade by the Portuguese at Batavia as shown in Table 9.1 and the last of Macao's ships for the next several decades departed that port in June of 1645. This measure was taken, as the Governor-General informed the Heeren XVII, because trade with the Portuguese of Macao was detrimental to the VOC's commerce on Taiwan. With the Portuguese barred from trading at Batavia and excluded from the Japan and Manila markets, their access to silver was severely restricted, and the VOC was of the opinion that Portuguese trade with China was almost impossible to sustain.[13]

The imbalance of power between the VOC and the Estado da India with its unfavourable consequences for Portuguese country traders at Macao, although apparent to some much earlier, became quite clear in 1645. Frei Gonsalvo Veloso de São José and Francisco Zusarte arrived in Batavia from Goa to negotiate with the VOC on the anchorage, passage and customs duties Portuguese shipping were to pay in the future at Malacca and to determine the compensation the Company would pay the Portuguese for their ships and cargoes that it had captured in 1644.[14]

Agreement was reached on both issues by the emissaries of the Estado da India and the VOC in May of 1645. The Portuguese and the VOC initially disagreed over the exact amount of compensation, but Francisco Zusarte returned to Goa in 1645 with an agreement which the country traders of the Estado da India did not like but were resigned to accept.[15]

The Portuguese were obliged to pay the VOC passage, anchorage and customs duties at Malacca. Passage fees for any type of Portuguese shipping, Crown or country trader, en route to or from China or India were assessed at a fixed rate of 320 rijksdaalders (rsd) per vessel in one direction. If these ships traded with the VOC or any of Malacca's inhabitants, customs duties were collected by the Company at the rate of 5 per cent on the value of all disembarked goods.[16] In 1664, after the cessation of Dutch–Portuguese hostilities, the Governor-General and the Council of the Indies resolved to increase the passage fee at Malacca for Portuguese ships on a graduated scale of 300 to 500 rsd for small to large vessels with customs duties at 10 per cent. Customs duties on imports rose to 20 per cent and exports to 15 per cent in 1678 on the orders of the Heeren XVII in order to compensate the Company for the decline of Malacca's trade receipts and the increase of the Portuguese and Muslim trade at Aceh and Kedah.[17]

Portuguese Crown and country traders paid passage and customs duties at Malacca from 1646 to 1652 and more sporadically from 1664 to 1683.[18] The Portuguese country traders' severely diminished capability to engage large numbers of ships and, perhaps, capital was commented upon in the VOC's appraisal of their trade, and the frequency of arrivals is shown in Table 9.2. Portuguese trade between Macao and the Estado da India, however tenuous, was maintained. The VOC policy of collecting passage and customs tolls remained a contentious practice that was resented by the Portuguese.

Open hostilities between the Portuguese and the VOC ceased over the years 1644 to 1652. During this truce, both antagonists sought to impede the expansion of the other's trade by diplomacy throughout the South China Sea region. The opportunities for the Portuguese country traders from Macao to contest the VOC in those specific markets oscillated on account of the deteriorating economic and political conditions in south China. The VOC, in stark contrast, was able to consolidate its economic and political position in the western portions of the Indonesian archipelago and its European and inter-Asian trades established an enviable profitability.

With the resumption of hostilities in 1652, although a plan to capture Macao was discussed, the Governor-General and the Council of the Indies determined that the VOC's strategic objectives were the sources of the Estado da India's supplies of cinnamon and pepper on Ceylon and the Malabar coast.[19] After tenacious Portuguese resistance, Ceylon was captured by the Company in 1658, and Cochin on the Malabar coast surrendered in 1663.[20]

The Company's decision to shift its strategic focus towards the Indian Ocean had important repercussions for the Dutch trade with China, which by 1652 was also being adversely affected by the continued Ming-Ch'ing dynastic confrontation

Table 9.2. *Portuguese shipping arrivals and departures at Malacca, 1645–82.*

	Arrivals								Departures								
Year	Macao	Cambodia	India	Goa	Cochin	Negapatnam	Masulipatnam	Unstated	Macao	Tonkin	Siam	Macassar	India	Goa	Cochin	Bengal	Unstated
1645				2	1	1			3		1						
1646	8		4						4					8			
1648	5			2		1			3					2	1	2	
1649	1			3					3								1
1650	2			1	1				2				2				
1651	2			1	1				2						2		
1664				1					1								
1665	2			1			1		2					1			
1666	1	1		2					2					2			
1667				4					2	1	1						
1669	3																
1672				4					4								
1677	1																
1679								1									
1680								1									
1681	1																
1682	1			2					2								

Sources: ARA, VOC 1374/KA 1263, *GM*, *DRB* and *Bouwstoffen*.

and more dramatically by the rise of Cheng forces in Fukien. The Dutch continued to utilise their base on Taiwan and experienced disruption in the supplies of various commodities apparently to a lesser degree than the Portuguese at Macao. These market dislocations and the necessity to establish open diplomatic and commercial relations with the Ch'ing dynasty led to a series of VOC trading and political initiatives at Canton from 1652 to 1659 and the despatch of the Pieter de Goyer and Jacob de Keyser embassy to Peking in 1655.[21]

Macao recognised the serious threat posed by the VOC's political and economic initiatives at Canton. The Portuguese were enjoying some improvement in their relations with Ch'ing officials at Canton as a result of the Portuguese policy of accommodation. The VOC merchant, Frederick Schedel, discovered the Chinese desire not to become involved in anti-Portuguese actions on the evening of 25–26 February 1653 at a dinner in Canton with the Viceroy of the Two Kwang and a Senado da Camara emissary. Schedel reported the disappointing news to Batavia that the Viceroy would not tolerate VOC–Portuguese hostilities in Chinese waters.[22] The success of Portuguese political initiatives in thwarting the VOC's negotiations and trade at Canton and Peking led Batavia to reconsider an attack on Macao.[23]

The VOC decisions to cease their trade was influenced not by the political situation at Canton or plans to attack Macao, but by commercial considerations.

The VOC's trade in the Canton region in 1659 had encountered severe competition and unfavourable trading conditions. Thirteen Portuguese country-trader ships had arrived at Macao from Macassar, Siam and Cambodia and six out of seven Cantonese junks successfully returned from their trading ventures at Manila, Johor and Japan (the seventh from Siam was lost). Market conditions at Canton and Macao were further influenced by price-fixing ordered by the Viceroy of the Two Kwang.[24] The VOC decided to augment their China trade at Taiwan from where they planned to attack Macao.

After the VOC's success in capturing Ceylon from the Portuguese, the demands upon the Governor-General and the Council of the Indies to re-allocate the Company's resources and manpower away from the Indian Ocean into the South China Sea were considered. The advocates for resources for the China trade and the attack on Macao saw ships, men and material utilised in other projects. The Company allocated significant additional resources to its forces in the South China Sea for a joint naval and military operation against Macassar in 1660.[25]

The VOC sought to strengthen its economic and political position in the South China Sea by eliminating foreign trade at Macassar and curbing that state's influence in the region. The additional benefit to the Company of an offensive against Macassar was to weaken Portuguese trade in China and India and dishearten Macao, an argument which it was hoped would convince the advocates for an immediate attack on Macao of the necessity for delay. At Batavia, those advocates of an immediate action against Macao were not dissuaded by such arguments and an attack was ordered for the end of October 1660. The Governor-General and the Council of the Indies declared that, 'if we delay any further and if we do not achieve our objective of chasing the Portuguese out of that corner, then perhaps the people from Macao, if there is no peace concluded between the Crown of Portugal and our country might try and seek the protection of the English or some other foreign nation.' The Company forsaw that 'under this pretext they would remain masters in their own land and perhaps in time rise up again and grow into one of the most important places in India as it used to be and this would be greatly to the detriment of the Company and the continuation of the northerly trade.'[26]

Although Batavia had found a number of ships and allotted 600 men for this attack, the VOC's representatives on Taiwan chose to interpret their orders in a different perspective. The Cheng threat to the VOC on Taiwan prompted the postponement of the Company's attack on Macao.[27] The attack was abandoned in 1661 when Dutch shipping and personnel losses, caused by a combination of hostilities between Cheng forces and adverse weather conditions, revealed the over-extension of VOC forces.[28] By 1662, the Company investigated what the reaction of the Ch'ing authorities on the south China coast to an attack on the Portuguese would be and discovered that the Manchu were strenuously opposed to such an action.

With the VOC's expulsion by Cheng forces from Taiwan in 1662, the rationale for an attack ended.[29] The Portuguese at Macao had taken a series of actions, including enlisting Ch'ing military support, which made the continuation of the Company's plans difficult and costly.[30] The VOC's efforts in China shifted to replying to the Cheng conquest of Taiwan.

With VOC intentions towards Macao deflected by events and Chinese forces, and the Estado da India exhausted by continued hostilities and the losses of Ceylon and Malabar, the Portuguese in Asia could only hope for a respite by an early declaration of peace in Europe. The news of peace between Portugal and the Netherlands reached the Estado da India in 1663, when the Viceroy, Antonio de Mello de Castro, despatched his emissary, the Jesuit Father A. Gomes, to Batavia to officially inform the VOC of peace in Europe. Father Gomes quickly discovered his diplomatic mission embroiled in a controversy over the VOC's policy towards Macassar. The Company had forcibly excluded Portuguese trade on Macassar, regardless of the stipulations in the peace treatly.[31] The Estado da India's emissary also learnt in 1664 of the VOC's increase in the rates it charged for anchorage, passage and customs duties at Malacca for Portuguese ships. With little option either to accept or renew hostilities, the Portuguese tacitly accepted the Dutch treatment and commercial restrictions.

There remained for Portuguese country traders from south China few markets in which their maritime trade was well received and profitable. Batavia was seen as a market with potential for Macao's traders. In 1661, the VOC permitted various Portuguese merchants who had been transported from Macassar en route to Macao to trade at Batavia and purchase a ship from the Company.[32] After the announcement of the peace treaty, the Portuguese traded only sporadically with Batavia on account of the Company's disinterest and preferred to concentrae their trade at Bantam on the island of Java.

The impediments to close trading relations between Macao and Batavia from 1664 to 1683 were created primarily by the Company and revolved around the VOC's interest in the China trade. After the loss of Taiwan, the Company embarked upon a series of inconsequential punitive actions along the south-eastern coast of China. Their China trade suffered and the Company had to reverse its policy of force by returning to the Canton region to negotiate with the Ch'ing by despatching the embassy of Pieter van Hoorn (1666–7). The Company hoped to benefit from Macao's poor relations with the Ch'ing authorities prior to the arrival of the Portuguese ambassador, Manuel de Saldanha.[33]

By 1669 the VOC's political initiatives and attempts to restructure its China trade had failed, and the Company decided to rely upon the resources of the vrij-burgers and the Chinese junk traders to supply Chinese products at Batavia. The vrij-burgers and the Chinese carried on smuggling trade in the Macao islands which met with sufficient success for the VOC to encourage its continuation.[34] This trade was a major source of friction between the VOC and the Portuguese at Macao, until the VOC limited the vrij-burgers' activities. The Senado da Camara and the capitão-geral of Macao attempted through diplomacy (the mission of Jeronimo de Abreu de Lima to Batavia in 1671 is the best documented) and correspondence to persuade the VOC to curtail and eliminate this practice.[35] Changes in the Ch'ing authorities towards the administration of foreign trade in the late 1670s alerted the Company that it had to constrain the vrij-burgers at a time when Batavia had independently decided that action was required.

Another source of friction between the Portuguese and the Dutch was the rapid expansion of Portuguese trade at Bantam from 1670 to 1682. Foreign trade at Bantam was carried on by English, Portuguese, Danish, French, Spanish, Chinese, Muslim and Javanese merchants and officials. By 1678 this trade had reached a sufficiently large volume and value for the VOC to apply political pressure at Bantam to have it curtailed. With the failure of these negotiations, the Company occupied Bantam in 1682 and banned all foreign trade by its competitors.[36]

The VOC's occupation of Bantam eliminated yet another market in the South China Sea for Portuguese country traders from Macao. The Heeren XVII, as a consequence of the reversals the Portuguese had suffered, were of the opinion that it might benefit the Company if they exchanged Cranganor (one of the former Estado da India possessions on the south-west Indian coast) for Macao. Batavia did not share the Heeren XVII's enthusiasm for such an exchange; Goa was even more lukewarm. The Governor-General and the Council of the Indies replied to the Heeren XVII that Batavia was no longer interested in the acquisition of more territory, especially territory that would have to be taken and held by force from the Chinese, even if a deal with the Portuguese Crown could be negotiated.[37]

Portuguese relations with the VOC and some of the points of friction between the Portuguese country traders and the Company did not terminate in the early 1680s. Although the Company went to great and successful lengths to exclude foreign competition in parts of the Indonesian archipelago, its trade with China was not satisfactory from the Heeren XVII and the Governor-General's vantage point. Ultimately, the cost and difficulty in maintaining a direct Company trade from Java with China was not to be borne by the VOC but by the Chinese junk and the Portuguese country trader from Macao.

The Portuguese from Macao, in certain instances, were able to alter and either balance or impose a temporary redress in their unfavourable position *vis-à-vis* Asian and European country traders and European Companies. This opportunity for redress occurred less often in the case of the Portuguese from Macao dealing directly with the representatives of the European Companies in China; the Portuguese from Macao had greater success in dealing with individuals in the Companies employ who sought to utilise the commercial facilities they offered to trade privately in China and India.[38]

At Macao, stable political and economic conditions in the Kwangtung region meant a marked improvement in the availability of supplies and an increase in exports. In the late seventeenth century, there was a recovery in the quantity of cargo exported from China in Macao's ships. The quality and the categories of Chinese produce exported by the Portuguese country traders and with which they competed against European Company and country traders and Chinese junk operators was modified.

Previously, Macao's country traders successfully competed for the small total market volume of quality Chinese textile goods, raw silk, silk and cotton piecegoods and gold. These goods, especially the silk textiles, commanded a relatively high unit cost price at Canton and had a high sale price and profit margin throughout Asia and Europe. Between 1684 and 1754, the Portuguese ceased exporting any significant quantity of Chinese textiles and concentrated upon the purchase of low-priced ballast cargoes with, usually, correspondingly low profit margins. Macao's country traders also acted as freight carriers on account of their financial debility for Chinese, Armenian and European merchants.

Macao's commercial dependence upon Canton's market and merchants dictated that the Portuguese dedicate their efforts to maintain good relations with the Chinese. By all accounts, the Portuguese perceived the reality in where the power lay to influence their continued survival. For most of this period, the resources of the Portuguese at Macao were allocated in maintaining Sino-Portuguese relations. The incorporation of Macao into Ch'ing China and their policy of accommodation towards Ch'ing authority occurred at this time. For the Portuguese country trader, the loss of the Portuguese Crown's claim of sovereignty over a piece of Chinese territory was unimportant as long as Portuguese communal authority was insured and commercial benefit could be obtained. Portuguese country, along with the rare Company, traders, after the imposition of the Canton system, were permitted to purchase their cargoes outside the co-hong. Certain commodities were upon occasion sold to them at slightly lower prices and they paid lower measurage duties than European Companies and country traders as a consequence of their accommodation to Chinese authority.[39]

In the late seventeenth and early eighteenth centuries, the Portuguese at Macao initially placed greater emphasis in dealing with the VOC than any other European Company. This emphasis stemmed from the Portuguese interest and involvement in the Batavia trade. After the VOC and the Dutch vrij-burgers ceased to compete directly against the Portuguese in the China market, these two antagonists evolved a *modus operandi* in their relations with the Portuguese bitterly resenting the toll collection policy operating against them at Malacca. During the Ch'ing ban on foreign trade from 1717 to 1727, Macao's country traders forced the Company to pay higher prices at Batavia for Chinese produce.[40] With the resumption of Chinese junk competition at Batavia and the VOC inauguration of direct trade to China in 1729, the Portuguese trade at Batavia diminished.

Portuguese interest at Macao in maintaining close formal relations with the VOC also dimmed. At Cochin on the Malabar coast and the major ports on Ceylon that were controlled by the VOC, in the early eighteenth century, the Company lamented the decline in their influence with the Portuguese at Macao. From the late 1710s until the 1750s, Macao country traders' ships called and traded at Cochin and on Ceylon. Portuguese activities on the Malabar coast demonstrated the impossibility in practice of the VOC establishing a pepper monopoly.

With the absence of direct VOC competition in the south China markets in the 1690s, the EIC from Europe and India and English country traders from EIC settlements in India were able to expand their China trade.[41] The rise of the EIC to prominence in the maritime trade of China was gradual. The EIC did not regularise its access to the Canton market until 1699.[42] Other European Companies, in particular the French, Ostend and the VOC, and English and Portuguese country traders, competed against the EIC at Canton in the purchase of export commodities for the European and Indian markets. While some of the EIC's ships traded via India instead of directly from Europe, the English and Portuguese country traders competed against the EIC in those Indian markets in the sale of Chinese commodities.

Macao was unable to influence the Chinese to prohibit the EIC, other Companies' and European country traders' commercial activities at Canton. Portuguese relations with the EIC and other Companies were kept at a distance in order that Macao avoid becoming responsible for their behaviour to the Chinese authorities. The supercargo system of arranging and negotiating cargoes at Canton also kept EIC contact with Macao to the minimum until the personnel from the Companies began to reside in China on a permanent basis and at Macao when not trading at Canton.[43]

The Portuguese at Macao maintained close contact with the EIC and English country traders in the Indian markets where both they and the Portuguese traded. From the late 1680s until 1750s, Portuguese country traders from Macao sailed to Madras on a regular, annual basis. Macao trading activity at that port in 1733 to 1735 forced the EIC to decide not to despatch any of the Company's ships to China in 1735.[44]

The sea customs, as import duties were called at Madras, and anchorage charges were a welcome supplement to the Honourable Company's revenue; the duties collected on Portuguese country traders' ships from Macao were considered significant and important to the EIC's prosperity. When English merchants at Madras complained of the competition from trading in 1739, the EIC's board explained their conduct, 'as to the Macao Men, they sold their China Cargoes and took in their returns here. This is a trade which has been carried on longer than any one of us can remember, and we need only remark, That the Customs paid by them on the imports from China are upwards of two Thousand four hundred pagodas.' In addition to customs duties, the EIC received good prices 'on the piece goods, Tin, Sandalwood, etc. of which their returning Cargoes consist,' which was mentioned 'to show how advantageous that trade is to the Company.'[45] The Portuguese import duty contribution to the sea customs on goods collected at Madras in 1739 amounted to almost 10 per cent of the total.[46]

In 1746 the EIC's directors in London ordered the President and Council at Fort St. George (Madras) to contract Macao's country traders to supply tea from China to Madras. Comsumption in England of low-priced teas, such as those the Portuguese were to supply, had grown to over a million pounds weight per annum. The Portuguese were selected to engage in this trade for EIC as a result of the similar role they played in supplying tea for the VOC at Batavia.[47] The EIC's directors resolution to proceed with this project wavered in 1748, after steps towards establishing a contract with Luis Coelho, a Portuguese country trader and

ship-owner at Macao, had been undertaken. The precise reasons for the EIC
directors' reconsideration of this project are unknown; they probably did not stem
from a fear of the necessary financial arrangements to secure large quantities of
tea. In dealing with the Chinese, the Portuguese ships would have to carry EIC
cash advances of 'one third or at least a fourth Part of their [the tea's] value to
be advanced to the China Merchants at Repondentia upon their Teas.'[48]

The Portuguese at Macao, also, had commercial transactions and relations with
other European Company and European and Asian country traders, in particular
the French and the Armenians. The Portuguese from Macao had acted as freight
carriers for the French on Bantam in the early 1680s. Upon arrival at Canton in
1704 French merchants wanted to reside at Macao; permission from the Senado
da Camara was not forthcoming in this case.[49] The French in India arranged to
trade with China in addition to their direct trade, via contacts with Macao country
traders. Throughout the first half of the eighteenth century, French ships on
rare occasions traded at Macao.[50]

The Macao Portuguese and the French developed elaborate trading contacts on
the south-west Indian coast in the 1740s. The French were established at Mahe
and the Portuguese were in search of pepper and sandalwood supplies and markets
to sell their Chinese produce, in particular sugar. The English at Tellicherry, also,
on the south-west Indian coast, observed with interest their activities; in 1746, the
French at Mahe had 1,400 *candils* of pepper in stock of which 1,000 candils had
been laden on two Macao country-trader ships for China.[51] These Portuguese and
French commercial transactions continued on the south-west Indian coast but it
was not until the latter half of the eighteenth century that the Portuguese country
traders at Macao despatched their ships to trade with the French on Mauritius.

In the late seventeenth and early eighteenth centuries, several Armenian
merchants, who along with the Sephardic Jewish community residing at Madras
had initiated the English country trade with Manila, came into contact with the
Portuguese from Macao and traded in south China. Relations between the
Portuguese and Armenians were cordial; a few Armenian merchants were active
in the China trade from Madras by despatching their own ships but, usually,
especially in the eighteenth century, by freighting their goods on Portuguese ships
from Macao. Armenian merchants, also, carried on their China trade by investing
and freighting their goods on Portuguese Crown and Macao country trader ships
from Goa to Macao.[52]

The Portuguese at Macao, as a result of the existence of numerous European
Companies and European and Asian country traders with an enormous diversity
in their capabilities and interest in the China trade, developed modest commercial
opportunities. The creation and the exploitation of such opportunities was
supported by the Macao country traders' pragmatic commercial attitudes and
methods which they utilised to insure their communal survival. In the late
seventeenth and early eighteenth centuries, the Portuguese country traders from
Macao dealt with almost any and all merchants, European and Asian, on the basis
of generating profitable trade and commercial advantage for their position at
Macao.

Although the Portuguese had long ceased being a serious imperial contender, Macao's merchants had developed commercial roles *vis-à-vis* the other Europeans in China. Accommodating their economic capabilities to the reality of their political position, Portuguese society was scorned by recently arrived European observers but used to mutual advantage by those old Asian hands that knew how to appreciate merchant skills and knowledge that they lacked. Portuguese society at Macao survived.

IO

CONCLUSION

The survival of empire or rather the survival of a Portuguese community and its society in China in the late seventeenth and early eighteenth centuries suggests that the nature of Portuguese colonial society and its contribution to the maritime trade of Asia require a re-evaluation of their significance. The Portuguese imperial experience in Asia may be approached from the Crown's or the casados perspective. Regardless of temporary successes of talented fidalgo administrators and the gains for the state, and individuals involved throughout the Estado da India for the Crown, the empire appears to have been an abject failure in financial and political terms but it was a responsibility that was retained for prestige, honour, religion and the elusive hope for gain that the Crown would not relinquish.

For the casados, whether reinol or mestiço, whose activities as ship-owners, operators and investors in the country trade are very much a central focus of this study, and the society that they created and maintained in China, the empire was less of a failure than for the Crown. Governors, judges and other Crown-appointed administrators arrived at Macao from Portugal or India recognising that their stay was short and invariably departed complaining of the intransigence of the casados towards the Crown's authority. Casados, lacking some of the fidalgos attitudes, did not possess the same mobility; married or living with a concubine, the Macao country traders knew from a very early date that their community's existence rested upon their imposing or maintaining good relations with Chinese merchants and officials and also upon their taking advantage of the trading opportunities in south China, the South China Sea and the Indian Ocean.

A numerically small community, Portuguese society in China and the South China Sea, as seen through the perspective of the casado/country trader at Macao, duplicated two continental Portuguese institutions in particular, the Senado da Camara and the Santa Casa da Misericordia, which effectively encompassed and represented the divergent political and commercial interests of the powerful within the local community. These communal institutions commanded the attention of the Crown's administrators and the Church's representatives; the Senado da Camara parried the Crown's efforts to incorporate the community's resources for imperial and military policies which the country trader neither sought nor was prepared to sustain. The Santa Casa da Misericordia provided necessary social services, ameliorated a harsh existence in an age with rudimentary medical knowledge and practice, and ensured the financial support of fortunate orphans and widows. By jealously maintaining their collective powers as a municipality, the Portuguese country traders at Macao through their election to the Senado da Camara officially negotiated on behalf of the community with Chinese and other Asian representatives on political and economic issues.

Faced with the collective strength as well as the eternal bickering amongst differing groups of casados, the influence of the Crown and the Church was relegated to significant but selective roles within local society which were expanded only under special or dramatic circumstances. The Crown's interest in the Portuguese communities in China and the South China Sea, which were initially outside the parameters desired by Lisbon or Goa, was to derive a financial benefit from the casados participation in inter-Asian trade and the supply of commodities from China and the South China Sea to India for Europe. Criticism of the Crown's inability to control those communities and the activities of the lançados/casados has failed to recognise the reality of the Crown's limited interest, capability and resources for such a policy. The Crown, instead, sought to benefit from the activities of the Macao country traders by imposing its claim upon and collecting revenue from the sale of the Japan voyage at Goa to various fidalgos who invariably relied upon the casados to finance, freight and, in exceptional cases, invest in the voyage. The Crown's monopoly of the Japan voyage did not seriously impede the growth of private enterprise at Macao, Japan and Manila, where the casados' activities demonstrated a capacity for innovative commercial behaviour and expertise in handling large amounts of capital equal to any contemporary northern European Company. It was only in the 1630s that the Crown administered the Japan and Manila voyages; even then Portuguese country traders were active in the Japan and Manila trades and actually diversified their operations in the South China Sea, most notably at Macassar.

The Catholic Church, so often ignored or separated from the activities of the Iberian powers or communities in Asia and elsewhere, was a fundamental component in Portuguese society. Nominally supported by the Crown, the Catholic missionary activities under the aegis of the Padroado played an active role in local society. The missionaries had influence with some of the casados as a result of the respected and feared position of the religious in Portuguese communities. The Padroado's organisation and talented manpower played an important role in maintaining Portuguese relations with Chinese officials at Macao, Canton and Peking. The Jesuits, in particular, were involved in trade and finance as an ally of certain country traders but also as competitors; they were ship-owners, investors and added an inter-regional aspect to their own everyday finance by relying on funding from revenue collected from small estates in northern India for supplementary support.

The nature and structure of Portuguese colonial society, with its emphasis on its various institutions which manifested a strong communal self-interest for the local elite and powerful private merchants, helps explain Macao's survival *vis-à-vis* the rest of the Estado da India. The adoption by Macao's country traders of relatively non-dogmatic attitudes in their relations with the Chinese also contributed to their survival, although their city became in all but name incorporated into Ch-ing

China with specific and important exceptions for the Portuguese in the regulations of their community and its commercial matters. The Portuguese country traders also demonstrated a pragmatic attitude towards advocating the exclusion and ultimately adjusting as best they could to the presence of the European Companies and European and Asian country traders at Macao or Canton. Despite relations which included violent conflict and confrontation, the political and commercial activities of the Portuguese country traders are a classic case study of the extent to which a European and mestiço community developed and maintained itself in partnership with other Asians and Europeans, in the era before European dominion was established.

Although the pragmatic nature of Portuguese society was one of its strengths, there were obvious limitations in its structure, not to mention physical resources and military capabilities, that inhibited its renewal and growth. The most glaring weakness was the general absence of discipline by the country traders, who were un-regulated entrepreneurs. They demonstrated in the Batavia trade a lemming-like propensity towards relying upon only one market for high profits and despatching too large a number of their ships to one port, thereby lowering the return on that trade and investment for all of Macao's merchants. Their financial ingenuity in modifying and regularising the utilisation of local institutions, such as the Santa Casa da Misericordia, for the purpose of investing the community's limited capital resources into maritime trade was laudable; but fraudulent efforts perpetrated and perpetuated by certain country traders to evade repayment demonstrated the ability for the powerful economic groups to dominate Portuguese society for their benefit. That is not to say that the Portuguese country trader was inherently more of a scoundrel or more easily corrupted than his English, Dutch, Chinese or Indian counterpart.

Portuguese commercial activities in China made an important contribution to the maritime trade of Asia. Prior to the Portuguese loss of Malacca and the Japan and Manila trades in the early 1640s, their contribution centred on maintaining the direct exchange by sea of merchandise to and from China and India in which the Chinese had participated in the fifteenth century. The Portuguese occupied an important middleman role in the trade from China to Japan and as a consequence were major participants in the transfer of silver bullion from Japan and the New World via Manila to China which stimulated the late Ming economy and in particular the Canton market. The Portuguese country trader from Macao joined other casados from the Estado da India in connecting Manila's market with India – a totally new but fledgling facet in the structure of Asian trade.

The Portuguese dependence upon supplies of Chinese merchandise from Canton and their sales of Indian and Japanese goods at the Canton market strongly supports the characterisation of their activities as an adjunct of that market. Their relationship with Canton's quevees and Chinese officials was far more dynamic than has been previously held. There is evidence that the Portuguese coerced Cantonese merchants to send fewer of their own vessels to trade at Manila in favour of Cantonese merchants' goods being carried by Portuguese ships; Chinese merchants and money lenders helped finance Portuguese trade to Japan. Canton's market and maritime trade, as a result of the Portuguese presence, benefited and, perhaps, expanded faster than many Sinologists, who have concentrated the focus of their research on the activities of the great maritime traditions of the Fukien and Chekiang ports, care to admit.

Portuguese commercial activities in the South China Sea also enhanced Asian trade; after their expulsion from the extreme eastern Indonesian archipelago, in the Moluccas, the decline of Malacca's participation in the East–West spice trade in the late sixteenth century and the arrival of the English and Dutch, the Portuguese casados expanded their political, commercial and military activities in the Celebes and the Lesser Sunda islands in the early seventeenth century. This development coincided with the rise of Macassar, a state in whose fortunes the Portuguese country traders were actively involved; from that state, the Portuguese casados were able to continue to trade for spices and sandalwood. They eagerly supported certain innovations in the region's maritime trade by investing in goods, primarily Indian textiles, on ships sailing to Manila and by shipping gold bullion and mas from Macassar to India. In other markets, Tonkin, for example, the Portuguese country traders demonstrated that their knowledge of the importance of relatively un-exploited commodities such as caixas was very finely developed and, along with their alliance with the Jesuits of the Padroado, enabled them to modestly maintain their commerce in highly competitive markets.

The Portuguese country traders from Macao continued to search for profitable markets further afield and outside of the South China Sea in the Indian Ocean in the early eighteenth century. One of their strengths was the ability to absorb the loss of a number of markets and to continue the search. The Canton market developed at the same time with the arrival of the European Company and country traders which dominated the lucrative international trade to Europe and competed in the inter-regional trade from India to China while the Chinese junks expanded and controlled most of the maritime trade of the South China Sea. The Portuguese at Macao possessed two real options, to compete for and occupy the role of selling Chinese produce to the VOC at Batavia, and to trade low-cost Chinese items in the Indian Ocean markets in exchange for small amounts of silver and the ballast cargo commodities from the South China Sea and India.

The sheer variety of the commercial methods and practices of the Portuguese country trader mirrored their pragmatic and non-dogmatic attitudes towards trade and their survival. In their accumulated experience in markets from Japan to Malabar over almost a century and a quarter, the Portuguese country traders at Macao demonstrated an ability and willingness to attempt to impose their claim of exclusive rights and compete violently for commercial advantage equal to any rival when their resources permitted. They relied upon Asian money-lenders, primarily, for their finances but their communal capital resources were surprisingly successful in supporting modest trading activities. When those favourable conditions were absent, they tried to deny other traders any commercial opportunity by intrigue, were willing to freight their goods on board the ships of Asian merchants, and would carry freight for Chinese, Armenian and European merchants in their own ships. There were few commercial arrangements that the Portuguese from Macao were not willing to attempt in order to produce a profit and ensure their ability to continue trading. Portuguese trade and society in China and the South China Sea in the mid seventeenth and first half of the eighteenth centuries reveals that it is not always the activities of the most powerful commercial groups – European or Asian – which provide a new perspective and a fascinating insight into the maritime trade of Asia.

NOTES

Most of the archives that were used in this study are known to the specialist, and in general the method of citing the archive poses few problems. After giving the abbreviation of the archive, the collection, or in absence of specific collection the codex number, is mentioned along with the folio or page number. In a few rare cases, where there was no folio number or indifferent and confusing pagination, the date of the document is given. For the Spanish archives, references follow their style, that is the abbreviation for the archive, collection, the *legajo* and *ramo*, in the absence of a *ramo*, the folio, and if it was lacking, the date of the document.

In the notes, in order to avoid confusion, only archival and printed archival records are abbreviated. Printed archival records with more than one series, as is the case of the *Archivos de Macau*, are indicated by 1st, 2nd, 3rd and followed with roman numerals for the volume and arabic numerals for the page. Author's names and titles of books and articles are shortened in a conventional manner in the notes of each chapter for convenience so that the reader is not forced to return to the initial citation in an earlier chapter. For complete references to these archival and printed records, consult the bibliography.

ABBREVIATIONS

MANUSCRIPT SOURCES

Portuguese Archives

AHMF	*Arquivo Histórico do Ministerio das Finanças*, Lisbon
Macao	*Maços de Macau* collection
ANTT	*Arquivo Nacional da Torre do Tombo*, Lisbon
LM	*Livros das Monções* collection
Ajuda	*Biblioteca da Ajuda*, Lisbon
JA	*Jesuitas na Asia* collection
BNL	*Biblioteca Nacional*, Lisbon
Pombalina	*Pombalina* collection
SGL	*Sociedade da Geografia*, Lisbon
Reservados	*Reservados* collection
Evora	*Biblioteca Pública e Arquivo Distrital*, Evora
Cadaval	private library and manuscript collection of the Cadaval family, Muge
SCM	*Santa Casa da Misericordia*, Macau

Indian Archives

HAG	Historical Archive of Goa
MR	*Monções do Reino* collection
Fazenda	*Conselho da Fazenda* collection
Regimentos	*Regimento e Instruções*, collection
Japão	*Japão* collection
Macao	*Macao* collection
Provisões	*Provisões* collection
Fianças	*Fianças* collection
Régias	*Senado de Goa – Carta Régias* collection

[The abbreviations, the numbers of the codices and the titles of these collections are those found in Pissurlencar's *Roteiro*.]

Spanish Archives

AHN	*Archivo Histórico Nacional*, Madrid
Jesuitas	*Jesuitas* collection
BNM	*Biblioteca Nacional*, Madrid
Jesuitas	*Jesuitas* collection
AGI	*Archivo General de Indias*, Seville
Filipinas	*Audiencia de Filipinas* collection
Patronato	*Patronato* collection
Mexico	*Audiencia de Mexico* collection
Indiferente General	*Indiferente General* collection
Escribania	*Escribanía de Camara* collection
AGS	*Archivo General de Simancas*
Sec. Prov.	*Secretarias Provinciales* collection

Dutch Archives

ARA	*Algemeen Rijksarchief*, The Hague
VOC/KA	*Koloniale Archieven Oost-Indie: Archieven van de Vereenigde Oost-Indische compagnie* collection

[The General State Archives at the Hague is in the process of switching the method of citing the Dutch East India Company records from KA to VOC with the codex number; consequently, both are given in the notes. The majority of the references from this archive and collection used in this study are from the *Overgekomen brieven* collection of the VOC materials. The Batavia *resolution* are cited VOC/KA number and the date of the resolution as it is found in the original documentation.]

British Archives

BM	British Museum, London
Add. Mss.	Additional Manuscripts collection
IOR	India Office Records, London
Celebes	Factory Records, Celebes
Java	Factory Records, Java

PRINTED SOURCES

AM	*Arquivos de Macau*
APO	*Archivo Portuguez Oriental* [Cunha-Rivara edition]
Doc. Rem. da India	*Documentos Remitidos do Estado da India ou Livros das Monções*
GM	*Generale Missiven van Gouverneurs-Generaal en Radan aan Heeren XVII der Vereenigde Oostindische Compagnie*
DRB	*Dagh-register gehouden in 't Casteel Batavia*
Opkomst	*De Opkomst van het Nederlandsch Gezag in Oost-Indie*
Bouwstoffen	*Bouwstoffen voor de Geschiedenis der Nederlanders in den Maleischen Archipel*
B & R	*The Philippine Islands*
	Records of Fort St. George:
Madras	*The Diary and Consultation Books*
England Despatches	*Despatches from England*
Ft. St. David	*Fort St. David Consultations*
Letters Ft. St. David	*Letter to Fort St. David*
Tellicherry	*Tellicherry Consultations*
Letters Tellicherry	*Letter to Tellicherry*
Tellicherry Letters	*Letters from Tellicherry*
Anjengo	*Anjengo Consultations*

I. MARITIME TRADE IN ASIA

1 cf. M. N. Pearson, 'The Indian Ocean and the Portuguese in the Sixteenth Century', a paper presented at the Second International Seminar on Indo-Portuguese History, Lisbon, 20–24 October, 1980.

2 cf. M. A. P. Meilink-Roelofsz, *Asian Trade and European Influence in the Indonesian Archipelago, between 1500 and about 1630*, The Hague, 1962, reprinted 1969, 27–88 and 136–72; and A. Cortesão, tr., *The Suma Oriental of Tomé Pires*, London, 1944, reprint, 1967.

3 cf. Cortesão, *The Suma Oriental*, 118 and 123–8.

4 cf. J. K. Fairbank, 'A Preliminary Framework', in J. K. Fairbank, ed., *The Chinese World Order: Traditional China's Foreign Relations*, Cambridge, Mass., 1968, 3.

5 cf. Wang Gungwu, 'Early Ming Relations with Southeast Asia: A Background Essay', in Fairbank, *Chinese World Order*, 56, and for Malacca's early relations with China, cf. by the same author, 'The Opening of Relations between China and Malacca, 1403–1405', in J. S. Bastin and R. Roolvink, eds., *Malayan and Indonesian Studies*, Oxford, 1964, 87–104.

6 Cf. Lo Jung-Pang, 'The Decline of the Early Ming Navy', *Oriens Extremus*, 5 (1958–9), 149–68.

7 cf. Wang Gungwu '"Public" and "Private" overseas trade in Chinese history', in M. Mollat, ed., *Sociétés et Compagnies de Commerce en Orient et dans l'Océan Indien*, Paris, 1970, 215–26, for a discussion of the public and private elements in China's maritime trade; cf. B. Wiethoff, *Die Chinesische Seeverbotspolitik und der private Überseehandel von 1368 bis 1567*, Hamburg, 1963 and by the same author, *China's Dritte Grenze: Der Traditionelle Chinesische Staat und der Kustennahe Seeraum*, Wiesbaden, 1969, for the conflicts within local Chinese society associated with the administration of maritime trade.

8 For one example of the hui-kuan in the overseas Chinese expansion in the South China Sea region, cf. Ch'en Ching-Ho, *Historical Notes on Hoi-An (Faifo)*, Carbondale, 1973, 35–58, 95–8. For the technical and financial sophistication of the late Ming merchant and the high levels of capitalisation, cf. J. Needham and R. Huang, 'The Nature of Chinese Society – A Technical Interpretation', *Journal of Oriental Studies*, 12 (1974), 1–16.

9 For Shanghai, cf. M. Elvin, 'Market Towns and Waterways: The County of Shanghai from 1480 to 1910', for Ning-po, cf. Yoshinobu Shiba, 'Ning-po and Its Hinterland', both of which are in G. W. Skinner, ed., *The City in Late Imperial China*, Stanford, 1977, 441–73 and 391–439. For the Fukien region, cf. E. S. Rawski, *Agricultural Change and the Peasant Economy of South*

China, Cambridge, Mass., 1972, Ng Chin-Keong, 'The Fukienese Maritime Trade in the Second Half of the Ming Period – Government Policy and Elite Groups' Attitudes,' *Nanyang University Journal*, 5, pt. 2 (1971), 81–100; and by the same author, 'A Study on the Peasant Society of South Fukien, 1506–1644', *Nanyang University Journal*, 6 (1972), 189–212.

10 cf. Ho Ping-ti, *Studies on the Population of China*, 1368–1953, Cambridge, Mass., 1959, for the growth in China's population in the late Ming and the Ch'ing; cf. J. Needham, *Science and Civilization in China*, 5 vols. in 8 parts, Cambridge, 1954–80, IV, pt. 3, 379–699, for the development of Chinese maritime technology; cf. D. H. Perkins, *Agricultural Development in China, 1368–1968*, Chicago, 1969, for a general introduction; recent research has either investigated one region or the development of a single commodity in agriculture and its manufacture, for the Fukien region cf. Rawski, *Agricultural Change*; cotton, cf. C. Dietrich, 'Cotton Culture and Manufacture in Early Ch'ing China', in W. E. Willmot, ed., *Economic Organisation in Chinese Society*, Stanford, 1972, 109–35; and silk, cf. E-tu Zen Sun, 'Sericulture and Silk Textile Production in Ch'ing China', in Willmott, ed., *Economic Organisation*, 79–108. For a review of recent Chinese and Japanese historiography on these topics, cf. R. H. Myers, 'Some Issues on Economic Organisation during the Ming and Ch'ing Periods: A Review Article', *Ch'ing-shih wen-t'i*, 3:2 (1974), 77–93, and by the same author, 'The "Sprouts of Capitalism" in Agricultural Development during the mid-Ch'ing Period', *Ch'ing-shih wen-t'i*, 3:6 (1976), 84–9.

11 cf. Rawski, *Agricultural Change*, 77, 86–7, indicates that money-lending and commerce were more profitable than rents from agricultural production but that land prices in Chang-chou in south Fukien were rising in the late Ming period and land was being purchased for its relative security.

12 cf. K. N. Chaudhuri, *The Trading World of Asia and the English East India Company, 1660–1760*, Cambridge, 1978, 313, 329–30, for a description of the importance of ballast, gruff or coarse goods to the Company traders.

13 cf. C. Dietrich, 'Cotton Culture', 133, which shows cotton producers in southern Hopei, Hupeh and Honan were marketing cotton fibre in Fukien, and Kwangtung, amongst other provinces. The most famous cotton textile manufactures for the internal market were found in the lower Yangtze area around Sung-chiang Prefecture and apparently marketed some of their production down the coastal route to Fukien and Kwangtung.

14 cf. J. L. Blussé, 'The Dutch Occupation of the Pescadores (1622–1624)', *Transactions of the International Conference of Orientalists in Japan*, 18 (1973), 41–2.

15 cf. *GM*, I, 136–7, describes the forty Chinese junks from south China to Japan as each carrying ten, twenty or thirty picols of silks, quantities of sugar and porcelain, cf. Kato Eiichi, 'The Japanese–Dutch Trade in the Formative Period of the Seclusion Policy, Particularly on the Raw Silk Trade by the Dutch Factory at Hirado 1620–1640', *Acta Asiatica*, 30 (1976), 34–84, supports the generale missieven's characterisation of the contemporary size and cargo capacity of Chinese junks.

16 cf. A. B. Woodside, *Vietnam and the Chinese Model*, Cambridge, Mass., 1971, 9–18, 234–76, for a description of Vietnamese concepts of kingship, creation of a tributary system on the Chinese model and its historical reality, and the Nguyen approaches to maritime trade in the early nineteenth century. For similar views of the power of the monarch and his role in trade and foreign relations, cf. Dang Phu'o'ng-Nghi, *Les Institutions Publiques du Viet-Nam au XVIIIe Siècle*, Paris, 1969, 41–52 and Nguyen Thanh-Nha, *Tableau Economique du Vietnam aux XVIIe et XVIIIe Siècles*, Paris, 1970, 183–227.

17 cf. Truong Buu Lam, 'Intervention versus Tribute in Sino-Vietnamese Relations, 1788–1790', in Fairbank, *The Chinese World Order*, 165–79.

18 cf. Woodside, *Vietnam and the Chinese Model*, 247–8, and M. Cotter, 'Towards a Social History of the Vietnamese Southward Movement', *Journal of Southeast Asian History*, 9 (1968), 12–24.

19 cf. Wang Gung-Wu, 'Early Ming Relations, in Fairbank, *Chinese World Order*, 58–68, for Siam and Cambodia relations with China in the early Ming; S. Prombon, 'Sino-Siamese Tributary Relations, 1282–1853', Ph.D. dissertation, University of Wisconsin, 1971, for an introduction to this subject; S. Viraphol, *Tribute and Profit: Sino-Siamese Trade, 1652–1853*, Cambridge, Mass., 1977, and J. W. Cushman, 'Fields from the Sea: Chinese Junk Trade with Siam During the Late Eighteenth Century and Early Nineteenth Century', Ph.D. dissertation, Cornell University, 1975.

20 cf. M. Mancall, 'The Ch'ing Tribute System: an Interpretive Essay', in Fairbank, *Chinese World Order*, 68–70. Kingship and its importance in South-east Asia as well as Siam has been the subject of intense scrutiny, cf. R. von Heine-Geldern, *Conceptions of State and Kingship in Southeast Asia*, Ithaca, 1956, H. G. Quaritch Wales, *Ancient Siamese Government and Administration*, London, 1934, and J. Kemp, *Aspects of Siamese Kingship in the Seventeenth Century*, Bangkok, 1969.

21 cf. O. W. Wolters, 'Ayudhya and the Rearward Part of the World', *Journal of the Royal Asiatic Society* (1968), pts. 3 and 4, 166–78.

22 cf. B. Watson Andaya, 'The Nature of the State in the Eighteenth Century Perak', in A. Reid and L. Castles, eds., *Pre-Colonial State Systems in Southeast Asia*, Kuala Lumpur, 1975, 24–6.

23 cf. Woodside, *Vietnam and the Chinese Model*, 235.

24 cf. L. Y. Andaya, 'The Structure of Power in Seventeenth Century Johor', in Reid and Castles, *Pre-Colonial State Systems*, 2.

25 State-to-state or ruler-to-ruler communication and the reception of such letters and the ambassadors that bore them is an intriguing subject, cf. *DRB, 1631–1634*, 6 for the VOC's reception of a letter from the King of Cambodia in 1631. Whether the Portuguese, Dutch and other Europeans perceived the theoretical and ritual importance of such ceremonies is dubious but they participated in ceremonial procedures common to the South China Sea. The Europeans also imposed Western contractual relationships that did not have a functional indigenous state co-efficient, cf. L. Y. Andaya, 'Treaty Conceptions and Misconceptions: a case study from South Sulawesi', *Bijdragen tot de Taal-, Land- en Volkenkunde*, 134 (1978), 275–95.

26 cf. Woodside, *Vietnam*, 34; R. B. Smith's articles on Confucian thought advocate a slightly different appreciation of its permeation of Vietnamese society, 'The Cycle of Confucianization in Vietnam', in W. F. Vella, ed., *Aspects of Vietnamese History*, Honolulu, 1973, 1–29 and 'Politics and Society in Viet-Nam during the Early Nguyen Period (1802–62)', *Journal of the Royal Asiatic Society* (1974), pt. 2, 153–69.

27 cf. J. C. van Leur, *Indonesian Trade and Society*, second edition, The Hague, 1967, and Meilink-Roelofsz, *Asian Trade*.

2. IMPERIAL FOUNDATIONS: THE ESTADO DA INDIA AND MACAO

1 cf. C. R. Boxer, *The Portuguese Seaborne Empire: 1415–1825*, New York, 1969, 52–61 and J. Duffy, *Shipwreck and Empire*, Cambridge, Mass., 1955.

2 cf. N. Steensgaard, *Carracks, Caravans and Companies: the structural crisis in the European–Asian trade in the early 17th century*, Copenhagen, 1972, 81–113 and K. N. Chaudhuri, *The Trading World of Asia and the English East India Company, 1660–1760*, Cambridge, 1978, 4–7.

3 cf. M. N. Pearson, 'Goa during the first Century of Portuguese Rule', *Itinerario*, 8:1 (1984), 36–57.

4 cf. V. Magalhães Godinho, *Os Descobrimentos e a Economia Mundial*, 2 vols., Lisbon, 1963, I, 50.

5 cf. J. V. Mills, tr., 'Description of Malacca, and Meridional India and Cathay', *Journal of the Malayan Branch of the Royal Asiastic Society* (1930), pt. 1, 19–20 and A. Cortesão, ed., *The Suma Oriental of Tomé Pires*, 2 vols., London, 1944, reprint 1967, 268–78.

6 cf. Lien-Shang Yang, 'Historical Notes on the Chinese World Order', in J. K. Fairbank, ed., *The Chinese World Order: Traditional China's Foreign Relations*, Cambridge, Mass., 1968, 31–3.

7 cf. C. R. Boxer, ed., *South China in the Sixteenth Century*, Cambridge, 1953, reprint 1967, xxi–xxiv.

8 cf. H. Bernard-Maitre, *Aux Portes de la Chine. Les Missionaires du Seizieme siècle, 1514–1583*, Tientsin, 1933.

9 cf. Kwan-wai So, *Japanese Piracy in Ming China During the Sixteenth Century*, East Lansing, 1975.

10 cf. J. E. Wills, Jr., 'Maritime China from Wang Chih to Shih Lang: Themes in Peripheral History', in J. D. Spence and J. E. Wills, Jr., eds., *From Ming to Ch'ing: Conquest, Region and Continuity in the Seventeenth Century*, New Haven, 1979, 210–13.

11 cf. J. M. Braga, *The Western Pioneers and their Discovery of Macao*, Macau, 1949, 84–6, 202–8.

12 cf. Wills, 'Maritime China', 213–15.

13 cf. W. S. Atwell, 'Notes on Silver, Foreign Trade, and the Late Ming Economy', *Ch'ing-shih wen-t'i*, 3:8 (1977), 5. For an idea of the low levels of silver production in Ming China, cf. R. Huang, *Taxation and Government Finance in Sixteenth Century Ming China*, Cambridge, 1974, 243.

14 cf. C. R. Boxer, *The Great Ship from Amacon: Annals of Macao and the Old Japan Trade, 1555–1640*, Lisbon, 1959, 1–171.

15 cf. AGS, Sec. Prov. 1461–1464, 1495, 1498, 1508, 1515, 1520, 1552 and 1553, for numerous Crown grants and approvals of requests from the Portuguese nobility to renounce and testate this voyage over the period 1601–27.

16 cf. HAG, Provisões, 1183, fol. 123; HAG, Fazenda, 1159, fols. 7–7v; HAG, Fazenda, 1161, fols. 28–28v, 100; HAG, Fazenda, 1162, fols. 42v–43, 90v; *Doc. Rem. da India*, I, 92, 126, 180, 182, 239, 338; II, 8, 189; and VI, 373, 374.

17 cf. ANTT, LM 38, fols. 349–55 and Boxer, *Great Ship*, 90, 245–65.

18 cf. C. R. Boxer, *Fidalgos in the Far East*, The Hague, 1948, reprint Oxford, 1968, 18.
19 cf. pp.170–1, 181–3, 189–90.
20 cf. AGI, Filipinas, leg. 18-B, 31/iv/1592.
21 cf. AGS, Sec. Prov. 1487, fols. 95v–96, BNM, 9419, fols. 75v–76, and Ajuda, JA, 49-V-5, fols. 172–3, 265v–66.
22 cf. Evora, CXVI/2–5, for the original papers of the first capitão-geral, Dom Felipe Mascarenhas, and Boxer, *Fidalgos*, 93–103, for particulars of the difficulties he had from the merchants and Jesuits in Macao in establishing the capitão-geral's authority.
23 cf. F. A. Dutra, 'Membership in the Order of Christ in the Seventeenth Century: Its Rights, Privileges and Obligations', *The Americas*, 27 (1970), 3–25.
24 For the career of Dom Miguel de Noronha, cf. his *Diário do terceiro conde de Linhares, vice-rei da Índia*, 2 vols., Lisbon, 1937–43 and A. R. Disney, *Twilight of the Pepper Empire; Portuguese Trade in Southwest India in the Early Seventeenth Century*, Cambridge, Mass., 1978, 95–7.
25 cf. Boxer, *Great Ship*, 140 and Disney, *Twilight of Empire*, 101–2.
26 cf. M. A. H. Fitzler, *O Cerco de Columbo*, Coimbra, 1928, 92–5.
27 cf. S. B. Schwartz, *Sovereignty in Colonial Brazil: The High Court of Bahia and its Judges, 1609–1751*, Berkeley, 1973, 1–21.
28 cf. C. R. Gonzalves Pereira, *Tribunal da Relação da Goa*, Lisbon, 1964 and his *História da Administração da Justiça no Estado da India*, 2 vols., Lisbon, 1964–5, and J. I. de Abranches Garcia, ed., *Arquivo da Relação de Goa*, 2 vols., Nova Goa, 1872–4.
29 cf. M. Teixeira, 'Os Ouvidores em Macau', *Boletim de Instituto Luis de Camões*, 10 (1976) 189–388.
30 cf. *AM*, 3rd, IX, 277 and 316–17.
31 cf. Boxer, *Portuguese Seaborne Empire*, 228–9.
32 For the activities of the Jesuits within the Padroado, in Portugal, cf. F. Rodriguez, *História da Companhia de Jesus na Assistencia de Portugal*, 7 vols., Oporto, 1931–50; in Brazil, cf. S. Leite, *História da Companhia de Jesus no Brasil, 1549–1760*, 10 vols., Rio de Janeiro, 1938–50; and in Japan, cf. C. R. Boxer, *The Christian Century in Japan, 1549–1650*, Berkeley, 1951; G. Elison, *Deus Destroyed*, Cambridge, Mass., 1973; M. Cooper, 'The Mechanics of the Macao–Nagasaki Silk Trade', *Monumenta Niponica*, 27 (1972), 423–33 and D. Pacheco, 'The Founding of the Port of Nagasaki and its Cession to the Society of Jesus', *Monumenta Niponica*, 25 (1970), 303–23.
33 cf. Boxer, *Christian Century*, 211; cf. L. Pfister, *Notices biographiques et bibliographiques sur les Jesuites de l'ancienne Mission de Chine, 1552–1773*, 2 vols., Shanghai, 1932–4, for biographical data which elucidate Professor Boxer's statement.
34 cf. Boxer, *Christian Century*, 48.
35 cf. A. F. Cardim, *Batalhas da Companhia de Jesus na sua gloriosa Provincia do Japão*, Lisbon, 1894.
36 cf. H. M. Robertson, *The Rise of Economic Individualism*, Cambridge, 1935, and the defence of this view by H. R. Trevor-Roper, *Religion, the Reformation and Social Change*, second edition, London, 1972, 34–5.
37 cf. pp. 189–93.
38 cf. B. W. Diffie and G. D. Winius, *Foundations of the Portuguese Empire, 1415–1580*, Minneapolis, 1977, 387–92, for Dr Winius' characterisation of Portuguese society in Macao.
39 cf. C. R. Boxer, *Portuguese Society in the Tropics: the Municipal Councils of Goa, Macao, Bahia and Luanda, 1510–1800*, Madison, 1965, 5–7.
40 *ibid.*, 9.
41 *ibid.*, 54.
42 cf. pp. 43–4, 60, 62, 79–80, 183–8.
43 cf. A. J. R. Russell-Wood, *Fidalgos and Philanthropists: The Santa Casa da Misericordia of Bahia, 1550–1755*, London, 1968, 1–23.
44 *ibid.*, 24–41 and for the activities of this institution at Goa, cf. J. F. Ferreira Martins, *História da Misericordia de Goa, 1520–1910*, 3 vols., Nova Goa, 1910–14.
45 A partial list of where the Portuguese established a Santa Casa da Misericodia in Asia includes: Ormuz in the Persian Gulf; Diu, Daman, Bassein, Chaul, Goa, Cochin, Cannanore, Mangalor, São Thomé de Meliapor and Negapatnam on the west and east coasts of India; Colombo on Ceylon; Malacca; Ambon, Tidore and Timor in the Indonesian archipelago; and Nagasaki and Bungo in Japan; cf. *Actas do IV Congresso das Misericordias*, 3 vols., Lisbon, 1959, I, 173.
46 cf. J. C. Soares, *Macau e a Assistencia*, Lisbon, 1950.
47 cf. Ajuda, 44-XIV-4, fols. 45–6, and HAG Régias, 7745, fols. 50v–51.
48 cf. Ajuda, JA, 49-V-5, fols. 154–155v, 179–179v, for copies of letters from the *Santa Casa da*

Misericordia of Macao to *Santa Casa da Misericordia* of Braga; SCM, 15, fols. 1–118, is a copy book of the earliest surviving last wills and testament at Macao.
49 cf. HAG, MR 68, fols. 39–39v.

3. POPULATION, PERSONALITY AND COMMUNAL POWER

1 cf. H. Furber, *Rival Empires of Trade in the Orient, 1600–1800*, Minneapolis, 1976, 322–4.
2 cf. T. R. de Souza, *Medieval Goa*, New Delhi, 1979, 115 and C. R. Boxer, *Macau na Epoca da Restauração*, Macau, 1942, 28.
3 cf. C. R. Boxer, *The Great Ship from Amacon*, Lisbon, 1959, 131.
4 For an excellent description of Goan society, cf. de Souza, *Medieval Goa*, 114–26.
5 cf. C. R. Boxer, *Fidalgos in the Far East, 1550–1770*, The Hague, 1948, reprint Oxford 1968, 127–8.
6 cf. C. R. Boxer, *Portuguese Society in the Tropics*, Madison, 1965, 65.
7 cf. C. R. Boxer, *Mary and Misogyny: Women in Iberian Expansion Overseas, 1415–1815*, London, 1975, 84.
8 cf. Boxer, *Fidalgos*, 127–8.
9 cf. AHU, Macao, Maço 4, n.d., appears to be 1774.
10 cf. Boxer, *The Great Ship*, 140.
11 cf. P. van Dam, *Beschrijvinge van de Oostindische Compagnie*, The Hague, 7 vols., [Rijks Geschiedkundige Publicatien. Grote Serie, vols. 63, 68, 74, 76, 83, 87, 963, 1927–54, LXVIII, 87, and 477.
12 A detailed list tabulating Portuguese shipping losses in the South China Sea from 1601 to 1683 was constructed but owing to its length could not be included in the present volume; but it is hoped it will be reproduced in an article. The principal sources used in reconstructing the magnitude of these losses were from different Dutch and Portuguese archival records: ARA, VOC 666/KA 568, VOC 667/KA 569, VOC 1075/KA 987, VOC 1083/KA 995, VOC 1087/KA 999, VOC 1088/KA 1000, VOC 1100/KA 1012, VOC 1102/KA 1014, VOC 1118/KA 1030, VOC 1218/KA 1130; Ajuda, JA, 49-IV-52, JA, 49-IV-61, JA, 49-V-3 and JA, 49-V-14; from printed records: *GM*, *DRB*, *Bouwstoffen* and *Doc. Rem. da India*; and secondary works, especially, N. MacLeod, *De Oost-Indische Compagnie als Zeemogenheid in Azië*, 2 vols., Rijswijk, 1927. No attempt was made to assign an arbitrary value for those entries without estimates of the cargo or ship value, consequently, the figure used, which was completed from values found in archival reports and converted from all other currencies to *guilders*, is very conservative.
13 cf. pp. 186–8.
14 cf. C. R. Boxer, *Francisco Vieira de Figueiredo: A Portuguese Merchant-Adventurer in South East Asia, 1624–1667*, The Hague, 1967, 48.
15 cf. p. 191.
16 For two studies, cf. Boxer, *Fidalgos* and by the same author, *Francisco Vieira de Figueiredo*.
17 cf. V. Rau, *O 'Livro de Rezão' de António Coelho Guerreiro*, Lisbon, 1956.
18 cf. BPL 876, in the Leiden University Library.
19 cf. AGI, Patronato, leg. 53. ramo 2.
20 cf. Boxer, *The Great Ship*, 42.
21 *ibid.*
22 *ibid.*
23 cf. C. R. Boxer, *The Christian Century in Japan, 1549–1650*, Berkeley, 1967, 118.
24 cf. *APO*, III, pt. 1, 481–2 and pt. 2, 545–6, 763–4 and 926–7.
25 cf. C. R. Boxer, '*Casados* and *Cabotagem* in the *Estado da India*, 16th and 17th centuries', a paper presented at the II International Seminar on Indo-Portuguese History, Lisbon, 20–24 October 1980; and A. A. de Piña, 'Macau no século XVII: Cartas de Francisco Carvalho Aranha', *Portugal em Africa*, 14 (1957), 343–60.
26 cf. Boxer, '*Casados*', 7, and C. R. Boxer, 'Friar Juan Pobre of Zamora and his lost and found *Ystoria* of 1598–1603', *Indiana University Bookman*, 10 (1969), 25–46.
27 cf. F. A. Dutra, 'Membership in the Order of Christ in the Seventeenth Century: Its Rights, Privileges, and Obligations', *The Americas*, 27 (1970), 3–25.
28 cf. Boxer, *Francisco Vieira de Figueiredo*, and by the same author, *Breve Relação da vida e feitos de Lopo e Inácio Sarmento de Carvalho, grandes capitães que no século XVII honraram Portugal no Oriente*, Macau, 1940.
29 cf. Boxer, *Macau na Epoca de Restauração*, 98.

30 cf. Boxer, *Fidalgos*, 70.
31 cf. Boxer, *The Great Ship*, 101.
32 cf. Boxer, *Fidalgos*, 79–90.
33 cf. Boxer, *The Great Ship*, 116–39 and 246–52.
34 cf. A. R. Disney, *Twilight of the Pepper Empire: Portuguese Trade in Southwest India in the Early Seventeenth Century*, Cambridge, Mass., 1978, 27, 97–8.
35 cf. Boxer, *The Great Ship*, 135.
36 cf. ANTT, LM 41, fol. 101–6.
37 cf. Boxer, *Macau na Epoca de Restauração*, 99–107.
38 cf. C. R. Boxer, *The Embassy of Captain Gonçalo de Siqueira de Souza to Japan in 1644–1647*, Macau, 1938.
39 cf. L. Bourdon, 'António Fialho Ferreira et le projet de liaison Macao–Lisbonne en droiture, 1640–1645', *Economia e Finanças, Anais do Instituto Superior de Ciencias Economia e Financieras*, 19 (1951), 101–28 and J. Gentil da Silva, 'Alguns elementos para a história do comercio da India de Portugal existentes na Biblioteca Nacional de Madrid', *Anais, Estados de História e Geografia da Expansão Portuguesa*, separate of vol. v, tomo II (1950), 92–7.
40 cf. C. R. Boxer, *Salvador de Sá and the Struggle for Brazil and Angola, 1602–1686*, London, 1952, 216.
41 cf. HAG, MR 66, fol. 310v and MR 50, fol. 222.
42 cf. HAG, MR 34, fol. 306.
43 cf. HAG, Embaixada, 1210 fol. 28–33 and J. F. Marques Pereira, 'Uma Resurreição Histórica (paginas ineditas d'um visitador dos jesuitas), (1665–1671)', *Ta-Sei-Yang-Kuo*, 2 (1900), 755–6.
44 G. V. Smith, *The Dutch in Seventeenth Century Thailand*, Carbondale, 1977, 8, 36, 75 and 113.
45 cf. *GM*, III, 326–7.
46 cf. HAG, Fazenda, 1171, fol. 250–2.
47 cf. *AM*, 1st, I, 152–75; 2nd, I, 21, 73–4, 147–50, 153–4, 157–8, 275–6, 277–8; 3rd, II, 305, 310, 335, 377, V, 320–1, 346–7 and VI, 8–9, 11, 15–16, 24–7, 30–9, 52–4, and 63–6.
48 cf. HAG, Correspondencia, 1265, fol. 9 and *GM*, IV, 691, 758, and 787–8.
49 cf. Boxer, *Portuguese Society*, 46.
50 cf. *GM*, IV, 760, V, 155–6, 175 and AHU, Macao, Maço 4, 390/xii/1746.

4. COUNTRY TRADERS AND CROWN MONOPOLY

1 cf. C. R. Boxer, ed., *Macau na Epoca de Restauração*, Macau, 1942, 36–7.
2 cf. Iwao Seiichi, 'Japanese Foreign Trade in the Sixteenth and Seventeenth Centuries', *Acta Asiatica*, 30 (1976), 6 and 9.
3 cf. Ajuda, JA, 49-V-8, fols. 511–11v.
4 cf. D. M. Brown, *Money Economy in Medieval Japan*, New Haven, 1951, 50–7.
5 cf. Kato Eiichi, 'The Japanese–Dutch Trade in the Formative Period of the Seclusion Policy: Particularly on the Raw Silk Trade by the Dutch Factory at Hirado, 1620–1640', *Acta Asiatica*, 30 (1976), 45–6.
6 *ibid.*, 48.
7 *ibid.*, 45–6.
8 cf. P. Chaunu, *Les Philippines et le Pacifique des Ibériques*, Paris, 1960, 148–55.
9 cf. J. S. Cummins, ed., *Sucessos de las Islas Filipinas*, Cambridge, 1971, 308.
10 cf. Kobata Atsushi, 'The Production and Uses of Gold and Silver in Sixteenth and Seventeenth Century Japan', *Economic History Review*, 2nd series, 18 (1965), 254.
11 *ibid.*
12 cf. *GM*, I, 341.
13 cf. *GM*, I, 736.
14 cf. P. van Dam, *Beschrijvinge van de Oostindische Compagnie*, The Hague, 7 vols., [Rijks Geschiedkundige Publicatien. Grote Serie, vols. 63, 68, 74, 83, 87, 96], 1927–54, LXXIV, 383–553; J. Hall, 'Notes on the Early Ch'ing Copper Trade with Japan', *Harvard Journal of Asiatic Studies*, 12 (1949), 444–61; K. Glamann, 'The Dutch East India Company's Trade in Japanese Copper 1645–1736', *Scandinavian Economic History Review*, 1 (1953), 41–99; and by the same author, *Dutch Asiatic Trade 1620–1740*, The Hague, 1958, 167–82.
15 G. B. Souza, 'Portuguese Trade and Society in China and the South China Sea, c. 1630–1754', unpublished Ph.D. dissertation, Cambridge University, 1981, 400.

16 cf. *GM*. I, 489, 514, 588, 659–60; *DRB, 1637*, 19–22; *Beschrijvinge*, LXXIV, 675; W. S. Atwell, 'Notes on Silver, Foreign Trade and the Late Ming Economy', *Ch'ing-shih wen-t'i*, 3 (1977), 1 and 15; C. R. Boxer, *The Great Ship from Amacon*, Lisbon, 1959, 61, 126–30, 136–45, and 149–53; C. R. Boxer, *Fidalgos in the Far East*, The Hague, 1948, reprint, 1968, 112; O. Nachod, *Die Beziehungen der Niederlandischen Ostindischen Kompagnie zu Japan in siebzehnten Jahrhundert*, Leipzig, 1897, Beilage 63, CCVIII; Brown, *Money Economy*, 62–4; Glamann, *Dutch Asiatic Trade*, 58; Iwao, 'Japanese Foreign Trade, 10–11; and Kobata, 'Production and Uses, 253.

17 cf. *GM*, I, 514 and Boxer, *Great Ship*, 141–5, 154–8, for the few existing examples of respondencia and consignment data.

18 cf. Atwell, 'Notes on Silver', 1 and Iwao, 'Japanese Foreign Trade', 10.

19 cf. Kato, 'Japanese–Dutch Trade', 47.

20 cf. Boxer, *Great Ship*, 96–7.

21 *ibid.*, 122.

22 cf. *DRB, 1631–1634*, 148–9, 152 and 157 for the VOC's opinion of these Portuguese efforts to evade the pancada in 1633.

23 *ibid.*, 250–1 and Boxer, *Great Ship*, 131.

24 cf. *GM*, I, 482–9 and *DRB, 1631–1634*, 447.

25 cf. *GM*, I, 514–15 and Boxer, *Great Ship*, 144.

26 cf. H. Hagenaer's report in I. Commelin, *Begin ende Voortgangh der Vereenighde Nederlantsche Geoctroyeerde Oost-Indische Compagnie*, 2 vols., Amsterdam, 1646, reprint in 4 vols., 1969, pagination separate by each voyage, 101; *GM*, I, 588–90.

27 cf. ARA, VOC 1124/KA 1035, fol. 52, which was reproduced in Boxer, *Great Ship*, 191–7; Commelin, *Begin ende Voortgangh*, 125 and 127.

28 cf. Boxer, *Great Ship*, 278–86.

29 *ibid.*, 153.

30 cf. C. R. Boxer, *The Christian Century in Japan, 1549–1650*, Berkeley, 1951, 375–82 for a description of the Shimabara rebellion.

31 cf. Boxer, *Great Ship*, 154–5.

32 cf. *GM*, I, 736–8, 741–2.

33 cf. *B & R*, III, 179–89.

34 *ibid.*, 273–85.

35 *ibid.*, 58, 65–6.

36 cf. P. J. Bakewell, *Silver Mining and Society in Colonial Mexico, Zacatecas 1546–1700*, Cambridge, 1971; D. A. Brading and H. E. Cross, 'Colonial Silver Mining: Mexico and Peru', *Hispanic American Historical Review*, 52 (1972), 545–79.

37 cf. J. L. Blussé, 'The Dutch Occupation of the Pescadores, 1622–1624', *Transactions of the International Conference of Orientalists in Japan*, 18 (1973), 41–2.

38 cf. W. W. Borah, *Silk Raising in Colonial Mexico*, Berkeley, 1943, 85–101; W. L. Shurz, *The Manila Galleon*, New York, 1939.

39 cf. Borah, *Silk Raising*, 100.

40 cf. AGI, Patronato, leg 24, ramos 60, 61, 62 and 65; leg. 25, ramos 7 and 13; and leg. 46, ramo 14, describe in detail the acclamation of King Philip II of Spain as King of Portugal in Macao.

41 cf. AGI, Patronato, leg. 24, ramo 57 and 59 for the letters of Father Alexandre Valignano and Dom João de Albuquerque to the Governor of the Philippines.

42 Based on Spanish archival materials, two ships traded at Manila from Macao in 1580, cf. Chaunu, *Les Philippines*, 148.

43 cf. B. V. Pires, *A Viagem de Comércio Macau–Manila nos Séculos XVI a XIX*, Macau, 1971, 9.

44 cf. *B & R*, VII, 64–76.

45 cf. W. W. Borah, *Early Colonial Trade and Navigation Between Mexico and Peru*, Berkeley, 1954, 118; Canate justified his actions by writing that 'the galleons had not sailed that year and that Peru was short of merchandise, including iron and copper for the mines.'

46 cf. BNL, 637, fols. 140–1v, for a roteiro, dated 1584, of the voyage from Macao across the Pacific; my thanks to Dr P.-Y. Manguin for this reference.

47 cf. Boxer, *Fidalgos*, 43–4, for particulars about da Gama's career; cf. AGI, Mexico, leg. 71, 18/ii/1592 and 4/iii/1592; leg. 121, ix/1601; AGI, Filipinas, leg. 18-B, 31/v/1592 and AGI, Indiferente General, leg. 614, 22/i/1609.

48 For a copy of the Crown's orders prohibiting trade between Macao and Manila, cf. BNM, 19152, fols. 37v–38.

49 cf. *B & R*, VII, 139.

50 cf. Cummins, *Sucessos*, 69–79 for a brief description of Dasmariñas' governorship.

51 cf. AGI, Patronato, leg. 25, ramo 39, which is translated in *B & R*, VIII, 174–96; Dasmariñas' decision to permit trade between Manila and Macao was supported by the Bishop and capitão of Malacca, cf. AGI, Patronato, 46, ramo 23.

52 cf. *B & R*, VIII, 182–3.

53 cf. AGI, Filipinas, leg. 18-B, 31/v/1592.

54 *ibid*.

55 cf. L. Knauth, *Confrontación Transpacífica, El Japón y el Nuevo Mundo Hispánico, 1542–1639*, Mexico City, 1972, 180–97.

56 cf. *B & R*, VIII, 78–95.

57 cf. Borah, *Silk Raising*, 97.

58 *ibid.*, 35.

59 Borah, *Early Colonial Trade*, 121; there was an extreme pricing difference, Chinese textiles sold for one-ninth of the price of Spanish cloth and the Mexican price was somewhere in between.

60 cf. C. R. Boxer, 'Portuguese and Spanish Rivalry in the Far East during the Seventeenth Century', *Journal Royal Asiatic Society* (1946), 150–64; (1947), 91–105.

61 cf. *B & R*, XI, 157 and XII, 29–45, for Manila's reaction to this proposal and its aid to André Furtado de Mendonça's squadron, which amounted to 22,270 *reals*. For his career, cf. C. R. Boxer and F. de Vasconcelos, *André Furtado de Mendonça, 1558–1610*, Lisbon, 1955.

62 cf. *B & R*, XIV, 214–17; BNM, 9419, fols. 70v–71; AGI, Indiferente General, leg. 583, 2/iii/1607 and AGI, Filipinas, leg. 329, 4/ii/1608.

63 cf. Bakewell, *Silver Mining*, 152–3.

64 cf. AGI, Filipinas, leg. 20, 16/vii/1610.

65 The annual total amount of 4,200 quintales was from all sources including the Philippines; Europe supplied the largest quantity, cf. AGI, Mexico, leg. 28, 5/i/1611.

66 cf. Bakewell, *Silver Mining*, 152.

67 *ibid*.

68 cf. *B & R*, XVII, 237–8.

69 *ibid.*, XVIII, 293–4.

70 *ibid.*, XXII, 134.

71 *ibid.*, 96–8.

72 *ibid.*, XXIV, 197–228.

73 cf. G. V. Smith, *The Dutch in Seventeenth Century Thailand*, Carbondale, 1977, 18–20.

74 cf. ANTT, LM 16, fol. 97; LM 20, fol. 93, 17/ii/1624; HAG, MR 14, fols. 161–61v, 230–40, and 241–42v; ANTT, LM 30, fol. 25, 67; LM 31, fol. 23 and *B & R*, XXII, 96–8.

75 cf. Cummins, *Sucessos*, 308–9.

76 cf. S. P. Sen, 'The Role of Indian Textiles in Southeast Asian Trade in the Seventeenth Century', *Journal of Southeast Asian History*, 3:2 (1962), 92–110. Dr Sen is correct when he describes the primary position of Indian textiles as a medium of exchange for the maritime trade of the Malay state systems in Southeast Asia, but demand for precious metals increased during this period throughout parts of the region.

77 cf. AGS, Sec. Prov., 1966, fols. 374–8, for a recommendation to the Crown in 1609 that the Portuguese at Malacca be ordered to stop the sale of Indian textiles for reals. For Crown orders against such activities, cf. *Doc. Rem. da Índia*, I, 294–5; II, 178–82 and 188–9.

78 cf. I. B. Watson, 'The Establishment of English Commerce in North-Western India in the Early Seventeenth Century', *Indian Economic and Social History Review*, 13 (1976), 375–91; N. Steensgaard, *Carracks, Caravans and Companies: The Structural Crisis in the European–Asian Trade in the Early 17th Century*, Copenhagen, 1972; and A. R. Disney, *Twilight of the Pepper Empire: Portuguese Trade in Southwest India in the Early Seventeenth Century*, Cambridge, Mass., 1978, 103–5, 161 and 164.

79 cf. *B & R*, XXIII, 30–3; for a description of the Portuguese trade in that commodity from south-west India to Europe, cf. Disney, *Twilight of Empire*, 116–17.

80 cf. *B & R*, XXIII, 29–86.

81 Dutch records of cargoes of captured Portuguese private merchants shipping confirm this description, cf. VOC 1101/KA 1013, fols. 444–44v.

82 cf. AGI, Filipinas, leg. 340, 6/iii/1608.

83 cf. *B & R*, XVIII, 318–19; Chaunu, *Les Philippines*, 155, also indicates that Portuguese shipping

originating at Cochin in the late 1620s, with no stop at Malacca arrived at Manila with cargoes of slaves.
84 cf. N. P. Cushner, *Landed Estates in the Colonial Philippines*, New Haven, 1976, 46–8.
85 cf. Disney, *Twilight of Empire*, 118–19.
86 cf. T. Raychaudhuri, *Jan Company in Coromandel, 1605–1690*, The Hague, 1962, 95–6.
87 *ibid.*, 97.
88 cf. *B & R*, XVIII, 220 and XIX, 69.
89 *ibid.*, XVIII, 194–203 and Knauth, *Confrontatión Transpacífica*, 299.
90 cf. *DRB, 1631–1634*, 447 and *GM*, I, 438 for reports on the activity of the Chinese pirate, Janglauw; for the Manchu challenge to the Ming, cf. J. E. Wills, Jr., 'Maritime China from Wang Chih to Shih Lang: Themes in Peripheral History', in J. D. Spence and J. E. Wills, Jr., eds., *From Ming to Ch'ing: Conquest, Region and Continuity in the Seventeenth Century*, New Haven, 1979, 203–38.
91 cf. *B & R*, XXV, 60; slightly earlier, in 1626, Fernando de Silva wrote, expressing a similar concern for the extent of Portuguese trade at Manila, that the Portuguese were 'draining the wealth of the citizens here', *B & R*, XXII, 96–8.
92 cf. AGI, Filipinas, leg. 27, 8/x/1632.
93 cf. de Naveda's report in *B & R*, XXV, 128.
94 cf. AGI, Filipinas, leg. 27, 27/ix/1634; 29/viii/1636; and leg. 41, 19/xii/1635 for papers concerning Don Juan Grau's memorial; leg. 340, 10/xi/1634, for a *real cedula* ordering the *Audiencia* of Manila to investigate and alleviate the damage caused by Portuguese trade from Macao in that city; and leg. 8, 11/vii/1636, for a letter from the Governor of the Philippines claiming that he planned to allow only one Portuguese ship from Macao to trade at Manila. The 'loan' was extracted in 1633 and prompted the Portuguese not to come to Manila from Macao in protest in 1634; D. Sebastian Hurtado de Corquera, in 1636, was instructed to judge the various claims and counter-claims, cf. *B & R*, XXVII, 49 and *AM*, 1st, II, 229–30.
95 cf. Atwell, 'Notes on Silver', 11–13 for a discussion of this incident and the importance of Don Pedro de Quiroga y Moya's activities at Acapulco upon Manila's trade; *B & R*, XXX, 51 for the registered and real values of the 1636 cargoes imported from the Philippines to New Spain.
96 cf. AGI, Mexico, leg. 33, fols. 203–4 for a letter from the Viceroy of New Spain informing the Crown of Quiroga's death from illness and the result of the commission he held to regulate and investigate the Manila galleon trade; for evidence of the Crown's adverse reaction to the abruptness of Quiroga's policies and its attempts to ameliorate them, cf. AGI, Filipinas, leg. 330, fols. 73v–75, leg. 340, fols. 27v–40.
97 cf. *B & R*, XXIX, 208–58 for a description of this Chinese uprising and its suppression by the Spanish.
98 cf. AGI, Escribanía, leg. 409-B, fols. 218–18v.
99 cf. AGI, Filipinas, leg. 330, fols. 153–54v for the *real cedula* of 1643; Escribanía, leg. 409-B, fols. 342–43v for papers that outline the cost of ship prepared by the Governor; Filipinas, leg. 22, fol. 73 for the news of Berastegui's expedition and the confiscation of the Crown's funds by the Portuguese of Macao in 1644.
100 cf. Cummins, *Sucessos*, 306–7.
101 cf. Schurz, *Manila Galleon*, 77, 184–6, 194 and Borah, *Early Colonial Trade*, 124–5.
102 cf. *B & R*, XXV, 111–44; the de Naveda report is found in the AGI, Filipinas, leg. 41, 19/xii/1635 and a copy in leg. 27, 1632; for the unpublished certificate of the values of the customs duties from the merchandise imported into Manila by the Chinese and the Portuguese from 1606–1632, prepared by the Crown's *visitador*, D. Francisco de Roxas y Oriate, cf. AGI, Filipinas, leg. 27, 23/ix/1632.
103 cf. AGI, Filipinas, leg. 27, 23/ix/1632.
104 cf. M. Pakse-Smith, ed., *History of Japan*, 2 vols., Kobe, 1931, New York, 2 vols. in 1, reprint 1972, 450, for an account of one of the 'Fleet of Defence' captures of a Portuguese junk, which was probably smuggling, near the Lubang islands in the Philippines with several Chinese junks in May of 1622.
105 Dutch observations of the Chinese junk activity on the Fukien–Chekiang coast confirm this statement, cf. *DRB, 1624–1629*, 130, 224, 305; *GM*, 201, 353–5; *DRB, 1631–1634*, 51, 119; and *GM*, II, 1. For the evolution of Dutch policy towards Chinese shipping and Reyersens attempts to negotiate the prohibition of Chinese navigation to Manila, cf. W. P. Groeneveldt, *De Nederlanders in China, Eerste Deel: De eerste bemoeingen om dem handel in China en de vestiging in de Pescadores, 1601–1624*, The Hague, 1898; and *DRB, 1624–1629*, 19–21.

106 cf. AGI, Filipinas, leg. 27, 23/ix/1632.
107 cf. Chaunu, *Les Philippines*, 204–5, tabulates the almojarifazgo figures.
108 cf. Borah, *Early Colonial Trade*, 123.
109 cf. Atwell, 'Notes on Silver', 2, and Schurz, *Manila Galleon*, 188–90.
110 cf. pp. 54–8.
111 cf. S. A. M. Adshead, 'The Seventeenth Century General Crisis in China', *Asian Profile*, 1:2 (1973), 271–80, for a preliminary discussion of the nature of the seventeenth-century crisis for China and Atwell's, 'Notes on Silver', 1–33.

5. MERCHANTS AND MARKETS

1 cf. P.-Y. Manguin, *Les Portugais sur les Côtes du Viêt-Nam et du Campá*, Paris, 1972; for Japan's expansion into the South China Sea, cf. N. Péri, 'Essai sur les relations du Japon et de l'Indochine aux XVIe et XVII e siècles', *Bulletin de l'École Française d'Extrême-Orient*, 23 (1923), 1–136 and Iwao Seiichi, *Nanyo Nihōnmachi no Kenkyū*, Tokyo, 1941, reprint 1967.
2 cf. *AM*, 1st, II, 3–4; I, 379–80; II, 67 and III, 61–3.
3 cf. C. Skinner, ed., *Sja'ir Perang Mengkasar* (*The Rymed Chronicle of the Macassar War*), The Hague, 1963, 2.
4 cf. J. Noorduyn, 'Origins of South Celebes Historical Writing', Soedjatmoko, M. Ali, G. J. Resink and G. M. Kahin, eds., *An Introduction to Indonesian Historiography*, Ithaca, 1965, 137–55 and his article, 'De Islamisering van Makasar', *Bijdragen tot de Taal-, Land-en Volkenkunde*, 112 (1956), 347–66.
5. cf. J. V. Mills, tr., 'Description of Malacca, and Meridional India and Cathay', *Journal of the Malayan Branch of the Royal Asiatic Society*, 8 (1930), pt. 1, 181.
6 cf. M. A. P. Meilink-Roelofsz, *Asian Trade and European Influence in the Indonesian Archipelago between 1500 and about 1630*, The Hague, 1962, reprint 1969, 86 and 164.
7 cf. J. Tissanier, *Relation du Voyage du P. Joseph Tissanier*, Paris, 1663, 59.
8 cf. Meilink-Roelofsz, *Asian Trade*, 163–4.
9 For the decline of Portuguese power in the Moluccas, cf. A. B. da Sá, ed., *Documentação para a História das Missões do Padroado Portugues do Oriente. Insulínda*, 5 vols., Lisbon, 1954–8, III, 193–508, IV, 164–464. New sources have emerged with the publication of the Jesuit annual letters concerning this mission, cf. H. Th. Th. Jacobs, ed., *Documenta Malucensia*, 2 vols., Rome, 1974–80.
10 cf. L. Y. Andaya, *The Kingdom of Johor, 1641–1728*, Kuala Lumpur, 1975, 117–18 and the literature cited therein for the importance of the *gaukeng* and *toManurung* tradition in Macassar's statecraft.
11 cf. J. Keuning, 'Ambonnezen, Portugeze en Nederlanders', *Indonesië*, 9 (1956), 135–69, for a fascinating description of Ambon society and the socio-economic implications of Islamic and European expansion.
12 ibid., 149.
13 cf. D. K. Bassett, 'English Trade in Celebes, 1613–1667', *Journal of the Malayan Branch of the Royal Asiatic Society*, 31 (1958), 1–39.
14 cf. W. Foster, ed., *The Journal of John Jourdain, 1608–1617*, Cambridge, 1905, 294.
15 cf. *Doc. Rem. da India*, I, 319, II, 417 and III, 125–6 and 190.
16 cf. J. W. Ijzerman, 'Het schip *De Eendracht* voor Makassar in December 1616', *Bijdragen tot de Taal-, Land- en Volkenkunde*, 78 (1922), 369–72 for a transcription of Jan Joosten's report; IOR, Celebes, p. 21 for Thomas Staverton's report which supports much of Joosten's evidence on the composition of the Portuguese trading community as that of private merchants.
17 cf. AGI, Filipinas, leg. 27, 21/vii/1621.
18 cf. *DRB, 1624–1629*, 124–6.
19 cf. *GM*, I, 182.
20 cf. Kennung, 'Ambonnezen, Portugezen', 153.
21 cf. *GM*, I, 264–5.
22 cf. *Bouwstoffen*, II, 252–60.
23 cf. D. K. Bassett, 'Changes in the Pattern of Malay Politics, 1629–c. 1655', *Journal of Southeast Asian History*, 10:3 (1969), 429–52. Dr Bassett's depiction of the period 1629–c. 1655 as one of change for the Malay world states of the Malay peninsula and Sumatra is also applicable to Java (Mataram), the Celebes (Macassar) and the Moluccas in the eastern Indonesian archipelago.

24 cf. A. Reid, 'Trade and the Problem of Royal Power in Aceh, Three Stages: c. 1550–1700', in A. Reid and L. Castles, *Pre-Colonial State Systems in Southeast Asia*, Kuala Lumpur, 1975, 45–55.

25 cf. C. R. Boxer, 'A Note on Portuguese Reactions to the Revival of the Red Sea Spice Trade and the Rise of Atjeh, 1540–1600', *Journal of Southeast Asian History*, 10:3 (1969), 415–28.

26 cf. *APO*, III, pt. 2, 627, for the embassy of Thomas Pinto sent by Dom Diogo Lobo, capitão of Malacca; this embassy received treatment by Atjehenese historians, cf. T. Iskandar, *De Hikajat Atjéh*, The Hague, 1958, 136–43 and commented upon by D. Lombard, *Le Sultanat d'Atjéh au temps d'Iskandar Muda, 1607–1636*, Paris, 1967, 227–33.

27 cf. Reid, 'Trade and the Problem', 49.

28 cf. Bassett, 'Changes in the Pattern', 430.

29 cf. C. R. Boxer, ed., 'The Achinese Attack on Malacca in 1629, as described in Contemporary Portuguese Sources' in J. S. Bastin, and R. Roolvink, eds., *Malayan and Indonesian Studies*, Oxford, 1964, 109–21.

30 cf. S. Moertono, *State and Statecraft in Old Java. A Study of the later Mataram Period, 16th to 19th century*, Ithaca, 1968. For English summaries of the impressive scholarship by two Dutch historians, cf. H. J. de Graaf and Th. G. Th. Pigeaud, *Islamic States in Java, 1500–1700*, The Hague, 1976, 1–51.

31 cf. Graaf and Pigeaud, *Islamic States*, 50.

32 *ibid.*, 38.

33 *ibid.*, 42.

34 cf. A. Botelho de Sousa, *Nuno Alvares Botelho*, Lisbon, 1940; for his defeat of the Aceh attack on Malacca in 1629, cf. Boxer, 'The Achinese Attack'.

35 For the alliances of Johor, Pahang and Patani with the Portuguese, cf. Bassett, 'Changes in the Pattern, 429–52, L. Y. Andaya, *The Kingdom of Johor*, 20–36 and A. Teeuw and D. K. Wyatt, *Hikayat Patani*, The Hague, 1970, 5–18. For Portuguese initiatives to Mataram, Aceh, Bantam, Palembang, Johor, Kedah, Perak and Macassar, cf. ANTT, LM 30, fol. 35, LM 39, fols. 9–9v, LM 41, fols. 55–55v, LM 43 fols. 201–3v, 205–5v, 208, 209, 211–12 and LM 48, fols. 136v–7, C. R. Boxer, 'Uma Obra Raríssima Impresa em Goa no Século XVII', *Boletim Internacional de Bibliografía Luso-Brasileira*, 8, (1967), 431–528, and H. J. de Graaf, *De regering van Sultan Agung, vorst van Mataram, 1613–1645, en die van zijn voorganger Panembahan Séda-Ing-Krapjak, 1601–1613*, The Hague, 1958, 164–72, and 223–32.

36 cf. Graaf, *De regering van Sultan Agung*, 188 and Graaf and Pigeaud, *Islamic States*, 44. Palembang joined but Jambi refused to support the idea of a Mataram–Portuguese alliance in 1632, cf. *DRB, 1631–1634*, 89, 111 and 113.

37 For a summary of the large-scale movements of pepper from the Indonesian archipelago in the international and regional markets during the sixteenth to the mid nineteenth centuries, cf. J. Bastin, *The Changing Balance of the Early Southeast Asian Pepper Trade*, Kuala Lumpur, 1960; K. Glamann, *Dutch–Asiatic Trade, 1620–1740*, The Hague, 1958, 73–90, 294–300 and K. N. Chaudhuri, *The Trading World of Asia and the English East India Company, 1660–1760*, Cambridge, 1978, 313–28. For tin, cf. G. W. Irwin, 'The Dutch and the Tin Trade of Malaya in the Seventeenth Century', in J. Ch'en and N. Tarling, eds., *Studies in the Social History of China and South-East Asia*, Cambridge, 1970, 267–87 and J. C. Jackson, 'Mining in 18th Century Bangka: The Pre-European Exploitation of a "Tin Island"', *Pacific Viewpoint*, 10:2 (1969), 28–54.

38 cf. *APO*, III, pt. 2, 762–3.

39 cf. ANTT, LM 38, fols. 252–52v.

40 cf. Meilink-Roelofsz, *Asian Trade*, 257–62 summarises the role of the Bantam, Jambi and Palembang markets as pepper suppliers.

41 For an authoritative account of his career, cf. C. R. Boxer, *Francisco Vieira de Figueiredo: A Portuguese Merchant–Adventurer in South East Asia, 1624–1667*, The Hague, 1967. For additional insights into Figueiredo's career and the cloth and cloves trade at Macassar, cf. Bassett, 'English Trade in Celebes', 1–39.

42 cf. IOR, Celebes, p. 66.

43 cf. IOR, Celebes, p. 53; *DRB, 1631–1634*, 13–14, 314–16, 342, 351, 384, 395, 403 and *GM*, I, 403–4, for reports of Portuguese intentions, the Matteram embassy to Macassar in 1631, the combined military actions of Macassar and the Portuguese against the VOC on Ambon, VOC attempts to discredit the Portuguese with the Mataram and plans to deny the Portuguese access to Macassar.

44 For the 1638 agreement between the VOC and Ternate about Ambon, cf. J. E. Herres, ed., *Corpus*

Diplomaticum Neerlando-Indicum, The Hague, 5 vols., 1907–38, I, 316–18; Keuning, 'Ambonnezen, Portugezen', 156–8, describes the VOC and the Ternate machinations on Ambon.

45 Five and four Macao ships arrived at Macassar in 1656 and 1660; in 1659, the VOC reported Macao's fleet comprising thirteen ships, cf. *GM*, III, 123–4, 281, and 283–4.

46 cf. C. R. Boxer, ed. and tr., *Macao na Epoca de Restauração*, Macau, 1942, 45–6.

47 cf. HAG, MR 19D, fols. 1036–50 and HAG, *Regimentos*, 1420, fols. 38v–51 for the instructions of Manoel Ramos and Romão de Lemos, the first and second *administradores das viagems de Japão*.

48 cf. ANTT, LM 34, fols. 63–6 for the Conde de Linhares detailed description to the administrador of the method of transferring customs duties that were collected at Macao to Malacca.

49 cf. *GM*, II, 12–13 and 68.

50 *ibid.*, 295, for a VOC report in 1646 which mentions a Company loss of 91,119 guilders in Surat cloth sales in the Indonesian archipelago on account of the Portuguese, English and Danish competition with Coromandel coast cloth at Macassar.

51 cf. *Bouwstoffen*, II, 393.

52 For Figueiredo's involvement with Mir Jumla, the nawab of Golconda, cf. T. Raychaudhuri, *Jan Company in Coromandel, 1605–1690*, The Hague, 1962, 47–50 and Boxer, *Figueiredo*, 8–11.

53 cf. C. R. Boxer, 'Asian Potentates and European Artillery in the Sixteenth–Eighteenth Centuries', *Journal of the Malayan Branch of the Royal Asiatic Society*, 38 (1965), 156–72.

54 cf. AGI, Filipinas, leg. 31, 8/v/1648.

55 cf. *Bouwstoffen*, III, 133–5.

56 *ibid.*

57 cf. *GM*, II, 270 and *Bouwstoffen*, III, 238.

58 For the VOC, English and Danish attempts to penetrate the Manila market in the 1640s, cf. M. P. H. Roessingh, 'Nederlandse Betrekkingen met de Philippijnen, 1600–1800', *Bijdragen tot de Taal-, Land- en Volkenkunde*, 124 (1968), 482–504; S. D. Quaison, *English 'Country Trade' with the Philippines, 1644–1765*, Quezon City, 1966, 17–24 and *GM*, II, 285.

59 cf. P. Chaunu, *Les Philippines et le Pacifique des Ibériques*, Paris, 1960, 204–8.

60 cf. AGI, Filipinas, 64, *Testimonios de visitas y registros de champanes y pataches que legaron al comercio de aquellas islas ocurridos desde el año de 1657 à 1686*, fols. 1–2v, 13v–15v, 23–5v, 27–8, 41–4, 79v–82, 101v–4v, 124v–32, 145–5v, 151v–3, 161–4v and 180v–83.

61 cf. *Bouwstoffen*, III, 12–13.

62 cf. *Bouwstoffen*, II, 351–2.

63 cf. *GM*, II, 270, 285, 288, 295, 313–14, 334–5, 374, 431–2, 479, 497–8, 598, 621 and 675–60; *Bouwstoffen*, III, 238, 255–6, 281–3, 329–31, 333–5, 341–2, 367, 454–5 and 463; and *DRB*, *1647–1648*, 28–9, 46, 83–7, 92, 124–6 and 136, for the VOC's reports on Portuguese and foreign trade in general at Macassar and the extent of their competition in the Indian textile trade in the Indonesian archipelago for the years, 1645–52.

64 The VOC also recognised that the absence of Chinese silk supplies at Manila was one of the factors that kept the demand for Indian textiles from Macassar at Manila buoyant, cf. *Bouwstoffen*, III, 454.

65 cf. V. Magalhães Godinho, *Os Descobrimentos e a Economia Mundial*, Lisbon, 2 vols., 1963–5, I, 338–67, 389–400 and 437–65 and Meilink-Roelofsz, *Asian Trade*, 25–6, 40, 84, 161, 164, 208–11, 246 and 273 for a discussion of the role of copper, gold and silver specie and bullion and primitive monies in sixteenth century Asia and the Estado da India.

66 cf. Magalhães Godinho, *Os Descobrimentos*, I, 436, for the amounts of silver exported from Portugal to Malacca for the purchase of pepper in the 1580s.

67 For a description of the Portuguese experience of trading with caixas in the Moluccas for spices, cf. Meilink-Roelofsz, *Asian Trade*, 161.

68 cf. N. Gervaise, *An Historical Description of Macassar*, London, 1701, reprint 1971, 84.

69 cf. IOR, Celebes, p. 19, 56–7; *GM*, I, 668.

70 cf. ARA, VOC 1134/KA 1043, fols. 422–6.

71 cf. IOR, Celebes, p. 56–7.

72 cf. *GM*, II, 139 and *Bouwstoffen*, III, 320–1.

73 cf. *GM*, II, 288 and *Bouwstoffen*, III, 281–3.

74 cf. *GM*, II, 313–14 and *Bouwstoffen*, III, 341.

75 For the VOC–Macassar war (1653–5), cf. Boxer, *Figueiredo*, 11–19, F. W. Stapel, *Het Bongaais Verdrag*, Groningen and The Hague, 1922, 46–50 and L. Bor, *Amboinse Oorlogen door Arnold de Vlaming van Oudshoorn als Superintendent over d'Oosterse gewesten oorlogastig ten ein gebracht*, Delft, 1663, 141–95.

76 cf. IOR, Celebes, p. 111–13, 141 and 148.
77 cf. *DRB, 1647–1648*, 83–7 and IOR, Celebes, p. 145, and 193–9.
78 cf. *DRB, 1663*, 228–33.
79 cf. *GM*, III, 468–9 and IOR, Celebes, p. 285.
80 cf. HAG, Regimentos, 1422, fols. 10–10v.
81 cf. *DRB, 1643–1644*, 6, and 60.
82 G. B. Souza, 'Portuguese Trade and Society in China and the South China Sea, c. 1630–1754', unpublished Ph.D. dissertation, Cambridge University, 1981, 400.
83 cf. *GM*, II, 263.
84 cf. H. J. de Graaf, *De Regering van Sunan Mangku-Rat I Tegal-Wangi, vorst van Mataram, 1646–1677*, The Hague, 2 vols., 1961–2, I, 53–81 and Graaf and Pigeaud, *Islamic States*, 53–74.
85 cf. HAG, Regimentos, 1422, fols. 10–10v.
86 cf. *DRB, 1647–1648*, 22–3, 28–31, and 46, for the VOC's description of Figueiredo's reception at Bantam and his embassy at Batavia on behalf of both the Estado da India and the Kingdom of Goa. As Macassar's ambassador, he was to negotiate the restitution from the VOC for a ship and its goods that they had taken while it was en route from Macassar to Manila in 1646.
87 For the Jesuit mission on Macassar, cf. A. F. Cardim, *Batalhas da Campanhia de Jesus na sua Gloriosa Provincia do Japão*, Lisbon, 1894, 283–6.
88 cf. *DRB, 1653*, 21–2 and 158, *GM*, II, 686, for a description of how the Portuguese country trader, M. Cruz, arranged this trade at Jambi from Japara.
89 For Father A. F. Cardim's account of the capture of Portuguese shipping off Java and in the South China Sea before the end of the truce, cf. Ajuda, JA, 49-IV-61, fols. 532–56.
90 cf. Boxer, *Figueiredo*, 11–19 and 58–73.
91 cf. Sá, *Documentação*, V, 324.
92 Frei Lucas de Santa Catarina described the establishment of two Macassar communities on Timor at Manatuto and Adem, cf. Sá, *Documentação*, IV, 489.
93 cf. Sá, *Documentação*, IV, 502 and H. Leitão, *Os Portugueses em Solor e Timor de 1515 a 1702*, Lisbon, 1948, 207–26.
94 cf. HAG, Regimentos, 1422, fols. 10–10v.
95 cf. *DRB, 1643–1644*, 87 for the VOC complaints of Portuguese ill-treatment of their trading representatives in the Solor and Timor area in 1644; *GM*, II, 295 and *Bouwstoffen*, III, 320–2 and 329–31 for the Company's decision and its instructions to the commander in charge of the re-occupation of Fort Henricus.
96 cf. *GM*, II, 239 and *DRB, 1647–1648*, 146–7.
97 For a summary of the VOC's operations and employment of indigenous forces for the years 1652–7, cf. *GM*, II, 620–1, 683–5; *GM*, III, 13–15, 88–9 and 154; for an indication of the intensity of Portuguese efforts in the use of indigenous forces, and intimidation, including the murder of the rulers of Mena on Timor, cf. Boxer, *Figueiredo*, 19.
98 cf. *DRB, 1656–1657*, 11.
99 cf. *GM*, III, 215.
100 cf. *DRB, 1659*, 31, 35, and 222–3, ter Horst reported that the VOC's indigenous allies had left the field; the Portuguese claimed all of Timor and demanded that the VOC abandon Cupang before any negotiations could be undertaken.
101 For the VOC's decision to attack, its success and the Company's subsequent diplomatic negotiations, cf. Stapel, *Het Bongaais Verdrag* and L. K. Andaya, 'Treaty Conceptions and Misconceptions: a case study from South Sulawesi', *Bijdragen tot de Taal-, Land- en Volkenkunde*, 134 (1978), 275–95.
102 cf. L. Cadière, 'Le Mur de Dong-hoi. Étude sur l'éstablissement des Nguyen en Cochinchine', *Bulletin de l'École Française d'Extrême-Orient*, 6 (1906), 85–253.
103 cf. Péri, 'Éssai sur les relations', 30–1.
104 For a description of VOC trade with Tonkin and with some reference to Chinese and Portuguese competition, cf. W. J. M. Buch, 'La Compagnie des Indes Néerlandaises et l'Indochine', *Bulletin de l'École Française d'Extrême-Orient*, 36 (1936), 97–196 and 37 (1937), 121–237.
105 cf. J. Baldinotti, 'La Relation sur le Tonkin du P. Baldinotti', *Bulletin de l'École Française d'Extrême-Orient*, 3 (1903), 71–7 for the Jesuit report of the establishment of their mission in 1626.
106 cf. Cardim, *Batalhas*, 75.
107 cf. Ajuda, JA, 49-V-9, fol. 8v.
108 cf. Ajuda, 49-V-13, fols. 175–89v.

109 cf. J. M. Dixon, tr., 'Voyage of the Dutch Ship "Grol" from Hirado to Tongking', *Transactions of the Asiatic Society of Japan*, 9 (1883), 180–215.
110 cf. *DRB, 1641–1642*, 65, and 124–8.
111 cf. Ajuda, 49-V-31, fol. 92 and *DRB, 1661*, 456–68.
112 cf. Magalhães Godinho, *Os Descobrimentos*, I, 338–67, 389–400 and 437–65, for an encyclopedic treatment of the currencies of these regions; on the specific topic of these caixas as 'primitive money', cf. J. L. Blussé, 'Trojan Horse of Lead: The Picis in Early Seventeenth Century Java', in Fr. von Anrooij, D. H. A. Kolff, J. T. M. van Laanen, G. J. Telkamp, eds., *Between People and Statistics: Essays on Modern Indonesian History*, The Hague, 1979, 33–47.
113 cf. Nguyen Thanh-Nha, *Tableau Economique du Vietnam aux XVIIe et XVIIIe Siècles*, Paris, 1970, 86–90, 114–5 and 162–72.
114 cf. *GM*, II, 777–8.
115 cf. Nguyen Thanh-Nha, *Tableau Economique*, 86–7, 144–5 and 163–4.
116 cf. M. Johnson, 'The Cowrie Currencies of West Africa', *Journal of African History*, 11 (1970), 17.
117 cf. C. R. Boxer, *The Great Ship from Amacon*, Lisbon, 1959, 338–9.
118 cf. *GM*, II, 653–6.
119 cf. *AM*, 2nd, I, 255.
120 cf. Dixon, 'Voyage of the Dutch', 201, 205, 211, and 212.
121 cf. Buch, 'La Compagnie des Indes', 36 (1936), 164, 166, 169, 180; 37 (1937), 121, 124, 128–32 and *GM*, II, 425, for data on the VOC and Chinese exports of Tonkin raw silk and silk piecegoods from 1638 to 1650.
122 cf. *GM*, II, 297, and 300–1.
123 *ibid.*, 325–6.
124 *ibid.*, 300–1.
125 *ibid.*, 390–1.
126 *ibid.*, 653.
127 For the *Heeren XVII's* order prohibiting the contracting of the manufacture of copper coin at Batavia in 1640, cf. Blussé, 'Trojan Horse of Lead', 44.
128 cf. *GM*, II, 697.
129 *ibid.*; the VOC also described how the resident Chinese merchant community advanced money in the countryside, cf. *GM*, II, 699.
130 *ibid.*, 777–9.
131 *ibid.*, III, 109–11.
132 *DRB, 1661*, 49–53.
133 *ibid.*
134 *ibid.* and *GM*, III, 346.
135 *GM*, III, 450–1.
136 *ibid.*, 671.
137 *ibid.*, 813; IV, 3–4, 22, 62–4, 86–7, and 112, 158.
138 cf. D. K. Bassett, 'The Factory of the English East India Company at Bantam, 1602–1682', unpublished Ph.D., University of London, 1955.
139 cf. *ibid.*, 367 for a description of the Sultan's trade in the islands near Macao and with Manila. For the Sultan's trade in pepper in Tonkin in 1667, *GM*, III, 583.
140 cf. *GM*, III, 759.
141 cf. *DRB, 1676*, 16–17 and *DRB, 1678*, 761.
142 cf. Chaudhuri, *Trading World*, 538.
143 cf. J. W. Dawkins, *Zinc and Spelter*, London, 1950, reprint 1956.
144 cf. P. van Dam, *Beschrijvinge van de Oostindische Compagnie*, The Hague, 7 vols. [Rijks Geschiedkundige Publicatien. Grote Serie, vols. 63, 68, 74, 76, 83, 87, 96], 1927–54, LXIII, 129–37.
145 cf. Bassett, 'The Factory', 417–19.

6. COUNTRY TRADERS AND THE SEARCH FOR MARKETS

1 For a detailed description of the sultanate of Banjarmasin, cf. Goh Yoon Fong, 'Trade and Politics in Banjarmasin, 1700–1747', Ph.D. dissertation, University of London, 1969, and A. A. Cense, *De Kroniek van Banjarmasin*, Leiden, 1928.

2 cf. Goh Yoon Fong, 'Trade and Politics', 33–5 and Cense, *De Kroniek*, 116.

3 cf. Goh Yoon Fong, 'Trade and Politics', 39–42; J. E. Heeres and F. W. Stapel, eds., *Corpus Diplomaticum Neerlando-Indicum*, 6 vols., The Hague, 1907–55, II, 181–8.

4 G. B. Souza, 'Portuguese Trade and Society in China and the South China Sea, c. 1630–1754', unpublished Ph.D. dissertation, Cambridge University, 1981, 400.

5 cf. *GM*, III, 284 and P. van Dam, *Beschrijvinge van de Oostindische Compagnie*, 7 vols. [Rijks Geschiedkundige Publicatien. Grote Serie, vols. 63, 68, 76, 83, 87, 96], The Hague, 1927–54, LXXIV, 316–7.

6 cf. *GM*, III, 422.

7 cf. *DRB, 1677*, 105.

8 cf. *GM*, IV, 408.

9 cf. *ibid*., 234, 247, 278–80 and Goh Yoon Fong, 'Trade and Politics', 43.

10 cf. *GM*, IV, 342–3, and 408.

11 cf. Goh Yoon Fong, 'Trade and Politics', 44–5.

12 cf. *AM*, 3rd, I, 49–50.

13 *ibid*., 101.

14 cf. R. Nichol, 'The Mission of Father António Ventimiglia to Borneo', *The Brunei Museum Journal*, 2 (1972), 183–205. Mr Nichol's article relied upon Fr. Bartolomeo Ferro's, *Istoria Delle Missione De'Cherici Regolari Teatine*, Rome, 1705.

15 cf. *AM*, 3rd, I, 49–50.

16 *ibid*., 25–6, 49–50, 55, 69, 79–80, 101, 109 and 135–6.

17 cf. Ajuda, 51-VII-34, fols. 32v–4v, VOC 1500/KA 1390, fols. 572–75v, and *GM*, V, 520–2, and 626.

18 cf. Goh Yoon Fong, 'Trade and Politics', 195–6.

19 cf. R. Suntharalingam, 'The British in Banjarmasin: An Abortive Attempt at Settlement, 1700–1707', *Journal of Southeast Asian History*, 4 (1963), 33–50.

20 cf. Goh Yoon Fong, 'Trade and Politics', 152–5, 160–3.

21 *ibid*., 205–36 and J. A. van Hohendorff, 'Radicale Beschryving van Banjermasing', *Bijdragen tot de Taal-, Land- en Volkenkunde*, 8 (1861), 151–216.

22 For a summary of VOC, Dutch vrij-burger, Portuguese and Chinese trade in south China and at Batavia from 1682 to 1687, cf. van Dam, *Beschryvinge*, LXXIV, 752–67. For Vincent Paats embassy to Peking, cf. J. E. Wills, Jr., *Pepper, Guns and Parleys: The Dutch East India Company and China, 1662–1681*, Cambridge, Mass., 1974, 195–7 and J. Vixseboxse, *Een Hollandsch Gezentschap naar China in de Zeventiende Eeuw (1685–1687)*, Leiden, 1946, 110–14.

23 cf. *GM*, V, 220; ARA, VOC 1453/KA 1342, fols. 275v–8v and VOC 1462/KA 1351, fols. 27–38v.

24 For Dutch translations of this lost *Senado da Camara* correspondence to Batavia, cf. ARA, VOC 1485/KA 1375, fols. 207v–9, VOC 1490/KA 1381, fols. 374–8v and *GM*, V, 467, 499, 532–3, 590–1, and 626.

25 cf. *GM*, V, 407.

26 *ibid*., 627, and 661.

27 cf. ARA, VOC 1569/KA 1459, Malacca, fols. 207–7v.

28 cf. *GM*, VI, 357–8, 528 and ARA, VOC 1760/KA 1652, Malacca, fols. 63–5, and VOC 1776/KA 1668, Malacca 1, fols. 23–8.

29 cf. *GM*, VII, 178 and *AM*, 3rd, VI, 80–1.

30 There is a possibility that this Cantonese merchant, Lingua, was the same Leangua (Liangua) that the EIC supercargoes had dealings with several years later, cf. H. B. Morse, *Chronicles of the East India Company Trading to China*, Oxford, 5 vols., 1926–29, Taiwan reprint, 1975, I, 104, 126 and 138.

31 cf. *AM*, 3rd, I, 23–4.

32 *ibid*., II, 84.

33 cf. J. de Hullu, 'Over den Chinaschen Handel der Oost-Indische Compagnie in de Eerste Dertig Jaar van de 18e eeuw', *Bijdragen tot de Taal-, Land- en Volkenkunde*, 73 (1917), 32–151 and J. L. Blussé, 'Chinese Trade to Batavia During the Days of the VOC', *Archipel*, 18 (1979), 195–213. For the VOC's reports of the trade for the years 1718 to 1724, cf. *GM*, VII, 349–50, 378, 394, 412, 427–8, 513–14, 545–6, 637, 655–6, 681, 704–5 and 741; *Opkmost*, IX, 77–86.

34 cf. *AM*, 1st, I, 37–8; 3rd, II, 294–5, 301–2, 323–5, 330–1, 343–6, 349–50, 357, 362–3 and 365–9; 3rd, III, 30–1; 3rd, IX, 154 and XV, 152–4 and 159.

35 cf. G. B. Souza, 'Notes on the *Algemeen Rijksarchief* and its Importance for the Study of Portuguese, Asian and Inter-Asian Maritime Trade', *Itinerario*, 4:2, (1980), 48–56.

36 cf. E. W. Hutchinson, tr., *1688 Revolution in Siam: The Memoir of Father de Bèze*, S.J., Hong Kong, 1968, 40–6.
37 cf. Dam, *Beschryvinge*, LXXIV, 756 and ARA, VOC 1403/KA 1292, fols. 339v–47.
38 cf. Dam, *Beschryvinge*, LXXIV, 760–1.
39 cf. ARA, VOC 2708/KA 2600, fol. 138.
40 cf. K. Glamann, *Dutch–Asiatic Trade, 1620–1740*, The Hague, 1958, 217.
41 *ibid.*, 217–8.
42 For descriptions of the different teas, cf. Chaudhuri, *Trading World*, 213–14.
43 cf. Chaudhuri, *Trading World*, 391, 403, and 405.
44 cf. Glamann, *Dutch–Asiatic Trade*, 220.
45 cf. J. C. Jackson, 'Mining in Eighteenth Century Bangka: The Pre-European Exploitation of a "Tin Island"', *Pacific Viewpoint*, 10 (1969), 28–54.
46 For the EIC's activities on the west coast of Sumatra, cf. J. Kathirithamby-Wells, *The British West Sumatran Presidency (1760–85)*, Kuala Lumpur, 1977, 1–55 and J. Bastin, ed., *The British in West Sumatra, 1760–85*, Kuala Lumpur, 1965. For trends in the purchase of pepper by the EIC in the early eighteenth century on the Malabar coast as compared to Sumatra, cf. Chaudhuri, *Trading World*, 324–5.
47 cf. H. K. s'Jacob, ed., *De Nederlanders in Kerala, 1663–1701*, The Hague, 1976, and A. Das Gupta, *Malabar in Asian Trade, 1740–1800*, Cambridge, 1967.
48 cf. *GM*, VII, 92, for an example of 'smuggling' by a Macao ship at Palembang in 1714.
49 cf. Glamann, *Dutch–Asiatic Trade*, 216.
50 For Manila's maritime trade in the eighteenth century, cf. P. Chaunù, *Les Philippines et le Pacifique des Ibériques*, Paris, 1960, S. D. Quiason, *English 'Country Trade' with the Philippines 1644–1765*, Quezon City, 1966 and W. E. Cheong, 'Canton and Manila in the Eighteenth Century', in J. Ch'en and N. Tarling, eds., *Studies in the Social History of China and South-east Asia*, Cambridge, 1970, 227–45.
51 cf. *GM*, V, 787, 815, and 832.
52 cf. C. R. Boxer, '*Plata es Sangre*: Sidelights on the Drain of Spanish–American Silver in the Far East, 1550–1700', *Philippine Studies*, 18 (1970), 457–75.
53 cf. *GM*, VII, 76, and 133.
54 cf. J. W. Cushman, 'Duke Ch'ing-Fu Deliberates: a Mid-Eighteenth Century Reassessment of Sino-Nanyang Commercial Relations', *Pepper on Far Eastern History*, 17 (1978), 137–56.
55 For an authoritative description of the conditions on the Malabar coast at this time, cf. A. Das Gupta, *Malabar in Asian Trade, 1740–1800*, Cambridge, 1967.
56 *ibid.*, 4.
57 cf. ARA, VOC 2863/KA 2755 to 3668/KA 3560.
58 cf. K. Glamann, *Dutch–Asiatic Trade*, 164–6.
59 cf. Das Gupta, *Malabar in Asian Trade*, 99.
60 For the low unit cost of sugar, 3 to 5 taels/picol of sugar or candy in 1751, cf. Morse, *Chronicles*, I, 291; for the rising price of pepper on the Malabar coast, cf. Das Gupta, *Malabar in Asian Trade*, 25.
61 cf. HAG, Fazenda, 1179, fols. 73v–6v, and *AM*, 3rd, VII, 108–14 and 133–4 for the relevant documentation which describes the relationship of the rendeiro of the collection of Goa's customs duties to Macao's shipping south of Goa to Cape Comorin.
62 For the peace treaties between the *Estado da India* and the Zamorin of Calicut between 1696 and 1735, cf. J. F. J. Biker, ed., *Collecção de Tratados e Concertos de Pazes que o Estado da India Portugueza fez com os Reis e Senhores com quem teve Relações nas partas da Asia e Africa Oriental*, Lisbon, 14 vols., 1881–7, IV, 288–91, VI, 16–21, 23–5, and 179–82.
63 cf. *Letters Tellicherry*, VII, 18–20.
64 cf. *Tellicherry*, XVI, 149, 152 and *Letters Tellicherry*, VI, 34.
65 cf. *Tellicherry*, XIII, 111, 123; XIV, 16, 115, 123, XVIII, 197, 209; *Letters Ft. St. David*, III, 36; *Letters Tellicherry*, XI, 13, 19, 21, 29; *Tellicherry Letters*, VII, 22, and 28.
66 cf. *Anjengo*, IIA, 35.
67 cf. *Anjengo*, IIB, 93, 99–100, and 108.

7. IMPERIAL RELATIONS: MACAO AND THE ESTADO DA INDIA

1 cf. A. R. Disney, *Twilight of the Pepper Empire: Portuguese Trade in Southwest India in the Early Seventeenth Century*, Cambridge, Mass., 1978, 10–13; the depiction of commercial rivalry between Cochin and Goa is evident in contemporary reports published in *APO*, III, pt. 1, 212–13, 289, 353–4, 491–2; III, pt. 2, 626–31 and 891–3 and supported in AGS, Sec. Prov. 1550 and 1551.

2 cf. N. Steensgaard, *Carracks, Caravans and Companies*, Copenhagen, 1973, 81–113 and K. N. Chaudhuri, *The Trading World of Asia and the English East India Company, 1660–1760*, Cambridge, 1978, 4–7, for a discussion of the Crown monopoly system.

3 cf. HAG, MR 37, fols. 123–23v, 133–36; MR 38A, fol. 4, 128–29v; MR 39, fol. 2; MR 41, fol. 260; MR 48, fol. 117–19v; HAG, Fazenda, 1170, fols. 12v–13v, 65–65v, 68v–9v, 125–130v and 132v.

4 cf. C. R. Boxer, *Portuguese Society in the Tropics*, Madison, 1965, 57–9.

5 cf. H. T. Colenbrander and W. P. Coolhaas, eds, *Jan Pietersz. Coen, Bescheiden omtrent zijn bedrijf in Indië*, The Hague, 7 vols., 1919–23, I, 690.

6 *ibid.*, and H. Furber, *Rival Empires of Trade in the Orient, 1600–1800*, Minneapolis, 1976, 188.

7 cf. P. van Dam, *Beschrijvinge van de Oostindische Compagnie*, 7 vols., The Hague, [Rijks Geschiedkundige Publicatien. Grote Serie, vols. 63, 68, 74, 76, 83, 87, 96], 1927–54, LXXXVII, 477, the actual value was 3,389,772 guilders.

8 cf. Colenbrander, *Coen*, I, 690.

9 cf. Disney, *Twilight of the Empire*, 24.

10 cf. A. de Santa Maria, *História da Fundação do Real Convento de Santa Monica da Cidade de Goa*, Lisbon, 1699, 334–43, the relevant passages were translated by F. Cotta, 'Portuguese Losses in the Indian Seas (1629–1636)', *Journal of the Asiatic Society of Bengal*, 11 (1915), 205–15.

11 *ibid.*

12 See p. 34, n. 12.

13 This argument stresses sophistication and equality of the Portuguese country trader with most of their Asian and European competition not superiority in economic or sailing techniques, cf. C. R. Boxer, 'Portuguese *Roteiros* 1500–1700', *Mariner's Mirror*, 20 (1934), 171–86 and 'Some Early Portuguese Bills of Lading 1625–1708', *Mariner's Mirror*, 25 (1939), 24–34, who demonstrated that the Portuguese commercial techniques were equal to the European Companies. In the South China Sea, surviving Portuguese roteiros from 1634–55 reveal a technical knowledge of the region equal to any group in that area, cf. Cadaval, 972, and SGL, Reservados, 146/B/5, for the roteiros of Gaspar Pereira dos Reis, João Preto, Francisco Pires and others.

14 cf. Ajuda, JA, 49-V-5, fols. 207v–11v.

15 cf. Ajuda, JA, 49-V-5, fols. 206v–207v.

16 cf. G. V. Scammell, 'Indigenous assistance in the establishment of Portuguese power in Asia', *Modern Asian Studies*, 14 (1980), 1–11; A. Cortesão, ed., *The Suma Oriental of Tomé Pires*, 2 vols., London, 1944, reprint 1967, 283–5 and M. N. Pearson, *Merchants and Rulers in Guajarat*, Berkeley, 1976, 110 for instances of Portuguese traders utilisation of Malacca and Gujarati brokerage facilities.

17 cf. Boxer, *Fidalgos*, 13; H. Leitão and J. V. Lopes, *Dicionário da Linguagem de Marinha Antigua e Actual*, Lisbon, 1974, 283, and 368.

18 cf. Boxer, *Fidalgos*, 27 and Leitão and Lopes, *Dicionário*, 155, 284 and 398.

19 cf. N. MacLeod, *De Oost-Indische Compagnie als Zeemogenheid in Azie*, 2 vols., Rijswijk, 1927, II, 3, 6, 202–8, 218 and 224.

20 cf. M. A. P. Meilink-Roelofsz, *Asian Trade and European Influence in the Indonesian Archipelago between 1500 and about 1630*, The Hague, 1962, reprint 1969, 128–29, 175, and C. R. Boxer, *The Great Ship from Amacon*, Lisbon, 1959, 13 and 210 for comparisons of the Portuguese carrack to VOC and EIC shipping.

21 cf. HAG, MR 6A, fol. 56 and HAG, Fazenda, 1159, fols. 51v–3.

22 cf. ANTT, LM 25, fol. 62; LM 26, fol. 230; LM 27, fol. 3; LM 28, fol. 352; LM 30, fol. 53; LM 31, fols. 109, 111, 432; LM 33, fol. 47; LM 36, fol. 176, 513–14; LM 38, fols. 405v, 410; and LM 39, fol. 53.

23 cf. ARA, VOC 1134/KA 1043, fols. 431–2.

24 cf. HAG, Fazenda, 1168, fols. 36–36v and 274–6.

25 cf. Meilink-Roelofsz, *Asian Trade*, 173–206.

26 For conditions on the passage to the East, cf. J. Duffy, *Shipwreck and Empire*, Cambridge, Mass., 1955 and C. R. Boxer, ed. and tr., *The Tragic History of the Sea, 1589–1622*. Cambridge, 1959.

27 cf. *DRB, 1631–1634*, 294, 386–9, and 410–11.

28 Cochin and Goa both had excellent shipyards and it was customary that when necessary the Portuguese could build vessels of 300 tons or more in Cambodia, Siam and near Macassar, cf. *DRB, 1631–1634*, 43; for an example of a Portuguese purchase of foreign shipping, cf. *DRB, 1624–1629*, 278 and 282.

29 cf. Ajuda, JA, 49-V-5, fols. 514v–17v, and Ajuda, JA, 49-V-6, fols. 133v–4.

30 cf. Ajuda, JA, 49-V-5, fols. 361–61v.

31 cf. Ajuda, JA, 49-V-6, fols. 258v–67, for a detailed report on the excesses associated with the municipal elections of 1626.

32 N. Steensgaard, 'European Shipping to Asia, 1497–1700', *Scandinavian Economic History Review*, 18, (1970), 1–11, shows that the Portuguese Crown despatched a total of forty-one ships to India over the period 1681–1701.

33 cf. M. N. Pearson, 'Indigenous Dominance in a Colonial Economy. The Goa *Rendas*, 1600–1670', *Mare Luso-Indicum*, 2 (1973), 63.

34 cf. A. Das Gupta, *Indian Merchants and the Decline of Surat, c. 1700–1750*, Wiesbaden, 1979, for conditions at Surat; early Macao country trader 'smuggling' on the Malabar coast, cf. H. K. s'Jacob, ed., *De Nederlanders in Kerala, 1663–1701*, The Hague, 1976, 278, and 354.

35 cf. *AM*, 3rd, II, 94–5.

36 cf. E. V. Axelson, *The Portuguese in South-East Africa, 1600–1700*, London, 1960, 115, 119–20, 130, 132–3, 135–6 and 144–8, which briefly outlines the importance of this institution for seventeenth century Portuguese imperial administration in Africa.

37 For the *carta regia* (Crown letter) that exempted Macao from the collection and payment of these customs duties, cf. *AM*, 3rd, IX, 6–7; for the War of the Spanish Succession and a background to conditions in early eighteenth century Portugal, cf. E. Prestage, *Portugal and the War of the Spanish Succession*, Cambridge, 1938 and A. D. Francis' two studies, *The Methuens and Portugal*, Cambridge, 1966 and *The First Peninsular War, 1702–1713*, London, 1975.

38 cf. *AM*, 3rd, II, 215–16; for the efforts of the *Estado da India* against these pirates, the Muscat Arabs and the Maratha, cf. H. Furber, *Bombay Presidency in the mid-Eighteenth Century*, New York, 1965, 37–8, 40–4, and P. S. Pissurlencar (tr. P. R. Kakodkar), *The Portuguese and the Marathas*, Bombay, 1975.

39 cf. AHU, Macao, 2, 15–21/xii/1714 and 4/iii/1716.

40 *ibid.*, and *AM*, 3rd, IX, 107.

41 cf. *AM*, 3rd, XV, 287–90; Das Gupta, *Indian Merchants*, 63, 74, 137–8 and 290.

42 cf. AHU, 475, fols. 1–5v.

43 cf. *AM*, 3rd, VI, 98–9.

44 cf. Evora, CXV/1–38, pages 336–75, and Furber, *Bombay Presidency*, 5.

45 cf. A. R. Disney, *Twilight of the Pepper Empire*, Cambridge, Mass. 1978 and C. R. de Silva, 'The Portuguese East India Company, 1628–1633', *Luso-Brazilian Review*, 11 (1974), 152–205.

46 cf. J. H. da Cunha Rivara, 'A Companhia do Comercio', *O Chronista de Tissuary*, 17–20 (1867), 99–104, 123–31, 147–55 and 171–83; Evora, CV/1–17, fols. 40v–49; HAG, MR 60, fol. 201; and Ajuda, 51-VIII-34, fols. 25v–26.

47 For the Companhia de Macao, cf. Ajuda, JA, 49-V-26, fols. 578v–86; AHU, Macao, 2, 21/i/1710, 16/iii/1713; *AM*, 3rd, II, 311–16; and *AM*, 3rd, V, 172. For the Companhia da Fabrica Real da Seda, cf. AHU, Macao, 16, 3/i/1741; AHU, Macao, 10, 30/iii/1742, AHU, Macao, 3, 21/i/1744, Ajuda, JA, 49-V-29, fol. 235–50v and *AM*, 3rd, III, 223–4. For Felix von Oldenburg's activities, cf. M. A. H. Fitzler, *Die Handelsgeschellschaft Felix von Oldenburg und Co. 1753–60*, Stuttgart, 1931; BNL, Pombalina, 651, fols. 434–59 and 652. For the Companhia Geral do Grão Pará e Maranhão, cf. AHU, Macao, 15, 5/i/1759; AHMF, XV/R/199, XV/T/51–62, XV/T/292, XV/U/16–28 and XV/U/254. One account of a voyage for this company to China was published, *Diário de Negociação de Macau*, Lisbon, 1970.

48 cf. HAG, Provisões, 7571, and AM, 2nd, I, 9.

49 cf. HAG, MR68, fols. 23–23v.

50 cf. AHU, Macao, 1, 20/iii/1695.

51 cf. AHU, Macao, 2, 30/xii/1709.

52 For indigenous and European piracy in the Indian Ocean and the South China Sea in the 1680s to 1750s, cf. A. Toussaint, 'La Course et al Piraterie dans l'Ocean Indien', in M. Mollat, ed., *Course et Piraterie: Études présentées à la Commission Internationale d'Histoire Maritime à l'occasion de*

son *XVe colloque international pendant le XIVE Congrès International des Sciences historiques*, 2 vols., Paris, 1975, II, 703–43.

53 cf. Ajuda, 51-VII-34, fol. 82v, and HAG, Regimentos, 1425 and 1426 for the Crown's instructions, which included permission to accept freight, for the frigates that sailed from Goa to Macao from 1698 to 1714.

54 cf. *AM*, 3rd, IX, 84 and XV, 131 and 132, and AHU, 475, fols. 1–5v.

55 cf. *AM*, 3rd, III, 163–7, VII, 13–17 and XV, 241–3, 246, 259, 263–4, 273–5 and 329–30.

56 cf. *AM*, 3rd, III, 211–12; for an introductory summary of Portuguese–Maratha relations, cf. A. Lobato, *Relações Luso-Maratas, 1658–1737*, Lisbon, 1965 and Pissurlencar, *The Portuguese and the Marathas*.

57 There is as yet no integrated study, utilising Portuguese and Dutch archival materials, that explores Timorese society and its economic relations with the Portuguese and Dutch, cf. C. R. Boxer, *Fidalgos in the Far East, 1550–1770*, The Hague, 1948, reprint Oxford, 1968, 174–98; A. T. de Matos, *Timor Português, 1515–1769*, Lisbon, 1974; H. Leitão, *Os Portugueses em Solor e Timor de 1515 à 1702*, Lisbon, 1948, and *Vinte e Oito Anos de História de Timor, 1698 à 1725*, Lisbon, 1952; and A. F. de Morais, *Solor e Timor*, Lisbon, 1944 and *Subsídios para a História de Timor*, Bastora, 1934.

58 cf. *GM*, III, 681, 757, 902, 920; *GM*, IV, 191, 194, 273, 530, 612; *GM*, V, 116, 210–1, 311 and 397.

59 cf. *GM*, V, 459, 624, 684–5 and 753.

60 Cf. *GM*, V, 397.

61 cf. *GM*, V, 459, and Ajuda, 51-VII-34, fols. 23–5.

62 cf. C. R. Boxer, *António Coelho Guerreiro e as Relações entre Macau e Timor no começo do século XVIII*, Macau, 1940 and V. Rau, *O 'Livro de Rezão' de António Coelho Guerreiro*, Lisbon, 1956.

63 cf. Rau, *O 'Livro de Rezão'*, 21–233, 90–3.

64 cf. *GM*, VI, 539.

65 cf. *GM*, VI, 764 and AHU, Timor, 2, 25/x/1706.

66 cf. *AM*, 3rd, VI, 70–1 and 102–103.

67 cf. AHU, Macao, 4, 30/xii/1746.

68 A detailed list tabulating Portuguese shipping losses in the South China Sea from 1683–1754 was constructed primarily from printed records: *GM* and *AM*, but owing to its length could not be included in the present volume.

69 cf. Ajuda, JA, 51-VII-34, fol. 82v; *AM*, 3rd, I, 223, 225–7; and *GM*, VI, 57.

70 cf. *AM*, 2nd, I, 279–80.

71 cf. Ajuda, JA, 49-V-19, fols. 573–5.

72 cf. *AM*, 3rd, V, 202 and VI, 19–20.

73 cf. *AM*, 3rd, III, 232–4.

74 cf. AHU, Macao, 2, 30/xii/1709 which re-iterated the Crown's alvara of 1698.

75 cf. SCM, 15, fols. 64v–6 and 68v–70v.

76 cf. Ajuda, JA, 49-V-27, fols. 568–9.

77 cf. SCM, 88, fol. 8v and SCM, 15, fols. 72–5v.

78 cf. AHU, Macao, 2, 8/viii/1728.

79 cf. AHU, Macao, 4, 25/xii/1735.

80 cf. SCM, 88, fols. 55–80.

81 cf. SCM, 34, fols. 30v–85 for the deliberations of the Mesa for the years 1746 to 1754.

82 cf. C. R. Boxer and C. de Azevedo, *Fort Jesus and the Portuguese in Mombasa, 1593–1729*, London, 1960, 75–83, Evora, CXV/1–38, fols. 324, 330 and 334 and HAG, Fazenda, 1179, fol. 96v.

83 cf. HAG, MR43, fol. 139.

84 cf. J. D. Spence, *To Change China: Western Advisers in China, 1620 to 1960*, Boston, 1969 and throughout J. Needham, *Science and Civilization in China*, 5 vols. in 8 parts, Cambridge, 1954–80.

85 cf. M. Mancall, *Russia and China: Their Diplomatic Relations to 1728*, Cambridge, Mass., 1971, and J. Sebes, ed., *The Jesuits and the Sino-Russian Treaty of Nerchinsk, 1689: The Diary of Thomas Pereira, S.J.*, Rome, 1961.

86 cf. HAG, Japão, 1890, fols. 6–32, for a record of the revenues and expenses of the Province of Japan for the years 1604–14, Ajuda, JA, 49-V-6, fols. 4v for an example of a *conhecimento* (letter of credit) used in the transfer of the Crown's contribution from Malacca, and Ambrósio de Piña, 'Macau no Seculo XVII. Cartas de Francisco Carvalho Aranha', *Portugal em Africa*, 14 (1957), 343–60, for further particulars on this type of capital transfer. For the Province of Japan's revenues, expenditures, direct investments in freight and respondencia for 1617 and 1618, cf. Ajuda, JA,

49-V-7, fols. 101–9v and 127–42; for the expenditures from 1616–39 and the donations and legacies left to the mission, 1626–41, cf. Ajuda, JA, 49-IV-66, fol. 43 and 49-V-8, fols. 146v–53.

87 cf. Ajuda, JA, 49-IV-56, fols. 198–202v and 204–4v.

88 cf. HAG, MR 33, fols. 83–9 and 311.

89 cf. HAG, Japão, 825.

90 cf. Ajuda, JA, 49-V-28, fols. 289v–96v.

91 cf. HAG, Macao, 2001.

92 cf. A. B. Braganza Pereira, 'Os Portugueses em Baçaim', *O Oriente Português*, separate (1935), 34, 36–9 and R. S. de Brito, *Goa e as Praças do Norte*, Lisbon, 1960. For a description of how the Estado da India incorporated existing Hindu land-tenure relationships in the sixteenth century for its own purposes, cf. A. D'Costa, 'The Demolition of the Temples in the Islands of Goa in 1540 and the Disposal of the Temple Lands', *Neue Zeitschrift für Missionswissenschaft*, 18, (1962), 161–76.

93 cf. Ajuda, JA, 49-V-13, fols. 133–36v.

94 cf. Ajuda, JA, 49-IV-65, fols. 365v–74.

95 There are several summaries of the Province of Japan's revenues and expenditures that were consulted that permit this assessment, which if anything is underestimated, cf. HAG, MR 19C, fols. 735v–6v and 744–5v for a Jesuit report to the Estado da India in 1634 and the investigation of Dezembargador Sebastião Soares Paes in 1635; Ajuda, JA, 49-IV-66, fols. 72–3, 85–7, 91–3, 94v–9v and 101–3, for Jesuit reports that catalogue their finances and benefactions received for the College of Macao, Province of Japan, Vice-Province of China, and the Tonkin Mission from the sixteenth and into the early eighteenth century; Ajuda, JA, 49-V-27, fols. 634–6v, for Father Joseph Anselmo's report to the Viceroy of the Estado da India in 1719 of the Province of Japan's revenues and expenditures and Ajuda, JA, 49-V-28, fols. 289v–96v, 359–62 and 369–76v for Jesuit summaries of their revenues and expenditures, 1612–1727, 1728 and 1730.

96 cf. Ajuda, JA, 49-V-24, fols. 266–7.

8. IMPERIAL SURVIVAL: SINO-PORTUGUESE RELATIONS FROM MING TO CH'ING

1 cf. C. R. Boxer, *Macao na Epoca de Restauração*, Macau, 1942, 69 and 89.

2 *ibid.*, 38 and 87–9.

3 *ibid.*, 38.

4 *ibid.*, 54–5 and 87.

5 *ibid.*, 89.

6 cf. D. Barbosa Machado, *Bibliotheca Lusitana*, 4 vols., Coimbra, 1966, II, 316–17.

7 cf. ARA VOC 1075/KA 987, fols. 228v–32 for de Matos' description of Portuguese commercial practices; M. Múrias, ed., *Instrução para of Bispo de Pequim*, Lisbon, 1943, 116–18.

8 cf. ANTT, LM 7, fol. 162; LM 20, fol. 7; LM 23, fol. 437; LM 24, fols. 41–41v; LM 25, fol. 102; and LM 26, fol. 282.

9 cf. ARA VOC 1075/KA 987, fols. 224–24v.

10 cf. Boxer, *Macau na Epoca*, 34–5.

11 cf. C. R. Boxer, *Fidalgos in the Far East, 1550–1770*, The Hague, 1948, reprint Oxford, 1968, 125.

12 cf. ARA, VOC 1075/KA 987, fols. 224v–27v.

13 *ibid.*

14 cf. C. R. Boxer, 'Portuguese Military Expeditions in Aid of the Ming against the Manchus, 1621–1647', *T'ien-hsia Monthly*, 7:1 (1938), 24–50.

15 cf. J. E. Wills, Jr., 'Maritime China from Wang Chih to Shih Lang', in J. E. Wills, Jr. and J. D. Spence, *From Ming to Ch'ing: Conquest, Region and Continuity in the Seventeenth Century*, New Haven, 1979, 223–8.

16 cf. RAH, Jesuitas, 7236, fols. 1025–48.

17 cf. Boxer, 'Portuguese Military Expeditions', 34–5.

18 cf. Ajuda, JA, 49-IV-61, fols. 105–9 and Ajuda, 50-V-38, fols. 232–34v.

19 cf. Ajuda, JA, 49-IV-61, fols. 105–9.

20 cf. Ajuda, 50-V-38, fols. 138–79v.

21 cf. Ajuda, 50-V-38, fols. 232–34v.

22 cf. J. E. Wills, Jr., *Pepper, Guns and Parleys: The Dutch East India Company and China, 1662–1681*, Cambridge, Mass., 1974, and his article, 'Ch'ing Relations with the Dutch, 1662–1690', in J. K. Fairbank, ed., *The Chinese World Order*, Cambridge, Mass., 1968, 225–56.

23 cf. Wills, 'Maritime China', 225–6.
24 cf. Hsieh Kuo-chen, 'A Study of the Evacuation of the Southeast Coast in the Early Ch'ing', *Chinese Social and Political Science Review*, 15 (1931), 559–96 and L. D. Kessler, *K'ang-hsi and the Consolidation of Ch'ing Rule, 1661–1684*, Chicago, 1976, 39–45.
25 cf. J. F. Marques Pereira, comp., 'Uma Resurreição Histórica (Paginas inéditas d'um visitador dos Jesuitas, 1665–1671)', *Ta-Ssi-Yang-Kuo*, 1:2 (1899), 114.
26 cf. Kessler, *K'ang-hsi*, 81–90 and Wills, *Pepper*, 154–7.
27 cf. Wills, *Pepper*, 157–78.
28 cf. AHN, Jesuitas, leg. 270, number 96, 29/i/1680.
29 cf. P'eng Tse-i, 'Ch'ing-tai Kuang-tung yang-hang chih-tu ti ch'i-yuan' [The Origin of the system of foreign trade guilds in Kwangtung during the Ch'ing period], *Li-shih yen-chiu*, 1 (1957), 9.
30 cf. *GM*, IV, 616–17, and P. van Dam, *Beschrijvinge van de Oostindische Compagnie*, The Hague, 7 vols. [Rijks Geschiedkundige Publicatien. Grote Serie, vols. 63, 68, 74, 76, 83, 87, 96], 1927–54, LXXIV, 752–67.
31 cf. Wills, 'Maritime China', 228–32 for Shih Lang and A. W. Hummel, *Eminent Chinese of the Ch'ing Period*, Washington, 1943, Tapei reprint, 1975, 899–900, for Yao Ch'i-shêng's contributions to the Ch'ing success.
32 cf. S. H. L. Wu, *Passage to Power: K'ang-hsi and his Heir Apparent, 1661–1722*, Cambridge, Mass., 1979, 84.
33 cf. S. Viraphol, *Tribute and Profit: Sino-Siamese Trade 1652–1853*, Cambridge, Mass., 1977, 48–9.
34 cf. Wu, *Passage to Power*, 106–11.
35 cf. Lo-Shu Fu, ed., *A Documentary Chronicle of Sino-Western Relations, 1644–1820*, 2 vols., Tucson, 1966, I, 86.
36 cf. *AM*, 2nd, I, 15, 19–20, and 71.
37 cf. *AM*, 3rd, I, 89–90.
38 cf. Lo-Shu Fu, *Documentary Chronicle*, II, 41, note 324 and I, 110.
39 cf. *AM*, 3rd, I, 57.
40 cf. Wu, *Passage to Power*, 118 and H. B. Morse, *Chronicles of the East India Company Trading to China*, 5 vols., Oxford, 1926–9, Taiwan reprint, 1975, I, 135–45.
41 cf. AHU, Macao, 2, 30/xii/1709.
42 cf. Ajuda, JA, 49-V-27, fols. 359–68v.
43 cf. J. D. Spence, 'Chang Po-hsing and the K'ang-hsi Emperor', *Ch'ing shih wen-t'i*, 1:8 (1968), 6–7.
44 cf. *AM*, 3rd, II, 162–3.
45 cf. Boxer, *Fidalgos*, 222–3; for a series of prohibitions of this practice from 1703 to Pombal's order for its eradication, cf. *AM*, 3rd, II, 44–5; *APO*, VI, pt. 2, 15–16, 283–4 and 474–7.
46 cf. AHU, Macao, 2, 19/xii/1710.
47 cf. Lo-Shu Fu, *Documentary Chronicle*, I, 122 and Viraphol, *Tribute and Profit*, 55–7.
48 cf. Lo-Shu Fu, *Documentary Chronicle*, I, 123–7 and II, 495, note 422.
49 cf. Morse, *Chronicles*, I, 163–5.
50 cf. Lo-Shu Fu, *Documentary Chronicle*, II, 495, note 421.
51 *ibid.*, 159–60.
52 This account of the rebellion of Taiwan relies upon the biographies of Chu I-Kuei, Lan T'ing-yuan and Shih Shih-p'iao, cf. A. W. Hummel, *Eminent Chinese of the Ch'ing Period*, Washington, 1943, reprint Taipei, 1975, 181–2, 440–1 and 654–5.
53 cf. Wu, *Passage to Power*, 173 and 175; Lo-Shu Fu, *Documentary Chronicle*, I, 145–7 and P. M. d'Elia, *Il Lontano Confino e la Tragica Morte del P. João Mourão, S.I., Missionario in Cina, 1681–1726*, Lisbon, 1963.
54 cf. Lo-Shu Fu, *Documentary Chronicle*, I, 154–7.
55 cf. *AM*, 3rd, II, 259–60, 263–6, and 268–72.
56 cf. Lo-Shu Fu, *Documentary Chronicle*, I, 127.
57 cf. *AM*, 3rd, V, 332–4 and 337.
58 cf. Lo-Shu Fu, *Documentary Chronicle*, I, 138–9.
59 *ibid.*, I, 141, and Pu Hsin-Hsien, 'Resumen del comércio internacional de Macau en el siglo XVIII según los documentos en chino del Arquivo Nacional da Torre do Tombo', *Actas. Congresso Internacional de História dos Descobrimentos*, Lisbon, 1961, V, pt. 2, 195–205 for a description of this quota system.
60 cf. Evora, CXVI/2–6, for the original papers of Alexandre Mettello de Souza e Menezes; *AM*, 1st, I, 33–4; 3rd, III, 41–4, 46–7, and 69–71; VI, 113–18, 122–4, 126–9, and 161–3.

61 cf. Lo-Shu Fu, *Documentary Chronicle*, I, 157–9, 161–4 and 166.

62 *ibid.*, I, 169–70, and 172–4, for Ch'ien Lung's edicts; Morse, *Chronicles*, V, 21–44 and 85–98 and Virapol, *Tribute and Profit*, 133–4 for a description of the Canton system.

63 cf. Viraphol, *Tribute and Profit*, 124.

64 *ibid.*, 121–39.

65 cf. Luis G. Gomes, tr., *Ou Mun Kei-Lèok, Monografia de Macau*, Macau, 1950, 92; the *Ao-men chi-lueh* was written by two Kwang-tung provincial officials, Yin Kuang-jen and Chang Ju-lin, both of whom were personally acquainted with Macao in the 1730s and 40s.

66 cf. Lo-Shu Fu, *Documentary Chronicle*, I, 176.

67 *ibid.*, and Ajuda, JA, 49-V-29, fols. 112–13v.

68 cf. Lo-Shu Fu, *Documentary Chronicle*, I, 186–8; Boxer, *Fidalgos*, 142–3 and *AM*, 3rd, VI, 178–88 and 214.

69 cf. Francisco de Assiz Pacheco de Sampaio's report of 31 August, 1755, *Noticias das couzas succedidas na Embaixada, que levou à Corte de Pekim Francisco de Assíz Pacheco de Sampayo, mandado pelo Senhor Rey D. Jozé lo*, Lisbon, 1936. For records indicating Macao's preparations for the Embassy and the ambassador's inquiries as to the city's economic condition, cf. *AM*, 3rd, VII, 47–50, 53–5, 60–71, 74–5 and 87–94. For the Chinese reception of this embassy, cf. Lo-Shu Fu, *Documentary Chronicle*, I, 189–92.

9. MACAO, COMPANIES AND COUNTRY TRADERS:
THE OTHER EUROPEANS IN CHINA

1 cf. H. T. Colenbrander and W. P. Coolhaas, *Jan Pietersz. Coen, Bescheiden omtrent zijn bedrijf in Indië*, 7 vols., The Hague, 1919–53, VII, pt. 1, 20–2.

2 cf. A. R. Disney, *Twilight of the Pepper Empire: Portuguese Trade in Southwest India in the Early Seventeenth Century*, Cambridge, Mass., 1978, 148–54.

3 cf. H. B. Morse, *The Chronicles of the East India Company Trading to China, 1635–1834*, 5 vols., Oxford, 1926–29, Taiwan reprint, 1975, I, 14–30.

4 cf. *GM*, II, 140.

5 *ibid.*, 163.

6 *ibid.*, 184–5.

7 *ibid.*, 190–1, and 213–14.

8 *ibid.*, 213–14.

9 cf. K. W. Goonewardena, *The Foundation of Dutch in Ceylon, 1638–1658*, Amsterdam, 1958, 66–75, 81–100, and 107–32.

10 cf. ARA, VOC 667/KA 569, 19/iv/1644, 21/vii/1644 and 2/ix/1644.

11 cf. *GM*, II, 256.

12 cf. *GM*, II, 244–6; ARA, VOC 667/KA 569, 9/xi/1644 and VOC 1150/KA 1056, fols. 287–91v. For this unsuccessful Portuguese embassy to Japan, cf. C. R. Boxer, *The Embassy of Captain Gonçalo de Siqueira de Souza to Japan in 1644–1647*, Macau, 1938.

13 cf. *GM*, II, 271.

14 cf. HAG, Regimentos, 1421, fol. 91.

15 cf. ARA, Collective Sweers, Van Vliet, Specx, number 3: 'Oost-Indische brieven, extracten en acten sedert 1623 tot 1655', fols. 263–70, for Francisco Zusarte's letter to the Governor-General and Council of the Indies in 1645.

16 cf. ARA, VOC 668/KA 570, 16/v/1645.

17 cf. *DRB, 1664*, 204 and 413–14; *GM*, IV, 280–1, 302 and 384.

18 cf. *GM*, IV, 280–1 and 302.

19 cf. P. van Dam, *Beschrijvinge van de Oostindische Compagnie*, The Hague, 7 vols. [Rijks Geschiedkundige Publicatien. Grote Serie, vols. 63, 68, 74, 76, 83, 87, 96], 1927–54, LXXXIV, 701–3.

20 For Ceylon, cf. S. Arasaratnam, *Dutch Power in Ceylon, 1658–1687*, Amsterdam, 1958, Goonewardena, *Foundation of Dutch Power* and G. D. Winius, *The Fatal History of Portuguese Ceylon*, Cambridge, Mass., 1971; for Malabar, M. A. P. Roelofsz, *De Vestiging der Nederlanders ter Kuste Malabar*, The Hague, 1943; T. I. Poonen, *A Survey of the Rise of Dutch Power in Malabar, 1603–1678*, Trichinopoly, 1948; and H. K. s'Jacob, ed., *De Nederlanders in Kerala, 1663–1701*, The Hague, 1976.

21 cf. *GM*, III, 123–4, 175–9, 183, 199–200, 281; *DRB, 1653*, 51–62, 159–63; *DRB, 1656–1657*,

38, 69–70, 130, 132–3; *DRB, 1659*, 117, 128; J. Nieuhoff (J. Ogilby, tr.), *An Embassy from the East India Company of the United Province to the Grand Tartar Cham Emperor of China*, London, 1669, n.d. reprint.

22 cf. ARA, VOC 1197/KA 1088, fols. 612–42 and fols. 623v–4.

23 cf. *DRB, 1653*, 51–62, 159–163; and Dam, *Beschryvinge* LXXIV, 704–9.

24 cf. *GM*, III, 281.

25 cf. W. E. van Dam van Isselt, 'Mr. Johan van Dam en zijne tuchtiging van Makassar in 1660', *Bijdragen tot de Taal-, Land- en Volkenkunde*, 60 (1908), 1–44.

26 cf. *GM*, III, 359.

27 cf. W. Campbell, *Formosa Under the Dutch*, London, 1903, reprint 1967, 469–74.

28 cf. *GM*, III, 388; *DRB, 1661*, 61–5; since 2/ix/1660, the VOC on Taiwan had lost five ships, two small *fluyts* (the *Worcum, Goes, Hector, Koukercke, Immenhorn, Kortenhoef* and the *Urk*), and 1,200 men.

29 cf. *GM*, III, 441.

30 cf. Wills, *Pepper*, 25–8.

31 cf. *DRB, 1663*, 75, 97–8, and 628–32.

32 cf. *DRB, 1664*, 67, 70–71, 79 and 86.

33 cf. Wills, *Pepper*, 136–44; *GM*, III, 667, 685; ARA, VOC 1272/KA 1162, fols. 1101–1224; *DRB, 1668–1669*, 287–301, 313, 324, 326, 342, 346, 347, 352, 453, 462; and Dam, *Beschryvinge*, LXXIV, 742–3.

34 cf. *GM*, III, 712, 719, 759, 810, 868, 949; *GM*, IV, 46, 89, 220–1, 488, 542, 545 and 616–17.

35 cf. *DRB, 1670–1671*, 274–5, 277, 280–1 and *DRB, 1673*, 91–3.

36 *DRB, 1678*, 154; and D. K. Bassett, 'The Factory of the English East India Company at Bantam', Ph.D. Dissertation, University of London, 1955.

37 cf. *GM*, IV, 575; HAG, MR 47, fols. 2–5.

38 cf. *Madras*, XVII, 18 and XLVII, 74–7 for evidence of English merchant involvement in freighting goods on board Macao shipping for China from Madras and from Macao for Batavia in 1697 and 1727.

39 cf. AHU, Macao, 9, 27/x/1770.

40 cf. F. Valentijn, *Oud en Nieuw Oost-Indien*, 4 vols., in 8 books, Dordrecht, 1724–6, IV, pt. 2, 4.

41 cf. H. Furber, *Rival Empires of Trade in the Orient, 1600–1800*, Minneapolis, 1976, 125–84 and P. J. Marshall, *East Indian Fortunes: The British in Bengal in the Eighteenth Century*, Oxford, 1976.

42 cf. Morse, *Chronicles*, I, 85–98; the EIC frequented other Chinese ports until 1711 and tried to trade at Amoy and Chusan in 1735 and 1736.

43 *ibid.*, 66–77.

44 cf. *Madras*, LV, 68.

45 *ibid.*, LIX, 97.

46 The actual total for sea customs on goods collected by the EIC at Madras in 1739 was 19,912 pagodas, cf. *Madras*, LX, 15.

47 cf. *England Despatches*, XX, 61–3.

48 cf. *Letters Fort St. David*, III, 18–20.

49 cf. *AM*, 3rd, II, 70–1.

50 cf. *AM*, 3rd, III, 5.

51 cf. *Tellicherry Letters*, VI, 31–5.

52 cf. AHU, 475, fols. 1–5v.

PRIMARY SOURCES

There is a daunting mass of archival documentation in Europe and Asia pertaining to Portuguese society in Asia. Most of the existing materials record, primarily, the administrative history of the Crown's enterprises in partnership with and/or in conflict against Asian rulers and European competitors, and crisis and confrontation in the Estado da India between Crown administrators, the Church and the institutions representing local society. Rare are the glimpses, amidst the morass of documentation, into the personalities of the country traders that were influential and responsible for Portuguese participation in the maritime trade of Asia.

Rarer, still, are the traces of Portuguese country traders' economic organisation, commercial methods – their account books, correspondence – and the legal instruments of business – amongst others, contracts and letters of exchange. Yet, it is those glimpses that reveal the side of Portuguese society which established the closest contact with Asian society and maintained an intimate relationship with indigenous merchants and rulers. Every effort, as this brief synopsis of the principal manuscript sources used in this study will attest, was made to discover new sources to obtain those glimpses of Portuguese society.

A systematic attempt was made to explore and examine original manuscript materials from a wide range of archival sources. My research in this field began while an undergraduate honours student at Stanford University in 1971. In addition to the principal sources mentioned in this study, investigation was undertaken in French, Italian, Brazilian and American archives and libraries, through personal visits and examination of microfilm copies of rare documentation.

Jesuit materials were consulted in Portuguese, Indian, Spanish, British and Italian archives. As an integral part of Portuguese society, Jesuit annual letters, histories, and other reports from Japan, China, Tonkin, Cochinchina and Macassar in particular chronicled political and economic information about the milieu in which they lived and were in contact. One Portuguese archive, the Ajuda Library with its *Jesuitas Na Asia* collection, houses an important single source of these reports. The Jesuits' archives in Rome house an even larger collection and were consulted; however, the *Jesuitas Na Asia* collection was preferred in that its size, location, and organisation permitted the incorporation of its materials into this study. There is still, despite an incredible beginning, a tremendous job of compilation, cataloguing, comparison and publishing to be done by Jesuit historians of the Japan and China mission documentation.

Portuguese and Indian archival materials form the core of the documentation consulted for this study. It was necessary to consult Spanish, Dutch and British archival records to obtain fundamental corroborative evidence of an economic nature concerning Portuguese trading and commercial activities.

Although all three countries' archives house sources of inestimable historical value, the Dutch materials for their sheer volume, detail, and organisation were the most useful for specific information on the markets, sales and purchases, shipping and other economic data in which the Portuguese were active.

The Portuguese archives document, primarily, the Crown's role in the administration of a far-flung empire. Copies of the correspondence sent by the Crown, its representatives and councils and the answers received from Viceroys, judges, religious and prominent servants of the Crown are to be found in several depositories in Lisbon and Evora.

In Lisbon, the *Arquivo Histórico Ultramarino*'s *Maços de Macao* collection and the *Arquivo Nacional da Torre do Tombos*' collection *Livros das Monções*, and in Evora, the *Biblioteca Pública e Arquivo Distrital de Evora*'s codex collection of the personal papers of Macao's first governor, were the principal sources consulted which document royal government in the East. The *maços* are the loose bundles of documents which record the results of the Overseas Council's deliberations on colonial affairs. The *livros das monções* or monsoon books are the Crown's letter orders and dispatches sent from Lisbon to the Viceroy of India yearly from 1605 tp 1655 with some later seventeenth-century documents. These materials are a smaller collection of similar, equally important, and more extensive documents housed in Goa.

The Ajuda Library houses the *Jesuitas Na Asia* collection. Of the some sixty codices examined, these materials included the Jesuits annual letters, reports and other documents, for the Japan, China, Tonkin, Cochinchina and Macassar missions in the seventeenth and, in the case of Tonkin, into the eighteenth centuries. Although these reports were not always chronologically complete, their consultation provided political and economic data not commented upon in other Portuguese sources. Father Simão da Cunha's report in the China missions annual letter of the Portuguese involvement in pirate suppression activities in Kwangtung province in the 1650s to win favour with the Manchu is an example of a little known incident in Sino-Portuguese relations which is described in colourful detail.

Macao

The existing archives of the Municipal Council of Macao are recorded in 316 volumes which date from 1630 to 1900 and represent only a portion of the original holdings. Although there are a small number of originals or copies of letters from the municipal council, dating from its establishment in 1583 to 1630, to be found scattered throughout Portuguese, Spanish, British and Dutch archives, there is a complete absence of them in Macao itself on account of loss via the damp, corrosive ink and lack of care. The transcribed seventeenth-century documents are copies made in the nineteenth century of incomplete records going back to 1630; the oldest original document dates from 1712. The bulk of the surviving seventeenth-century and early eighteenth-century materials are published in the *Archivos de Macau* of which there are three series, 1929–1931, 1939–1941, and 1964 to the present. The documents of this institution demonstrate the vital role it played in local government *vis-à-vis* the Crown and the Church in the maintenance and expansion of commercial and political relations with neighbouring states in East and Southeast Asia.

Macao's *Santa Casa de Misericordia* houses the more interesting original documentation. The records of this charitable lay brotherhood, which was established in 1569, are quite extensive from the mid seventeenth century to the present; its contents vary tremendously from accounts of the governing body of the institution, to official correspondence and ledger accounts. However, much of the material in the approximately 500 volumes is of the nineteenth and twentieth centuries. I examined thoroughly some ten codices which are largely early nineteenth century copies of documentation long since destroyed and which comprise much of the pre-1800 material. Codices 15, 18, 34, 73–6, 79 and 88 document the allocation of the *Santa Casa de Misericordia*'s economic resources. These funds were generated by the estates of deceased members, which were administered by the brotherhood and invested in rental properties accruing interest at fixed rate, loans granted on merchandise in maritime trade at 15–25 per cent interest, and in loans to the municipality at fixed rates of interest guaranteed in theory by municipal receipts from the collection of maritime duties and fees. Codices 73–6 (1672–1801) are contracts between the *Santa Casa de Misericordia* and the local recipients, the conditions, the amount borrowed, interest rate, repayment schedule, financial guarantor, on what ships, its owners and destination, and form only a portion of a collection which dates from 1762 to 1843.

INDIAN ARCHIVES

Since Goa was the administrative centre of royal government in Portuguese Asia, the Historical Archives of Goa contain the Viceroy of India's voluminous correspondence with Lisbon and the records of the local Treasury and State councils financial and political deliberations.

The *Livro das Monções do Reino* collection (1574–1914), in 467 folio volumes, originally comprised (or should have done) the orders and dispatches received yearly at Goa from Lisbon in the monsoon of September–October together with copies of the replies and reports sent from Goa to Portugal in the homeward-bound Indiamen of the following December–March. The collection begins in 1574 and continued without interruption until the twentieth century. I consulted some fifty odd volumes, most of which lacked indices, and contained material for my study to the end of the seventeenth century.

The first six codices, 1264–9 of the *Livros da Correspondencia de Macao (e de Timor e de Canara)* collection, were examined. These codices date from 1677 to 1766, contain copies of viceregal correspondence with Macao, Siam, Timor and Solor, the Jesuits in China and the problems of the Portuguese Padroado and the Chinese Rites, the Spanish in Manila and the Dutch Governor-General at Batavia. This collection presents the Viceroy's viewpoint without the Macao response, and its importance depended largely upon a rigorous comparison of these documents with those published in *Arquivos de Macao* which revealed the extent of compliance or defiance from local government in Macao.

Assentos do Conselho da Fazanda, codices 1159–1180, and *Petições despachadas do Conselho da Fazanda* codices 1127–30, were examined; their contents are of fundamental importance for the comprehension of the Crown's influence upon Portuguese economic activities in Asia, how these activities were organised and regulated by the Treasury Council in Goa. The deliberations of the Treasury Council reveal what amount of Crown support there was and when it was dispatched to Macao, requests for payment of overdue Crown donations to various religious orders in China and the attempts made to find or generate these funds from existing revenue and finally, its influence over the Crown's administration of trade at Manila, Timor and other areas of the region.

Portions of several diverse collections, codices 825, *Fundação do Seminario de Japão* (1729); 1497, *Contas do Colegio do Macau* (1693–1736); 1890, *Contas das Rendas das*

Provincias do Japão and 2001, *Legados da Produratura* (1738–1761) provide a new, invaluable source for understanding Jesuit financing of their missionary activity in the East and their involvement in Macao and India. Codes 1467 details the income derived by the Portuguese Jesuits of the China Mission from their property in north-west India and the other codices supplemented this data by providing the account books for the support of Japanese seminarists in Macao, from 1638 to 1750, for the Province of Japan at an earlier period 1604–1614, and for the legacies of deceased Portuguese administered by the Jesuit Procurador in Macao who invested this money in rental properties and the maritime trade of Macao, 1738–1761. These materials established that the Jesuits played an important economic role in financing the survival of Portuguese trade and society in China and the South China Sea.

SPANISH ARCHIVES

Although the Habsburg's incorporation of Portugal and its empire within the Spanish Crown from 1580 to 1640 provided for a certain autonomy of imperial control from Lisbon, some pertinent reports from Crown administrators and other representatives are to be found in Spanish archives, as well as additional Jesuit material. The prime Spanish source for royal governmental reports concerning Portugal and the Portuguese in Asia was at the *Archivo General de Simancas* especially in the *Secretarias Provinciales* codices from 1461 to 1553. The supplementary Jesuit material is to be found in Madrid in the *Archivo Histórico Nacional*'s *Jesuitas* collection, *legajos* 270–2.

Spanish materials, however, concerning the Philippines, and Mexico in the *Archivo General de Indias* were the truly surprising sources of new data on Portuguese trade in the seventeenth century from China to Manila, the comparison of the Portuguese trade with the Chinese junks to Manila, and the Portuguese arrangement with the Sultan of Macassar to trade illicitly at Manila from Macassar in the late 1640s to the late 1650s.

DUTCH ARCHIVES ·
THE HAGUE

The *Algemeen Rijksarchief* contains important, sometimes unique, sources which are invaluable as corroborative evidence for the study of the socio-economic and political activities of the Portuguese in Asia. It is one source, because of the Dutch East India Company's scrupulous record-keeping methods and its commercial orientation, that provides detailed observations of Portuguese Crown and local societies' economic behaviour and substantiates or contradicts earlier-held views on the economic orientation of the Portuguese Empire.

The materials used in this study was formed in the *Overgekomen Brieven, Inkomend Briefboek, Bataviaasch Uitgaand Briefboek, Resoulution van Gouverneur-General en Raden, Salmon Swears, et al., Hugo de Groot,* and the *Voorcompagnie* collections.

Reports to the Company's Directors in Holland, the Heeren XVII, from the Governor-General and the Council of the Indies and instructions from the Heeren XVII to Batavia are found primarily in the *Overgekomen Brieven*. These *Generale Missiven* serve as an introduction to overall Dutch East India company [the *Vereenigde Oost-Indische Compagnie*, the VOC] economic, political and military policies towards the Portuguese and Asian societies. Owing to the absence of such data elsewhere, these reports are a good general indicators of the economic habits of the Portuguese country trader and his method of operation in various Asian markets.

Reports from various VOC factory merchants and naval commanders to the Governor-
General and the Council of the Indies are, once again, found primarily in the *Overgekomen
Brieven*. These reports were usually compiled by the senior VOC representative at, and were
catalogued under the geographic location of the individual factory. The first several reports
from Dutch envoys in areas where the Portuguese were particularly well established often
illuminate aspects such as the size of the Portuguese community, its economic condition
and trading relations with local Asian society which are rarely seen, although not devoid
of presentation, in Portuguese or Jesuit accounts. They also include copies of or intelligence
estimates of the contents of letters of Asian monarchs to the Portuguese, such as those of
the King of Siam in 1631 and the Sultan of Palembang to Macao in 1644, results of Dutch
conversations with captured merchants and reports on Portuguese activities in areas
nominally of interest to the VOC such as Banjarmasin in 1691. The reports of the greatest
significance revolve around Portuguese and Dutch negotiations concerning trade at Batavia
and exemption from anchorage and passage fees at Malacca in the late seventeenth and early
eighteenth centuries.

The *dagh-registers* or daily journals of the commanders of various voyages and, more
important, the merchants from the outlying factories. They provide the Dutch East India
company's view of, negotiations with, and the Portuguese from Macao's commercial
capabilities and political relationship with indigenous society at different times and locations.
Although significant gaps in the published material for the period 1624–82 exist, and the
archival records for 1683 to the late eighteenth century have yet to be thoroughly utilized,
Batavia's dagh-register is the most famous. Its fame is justified in that its daily reports include
portions of reports from many of the outlying Dutch factories, letters from regional rulers
to and notices of arrival and transactions between foreign merchants and the VOC.

Other non-published journals were found to contain new material on the Portuguese
country traders from Macao; these included, for example, those of Siam (1633–37), Quinam
(1633), Macao (1642) and Canton (1653, 1688) and elaborated the extent of Portuguese
economic capabilities and political penetration at those locations. Only a small amount of
pertinent material was found in the Fort Zelandia dagh-register (1622–62). The Batavia and
Malacca dagh-registers were the most important collection of this type of material for this
study.

The VOC kept detailed reports on the cargo of captured Portuguese ships, especially in
the period 1621–37. These reports provide a tantalising introduction to and supplementary
information on the actual size of Portuguese country shipping and types of commodities
carried. Other reports on Portuguese, European and indigenous shipping movements and
commercial activities were prepared by the Dutch based on first-hand observation and
participation. Such reports from one geographic location did not however explain the totality
of the activities of Portuguese country traders and such generalisations required consultation
of all the available *Rijksarchief* reports for as many geographic locations as possible and
incorporated similar data from English, Spanish and Portuguese sources.

Pre-1715 materials concerning Portuguese trade at Batavia are found in the
dagh-register of Batavia and the *Generale Missiven*. After 1715 until 1792, the Company
prepared lists of all foreign shipping arriving and departing Batavia which separated into
two lists of foreign (non-Chinese) and Chinese. In the case of the non-Chinese, the date
of Portuguese arrivals and departures with destination, name of vessel, commander, size,
crew and armament was included. I could not find the reports for 1763, 1772, 1788 otherwise
the data is complete. The Chinese lists included similar information, the date of arrivals
and departures with destinations, name of the ship commander, its type, size, crew numbers;

other separate reports indicated the official numbers of Chinese immigrants. I could not find the reports for 1742 (which is comprehensible because of the events of that year), 1750, 1752, 1756, 1763, 1772 and 1788. The Dutch also kept account of their purchases and sales of commodities to the principal country traders at Batavia, the Chinese and the Portuguese, but did not, generally, differentiate between them; reports of such sales and purchases were found for one year in the 1670s four years in the 1680s, three years in the 1690s, four years in the 1700s, 1710–24, 1728–32, 1734, 1736, 1741–3 and 1745–64.

The dagh-registers of Malacca were found to contain records of the name and nationality of arriving and departing foreign ships, including indigenous, with their destinations, ship type, and from general to very specific cargo information for the periods 1681–1742 and 1777–1792. The structure of Macao's country trade to India and a general indication of the significant commodities and volume is provided from these records.

Records of Portuguese with Siam, Malabar, Surat, Bengal trade to Coromandel and Ceylon are also available. With the exception of Ceylon, these records have significant gaps over the period 1719–91.

There are a few original and Dutch précis of Portuguese correspondence in the *Rijksarchief.* The few existing examples of this type of material are significant in that they provide information about important incidents which are generally absent in the Portuguese archives. These materials consist of captured or received Portuguese correspondence; the earliest being those letters captured from the *Sta. Catharina* in 1603. There are a series of letters from the Jesuit rector of Macao to Goa in 1621 which were seized by the Company; they describe in great detail Portuguese commercial relations with the Chinese authorities and merchants at Canton. There are a few additional letters and petitions of the 1640s. The Dutch precis of letters from the Senado da Camara of Macao to the Company over the years 1682–95 are most important in that the originals in Macao no longer exist.

BRITISH ARCHIVES

The Portuguese and Jesuit materials in the *Additional Manuscript* collection of the British Museum also provided supplementary accounts of Portuguese royal government correspondence to and response from the Portuguese authorities in Asia.

A more accurate perspective of Portuguese activity in China was obtained by consulting the early English East India Company records in the India Office Library, in particular their merchants and supercargo reports from Macassar in the seventeenth century and Canton in the early eighteenth century.

BIBLIOGRAPHY

MANUSCRIPT SOURCES

Portuguese Archives
Arquivo Histórico do Ministerio das Finanças, Lisbon
  Codices: XV/R199; XV/T/51–62; XV/T/292; XV/U/16–28; XV/U/254
Arquivo Histórico Ultramarino, Lisbon
  Consultas Mixtas codices 13–18, 475, 1161
  Maços de Macau 1–4, 8–10, 13, 15, 16, 20
Arquivo Nacional da Torre do Tombo, Lisbon
  Livros das Monçoes 1–61
Biblioteca da Ajuda, Lisbon
  Codices: 44-XIV-4, 46-XIII-31, 50-V-27, 50-V-37, 50-V-38, 51-II-4, 51-VII-34
  Jesuitas na Asia: 49-IV-52, 49-V-56, 49-IV-61, 49-IV-65, 49-IV-66, 49–V–1 to 49-V-9,
    49-V-11, 49-V-13, to 49-V-20, 49-V-22, 49-V-24, 49-V-26 to 49-V-33, 49-VI-1
Biblioteca Nacional, Lisbon
  Codices: 637, 9445–7, 8548
  Pombalina: 642, 643, 651, 652
Sociedade de Geografia, Lisbon
  Reservados: 146/B/5
Biblioteca Pública e Arquivo Distrital de Evora, Evora
  Codices: CXV/1–30, CXV/1–37, CXV/1–38, CXV/2–9, CXVI/2–3, CXVI/2–5,
    CXVI/2–6, CXVI/2–11, CXVI/2–14, CXXII/2–11d
Casa de Cadaval, Muge
  Codices: 903, 972
Santa Casa da Misericordia, Macau
  Codices: 15, 18, 27, 34, 73–6, 79, 88

Indian Archives
Historical Archive of Goa, Goa
  Conselho da Fazenda: 1127–30, 1159–80
  Fianças: 1369
  Japão: 825, 848, 1890
  Macau: 1264–6, 1497, 2001
  Monçoes do Reino: 1–68, 72–81, 84–6B, 88, 92
  Provisões (da Fazenda): 7571
  Regimentos e Instruções: 1420–2, 1425–6
  Senado de Goa – Carta Régias: 7745

Spanish Archives

Archivo Histórico Nacional, Madrid
  Jesuitas: legajos 270–2
Biblioteca Nacional, Madrid
    Codices: 2352, 2371, 3015, 3217, 9414, 19152
Real Academia de la História, Madrid
  Jesuitas: legajos 7236, 7239
  Cortes: codices: 2165, 2665, 2666
  Papeles de los Jesuitas: volumes IV, LXXXIV, CLXXXV, CXCI
Archivo General de Indias, Seville
  Audiencia de Filipinas: legajos: 4, 6–9, 18-B, 20, 22–3, 27–8, 30–1, 41, 43, 64, 70, 79,
    84, 163, 266–7, 285, 329–30, 340, 350, 895, 942, 943
  Patronato: legajos: 24, 25, 46, 53, 263
  Audiencia de Mexico: 28, 31–3, 71, 102, 121
  Escribanía de Camara: legajo: 409–B
  Indiferente General: legajos: 536, 583, 614, 1450, 1872
Archivo General de Simancas, Simancas
  Secretarías Provinciales: 1461–4, 1469, 1471, 1473, 1479, 1494–5, 1498–9, 1508, 1512,
    1515–6, 1520, 1530, 1552–3

Dutch Archives

Algemeen Rijksarchief, The Hague
  Collectie Hugo de Groot: 22
  Collectie Sweers, Van Vliet, Specx: 3
  Voorcompagine 158: 60–3
  Koloniale Archieven Oost-Indie: Archieven van de Vereenigde Oost-Indische Compagnie:
    [The *Rijksarchief* is in the process of switching from referring to these collections and
    documents by KA to VOC numbers; the new VOC number is referred to here but
    both are given in the notes] 666–7, 1075, 1088, 1100–3, 1125, 1134, 1140, 1141, 1147,
    1197, 1272, 1377 to 2833

British Archives

British Museum, London
  Additional Manuscripts: 22842–56
India Office Records, London
  Factory Records: Celebes, Java, China and Japan

PRINTED SOURCES

Abranches Garcia, J. I. de, ed., *Arquivo da Relaçao de Goa*, 2 vols., Nova Goa, 1872–4.
Arquivos de Macau, first series, 3 vols., Macau, 1929–31, second series, 1 vol., 1941, third
    series, 28 vols., 1964–77.
Bastin, J. S., ed., *The British in West Sumatra, 1685–1825*, Kuala Lumpur, 1965.
Biker, J. F., ed., *Collecçao de Tratados e Concertos de Pazes que o Estado da India Portugueza
    fez com os Reis e Senhores com quem teve Relações nas Partes da Asia e Africa Oriental*,
    14 vols., Lisbon, 1881–7.
Blair, E. H. and Robertson, J. A., eds. *The Philippine Islands*, 55 vols., Cleveland, 1903–9.

Boxer, C. R., ed., *Azia Sinica e Japonica*, 2 vols., Macau, 1941–50.

Boxer, C. R. and Braga, J. M., eds., *Breve Relação da Jornada que Fez à Corte de Pekim o Senhor Manoel de Saldanha, Embaixador Extraordinario del Rey de Portugal ao Emperador da China, e Tartaria, 1667–1670*, Macau, 1942.

Bulhão Pato, A., and Silva Rego, A. de, eds., *Documentos Remettidos da Índia, ou Livros das Monções*, 8 vols., Lisbon, vols., 1–5, 1880–1935, vols., 6–8, 1974–7.

Chijs, J. A. van der, Colenbrander, H. T., Hullu, J. de, Haan, F. de and Fruin-Mees, W., eds., *Daghregister gehouden int Casteel Batavia vant passerende daer ter plaetse als over geheel Nederlandts India*, 31 vols., Batavia and The Hague, 1888–1931.

Chijs, J. A. van der, *Nederlandsch–Indisch Plakaatboek, 1602–1811*, 17 vols., Batavia and The Hague, 1885–1900.

Colenbrander, H. T. and Coolhaas, W. P., *Jan Pietersz. Coen, Bescheiden omtrent zijn bedrijf in Indië*, 7 vols., The Hague, 1919–53.

Commelin, I., *Begin ende Voortgangh van de Vereenighde Nederlantsche Geoctroyeerde Oost-Indische Compagnie*, 2 vols., Amsterdam, 1646, reprint, 4 vols., 1969.

Coolhaas, W. P., ed., *Generale Missiven van Gouverneurs-Generaal en Raden aan Heren XVII der Verenigde Oostindische Compagnie*, 7 vols., The Hague [Rijks Geschiedkundige Publicatien, Grote Serie, vols., 104, 112, 125, 134, 150, 159, 164], 1960–79.

Cunha Rivara, J. H. da, ed., *Archivo Portuguez–Oriental*, 6 vols., in 9, Nova Goa, 1857–76.

Dam, P. van, *Beschrijvinge van de Oostindische Compagnie*, 7 vols., The Hague [Rijks Geschiedkundige Publicatien. Grote Serie, vols., 63, 68, 74, 83, 87, 96], 1927–54.

Diário de Negociação de Macau, Lisbon, 1970.

Ferro, Fr. Bartolomeo, *Istoria Delle Missione De'Cherici Regolari Teatine*, Rome, 1705.

Heeres, H. E. and Stapel, F. W., eds. *Corpus Diplomaticum Neerlando-Indicum*, 6 vols., The Hague, 1907–55.

Jacobs, H. Th. Th. M., ed. and tr., *A Treatise on the Moluccas*, Rome, 1970.

Jacobs, H. Th. Th. M., ed., *Documenta Malucensia*, 2 vols., Rome, 1974–80.

Jonge, J. K. J. de, Deventer, M. L. van, and Roo, L. W. G. de, eds., *De Opkomst van het Nederlandsch Gezag in Oost-Indie*, 17 vols., The Hague and Amsterdam, 1862–1909.

Linhares, Conde de (Dom Miguel de Noronha), *Diário do terceiro conde de Linhares, vice-rei da Índia*, 2 vols., Lisbon, 1937–43.

Lo-Shu Fu, ed., *A Documentary Chronicle of Sino-Western Relations 1644–1820*, 2 vols., Tucson, 1966.

Marques Pereira, J. F., comp., 'Uma Resurreição Histórica (Paginas inéditas d'um visitador dos Jesuitas, 1665–1671)' *Ta-Ssi-Yang-Kuo*, 1:1 (1899), 31–41, 1:2 (1899), 113–19, 1:3 (1899), 181–8, 1:5 (1900), 305–10, 2:11 (1901), 693–702, 2:12 (1901), 747–63.

Mendes da Luz, F. P., comp., 'Livro das Cidades e fortalezas que a Coroa de Portugal tem nas partes da India, e das capitanias e seus cargos que nelas ha e da importancia deles', *Studia*, 6, (1960), 353–63.

Muller, H. P. N., *De Oost-Indische Compagnie in Cambodja en Laos*, The Hague, 1917.

Múrias, M., ed., *Instrução para o Bispo de Pequim* [1784] *e outros documentos para a história de Macau*, Lisbon, 1943.

Noticias das couzas succedidas na Embaixada, que levou á Corte de Pekim Francisco de Assís Pacheco de Sampayo, mandado pelo Senhor Rey D. Jozé I⁰, Lisbon, 1936.

Pakse-Smith, M., ed., *History of Japan*, 2 vols., Kobe, 1931, reprint, 2 vols. in 1, New York, 1972.

Pissurlencar, P. S., *Assentos do Conselho do Estado da India, 1618–1750*, 5 vols., Goa-Bastora, 1953–57.

Records of Fort St. George:
  The Diary and Consultation Books, 76 vols., Madras, 1910–47.
  Despatches from England, 24 vols., Madras, 1911–32.
  Despatches to England, 11 vols., Madras, 1919–32.
  Letters from Fort St. George, 40 vols., Madras, 1915–41.
  Letters to Fort St. George, 45 vols., Madras, 1916–46.
  Fort St. David Consultations, 42 vols., Madras, 1933–5.
  Letters to Fort St. David, 4 vols., Madras, 1935.
  Letters from Fort St. David, 4 vols., Madras, 1935–6.
  Tellicherry Consultations, 20 vols., Madras, 1932.
  Letters to Tellicherry, 12 vols., Madras, 1934.
  Letters from Tellicherry, 8 vols., Madras, 1934.
  Anjengo Consultations, 1–2b vols., Madras, 1935–6.
s'Jacob, H. K., ed., *De Nederlanders in Kerala 1663–1701*, The Hague, 1976.
Sá, A. B. de, ed., *Documentação para a História das Missões do Padroado Portugues do Oriente, Insulíndia*, 5 vols., Lisbon, 1954–8.
Sebes, J., *The Jesuits and the Sino-Russian Treaty of Nerchinsk, 1689: The Diary of Thomas Pereira, S.J.* Rome, 1961.
Silva Rego, A. da, ed. *Documentação para a História das Missões do Patdoado Portugues do Oriente, India*, 12 vols., Lisbon, 1947–58.
Tiele, P. A. and Heeres, J. E., eds. *Bouwstoffen voor de Geschiedenis der Nederlanders in den Maleischen Archipel*, 3 vols., The Hague, 1886–95.
Valentijn, F., *Oud en Nieuw Oost Indien*, 5 vols. in 8 parts, Dordrecht, 1724–6.
Wicki, J., *Documenta Indica*, 12 vols., Rome, 1948–72.

PRINTED SECONDARY SOURCES
Books
Actas, Congresso Internacional da História dos Descobrimentos, 5 vols., Lisbon, 1961.
Actas do III Colóquio Internacional de Estudos Luso-Brasileiros, 2 vols., Lisbon, 1960.
Actas do IV Congresso das Misericordias, 3 vols., Lisbon, 1959.
Alexandrowicz, C. H., *An Introduction to the History of the Law of Nations in the East Indies (16th, 17th and 18th Centuries)*, Oxford, 1967.
Andaya, L. Y., *The Kingdom of Johor, 1641–1728*, Kuala Lumpur, 1975.
Andaya, L. Y., *The Heritage of Arung Palakka: A History of South Sulawesi (Celebes) in the Seventeenth Century*, The Hague, 1981.
Anrooij, F. van, Kolff, D. H. A., Laanen, J. T. M. van, and Telkamp, G. J., eds., *Between People and Statistics: Essays Modern Indonesian History*, The Hague, 1979.
Arasaratnam, S., *Dutch Power in Ceylon, 1658–1687*, Amsterdam, 1958.
Audemard, L., *Les Jonques Chinoises*, Rotterdam, 1957.
Axelson, E. V., *The Portuguese in South-East Africa, 1600–1700*, London, 1960.
Bakewell, P. J., *Silver Mining and Society in Colonial Mexico: Zacatecas 1546–1700*, Cambridge, 1971.
Barbosa Machado, D., *Biblioteca Lusitana*, 4 vols., Coimbra, 1966.
Bastin, J. S., *The Changing Balance of the Early Southeast Asia Pepper Trade*, Kuala Lumpur, 1960.
Bastin, J. S. and Roolvink, R., eds. *Malayan and Indonesian Studies*, Oxford, 1964.

Bernard-Maitre, H., *Aux Portes de la Chine. Les Missionnaires du Seizième Siècle, 1514–1588*, Tientsin, 1933.

Bor, L., *Amboinse Oorlogen door Arnold de Vlaming van Oudshoorn als Superintendent over d'Oosterse gewesten oorlogastig ten eind gebracht*, Delft, 1663.

Borah, W. W., *Early Colonial Trade and Navigation between Mexico and Peru*, Berkeley, 1954.

Borah, W. W., *Silk Raising in Colonial Mexico*, Berkeley, 1943.

Botelho de Sousa, A., *Nuno Álvares Botelho*, Lisbon, 1940.

Botelho de Sousa, A., *Subsidios para a História militar maritima da India*, 4 vols., Lisbon, 1930–56.

Boxer, C. R., *The Christian Century in Japan, 1549–1650*, Berkeley, 1951.

Boxer, C. R., *The Dutch Seaborne Empire*, New York, 1965.

Boxer, C. R., *The Embassy of Captain Gonçalo de Siqueira de Souza to Japan in 1644–1647*, Macau, 1938.

Boxer, C. R., *Francisco Vieira de Figueiredo: A Portuguese Merchant-Adventurer in Southeast Asia, 1624–1667*, The Hague, 1967.

Boxer, C. R., *Fidalgos in the Far East, 1550–1770*, The Hague, 1948, reprint Oxford, 1968.

Boxer, C. R., *The Great Ship from Amacon: Annals of Macao and the Old Japan Trade, 1555–1640*, Lisbon, 1959.

Boxer, C. R., *Macau na Epoca de Restauração*, Macao, 1942.

Boxer, C. R., *Mary and Misogyny: Women in Iberian Expansion Overseas 1415–1815*, London, 1975.

Boxer, C. R., *The Portuguese Seaborne Empire: 1415–1825*, New York, 1969.

Boxer, C. R., *Portuguese Society in the Tropics: the municipal councils of Goa, Macao, Bahia, and Luanda, 1510–1800*, Madison, 1965.

Boxer, C. R., *Salvador de Sá and the Struggle for Brazil and Angola, 1602–1686*, London, 1952.

Boxer, C. R., ed., *South China in the Sixteenth Century*, Cambridge, 1953, reprint 1967.

Boxer, C. R., *The Tragic History of the Sea, 1589–1622*, Cambridge, 1959.

Boxer, C. R., and Alzevedo, C. de, *Fort Jesus and the Portuguese in Mombasa, 1593–1729*, London, 1960.

Braga, J. M., *The Western Pioneers and Their Discovery of Macao*, Macau, 1949.

Brito, R. S. de, *Goa e as Praças do Norte*, Lisbon, 1960.

Brown, D. M., *Money Economy in Medieval Japan*, New Haven, 1951.

Campbell, W., *Formosa under the Dutch*, London, 1903, reprint Taipei, 1967.

Cardim, A. F., *Batalhas da Companhia de Jesus na sua Gloriosa Provincia do Japão*, Lisbon, 1894.

Caron, L. J. J., *Het Handels – en Zeerecht in de Adatrechtsregelen van de Rechtskring Zuid-Celebes*, Bussum, 1937.

Castro, A. de, *As Possessões Portuguesas na Oceania*, Lisbon, 1867.

Cense, A. A., *De Kroniek van Banjarmasin*, Leiden, 1928.

Chang T'ien-tse, *Sino-Portuguese Trade from 1514 to 1644*, Leiden, 1933, reprint, 1968.

Chappoulie, H., *Rome et les missions d'Indochine au XVIIe siècle*, Paris, 1943.

Chaudhuri, K. N., *The Trading World of Asia and the English East Indian Company, 1660–1760*, Cambridge, 1978.

Chaunu, P., *Les Philippines et le Pacifique des Ibériques (XVIe, XVIIe, XVIII siècles)*, Paris, 1960.

Ch'en Ching-Ho, *Historical Notes on Hoi-An (Faifo)*, Carbondale, 1973.

Ch'en, J. and Tarling, N., eds., *Studies in the Social History of China and South East Asia*, Cambridge, 1970.

Cinatti Vaz Monteiro Gomes, R., *Esboço Histórico do Sândalo no Timor Português*, Lisbon, 1950

Cortesão, A., ed., *The Suma Oriental of Tomé Pires*, 2 vols., London, 1944, reprint, 1967.

Cummins, J. S., ed., *Sucessos de las Islas Filipinas*, Cambridge, 1971.

Cummins, J. S., ed., *Travels and Controversies of Friar Domingo Navarrete, 1616–1686*, 2 vols., London, 1962.

Cushner, N. P., *Landed Estates in the Colonial Philippines*, New Haven, 1976.

Dang Phu'o'ng-Nghi, *Les Institutions Publiques du Viet-Nam au XVIIIe siècle*, Paris, 1969.

Das Gupta, A., *Indian Merchants and the Decline of Surat, c. 1700–1750*, Wiesbaden, 1979.

Das Gupta, A., *Malabar in Asian Trade 1740–1800*, Cambridge, 1967.

Dawkins, J. M., *Zinc and Spelter*, London, 1950, reprint, 1956.

Dermigny, L., *La Chine et l'Occident: Le commerce à Canton au XVIIIe siècle*, 3 vols., Paris, 1964.

Diffie, B. W. and Winius, G. D., *Foundations of the Portuguese Empire 1415–1580*, Minneapolis, 1977.

Disney, A. R., *Twilight of the Pepper Empire: Portuguese Trade in Southwest India in the Early Seventeenth Century*, Cambridge, Mass., 1978.

Duffy, J., *Shipwreck and Empire*, Cambridge, Mass., 1955.

Elia, P. M. d', *Il Lontano Confino e la Tragica Morte del P. João Mourão, S.I., Missionario in Cina, 1681–1726*, Lisbon, 1963.

Elison, G., *Deus Destroyed*, Cambridge, Mass., 1973.

E-tu Zen Sun and Francis, J. de., eds., *Chinese Social History*, Washington, 1956.

Fairbank, J. K., ed., *The Chinese World Order*, Cambridge, Mass., 1968.

Ferreira Martins, J. F., *História da Misericordia de Goa 1520–1910*, 3 vols., Nova Goa, 1910–14.

Fitzler, M. A. H., *Die Handelsgesellschaft Felix von Oldenburg und Co. 1753–60*, Stuttgart, 1931.

Fitzler, M. A. H., *O Cerco de Columbo*, Coimbra, 1928.

Foster, W., ed., *The Journal of John Jourdain, 1608–1617*, Cambridge, 1905.

Francis, A. D., *The Methuens and Portugal*, Cambridge, 1966.

Francis, A. D., *The First Peninsular War, 1702–1713*, London, 1975.

Furber, H., *Bombay Presidency in the mid-Eighteenth Century*, New York, 1965.

Furber, H., *John Company at Work*, Harvard, 1951.

Furber, H., *Rival Empires of Trade in the Orient 1600–1800*, Minneapolis, 1976.

Gervaise, N. (H. S. O'Neill, tr.), *The Natural and Political History of the Kingdom of Siam*, Bangkok, 1928.

Giles, H. A., *A Chinese Biographical Dictionary*, London, 1898.

Gill, C., *Merchants and Mariners of the 18th Century*, London, 1961.

Glamann, K., *Dutch Asiatic Trade, 1620–1740*, The Hague, 1958.

Gobel, E., *Asiatisk Kompagnis Kinafarter, 1732–1772*, Årbog, 1978.

Gomes, L. G., tr., *Ou Mun Kei-Lèok, Monografia de Macau*, Macau, 1950.

Gonzalves Pereira, C. R., *História da Administração da Justiça no Estado da India*, 2 vols., Lisbon, 1964–5.

Gonzalves Pereira, C. R., *Tribunal da Relação da Goa*, Lisbon, 1964.

Goonewardena, K. W., *The Foundation of Dutch Power in Ceylon, 1638–1658*, Amsterdam, 1958.

Goor, J. van, *Kooplieden, Predikanten & Bestuurders Overzee. Beeldvorming en Plaatsbepaling in een andere Wereld*, Utrecht, 1982.

Graaf, H. J. de, *De Regering van Sulton Agung, Vorst van Mataram 1613–1645 en die van zijn Voorganger Panembahan Séda-Ing-Krapjak, 1601–1613*, The Hague, 1958.

Graaf, H. J. de, *De Regering van Sunan Mangku – Rat I Tegal-Wangi, Vorst van Mataram, 1646–1677*, 2 vols., The Hague, 1961–2.

Graaf, H. J. de, and Pigeaud, Th. G. Th., *Islamic States in Java, 1500–1700*, The Hague, 1976.

Groeneveldt, W. P., *De Nederlanders in China, Eerste Deel: De eerste Bemoeingen om den Handel in China en de Vestiging in de Pescadores, 1601–1624*, The Hague, 1898.

Heine-Geldern, R. von, *Conceptions of State and Kingship in Southeast Asia*, Ithaca, 1956.

Ho Ping-ti, *Studies on the Population of China, 1368–1953*, Cambridge, Mass., 1959.

Huang, R., *Taxation and Governmental Finance in Sixteenth Century Ming China*, Cambridge, 1975.

Hummel, A. W., *Eminent Chinese of the Ch'ing Period*, Washington, 1943, reprint Taipei, 1975.

Hutchinson, E. W., tr., *1688 Revolution in Siam: The Memoir of Father de Bèze, S.J.*, Hong Kong, 1968.

Iskander, T., *De Hikajat Atjéh*, The Hague, 1958.

Iwao Seiichi, *Nanyō Nihonmachi no Kenkyū*, Tokyo, 1941, reprint 1967.

Jörg, C. J. A., *Porselein als Handelswaar: De Porseleinhandel als Orderdeel van de Chinahandel van de V.O.C., 1729–1794*, Groningen, 1978.

Kathirithamby-Wells, J., *The British West Sumatran Presidency, 1760–85*, Kuala Lumpur, 1977.

Kemp, J., *Aspects of Siamese Kingship in the Seventeenth Century*, Bangkok, 1969.

Kessler, L. D., *K'ang-hsi and The Consolidation of Ch'ing Rule, 1661–1684*, Chicago, 1976.

Kling, B. B. and Pearson, M. N., eds., *The Age of Partnership: Europeans in Asia Before Dominion*, Honolulu, 1979.

Knauth, L., *Confrontación Transpacífica: El Japón y el Nuevo Mundo Hispánico, 1542–1639*, Mexico City, 1972.

Knowlton, Jr., E. C., tr., *The Conquest of Malacca*, Kuala Lumpur, 1970.

Kwan-wai So, *Japanese Piracy in Ming China During the Sixteenth Century*, East Lansing, 1975.

Le Than Khoi, *Le Viet Nam, Historie et Civilisation*, Paris, 1955.

Leitão, H., *Os Portugueses em Solor e Timor de 1516 a 1702*, Lisbon, 1948.

Leitão, H., *Vinte e Oito Anos de História de Timor, 1698 à 1725*, Lisbon, 1952.

Leitão, H. and Lopes, J. V., *Dicionário da Linguagem de Marinha Antiga e Actual*, Lisbon, 1974.

Leite, S., *História da companhia de Jesus no Brasil, 1549–1760*, 10 vols., Rio de Janeiro, 1938–50.

Leur, J. C. van, *Indonesian Trade and Society*, The Hague, 1955. Second edn., 1967.

Ljungstedet, A., *An Historical Sketch of the Portuguese Settlement in China*, Boston, 1835.

Lobato, A., *Relações Luso-Maratas, 1658–1737*, Lisbon, 1965.

Lombard, D., *Le Sultanat d'Atjéh au temp d'Iskander Muda, 1607–1838*, Paris, 1967.

MacLeod, N., *De Oost-Indische Compangnie als Zeemogendheid in Azië*, 2 vols., Rijswijk, 1927.

Magalhães Godinho, V., *Os Descobrimentos e a Economia Mundial*, 2 vols., Lisbon, 1963–5.

Mancall, M., *Russia and China: Their Diplomatic Relations to 1728*, Cambridge, Mass., 1971.

Manguin, P.-Y., *Les Portugais sur les Côtes du Viêt-Nam et du Campá*, Paris, 1972.

Marshall, P. J., *East India Fortunes: the British in Bengal in the Eighteenth Century*, Oxford, 1976.

Matos, A. T. de, *Timor Português, 1515–1769*, Lisbon, 1974.

Meilink-Roelofsz, M. A. P., *Asian Trade and European Influence in the Indonesian Archipelago, between 1500 and about 1630*, The Hague, 1962, reprint 1969.

Mendes da Luz, F. P., *O Conselho da India*, Lisbon, 1952.

Moertono, S., *State and Statecraft in Old Java: A Study of the Late Mataram Period, Sixteenth to Nineteenth Century*, Ithaca, 1968.

Mollat, M., ed., *Course et Piraterie: Etudes présentées à la Commission Internationale d'Histoire Maritime à l'Occasion de son XVe Colloque international pendant le XIVe Congrès International des Sciences historiques*, 2 vols., Paris, 1975.

Mollat, M., ed., *Sociétés et Compagnies de Commerce en Orient et dans l'Océan Indien*, Paris, 1970.

Montalto de Jesus, C. A., *Historic Macao*, Hong Kong, 1902.

Morais, A. F. de, *Solor e Timor*, Lisbon, 1944.

Morais, A. F. de, *Subsídios para a História de Timor*, Bastora, 1934.

Moreland, W. H. *From Akbar to Aurangzeb. A Study in Indian Economic History*, London, 1923.

Moreland, W. H., *India at the Death of Akbar*, London, 1920.

Morse, H. B., *Chronicles of the East India Company Trading to China, 1635–1834*, 5 vols., Oxford, 1926–9, reprint Taiwan, 1975.

Nachod, O., *Die Beziehungen der Niederländischen Ostindischen Kompagnie zu Japan im Siebzehnten Jahrhundert*, Leipzig, 1897.

Needham, J., *Science and Civilization in China*, 5 vols. in 8, Cambridge, 1954–80.

Nguyen Thanh-Nha, *Tableau Economique du Vietnam aux XVIIe et XVIIIe siècles*, Paris, 1970.

Nieuhoff, J. (J. Ogilby, tr.), *An Embassy from the East India Company of the United Provinces to the Grand Tartar Cham Emperor of China*, London, 1669, n.d. reprint.

Pearson, M. N., *Merchants and Rulers in Gujarat*, Berkeley, 1976.

Perkins, D. H., *Agricultural Development in China, 1368–1968*, Chicago, 1969.

Pfister, L., *Notices Biographiques et Bibliographique sur les Jesuites de l'Ancienne Mission de Chine 1552–1773*, 2 vols., Shanghai, 1932–4.

Pires, B. V., *A Viagem de Comércio Macau–Manila, nos Séculos XVI a XIX*, Macau, 1971.

Pissurlencar, P. S. (P. R. Kakodkar, tr.), *The Portuguese and the Marathas*, Bombay, 1975.

Pissurlencar, P. S., *Roteiro dos Arquivos da India Portuguesa*, Bastora and Goa, 1955.

Poonen, T. I., *The Rise of the Dutch Power in Malabar, 1603–1678*, Trichinopoly, 1948.

Prestage, E., *Portugal and the War of the Spanish Succession*, Cambridge, 1938.

Pritchard, E. H., *The Crucial Years of Early Anglo-Chinese Relations, 1750–1800*, Pullman, 1936.

Quaison, S. D., *English 'Country Trade' with the Philippines, 1644–1765*, Quezon City, 1966.

Quaritch Wales, H. G., *Ancient Siamese Government and Administration*, London, 1934.

Rau, V., *O 'Livro de Rezão' António Coelho Guerreiro*, Lisbon, 1956.

Rawski, E. S., *Agricultural Change and the Peasant Economy of South China*, Cambridge, Mass., 1972.

Raychaudhuri, T., *Jan Company in Coromandel 1605–1690*, The Hague, 1962.

Reid, A. and Castles, L., eds., *Pre-Colonial State Systems in Southeast Asia*, Kuala Lumpur, 1975.

Richards, D. S., ed., *Islam and the Trade of Asia*, Oxford, 1970.

Robertson, H. M., *The Rise of Economic Individualism*, Cambridge, 1935.

Rodriguez, F., *História da Companhia de Jesus na Assistencia de Portugal*, 7 vols., Oporto, 1931–50.

Roelofsz, M. A. P., *De Vestinging der Nederdanders ter Kuste Malabar*, The Hague, 1943.

Rosso, A. S., *Apostolic Legations to China of the Eighteenth Century*, South Pasadena, 1948.

Russell-Wood, A. J. R., *Fidalgos and Philanthropists: The Santa Casa da Misericordia of Bahia, 1550–1755*, Berkeley, 1968.

Santa Maria, A. de, *História da Fundação do Real Convento de Santa Monica da Cidade de Goa*, Lisbon, 1699.

Scammell, G. V., *The World Encompassed: The first European maritime empires, c. 800–1650*, Berkeley, 1981.

Scattergood, B. P., Temple, R. C. and Anstey, L. M., *The Scattergoods and the East India Company, 1681–1723*, privately printed, London, 1935.

Schrieke, B. J., *Indonesian Sociological Studies*, 2 vols., The Hague, 1955–7.

Schurz, W. L., *The Manila Galleon*, New York, 1939.

Schutte, J. F., *El 'Archivo del Japon', Vicisitudes del Archivo Jesuitico del Extremo Oriente y descripción del Fondo Existente en la Real Academia de la História de Madrid*, Madrid, 1964.

Schwartz, S. B., *Sovereignty in Colonial Brazil: The High Court of Bahia and its Judges, 1609–1751*, Berkeley, 1973.

Skinner, G. W., ed., *The City in Late Imperial China*, Stanford, 1977.

Skinner, C., ed., *Sja 'ir Perand Mengkasar (The Rhymed Chronicle of the Macassar War)*, The Hague, 1963.

Smith, G. V., *The Dutch in Seventeenth Century Thailand*, Carbondale, 1977.

Soares, J. C., *Macau e Assistencia*, Lisbon, 1950.

Soedjatmoko, Ali, M., Resink, G. J. and Kahin, G. M., eds., *An Introduction to Indonesian Historiography*, Ithaca, 1965.

Souza, T. R. de, *Medieval Goa*, New Delhi, 1979.

Spence, J. D., *To Change China: Western Advisers in China, 1620 to 1960*, Boston, 1969.

Spence, J. D. and Wills, Jr., J. E., eds., *From Ming to Ch'ing: Conquest, Region and Continuity in the Seventeenth Century*, New Haven, 1979.

Stapel, F. W., *Het Bongaais Verdrag*, Groningen and The Hague, 1922.

Steensgaard, N., *Carracks, Caravans, and Companies: the structural crisis in the European–Asian trade in the early 17th century*, Copenhagen, 1972.

Teeuw, A. and Wyatt, D. K., eds. *Hikayat Patani*, 2 vols., The Hague, 1970.

Terpstra, H., *De Factorij der Oostindische Compagnie te Patani*, The Hague, 1938.

Tissanier, J., *Relation du Voyage du P. Joseph Tissanier*, Paris, 1663.

Trevor-Roper, H. R., *Religion, the Reformation and Social Change*, second edition, London, 1972.

Vella, W. F., ed., *Aspects of Vietnamese History*, Honolulu, 1973.

Viraphol, S., *Tribute and Profit: Sino-Siamese Trade, 1652–1853*, Cambridge, Mass., 1977.

Vixseboxse, J., *Een Hollandsch Gezantschap naar China in de Zeventiende Eeuw, 1685–1687*, Leiden, 1946.

Volker, T., *Porcelain and the Dutch East India Company 1602–1682*, Leiden, 1954.

Watson, I. B., *Foundation for Empire: English Private Trade in India, 1659–1760*, New Delhi, 1980.

Wiethoff, B., *Chinas Dritte Grenze: Der Traditionelle Chinesische Staat und der Kustennahe Seeraum*, Wiesbaden, 1969.

Wiethoff, B., *Die Chinesische Seeverbotspolitik und der Private Überseehandel von 1368 bis 1567*, Hamburg, 1963.

Willmott, W. E., ed., *Economic Organisation in Chinese Society*, Stanford, 1972.

Wills, Jr., J. E., *Pepper, Guns and Parleys: The Dutch East India Company and China, 1662–1681*, Cambridge, Mass., 1974.

Wills, J. E. Jr., *Four Embassies: Maritime Europe and the Ch'ing Tribute System, 1666–1687*, New Haven, 1981.

Winius, G. D., *The Fatal History of Portuguese Ceylon*, Cambridge, Mass., 1971.

Wolters, O. W., *Early Indonesian Commerce: A Study of the Origins of Srívijaya*, Ithaca, 1967.

Woodside, A. B., *Vietnam and the Chinese Model*, Cambridge, Mass., 1971.

Wu, S. H. L., *Passage to Power: K'ang-hsi and his Heir Apparent, 1661–1722*, Cambridge, Mass., 1979.

Articles

Adshead, S. A. M., 'The Seventeenth Century General Crisis in China', *Asian Profile*, 1:2 (1973), 271–80.

Andaya, L. Y., 'Treaty Conceptions and Misconceptions: a case study from South Sulawesi', *Bijdragen tot de Taal-, Land- en Volkenkunde*, 134 (1978), 275–95.

Arasaratnam, S., 'The Indian merchants and their trading methods', *Indian Economic and Social History Review*, 3 (1966), 85–95.

Atwell, W. S., 'Notes on Silver, Foreign Trade, and the Late Ming Economy', *Ch'ing-shih wen-t'i*, 3:8 (1977), 1–33.

Baldinotti, J., 'La Relation sur le Tonkin du P. Baldinotti', *Bulletin de l'École Française d'Extrême-Orient*, 3 (1903), 71–7.

Barten, C., 'Hollandse Kooplieden op Bezoek Bij Concilievaders', *Archief voor de Geschiedenis van de Katholieke Kerk in Nederland*, 12 (1970), 75–120.

Bassett, D. K., 'Changes in the Pattern of Malay Politics, 1629–c. 1655', *Journal of Southeast Asian History*, 10:3 (1969), 429–52.

Bassett, D. K., 'English Trade in Celebes, 1613–1667', *Journal of the Malayan Branch of the Royal Asiatic Society*, 31 (1958), 1–39.

Bassett, D. K., 'The Trade of the English East India Company in the Far East, 1623–84', *Journal of the Royal Asiatic Society*, 104 (1960), 32–47, 145–57.

Blussé, J. L., 'Chinese Trade to Batavia During the Days of the VOC', *Archipel*, 18 (1979), 195–213.

Blussé, J. L., 'The Dutch Occupation of the Pescadores, 1622–1624', *Transactions of the International Conference of Orientalists in Japan*, 18 (1973), 28–44.

Blussé, J. L., 'Western Impact on Chinese Communities in Western Java at the Beginning of the Seventeenth Century', *Nampo Bunka*, 2 (1975), 26–57.

Bourdon, L., 'António Fialho Ferreira et le Projet de Liaison Macao–Lisbonne en Droiture, 1640–1645', *Economia e Finanças, Anais do Instituto Superior de Ciencias Economica e Financieras*, 19 (1951), 101–28.

Boxer, C. R., 'Asian Potentates and European Artillery in the Sixteenth–Eighteenth centuries', *Journal of the Malayan Branch of the Royal Asiatic Society*, 38:2 (1965), 156–72.

Boxer, C. R., 'Friar Juan Pobre of Zamora and his lost and found *Ystoria* of 1598–1603', *Indiana University Bookman*, 10 (1969), 25–46.

Boxer, C. R., 'A Note on Portuguese Reactions to the Revival of the Red Sea Spice Trade and the Rise of Atjeh, 1540–1600', *Journal of Southeast Asian History*, 10:3 (1969), 415–28.

Boxer, C. R., 'Macao as a Religious and Commercial Entrepôt in the Sixteenth and Seventeenth Centuries', *Acta Asiatica*, 26 (1974), 64–90.

Boxer, C. R., '*Plata Es Sangre*: Sidelights on the Drain of Spanish–American Silver in the Far East, 1550–1700', *Philippine Studies*, 18 (1970), 457–75.

Boxer, C. R., 'Portuguese Military Expeditions in Aid of the Mings against the Manchus, 1621–1647', *T'ien-hsia Monthly*, 7:1 (1938), 24–50.

Boxer, C. R., 'Portuguese Roteiros 1500–1700', *Mariner's Mirror*, 20 (1934), 171–86.

Boxer, C. R., 'Portuguese and Spanish Rivalry in the Far East during the Seventeenth Century', *Journal Royal Asiatic Society* (1946), 150–64; (1947), 91–105.

Boxer, C. R., 'The Rise and Fall of Nicholas Iquan', *T'ien-hsia Monthly*, 11:5 (1939), 401–39.

Boxer, C. R., 'Some Early Portuguese Bills of Lading, 1625–1708', *Mariner's Mirror*, 25 (1939), 24–34.

Boxer, C. R., 'Uma Obra Raríssima Impresa em Goa no Século XVII', *Boletim Internacional de Bibliografia Luso-Brasileira*, 8 (1967), 431–528.

Brading, D. A. and Cross, H. E., 'Colonial Silver Mining: Mexico and Peru', *Hispanic American Historical Review*, 52 (1972), 546–79.

Brading, D. A., 'Mexican Silver-Mining in the Eighteenth Century: the Revival of Zacatecas', *Hispanic American Historical Review*, 50 (1970), 665–81.

Braganza Pereira, A. B., 'Os Portugueses em Baçaim', *O Oriente Português*, separate (1935).

Buch, W. J. M., 'La Compagnie des Indes Néerlandaises et L'Indochine', *Bulletin de L'École Française d'Extrême-Orient*, 36 (1936), 97–196 and 37 (1937), 121–237.

Cadière, L., 'Le Mur de Dong-hoi. Étude sur l'établissement des Nguyen en Cochinchine', *Bulletin de l'École Française d'Extrême-Orient*, 6 (1906), 85–253.

Chang Te-ch'ang, 'The Economic Role of the Imperial Household', *Journal of Asian Studies*, 31 (1972), 243–73.

Coolhaas, W. P., 'Een Bron van het Historische Gedeelte van Hugo de Groots de Jure Praedae', *Bijdragen en Mededelingen van hiet Historisch Genootschap*, 79 (1965), 415–540.

Cooper, M., 'The Mechanics of the Macao–Nagasaki Silk Trade', *Monumenta Niponica*, 27 (1972), 423–33.

Cotta, F., 'Portuguese Losses in the Indian Seas (1629–1636)', *Journal of the Asiatic Society of Bengal*, 11 (1915), 205–15.

Cotter, M., 'Towards a Social History of the Vietnamese Southward Movement', *Journal of Southeast Asian History*, 9 (1968), 12–24.

Cunha Rivara, J. H. da, 'A Companhia do Comercio', *O Chronista de Tissuary*, 17–20 (1867), 99–104, 123–31, 147–55 and 171–83.

Chushman, J. W., 'Duke Ch'ing-Fu Deliberates: a Mid-Eighteenth Century Reassessment of Sino-Nanyang Commercial Relations', *Papers on Far Eastern History*, 17 (1978), 137–56.

D'Costa, A., 'The Demolition of the Temples in the Islands of Goa in 1540 and the Disposal of the Temple Lands', *Neue Zeitschrift für Missionswissenschaft*, 18 (1962), 161–76.

Dam van Isselt, W. E. van, 'Mr. Johan van Dam en zijne tuchtiging van Makassar in 1660', *Bijdragen tot de Taal-, Land- en Volkenkunde*, 60 (1908), 1–44.

Dixon, J. M., tr., 'Voyage of the Dutch Ship "Grol" from Hirado to Tongking', *Transactions of the Asiatic Society of Japan*, 9 (1883), 180–216.

Dutra, F. A., 'Membership in the Order of Christ in the Seventeenth Century: Its Rights, Privileges, and Obligations', *The Americas*, 27 (1970), 3–25.

Fischel, J. W., 'The Jewish Merchant Colony in Madras (Fort St. George) during the Eighteenth and Nineteenth Centuries', *Journal of the Economic and Social History of the Orient*, 3 (1960), 78–107, 175–95.

Glamann, K., 'The Dutch East India Company's Trade in Japanese Copper 1645–1736', *The Scandinavian Economic History Review*, 1 (1953), 40–79.

Glamann, K., 'The Danish Asiatic Company, 1732–1772', *The Scandinavian Economic History Review*, 8 (1960), 109–49.

Hall, J., 'Notes on the Early Ch'ing Copper Trade with Japan', *Harvard Journal of Asiatic Studies*, 12 (1949), 444–61.

Hohendorff, J. A. van, 'Radicale Beschrijving van Banjermassing', *Bijdragen tot de Taal-, Land- en Volkenkunde*, 8 (1861), 151–216.

Horst, W. A., 'De Peperhandel van de Vereenigde Oostindische Compagnie', *Bijdragen voor Vaderlandsche Geschiedenis en Oudheidkunde*, eighth series, 3 (1941), 95–103.

Hsieh Kuo-chen, 'A Study of the Evacuation of the Southeast Coast in The Early Ch'ing', *Chinese Social and Political Science Review*, 15 (1931), 559–96.

Hullu, J. de, 'Over den Chinaschen Handel der Oost-Indische Compagnie in de eerste dertig jaar van de 18ᵉ eeuw', *Bijdragen tot de Taal-, Lande- en Volkenkunde*, 73 (1917), 32–151.

Ijzerman, J. W., 'Het schip *De Eendracht* voor Makasar in December 1616', *Bijdragen tot de Taal-, Land- en Volkenkunde*, 78 (1922), 343–72.

Iria, A., 'Elementos de estudo acerca da possivel contribuição portuguesa para a organização de Museu histórico de Malaca', *Studia*, 5 (1960), 47–134; 6 (1960), 57–120; 7 (1961), 107–150; and 8 (1961), 257–334.

Ishii Yoneo, 'Seventeenth Century Japanese Documents about Siam', *Journal of the Siam Society*, 59 (1971), 161–74.

Iwao Seiichi, 'Japanese Foreign Trade in the sixteenth and seventeenth centuries', *Acta Asiatica*, 30 (1976), 1–18.

Iwao Seiichi, 'Li Tan, Chief of the Chinese Residents at Hirado, Japan in the Last Days of the Ming Dynasty', *Memoirs of the Research Department of the Toyo Bunko*, 17 (1958), 27–83.

Jackson, J. C., 'Mining in 18th Century Bangka: The Pre-European Exploitation of a "Tin Island"', *Pacific Viewpoint*, 10:2 (1969), 28–54.

Johnson, M., 'The Cowrie Currencies of West Africa', *Journal of African History*, 11 (1970), 17–49, 331–53.

Kato Eiichi, 'The Japanese–Dutch trade in the formative period of the seclusion policy, particularly on the raw silk trade by the Dutch Factory at Hirado, 1620–1640', *Acta Asiatica*, 30 (1976), 34–84.

Keuning, J., 'Ambonnezen, Portugezen en Nederlanders', *Indonesië*, 9 (1956), 135–69.

Kobata Atsushi, 'The Production and Uses of Gold and Silver in Sixteenth and Seventeenth-Century Japan', *Economic History Review*, second series, 18:2 (1965), 245–66.

Koorders, S. H., 'A Note on Sandalwood', *The Indian Forester*, 20 (1894), 321–3.

Lo Jung-Pang, 'The Decline of the Early Ming Navy', *Oriens Extremus*, 5 (1958–9), 149–68.

Lo-shu Fu, 'The Two Portuguese Embassies to China during the K'ang-hsi Period', *T'oung-pao*, 43 (1955), 75–94.

Mauro, F., 'Towards an "International Model": European Overseas Expansion between 1500 and 1800', *Economic History Review*, second series, 14 (1961), 1–17.

Meilink-Roelofsz, M. A. P., 'De Europese Expansie in Azië', *Bijdragen tot de Taal-, Land- en Volkenkunde*, 135 (1979), 403–42.

Meilink-Roelofsz, M. A. P., 'The structures of Trade in Asia in the Sixteenth and Seventeenth Centuries. A Critical Appraisal', *Mare Luso-Indicum*, 4 (1980), 1–43.

Mills, J. V., tr., 'Destruction of Malaca, Meridional India and Cathay', *Journal of the Malayan Branch of the Royal Asiatic Society*, 8, part 1 (1930), 1–288.

Myers, R. H., 'Some Issues on Economic Organization during the Ming and Ch'ing Periods: A Review Article', *Ch'ing-shih wen-t'i*, 3:2 (1974), 77–93.

Myers, R. H., 'The "Sprouts of Capitalism" in Agricultural Development during the mid-Ch'ing Period', *Ch'ing-shih wen-t'i*, 3:6 (1976), 84–9.

Needham, J. and Huang, R., 'The Nature of Chinese Soceity – A Technical Interpretation', *Journal of Oriental Studies*, 12 (1974), 1–16.

Nicholl, R., 'The Mission of Father António Ventimiglia to Borneo', *The Brunei Museum Journal*, 2 (1972), 183–205.

Ng Chin-keong, 'A Study on the Peasant Society of South Fukien, 1506–1644', *Nanyang University Journal*, 6 (1962), 189–212.

Ng Chin-keong, 'The Fukinese Maritime Trade in the Second Half of the Ming Period – Government Policy and Elite Groups' Attitudes', *Nanyang University Journal*, 5, pt. 2 (1971), 81–100.

Noorduyn, J., 'De Islamisering van Makasar', *Bijdragen tot de Taal-, Land- en Volkenkunde*, 112 (1956), 347–66.

Noorduyn, J., 'Majapahit in the Fifteenth Century', *Bijdragen tot de Taal-, Land- en Volkenkunde*, 134 (1978), 207–74.

Pacheco, D., 'The Founding of the Port of Nagasaki and its Cession to the Society of Jesus', *Monumenta Niponica*, 25 (1970), 303–27.

Pearson, M. N., 'Goa during the first Century of Portuguese Rule', *Itinerario*, 8:1 (1984), 36–57.

Pearson, M. N., 'Indigenous Dominance in a Colonial Economy. The Goa *Rendas*, 1600–1670', *Mare Luso-Indicum*, 2 (1972), 61–73.

Pelliot, P., 'Un Ouvrage sur les Premiers Temps de Macao', *T'oung-pao*, 31 (1935), 58–94.

P'eng Tse-i, 'Ch'ing-tai Kuang-tung yang-hang chih-tu ti ch'i-yuan', [The Origin of the System of Foreign Trade Guilds in Kwangtung during the Ch'ing Period], *Li-shih yen-chiu*, 1 (1957), 1–25.

Péri, N., 'Essai sur les Relations du Japon et de l'Indochine aux XVIe et XVIIe Siècles', *Bulletin de L'École Française d'Extrême-Orient*, 23 (1923), 1–136.

Petech, L., 'Some Remarks on the Portuguese Embassies to China in the K'ang-hsi Period', *T'oung pao*, 44 (1956), 227–41.

Piña, A. de, 'Macau no Século XVII: Cartas de Francisco Carvalho Aranha', *Portugal em Africa*, 14 (1957), 343–60.

Reid, A., 'Sixteenth Century Turkish Influence in Western Indonesia', *Journal of Southeast Asian History*, 10:3 (1969), 395–414.

Roessingh, M. P. H., 'Nederlandse Betrekkingen met de Philippijen, 1600–1800', *Bijdragen tot de Taal-, Land- en Volkenkunde*, 124 (1968), 482–504.

Scammell, G. V., 'Indigenous Assistance in the Establishment of Portuguese Power in Asia', *Modern Asian Studies*, 14 (1980), 1–11.

Sen, S. P., 'The Role of Indian Textiles in South-East Asian Trade in the Seventeenth Century', *Journal of Southeast Asian History*, 3:2 (1962), 92–110.

Silva, C. R. de, 'The Portuguese East India Company, 1628–1633', *Luso-Brazilian Review*, 11 (1974), 152–205.

Silva, J. Gentil da, 'Alguns elementos para a história do comercio da India de Portugal existentes na Biblioteca Nacional de Madrid', *Anias, Estados de História e Geografia da Expansão Portuguesa*, separate of vol V, tomo II (1950), 92–7.

Smith, R. B., 'Politics and Society in Viet-Nam during the Early Nguyen Period (1802–62)', *Journal of the Royal Asiatic Society* (1974), pt. 2, 153–69.

Souza, G. B., 'Notes on the *Algemeen Rijksarchief* and its Importance for the Study of Portuguese, Asian and Inter-Asian Maritime Trade', *Itinerario*, 4:2 (1980), 48–56.

Spence, J. D., 'Chang Po-hsing and the K'ang-hsi Emperor', *Ch'ing-shih wen-t'i*, 1:8 (1968), 3–9.

Steensgaard, N., 'European Shipping to Asia, 1497–1700', *Scandinavian Economic History Review*, 18 (1970), 1–11.

Suntharalingam, R., 'The British in Banjarmasin: An Abortive Attempt at Settlement, 1700–1707', *Journal of Southeast Asian History*, 4 (1963), 33–50.

Teixeira, M., 'Os Ouvidores em Macau', *Boletim de Instituto Luis de Camões*, 10 (1976), 189–388.

Tiele, P. A., 'Verklaring van Martinius Apius van het Geen Hem en zijne Medegevangenen van de Vloot van Jacob van Neck in 1602 te Macao is Overkomen', *Bijdragen en Mededelingen van hiet Historisch Genootschap*, 6 (1883), 228–42.

Toby, R. P., 'Reopening the Question of Sakoku: Diplomacy in the Legitimation of the Tokugawa Bakufu', *Journal of Japanese Studies*, 3 (1977), 323–63.

Watson, I. B., 'The Establishment of English Commerce in North-Western India in the Early Seventeenth Century', *Indian Economic and Social History Review* 13 (1976), 375–91.

Wills, Jr., J. E., 'Early Sino-European Relations: Problems, opportunities, Archives', *Ch'ing-shih wen-t'i*, 3:2 (1974), 50–76.

Wolters, O. W., 'Ayudhya and the Rearward Part of the World', *Journal of the Royal Asiatic Society* (1968), pts. 3 and 4, 166–78.

UNPUBLISHED DISSERTATIONS

Bassett, D. K., 'The Factory of the English East India Company at Bantam, 1602–1682', Ph.D. dissertation, University of London, 1955.

Cushman, J. W., 'Fields from the Sea: Chinese Junk Trade with Siam During the Late Eighteenth Century and Early Nineteenth Century', Ph.D. dissertation, Cornell University, 1975.

Goh Yoon Fong, 'Trade and Politics in Banjarmasin, 1700–1747', Ph.D. dissertation, University of London, 1969.

Manguin, P.-Y., 'Les Nguyen, Macau et le Portugal: Aspects Politiques et Commerciaux d'une Relation Privilegiée, 1773–1802', Thèse de IIIe cicle, Université de Paris IV, 1978.

Promboon, S., 'Sino-Siamese Tributary Relations, 1282–1853', Ph.D. dissertation, University of Wisconsin, 1971.

INDEX